KINGS
&QUEENS

KINGS & QUEENS

A CHRONICLE OF HISTORY'S MOST INTERESTING MONARCHIES

BRENDA RALPH LEWIS

amber
BOOKS

This edition published in 2017

© 2005 and 2008 Amber Books Ltd

Previously published as *Dark History of the Kings & Queens of Europe* and *Dark History of the Kings & Queens of England*

ISBN: 978-1-78274-478-8

Published by
Amber Books Ltd
74–77 White Lion Street
London
N1 9PF
United Kingdom
www.amberbooks.co.uk
Appstore: itunes.com/apps/amberbooksltd
Facebook: www.facebook.com/amberbooks
Twitter: @amberbooks

Project Editors: James Bennett and Sarah Uttridge
Picture Research: Terry Forshaw, Natasha Jones and Kate Green
Design: Zoe Mellors and Jerry Williams

Manufactured in China

4 6 8 10 9 7 5 3 2

CONTENTS
THE KINGS & QUEENS OF EUROPE

THE KINGS & QUEENS OF ENGLAND

WESTERN PART OF THE MEDITERRANEAN SEA WITH THE COASTS OF SPAIN FRANCE ITALY BARBARY.

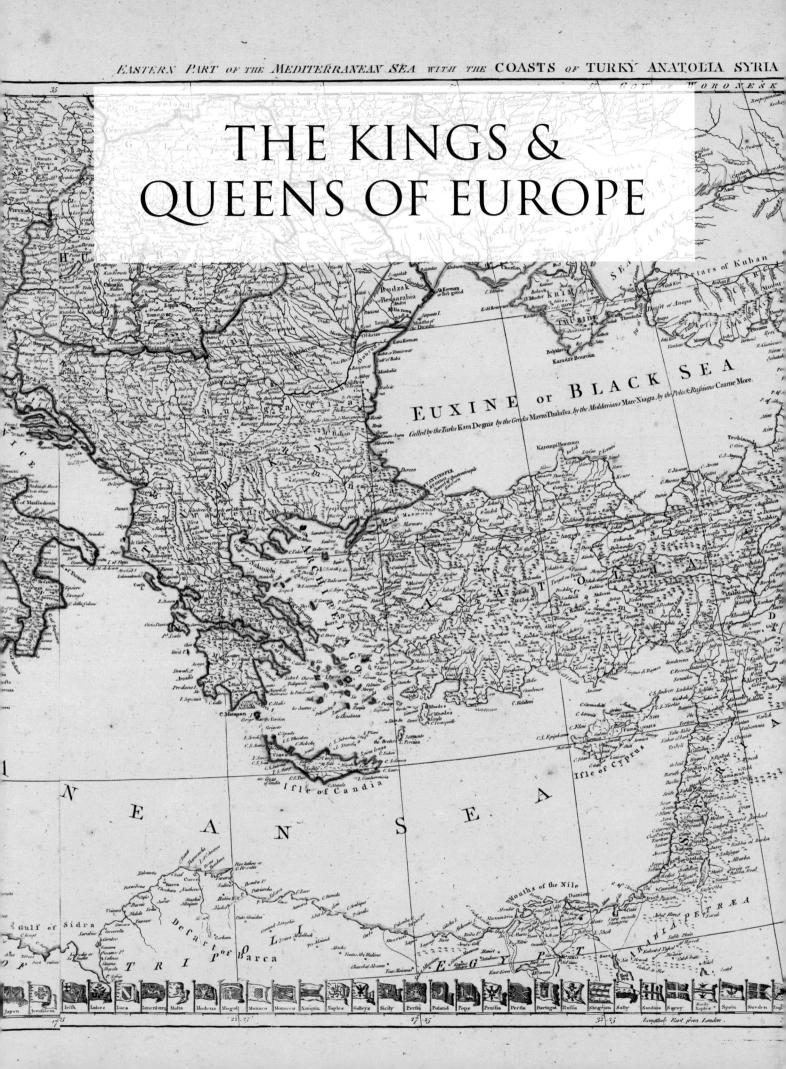

THE KINGS & QUEENS OF EUROPE

INTRODUCTION

History can be dark in many ways, and the royal history of continental Europe is no exception. For example, in the fifteenth and sixteenth centuries, Elizabeth Bathory and Gilles de Rais were mass murderers. De Rais and the horrors he perpetrated at his castle entered French folklore in tales of the barbaric Bluebeard, who murdered seven wives and hung their bodies in a blood-drenched cupboard. In the nineteenth century, King Leopold II of Belgium reduced the population of the Congo, in Africa, by 70 per cent, through the appalling punishments and brute exploitation practised in his colony, the Congo Free State.

✦

Vlad III Dracul, a fifteenth-century Prince of Wallachia (now part of Romania), also entered the shock-horror annals of Europe. He was probably the model for Count Dracula, the blood-sucking vampire in Bram Stoker's novel *Dracula*, published in 1897. The real Vlad Dracul went a great deal further: he specialized in impaling his enemies by having stakes driven through their bodies, and afterwards leaving them to die a slow, horrifically agonizing death.

Several kings of France appear in the cast list. The most notorious was the fourteenth-century King Philip IV, who coveted the wealth and feared the power and influence of the Knights Templar, the most prestigious of the crusader military orders. Philip devised a truly evil plot to destroy them. Hundreds of Templars died or were crippled after being tortured to confess.

Two later French kings, Louis XIV and Louis XV, were more civilized, but still reprehensible. They

specialized in debauchery. Louis XV had his own private brothel near the Palace of Versailles where he regularly serviced a bevy of young girls. In the seventeenth and eighteenth centuries, kings were expected to have a mistress as a consolation prize for their duty to enter an arranged marriage and produce heirs to the throne. Both Louis XIV and Louis XV gained a great deal of 'consolation' by way of this tradition.

Not all the dark history in this book deals with barbarity, wickedness or immorality. Some royal lives were ruined by the insanity that ran in their families because of the unwise practice of inbreeding.

This was supposed to keep the dynastic line 'pure' and retain royal power, wealth and influence within the family. But inbreeding ran too close to incest and produced monsters so damaged in body and mind that their families dared not reveal the truth.

The Spanish Hapsburgs and the Wittelsbachs of

'The Family of Louis XIV' painted in 1711 by Nicolas de Largillière. The picture shows some of the legitimate heirs of King Louis (third from left) but his many illegitimate children were not, of course, included. The small child pictured was the King's great-grandson and successor in debauchery, the future King Louis XV.

Bavaria were riddled with insanity and its appalling manifestations. They suffered lifelong torment, which included morbid fears, hallucinations and murderous violence. The pity of it was that some of them knew they were losing their minds, yet were inexorably swept on into the maelstrom of madness. Another scourge, haemophilia, the dreaded 'bleeding disease', wrecked two European royal families and ruined many lives.

Scandal, of course, proliferates in dark history. King Ludwig II of Bavaria was revealed as a hapless old fool over his infatuation with the femme fatal Lola Montez, who cost him his throne. Queen Christina of Sweden, whose gender was uncertain, scandalized Paris and Rome with her eccentric behaviour. The royal families of Netherlands and Monaco, together with King Carol II of Romania, provided years of salacious copy for the intrusive modern media. This is not a book for the faint-hearted. It took a strong stomach to write it. It could require another to read it.

n lan de noſtre ſeigneur mil ꝑ
v. lix. templiers a pare
le moulin aburent apꝛes leo

PHILIP IV OF FRANCE AND THE KNIGHTS TEMPLAR

Grand Master Jacques de Molai had nothing to lose when he appeared before an assembly of French prelates to confess, yet again, to a roster of terrible charges first laid against his Order of the Temple of Solomon in 1307.

✦

The accusations, which were entirely bogus, were the work of the Grand Master's implacable enemy, Philip IV of France. They included denying Christ and his apostles, blasphemy, sodomy and other homosexual practices that were said to be rife within the Order, which was better known

Left: Falsely accused of crimes by Philip IV of France, the Knights Templar burn while Philip (on horseback) looks on.
Above: Jacques de Molai became Grand Master of the Templar Order in 1295.

as the Knights Templar. It was now seven years since these accusations had first been made against the Order, but whatever happened on this day – 18 March 1314 – de Molai knew that the least he could expect was to spend whatever remained of his life in the stinking holes that served as prisons in medieval times.

Last-minute resolve
De Molai was about 70 years old, which in his times was considered extreme old age. He was deeply ashamed because, terrified of the agonies of torture and

death by fire at the stake, he had already confessed to some of the charges against him. Now, he was required to reaffirm his 'guilt' and do it before the crowd of onlookers gathered around a scaffold before the Cathedral of Notre Dame in Paris. This time, though, he had found a latent courage and, though well aware of the consequences, he was resolved to recant.

'It is only right,' he told the crowd, 'that at so solemn a moment, when my life has so little time to run, I should reveal the deception that has been practised and speak up for the truth. Before Heaven and Earth and all of you … I admit I am guilty of the grossest iniquity. But the iniquity is that, to my shame and dishonour, I have suffered myself … to give utterance to falsehoods in admitting the disgusting charges laid against the Order … I declare, and I must declare, that the Order is innocent … I disdain to seek wretched and disgraceful existence by grafting another lie upon the original falsehood.'

This pronouncement by the most senior of all Templars created uproar and dismay, all the more so because de Molai was backed by another prominent

Templar, Guy de Charnay, Preceptor of Normandy. Before de Molai could say anything else, the two men were summarily seized and dragged back to prison. Two other Templars, Hugues de Rairaud and Geoffroi de Goneville, were either less courageous or less despairing; they distanced themselves from the Grand Master and Preceptor. The damage had been done and the Order of the Temple of Solomon and its Grand Master stood on the brink of ultimate punishment.

All that was left after de Molai and de Charnay were burned at the stake in 1314 was blackened bones and ashes, and nothing could have symbolized more starkly the tragedy and ruin that overtook the Knights Templar between 1307 and 1314. King Philip IV's revenge was complete.

An order of protection

The Templars had been among the first of the military and religious orders formed to manage the new situation in the Holy Land that followed the brilliant success of Christian arms in the First Crusade of 1095–1099. The Muslim forces were

PHILIP'S LONG-AWAITED REVENGE

King Philip IV had waited a long time for this moment, the moment when he could destroy the Templars once and for all. His motives included greed for the Templars' wealth and fear and jealousy of their power. His method was accusation of the worst possible kind. Now, after a seven-year campaign of lies, fake evidence and false witnesses in court, Philip was not going to let de Molai, his prize captive, get away with uncovering his duplicity. A few hours after the Grand Master made his recantation, he and de Charnay were taken to the Ile-des-Javiaux, an eyot in the River Seine that lay between the royal gardens and the

convent of Saint-Augustin. They were tied to stakes, the wood beneath them was lit and the two men burned to death. According to witnesses, de Molai and de Charnay met their terrible end with dignity, calm and courage. To many who saw them die, they became instant martyrs. Some waited until the ashes had cooled in order to sift through for bones that they could keep and revere as holy relics.

Philip IV, nicknamed The Fair, became King of France in 1285. Apart from the Knights Templar, Philip also quarrelled with Pope Boniface VIII, installing in 1305 his own rival pope, Clement V, at Avignon.

This painting by the French artist François Marius Granet depicts the inauguration of a Knight Templar. He painted many scenes inside churches and monasteries and, like many, was fascinated by the Templars.

decisively defeated, and Crusader realms were set up in Tripoli, Antioch, Edessa and, most prestigious of all, Jerusalem, which had fallen on 15 July 1099 after a long and bloody siege. The new Christian acquisitions needed defence and succour; for this purpose, military and religious orders of chivalry were created soon after the end of the First Crusade.

These included the Knights of the Holy Sepulchre, whose task was to defend this most important centre of Christian worship in Jerusalem; the Orders of the Hospital of St John of Jerusalem, known as the Knights Hospitaller, who provided medical services; and the Knights Templar. Like the Hospitallers, the Templars, who formed in 1118, were mainly composed of Frankish knights. Their task was to provide armed escort and protection for the pilgrims who made the long and arduous journey to the Holy Land.

Jerusalem was the emotional focus of these pilgrimages, which were large-scale events even before the Muslims captured the city in AD 638. But travelling to, or merely being in, the Holy Land could be a perilous business. Unarmed pilgrims were ambushed, robbed, killed, kidnapped and even sold into slavery by bandits who specialized in swift hit-and-run tactics, then melted away into the desert landscape. The first Knights Templar who volunteered to guard and protect the pilgrims against such merciless enemies were only nine in number, but were otherwise well suited to the task.

Noble knights

All of the Templars were of noble birth, all well connected to powerful families. All came from the area around Champagne and Burgundy in northeast France, and their leader, Huges de Payens, who was born near Troyes, was probably a cousin as well as a vassal of Hugh, Comte de Champagne. The comte was one of the mightiest and most prestigious magnates in France, devoted to the cause of crusade and virtually independent of the French king. He was undoubtedly

This painting shows the inauguration in 1295 of the 54-year-old Jacques de Molai as Grand Master of the Templar Order. We know very little about de Molai's life up to this point, but he has become the most famous of the Templars' Grand Masters.

his cousin's richest and most powerful patron, but the Knights Templar did not take their cue from his kind of eminence. Instead, they opted for the poverty, chastity, obedience and humility of monks, willing to beg for their food and lead pure, exemplary lives. Their original name, the Poor Knights of Christ and the Temple of Solomon, said a great deal about them.

Changing focus

In time, however, the realities of life and the nature of Christian society in the Holy Land worked together to change this emphasis. The Templars retained their martial identity and were, in fact, the most effective of all the military orders in the field. But though they exemplified the two great passions of medieval times – fervent faith and fighting prowess – they soon became celebrities, thrilling the popular imagination as valiant champions of Christ, with God undoubtedly on their side.

They also attracted rich, powerful backers, including the Pope himself. Only 10 or 12 years after the Order was founded, prominent magnates such as Fulk, Count of Anjou (afterwards the fourth Crusader King of Jerusalem) and Thibaud II, a later Comte de Champagne, both became Templars and gifted large sums of money to the Order. Fulk's contribution alone was 30 pounds of silver a year.

Other, rich revenues together with fine properties were lavished on the Templars by aristocrats and churchmen on a scale that gave the knights a status they had neither sought nor envisaged. They became wealthy, privileged and both politically and diplomatically significant. Eventually, it was reckoned that the Templars owned 900 estates, many of them donated to the Order by new recruits from prominent families, who were not allowed to own personal property. In time, the Order established itself in England, Italy, Cyprus, Germany and France, where it owned a

A Knight Templar in action on horseback, from a fourteenth-century manuscript.

Philip IV of France seated 'in majesty' on his throne, flanked by two lions. Philip was killed when he was mauled by a wild boar during a hunting trip. All three of his sons eventually became kings of France.

total of 870 castles, schools and houses. In addition, the Templars established major castles in the Holy Land – at Jaffa, Acre, Sidon, Safed and elsewhere. But the favours the Templars attracted went beyond the merely material. They were given special papal protection,

Muslim forces successfully challenged crusader power in the Holy Land, sending crusading zeal into decline.

and a Bull of 1139 issued by Pope Innocent II declared them exempt from any other jurisdiction, whether Church or government. The properties the Templars acquired were tax-free: they did not even have to pay the usual ecclesiastical tithes.

Honest money men

Possibly the most significant concession that Rome made to the Templars was to exempt them from the ban on usury, which had long ago acquired a bad name in the Christian world. This enabled the Order to set up banks and other financial institutions which eventually embraced most of the banking functions common today – current accounts, safe deposits, loans and credit, international money transfers, trustee services, strongholds for keeping secure jewellery, gold or other treasure, and armed guards when it was in transit. The Templars inspired such trust in their honesty and efficiency that several European princes and even some wealthy Muslims allowed them to handle their not insubstantial treasuries. Still, the picture was not all

PHILIPPE   LE BEL

glorious. The lavish favours, the special treatment, the mass of wealth and the extraordinary privileges the Templars acquired meant that they were soon regarded as spoiled darlings and were, of course, deeply resented as such. Already, by 1295, when Jacques de Molai became Grand Master of the Order, the Templars were being regularly accused of loving luxury, glorying in wealth and fame, and encouraging the sin of pride, and even arrogance. In 1307, de Molai was personally attacked for failing to emulate the self-denial practised

two centuries earlier by Huges de Payens. In the demanding world of Christian piety, these were very serious accusations. What is more, they arose in full force at a time Muslim forces successfully challenged crusader power in the Holy Land, sending crusading zeal into decline. The Muslim forces reoccupied the

This medieval manuscript depicts the destruction of the Knights Templar and the death of King Philip IV, who survived martyred Jacques de Molai by only eight months.

Crusader kingdoms and other territory in 'infidel' hands and, by 1303, had the last Crusaders confined to the tiny island of Arwad, some 1.8 miles (3km) off the coast of present-day Syria in the Mediterranean Sea. There was talk in Europe of another crusade, but it failed to arouse sufficient interest.

Decline of crusaders

This ignominious failure badly damaged the standing of the military orders which had been an integral part of the crusading scene for more than 200 years. It was far worse than simple loss of face. The success and glory, and the certainty that God approved crusader endeavours, had gone as well. Inevitably, to the superstitious mindset of medieval times, their place was filled by fears that the devil and all his works

Two Knights Templar, tied back to back, are burned for heresy. This was a scene which occurred in several parts of France, and was normally attended by large crowds.

TORTURE AS AN INTERROGATION METHOD

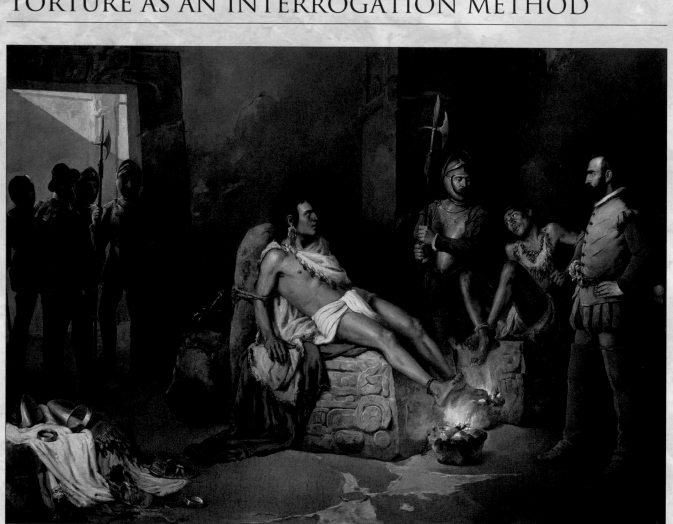

Torture by burning the feet persisted even beyond the medieval period. In this painting, an Aztec priest is tortured by Spanish conquistadores, in the early 1520s.

Medieval torture had numerous refinements. Prisoners were stretched on the rack, so dislocating their joints. Thumbscrews, toe-screws or foot-crushing boots were used to shatter their bones. Their mouths were forced open so wide that their jaws cracked. Their teeth or fingernails were pulled out. Their legs were immobilized in iron frames and grease spread over the soles of their feet and set on fire. The agony was so intense and the damage so great that the heel bones of one priest, Bernard de Vado, dropped out through his scorched skin. De Vado confessed, but later retracted his confession and gave his flame-blackened heel bones to his inquisitors as a memento.

Although many Templars died under torture, still stoutly proclaiming their innocence, de Vado's brand of impudent courage was not all that common and the confession rate was high. All but four of the 138 Knights Templar interrogated in Paris confessed to the charges against them, perhaps taking their cue from Grand Master de Molai whose arms, legs and testicles were flayed before he gave in and signed. Other high-profile Templars, including Guy de Charnay, Preceptor of Normandy, and Huges de Pairaud also capitulated. De Piraud was in a particularly invidious position, for several of his fellow Templars had named him as the man who led them astray.

had wormed their subversive way into the Church. In fact, the failure of the Crusades and the decline of crusading gave King Philip IV of France just the opportunity he needed to strike at the two most prestigious institutions of the Christian world: the papacy and the Templars.

The beginning of the end

King Philip's first target was Pope Boniface VIII, who had declared in 1301, 'God has set popes over kings and kingdoms.' This was a direct attack against the growing self-confidence which European monarchs had in their own glory and greatness.

In response, Philip sent in the 'heavy mob'. On 7 September 1303, French troops headed by Guillaume

One of the many forms of medieval torture was strappado, seen here being applied to a prisoner while his inquisitor looks on. Strappado involved tying up a victim's hands with rope behind his back, then suspending him in the air, dislocating his arms.

The Templars, King Philip contended, were not only guilty of blasphemy and homosexuality, but also of cannibalism, infanticide and child abuse, and dabbling in witchcraft and the supernatural.

de Nogaret, the king's chief minister, appeared at the Pope's private retreat in Agnani, near Rome, and demanded that Boniface resign. When Boniface refused, Nogaret is said to have beaten him up and threatened him with execution, although there appears to be little hard evidence for this. The Pope was released after three days, but never got over the shock. Whatever Nogaret did to him was more than enough for a man of 86 who probably thought his person was sacrosanct. Boniface died a month later, on 11 October 1303.

Vicious assault

Conditions were now ideal for King Philip's assault on the Knights Templar, and he pulled no punches, couching his accusations, issued on 13 September 1307, in the language of overkill.

'A bitter thing, a lamentable thing, a thing which is horrible to contemplate, terrible to hear of, a detestable crime, an execrable evil,' was how the King described the 'abominable work' of the Templars, whom he claimed surpassed 'unreasoning beasts in their astonishing bestiality (and) exposed themselves to all the supremely abominable cries which even the sensuality of unreasoning beasts abhors and avoids'.

This statement, with its blatant appeal to medieval superstition and fears of depraved sexuality, set the stage for the accusations finalized in the summer of 1308. The Templars, King Philip contended, were not only guilty of blasphemy and homosexuality, but also of cannibalism, infanticide and child abuse, and dabbling in witchcraft and the supernatural. It was also alleged that they worshipped the Baphomet, the devil in the form of an embalmed head or idol with a goat's beard and cloven hooves.

King Philip IV watches as Knights Templar are led to their deaths. The stakes on which they will be burned are shown top right.

After this, Philip spent the next month organizing mass arrests. On 13 October 1307, all over France, some 15,000 Templars and others associated with them – servants, tenants, farmers, shepherds – were seized and thrown in to the royal dungeons or imprisoned in castles. Subsequently, friars were dispatched to churches all over France to preach against the Templars and so rouse popular fury against them.

The proportion of senior Templars detained was relatively small, only around one in 20: they comprised 138 knights and some 500 sergeants and other 'brothers' of the Order. King Philip had, however, apprehended the most important leaders, including Grand Master Jacques de Molai who, only the day before his arrest, had been in high royal favour, serving as pallbearer at the funeral of the king's sister. Philip lost no time appropriating Templar land and property, which he had ordered to be surveyed before the arrests were made. But he never got his hands on the Order's records: despite intensive searches, the documents disappeared, either burned, hidden or spirited away by some 50 knights who were apparently forewarned of the arrests and made their escape by sea from the port of La Rochelle.

The lack of documentary evidence that the records might have provided was not a problem for the prosecution. Prosecutors in medieval courts relied on confessions extracted from the accused or from witnesses willing to fill in the fine detail of the charges. Not all of them were honest, and some had their own agendas. For example, the first allegations of Templar misconduct to reach King Philip, in 1305, came from one Esquin de Floyran, a criminal who purported to be a one-time member of the Order and clearly harboured a grudge against the Templars. Philip was de Floyran's second try: his first bid to poison the Templars' reputation, at the court of King James II of Aragon, failed to convince. Whether King Philip was seeking a cover to conceal his intentions or was more susceptible than James is not precisely known, but he was certainly willing to act on information received.

Increasing machinations

The king also sent agents to locate other dissident Templars. Among several malcontents, Brother Etienne de Troyes and Jean de Folliaco proved particularly useful: both of them alleged that they had been forced to deny Christ and his apostles. De Troyes went further: he recounted how he was forced to spit upon the cross, receive homosexual attentions and venerate an idol in the form of a severed head. Dramatic testimony such as this, designed to shock and awe a courtroom, gave impetus to the guilt by accusation that underlay trials of this nature.

Likewise, torture to extract confessions was a recognized procedure, probably on the premise that the devil could be encouraged by pain to disgorge his evil secrets. The Roman Inquisition set up in 1231 by Pope Gregory IX was permitted to use torture in 1252, but, short of that, psychological pressure was exerted. Prisoners were kept awake and starved. Only if they refused to confess at this stage did the Inquisition proceed to the next level and begin the torture.

Ultimately, King Philip's inquisition extracted confessions from most of the Templars in France, in exchange for promises of pardon and freedom. The victims soon discovered just how cynical these promises were. When the torture ceased, they were invariably taken back to their icy, unhealthy cells, where there was no straw to lie on and no covering to keep out the cold.

'The human tongue,' an anonymous, pro-Templar chronicler wrote in 1308, 'cannot express the punishments, afflictions, miseries, taunts and dire kinds of torture suffered by the … innocents.… The truth kills them, and lies liberate them from death.'

A few Templars were displayed for propaganda purposes. They were sent to repeat their confessions before tribunals. Others, however, reneged, including Huges de Pairaud and Grand Master de Molai. In 1309, both Pairaud and de Molai withdrew their confessions in the presence of two cardinals sent to Paris by Pope Clement V to report on the Templar trials. The Pope was initially minded to protest against the persecution of the Order, but later changed his mind in the face of threats from King Philip, including hints that his life would be in danger if he refused to toe the royal line.

> **The Templars had no hope of just treatment, for Philip did everything possible to 'fix' the final judgment against them. Anyone who confessed, then withdrew his confession could be condemned to burn as a lapsed heretic.**

That line was profoundly cynical. The Templars had no hope of just treatment, for Philip did everything possible to 'fix' the final judgment against them. Anyone who confessed, then withdrew his confession could be condemned to burn as a lapsed heretic. Philip's sinister protegé, the lawyer Guillaume de Nogaret, circulated anti-Templar rumours even while the accused were still giving evidence in court. The king packed the courtroom with hostile witnesses and brought in theologians from the University of Paris to trumpet his credentials as a champion of Christ and the Church, valiantly fighting the 'depraved' Templar Order.

The final blow

At last, in 1310, King Philip took steps to bring the cycle of confession and retraction to an end. On 12 May of that year, 54 Templars, all lapsed heretics, were taken to open country near the Pont St Antoine des Champs, outside Paris, and were burned at the stake by slow fire. Another 67 died the same way by the end of the month.

SLAUGHTER IN THE CASTLE: GILLES DE LAVAL, BARON DE RAIS

Outwardly, Gilles de Laval, Seigneur de Rais (1404–1444), gave no sign of the murderous nature that would one day appall the whole of Christian Europe. Instead, he appeared to be a valiant warrior and a generous patron of music, literature and art. He was also renowned for his religious piety and his charity towards the poor. Yet beneath this prestigious mask lay an undercurrent of extraordinary sadism.

After the death of his parents in 1415, Gilles de Laval was brought up by his godfather Jean de Craon. While in de Craon's indulgent care, Gilles developed into a spoiled brat, intent on having his way in everything. No one, it appears, attempted to rein him in. When he was 16, Gilles kidnapped a rich heiress whom he afterwards married. In time, he squandered both her fortune and his own. His conduct in battle was also less than honourable, for he showed an early taste for bloodletting and pillage.

CHILD SACRIFICE

The symptoms of depravity went unrecognized or perhaps ignored for several years, until Gilles retired from military service and took up residence at the castle of Tiffauges, near Nantes in western France. At Tiffauges, Gilles began experimenting with the occult and was persuaded by a Florentine sorceress that he could regain his lost fortune by sacrificing children to a demon called Barron. Before long, children, most of them young boys who had been sent to Tiffauges to beg for money, were failing to return home.

In time, fearful stories began to filter out of Tiffauges, stories of sexual orgies as well as allegations of torture, sodomy and black magic. At first, given Gilles's heroic reputation, these stories were dismissed as mere gossip and impossible to believe when they involved so illustrious a figure as the Seigneur de Rais. Until the Seigneur made a big mistake.

On 15 May 1440, he had an argument with a clergyman, Jean le Ferron, over the ownership of a château. In a rage, Gilles de Laval seized le Ferron and held him captive. This was so much out of character for a much-respected, devout and chivalrous

Gilles de Laval, Seigneur (Lord) de Rais seen seizing a young boy, doubtless to add to his roster of slaughtered victims.

knight that Jean de Malestroit, the influential Bishop of Nantes, decided to investigate Gilles de Laval's activities. What he uncovered at Tiffauges was utterly horrific and, in September 1440, Gilles de Laval was arrested and threatened with torture. Faced with this ghastly prospect, Gilles preferred to confess to a long list of hideous crimes.

Parts of his confession were so gruesome that, at his trial, many of the details were removed from the record. These and other evidence, which included the bodies of 50 young boys dug up inside Gilles's castle, revealed that the illustrious Seigneur de Rais had committed satanism, heresy, sodomy, apostasy, sacrilege, kidnapping and the torture, murder and mutilation of between 80 and 200 children. The children were usually beheaded, and the court heard how the Seigneur's accomplices, Henriet and Poitou, used to place the severed heads on display so that they could choose which one they liked best.

'CARNAL DELIGHT'

In the courtroom, Gilles de Laval seemed to be two totally contradictory people. One moment, he was the fierce, proud nobleman, insulting the judge for daring to bring him to trial. The next, he would assert his devout Christian faith, then break down in tears. However he behaved, he made no secret of how much he enjoyed watching his young victims die slow, agonizing deaths. When asked for an explanation, he replied that it was for the 'pleasure and carnal delight' the spectacle afforded him. Gilles de Laval, Henriet and Poitou were hung for their crimes in October 1444. Gilles was simultaneously burned.

Those who lived in the harsh, cruel world of medieval Europe did not shock easily, but Gilles de Laval, Seigneur de Rais, had committed so many of the worst possible crimes that he became a universal symbol of evil. His name soon entered European legend and, as so often happens, he was invoked by parents as a bogeyman to frighten children into obedience. The folk tale of Bluebeard, first recorded by Charles Perrault in his *History or Tales of Past Times* (1697) may also derive from the grisly story of Gilles de Laval. Bluebeard was a rich nobleman who murdered seven of his wives and hung their bodies on the walls of a blood-drenched room in his castle. The Seigneur de Rais slaughtered 30 times that number. This dubious achievement enabled him to retain his place among the world's most prolific and horrific serial killers.

The seal of Gilles de Laval, Seigneur de Rais, showing him on horseback, sword in hand. This design was typical of aristocrats who were military leaders as well as feudal lords and great landowners.

Pope Clement V, elected in 1305, collaborated with King Philip IV of France in the destruction of the Templars. Like Philip, he died in 1314 shortly after the Templar knights were finally eliminated.

Others who had always denied the accusations were imprisoned for life. Only those who confessed and stood by their confessions had a hope of escaping prison. Eventually, on 5 June 1311, after sessions lasting more than two years, the trials were brought to a close.

Dividing the loot

Eight months later, Pope Clement V issued a Papal Bull formally suppressing the Templar Order. Templar property, which King Philip had been persuaded to relinquish, was handed over to the Knights Hospitaller. Philip kept 10 per cent as his commission on the deal. Some of the property passed into other hands in Germany, Italy and Cyprus, while in England it was initially given to guardians appointed by the king Edward II. Afterwards, Edward, who had a penchant for expensive homosexual favourites, gave it to his boyfriend of the moment, Piers Gaveston. In 1312, however, the year Gaveston was murdered by Edward's infuriated nobles, the pope ordered

that Templar lands should be handed over to the Hospitallers and, despite resistance from the English king, the transfer was duly effected in November 1313.

The following month, Jacques de Molai and the three other senior Templars were again put on trial in Paris, this time before a formidable battery of experts – cardinals, prelates, theologians and lawyers. After a trial lasting three months, fresh confessions were expected, but de Molai refused to deliver. Instead, he stood by his last recantation and died in the flames without flinching, so redeeming himself and his honour in what was his finest as well as his final hour.

Philip IV did not live long to enjoy his triumph over the Templars or the Pope, who learned a salutary lesson about royal egos and never again attempted to place themselves above kings. Philip died on 29 November 1314, eight months after Jacques de Molai. Some said the cause of death was the will of God; others, hardly less judgmental, called it guilty conscience.

Medieval orders of chivalry like the Templars expressed their military ethos in mighty castles that exuded an air of power. This impressive castle was built by the Knights of St. John Hospitaller on Rhodes after they subjugated the island in 1309.

ELIZABETH BATHORY
THE BLOOD COUNTESS

Elizabeth (Erzsébet) Bathory (1561–1614) belonged to one of the richest and most influential families in sixteenth-century Hungary. Members of this powerful Protestant family had been rulers of Poland and Transylvania – warlords, political leaders, clerics, judges and landowners on a vast scale. One of them, Stephan Bathory, fought with Vlad III Dracul – the model for Count Dracula – during his wars against the Turks. Elizabeth, who was born in 1560 or 1561, was herself a niece of another Stephan Bathory, who was King of Poland.

✦

With her prestigious connections and the promise of extraordinary beauty she already showed at a very young age, Elizabeth was a great 'catch' for an ambitious husband, and several suitors showed an interest after she was placed on the

Left: A portrait of Stephan Bathory, King of Poland from 1576 to 1586, the uncle of Elizabeth Bathory.
Above: Elizabeth Bathory looks innocent in this portrait but she was one of history's most infamous torturers and serial killers.

'marriage market' in around 1570. The successful suitor was Count Ferenc Nadasdy, aged 25, who sought to increase his renown through his marriage: this was why he took the unusual step of adopting the Bathory surname as his own, rather than Elizabeth adopting his.

All the same, Nadasdy possessed his own prestige. He was wealthy, a famous war hero and an athlete, although even his mother admitted that he was 'no scholar'. Elizabeth, by contrast, was well educated and able to read and write Hungarian, Greek, German and Latin. This disparity was of little consequence in an age of political marriages, when royal or noble males earned renown by their exploits on the battlefield and literacy was regarded as an inferior activity fit only for clerics and women.

What Elizabeth and Nadasdy shared, though, was much more important to the events that marked their marriage, which took place on 8 May 1575, when she was aged 14: both of them were sadists.

An inherited excess?

Nadasdy had a furious temper which, when roused, prompted savage beatings and floggings, and earned him the nickname of the 'Black Hero of Hungary'. Nadasdy's cruelties, however, paled beside his wife's, which afterwards led to the most horrific scandal that ever occurred among the nobility of Eastern Europe. What was more, where Nadasdy had his limits and was disgusted by some of Elizabeth's excesses, her brand of cruelty seemed to know no bounds. Subsequently, she became known as the 'Blood Countess' and, although it was a fearful nickname, it actually understated the nature and extent of her crimes.

One source of Elizabeth's frightening behaviour derived from the Bathory family and their practice, common among European aristocracy, of inbreeding to preserve the 'purity' of the noble line. Both of Elizabeth's parents, György and Anna, belonged to the Bathory family, which produced many examples of mental derangement, including schizophrenia, sadomasochism, bisexuality and the purely sadistic streak which Elizabeth inherited.

Count Ferenc Nadasdy might look like an innocent young man here, but his horrific crimes, carried out with his wife Elizabeth Bathory, make him worthy of infamy.

GRISLY SPECTACLE

As a child, Elizabeth Bathory witnessed a display of public execution that was in many ways typical of the period, one which involved the execution of a gypsy who had been sentenced to death for treason. In the sixteenth century, and for a long time afterwards, gypsies were considered to be barely human and in some places were liable to be shot on sight, like animals. This perception may have explained the unusual nature of the execution Elizabeth witnessed. First, the belly of a live horse was dissected. The gypsy

was pushed into it and sewn up inside. The spectacle proceeded as the horse writhed in agony amid blood and gore, while the hapless gypsy struggled in its belly in a hopeless bid to escape. Only when both horse and gypsy lay still, and evidently dead, did the barbaric spectacle come to an end and the onlookers start to disperse. Whether or not this ghastly event triggered Elizabeth's dormant brutality is a matter of conjecture, but it is at least possible that it had some influence on her future actions, which were callous in the extreme.

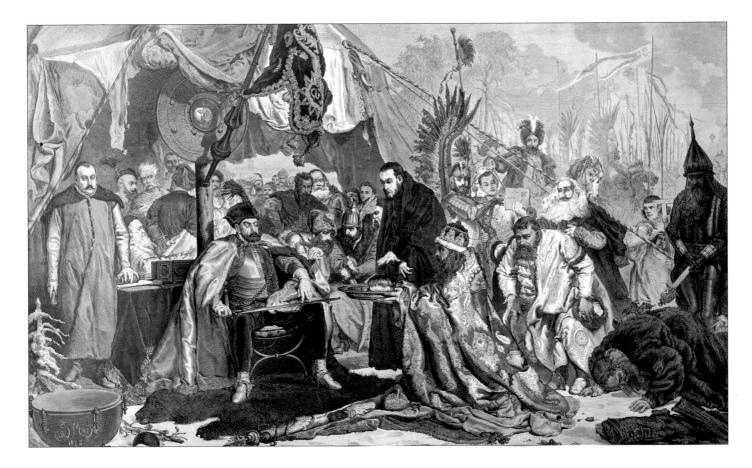

Stephan Bathory, the uncle of Elizabeth, is regarded as one of Poland's greatest kings. He is pictured here at the siege of Pskov, during the Livonian wars of the 1500s.

Elizabeth also displayed dismaying symptoms of her own. At age four or five, she began to have epileptic fits. She became prone to seizures that brought on violent, uncontrollable rages. She suffered extreme mood swings, one moment being cold and aloof, the next changing to murderous outbursts of temper. Elizabeth's instability was not helped by her upbringing. She was badly spoiled as a child, for a girl in her high position was considered too privileged to be disciplined by any of the numerous governesses who took charge of her. As a result, Elizabeth grew up vain, imperious and preoccupied with her own beauty. She was also susceptible to the callous and barbaric nature of the time and place in which she lived. Public executions, for example, were treated as a form of entertainment, which can hardly have helped to curb her instincts for cruelty and callousness.

This callousness was further encouraged by the circumstances of Elizabeth's married life. As a warlord, her husband was frequently absent from their home, the Castle of Cachtice, high up in the Carpathian Mountains of northwest Hungary. The military campaigns he conducted against the Ottoman Turks were prolonged; in the gloom

---

Where Nadasdy had his limits and was disgusted by some of Elizabeth's excesses, her brand of cruelty seemed to know no bounds. Subsequently, she became known as the 'Blood Countess'.

---

and boredom of the castle, Elizabeth had plenty of time to develop skills in the 'dark arts' and the finer points of torture. She had the opportunity, too, for her companions at Cachtice were her Aunt Klara, a sadomasochist and expert in flagellation, and Thorko, a retainer, who introduced Elizabeth to occult practices. She quickly moved on to experiments with potions, drugs, powders and herbal, possibly toxic brews.

Castle Cachtice, where
Elizabeth Bathory committed
her crimes, is in present day
Slovakia. Built in the
mid-13th century, it was
a wedding gift from the
Nadasdy family on Elizabeth's
marriage to Ferenc Nadasdy
in 1575.

AN OBSESSION WITH BLOOD ... AND YOUTH

Star-kicking was definitely a depraved formed of torture, but even this was not the ultimate extreme to which Elizabeth was willing to go. As she aged, she became obsessed with preserving her beauty and particularly the creamy smoothness of her skin. One day, a servant girl accidentally pulled Elizabeth's hair while brushing it, and received a slap in the face from her mistress that was so hard it made her nose bleed. As the girl wiped away the blood spots that had splashed her hand, Elizabeth thought she noticed that the skin where it had fallen seemed regenerated. At that, Elizabeth reputedly had the young girl's throat cut. She drained her blood into a vat and bathed in it while it was still warm. This, it seems, became regular practice at Castle Cachtice, with dozens of girls – all virgins – murdered to provide blood baths for the countess. Local gossip whispered that Elizabeth did not content herself with bathing in blood, but actually drank it and even ate the flesh of her victims after she bit their necks and breasts.

Elizabeth's husband, Count Ferenc Nadasdy, shared the gruesome tastes of his wife Elizabeth, but was completely outclassed by her cruelty.

Spiralling appetites

Somewhere along the line, Elizabeth discovered the delights of torturing the most vulnerable among her servants, the adolescent girls who were the general dogsbodies of their class. They were the least likely, through fear of the consequences, to tell tales about their mistress's behaviour. Elizabeth ensured that they kept their mouths shut about what went on at Castle Cachtice by employing five of her most trusted servants to make certain that they remained silent.

The slightest mistake or omission could be the excuse for excessive punishment. Elizabeth once sewed up the mouth of a girl who talked too much. Girls were beaten until they bled, then thrashed again with stinging nettles. This was nothing, though, to the punishments given servants suspected of stealing; Elizabeth would order them to strip, then torture them by placing red-hot coins on their skin.

Not that misbehaviour was required. Elizabeth would kill, torture and mutilate just for the thrill of it. Reportedly, she would tear the head of a servant apart, by exerting pressure on the sides of the mouth until they tore away and the neck snapped. Before long, Elizabeth had a collection of instruments for inflicting pain. Among them were tongs and pincers which were heated until red-hot, then used to tear flesh; spiked cages for impaling the girls alive; and red-hot irons to brand them. Girls were set on fire and left to burn to death while Elizabeth watched, often squealing with delight at the spectacle. Even Ferenc Nadasdy, no stranger to the horrors of the battlefield where mutilations were common, walked out of the room rather than watch these tortures.

> The slightest mistake or omission could be the excuse for excessive punishment. Elizabeth once sewed up the mouth of a girl who talked too much. Girls were beaten until they bled, then thrashed again with stinging nettles.

Other girls were covered in honey, then left tied to trees, where birds pecked at their flesh and insects devoured them. The 'water torture', another speciality at Castle Cachtice, involved stripping girls naked and leaving them outside in winter on days when the temperature fell below freezing point, until they froze to death. Sometimes their bodies were thrown over the castle walls to be eaten by wolves. One of Elizabeth's favourites was the torture known as 'star-kicking'. Pieces of oiled paper were placed between the girls' toes and set on fire. The victims jumped, jerked and kicked in futile attempts to get rid of the paper, but the oil made sure it remained in place while it burned, and the torture continued.

Powerful aristocracy

By this time, the slaughter and torture at Castle Cachtice had been going on for several years and at some point, despite Elizabeth's precautions, news of her activities was bound to get out. The hundreds of girls who had mysteriously vanished, the mutilated bodies found around the castle, the atmosphere of terror that prevailed in the surrounding countryside – these were impossible to ignore. And yet for a long time they were.

The power of the aristocracy in sixteenth-century Europe was so great that it was possible for them to frighten witnesses into silence and so escape official detection and, with that, justice. Local peasants dared not speak out for fear of reprisals. Parents who had lost their young daughters were powerless against the mighty Bathory family. The Church kept quiet, fearing Bathory revenge. Other nobles who came to know of the rumours or acquired more solid information from their own grapevines remained silent, rather than

betray one of their own, however bloodthirsty. Besides this, peasants, men and women alike, were serfs and therefore the property of their employers. Nobles such as Elizabeth Bathory could do anything they liked with their property.

The inevitable end

Elizabeth's 'reign of terror' was bound to end at some time, if only because, in around 1609, after more than 30 years, she ran out of local girls. By then, Elizabeth had managed to extinguish an entire generation of

females in the area around the Bathory estates, and although she was able to 'buy' a few more girls from poor peasants, ostensibly 'for a life of security in the service of the mighty House of Bathory', she needed to extend her reach. Looking further afield, Elizabeth decided on a new approach. At Castle Cachtice, she established a 'school' for girls for the minor nobility, where she intended, she said, to 'teach them the social graces' appropriate to their class.

It was not long before these girls, too, went missing, presumed dead. Istvan Magyari, a priest from a village near Cachtice Castle who had long suspected that a

> **Before long, Elizabeth had a collection of instruments for inflicting pain. Among them were tongs and pincers which were heated until red-hot, then used to tear flesh; spiked cages for impaling the girls alive; and red-hot irons to brand them.**

nightmare scenario was being acted out within the castle, found the courage to go to the local authorities and tell them what he knew. This time, they listened. They might have been willing to keep quiet about the mass deaths of peasant girls, but now the girls involved were of noble birth – that could not be so easily overlooked.

The Bathory family, who were well aware of what Elizabeth was doing, had worked for years to prevent any enquiry into her activities and labelled any news that *did* get out as local gossip or ignorant superstition. These tactics would no longer work. Magyari's evidence reached the ears of King Matthias of Hungary, who immediately ordered an investigation. This action may have reflected much more than shock and dismay at alleged atrocities. The king, it seems, had an agenda of his own, and saw an

This nineteenth-century illustration shows Elizabeth Bathory, right, seated in Cachtice Castle, commanding her servants to torture a number of local girls who have been stripped naked.

NOTORIETY BEYOND THE GRAVE

Notorious in life, Elizabeth Bathory soon became controversial in death. Her family wanted her buried at Cachtice, but the local populace objected strongly to the idea of her being close to their own homes, and interred in consecrated ground, too. There were also superstitious reasons for wanting Elizabeth buried far away from Cachtice.

Like Vlad Dracul more than a century before her, she was equated by popular myth with witches, warlocks and sorcerers whose black arts endangered the souls of honest Christians. Rather than being buried at the castle, Elizabeth was buried instead at Ecsed, her birthplace in southern Hungary.

It was unusual for the mighty Bathorys to pay so much attention to the opinions of peasants, but quite possibly they realized that, at Cachtice, Elizabeth's grave might be subject to desecration or to satanist rituals, where demons were believed to make sacrifices to the devil. That could have been just as damaging, if not more so, to the Bathory name than the crimes Elizabeth never admitted and for which she never showed any remorse.

opportunity to impose control over his troublesome nobility by revealing dark doings within the powerful and prestigious Bathory family. Matthias ordered Count György Thurzo, Lord Palatine of Hungary, to lead a raid on Cachtice Castle and find out what was going on. Count Thurzo already knew, for he was a cousin of Elizabeth's and, as a Bathory relative, had played his part in the family's attempts to hide the ghastly truth.

But when he reached the Castle on 29 December 1610, Count Thurzo quickly discovered that Elizabeth's crimes were even more hideous than he had imagined. There was a dead girl lying in the main hall. Nearby, there was another girl whose body was full of holes. She was, amazingly, still alive. More girls, dead or dying, were found in cells. In the basement, yet more girls had been hung from the rafters. They had been slit open and their blood was dripping into large vats on the floor below, apparently ready for one of Elizabeth's blood baths. Count Thurzo ordered the basement floor dug up; beneath it, 50 bodies were found. A further search of the castle revealed a register that Elizabeth kept in her desk; it contained the names of some 650 murdered girls.

Countess Elizabeth Bathory, in a contemporary painting. The well-connected Hungarian aristocrat was considered lovely as a girl, but she sought to perpetuate her youthful beauty by bathing in the blood of young virgins.

> ## They might have been willing to keep quiet about the mass deaths of peasant girls, but now the girls involved were of noble birth – that could not be so easily overlooked.

Arrest and trial

Count Thurzo arrested Elizabeth and her four accomplices, Dorottya Szentes (known as Dorko), Ilona Jo, Katarina Benicka (a washerwoman), and the dwarf Janos Ujvary (who was also known as Ibis or Ficzko). One servant, Erszi Majorova, a recent addition to Elizabeth's staff, escaped when the others were apprehended at the castle, but was afterwards caught and arrested. While the accomplices were taken away, to be tortured into their confessions, Elizabeth remained at the castle under house arrest. As it was not permitted by law to arrest aristocrats and put them on trial, Elizabeth never testified in court. Instead, her accomplices took the full brunt of the accusations and suffered the penalties.

It appears that Elizabeth repeatedly asked for her case to be presented before the judges, even though in doing so she risked a public scandal and, if found guilty and executed, the loss of her extensive property to the Crown. This was probably why King Matthias, who was anxious to curb the power of the Bathorys, also wanted her to be put on trial, but the family still exerted too much influence to allow the royal demands to be met. They managed to keep her where her cousin Count Thurzo had left her, confined to her castle and beyond the reach of the king.

As far as the trial was concerned, Elizabeth's appearance in court would, in any case, have been superfluous. The evidence against her, drawn from the accounts given by 200 witnesses and the gruesome discoveries made by Count Thurzo, was more than enough to establish her guilt.

The first trial of Elizabeth's accomplices opened on 7 January 1611 and was heard before 20 judges headed

> **While the accomplices were taken away, Elizabeth remained at the castle under house arrest. But as it was not permitted by law to arrest aristocrats and put them on trial, Elizabeth never testified in court.**

by the Royal Supreme Court Judge Theodosius Syrmiensis de Szulo. The confessions of the accused, obtained by torture, were placed in evidence, and the accomplices were duly found guilty. At the second trial, one of Elizabeth's servants, Zusanna, told the court about the register that listed the 650 victims whose ill treatment and deaths Elizabeth had recorded in her own handwriting.

Sickening testimony

Inevitably, some of the testimony given in court was sickening, even by the standards of the early seventeenth century, when casual cruelty and savage punishments were considered justified ways of treating criminals. One young girl, a 12-year-old named Pola, had been abducted and imprisoned in Castle Cachtice, but managed to escape. Dorka and Ilona Jo pursued and caught her, and brought her back to the castle, where she was confronted by an enraged Elizabeth. Elizabeth forced Pola into a cage shaped like

a huge ball. The ball was hauled up by a pulley and, suddenly, dozens of sharp spikes shot out of the sides and into the cage. From down below, the dwarf Ficzko manipulated the ropes until Pola, trapped inside the narrow cage, was caught on the spikes. Eventually, the girl was sliced to death.

Even when she was ill, it seems that Elizabeth's taste for sadistic pleasures was as strong as ever. Once, she ordered Dorottya Szentes to bring a girl to her as she was lying in bed. Elizabeth sat up as Szentes dragged the girl in, and bit her on the cheek. She then tore a piece of flesh from the girl's shoulders with her teeth and next went to work on her breasts.

At their trial, Dorottya Szentes and Ilona Jo were declared to be witches, a 'fact' that was reflected in their punishments. Their fingers, which had 'dipped in the blood of Christians', were torn from their hands with red-hot pincers. The pair was then burned alive. The dwarf Ficzko was considered less guilty than the other accomplices, and he was beheaded before being burned to ashes. Erszi Majorova was also executed, on 24 January. The only accomplice to escape death was Katarina Beneczky, who was exonerated by the other defendants and also by the servant Zussanna. Beneczky was sentenced instead to life imprisonment.

Walled up

Elizabeth Bathory received the same penalty, not from any court of law, but at the insistence of her family. They had striven mightily to save her life as well as preserve the family honour, but they still regarded her as a menace and a fearful disgrace to the Bathory name. They determined that she should never be free again, so she was walled up within her bedchamber at Cachtice Castle. Although it would be practically impossible for her to escape from there, guards were placed in the bedroom to make doubly certain. Small slits were left open for ventilation and to allow food to be passed through to her. Elizabeth survived there for more than three years, until 21 August 1614, when she was found dead, face down, inside her narrow prison cell. She was 54 years old.

Victims of Vlad III Dracul, another Wallachian aristocrat and the inspiration for Dracula, are impaled on sharp stakes driven from one side of the body to the other. It is more likely that the agony was prolonged by using the body's orifices to drive the stakes through the internal organs.

VLAD III DRACUL, THE REAL COUNT DRACULA

Vlad III Dracul, meaning Vlad the 'Demon', or 'Dragon', earned for himself a reputation for extreme cruelty that went way beyond that of any other European ruler. Numerous myths, superstitions and horror stories grew up about Vlad, including one tale which told how he invited a crowd of beggars, elderly and sick people to his castle, where he treated them to a big banquet, before boarding up the castle and setting it on fire. All his 'guests' died. This, it seems, was Vlad's way of releasing them from their troubles.

Vlad's influence went beyond mere anecdote. It created a genre of horror stories based, most sensationally, on his rumoured habit of drinking the blood and eating the flesh of his victims. This made him the model for stories about blood-sucking vampires, which proliferated in southeastern Europe in medieval times.

CRUEL SUPERSTITIONS

It was not surprising that the fifteenth century in southeastern Europe was the source for lurid tales and fearsome superstitions. The area was barely civilized. It was rife with violence. Murderous vendettas were common. Violent crime was an everyday event. So were punishments such as hacking off limbs, gouging out eyes, maimings and mutilations. Vlad's favourite punishment, it seems, was impaling his enemies on stakes. Sometimes, rumour asserted, more than 20,000 men, women and children were impaled at one time. With this, Vlad acquired the nickname of Tepes, meaning the 'impaler'.

Long before the Irish author Bram Stoker is said to have used him as the basis for his novel *Dracula* (1897), Vlad III Dracul was being identified with the vampire legends that were rife in eastern Europe in medieval times.

Vlad was fairly typical, however, of local rulers who were faced with handling the excesses of a volatile region and often went over the top in their efforts to retain power and see to it that their dignity was preserved. Vlad was definitely one of this kind. On one occasion, he demanded that a group of Turkish diplomats remove their hats in his presence as a mark of their respect. They refused, telling him that it was not their custom to go bareheaded. Vlad made sure that they observed their custom for ever: he ordered their hats nailed to their heads.

Vlad III had no love for the Turks. In his youth, he and his younger brother, Radu, lived as hostages at the court of the Ottoman Turkish Sultan Murad II. The brothers were there to ensure the loyalty of their father, Vlad II, who had fended off a threatened Turkish invasion by agreeing to become the sultan's vassal.

A RECIPE FOR REVENGE

The young Vlad suffered greatly at the hands of the Turks. He was imprisoned in an underground dungeon and was frequently whipped for being rude and stubborn. Then, in 1447, when Vlad was aged 16, his father was assassinated by Wallachian *boyars* (noblemen) on the orders of John Hunyadi, who resented the submission Vlad II had made to the Turks. Vlad III was released and at once set out to avenge his father, and also his older brother Mircea, who had been blinded with hot stakes and buried alive by *boyars*. Vlad raised a Turkish army and returned home to thrash the forces of John Hunyadi and take power in Wallachia. His triumph was brief, for Hunyadi hit back and dethroned Vlad. In the next few years, the two rivals tussled for control, but at last, in 1456, Vlad emerged victorious. Whether he killed Hunyadi in battle or Hunyadi died of plague is not clear. Either way, Vlad's rival was gone and the throne of Wallachia was his.

Vlad then set about wreaking revenge on the *boyars* who had killed his father and elder brother. Apparently, he invited the *boyars* to his castle for an Eastertide feast, but when the meal was over he had them seized and flung into prison. The sick and old among them were impaled on stakes and left to die. The others were taken to a ruined fortress some 80 kilometres away. There, they were forced to build a new fortress, later called Castle Dracula. When it was finished, these *boyars* were in their turn impaled.

King Matthias Corvinus of neighbouring Hungary was so disgusted by Vlad's savagery that, in around 1462, he seized him and placed him under house arrest. But Vlad's imprisonment, which lasted for up to 12 years, failed to cure him of his sadistic habits. While he remained confined, the impaled bodies of rats, mice, birds and other small creatures were discovered all over his palace. Some were beheaded; others tarred and feathered.

INVADING ARMY

Nor had Vlad's reputation for cruelty faded while he was out of the way. Although he was admired by some for defending his kingdom against the marauding Turks, he was also deeply feared. This was so not only in Wallachia and the surrounding

kingdoms, but also among the Ottoman Turks. During his imprisonment, the Turks had seized Wallachia and planted their own candidate, Basarab cel Batrin, as its ruler. In 1475, after his release from house arrest, Vlad gathered a small army of around 4000 men and invaded Wallachia, intent on retrieving his crown for a third time. Although Vlad's army was comparatively few in number, his approach seemed to inspire such panic in the Ottomans that they fled.

Not long afterwards, the Ottoman Turks got their revenge. Vlad was killed in battle against them at Vaslui, near Bucharest in 1476. The Ottomans afterwards decapitated him and took his head back to their capital, Istanbul. There it was preserved in honey and put on display by the Sultan Mehmet II to show that Vlad Tepes, the Impaler, was well and truly dead.

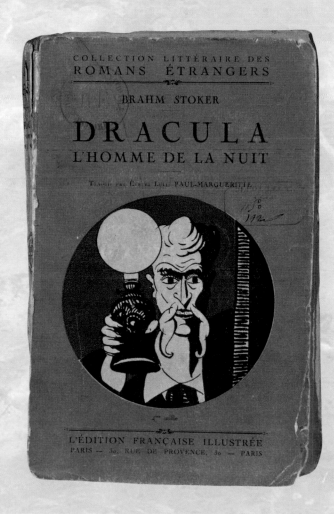

Bram Stoker's novel *Dracula*, published in 1897, was partly inspired by stories of Vlad III Dracul, although there are also similarities to the story of Elizabeth Bathory – both Dracula and Bathory had a fondness for human blood.

TWO FRENCH ROYAL RAKES: LOUIS XIV AND LOUIS XV

Louis XIV of France, the so-called 'Sun King', and his great-grandson and successor, Louis XV, were the greatest royal rakes Europe ever knew. Of the two, the fifteenth Louis was the more debauched and the less careful of his power and position. His most famous mistresses, the Marquise de Pompadour and the Comtesse du Barry, became influential figures while the king dallied elsewhere.

✦

This was something Louis XIV would never have permitted. The greatest of the absolute monarchs of Europe, he never doubted that power and influence rightfully lay in his hands. He

Left: Louis XIV, the Sun King, was the most absolute of absolute monarchs and the most powerful king France ever had.
Above: Louis XV matched his great-grandfather only in his appetite for debauchery.

never doubted, either, the truth of the Divine Right of Kings, which was impressed upon him at an early age. 'Kings are appointed by God,' he wrote as a child. 'They may do as they please.'

A later pronouncement, *'L'état c'ést moi!'* – 'I am the state!' – became his unofficial motto, and his greatness was expressed by his magnificent palace at Versailles, which was universally recognized as the most splendid of its kind. Many of the artistic, architectural and design features which Louis approved for Versailles came about through the influence on the king of his first – platonic – love, Marie Mancini, who arrived at Louis's court when she was aged 16. Marie was a niece of Cardinal Jules Mazarin, the king's chief minister during his minority. A bright, well-educated, cultured girl, she introduced Louis to great literature, painting, sculpture, philosophy and other intellectual subjects.

The expected political alliance

By 1657, Louis, aged 19, and Marie, 18, had fallen in love and wanted to marry. Sadly, though, Marie was not queen material. The marriage of a King of France needed to have a political purpose that brought his country diplomatic, trade, military or religious benefits. Despite her Mazarin connection, Marie Mancini afforded no such advantages, and that fact doomed any chance of her marrying the young king. Marie was sent away and Louis was heartbroken. The more prestigious union required of a king took place on 9 June 1660, when Louis married the Infanta Maria Theresa of Spain, who, unlike Marie Mancini, qualified as a consort with the 'right' ancestry.

These advantages, it seemed, overrode her rather alarming appearance and personality. Maria Theresa looked like a dwarf and had the overlong jaw known as the 'Hapsburg lip'. She was simpleminded, with no interests beyond cakes and sweets, her pets, her dwarf entertainers, playing cards and praying. But at least she rapidly provided Louis with the male heir all kings desired: the first of their six children, the Dauphin Louis, was born on 1 November 1661.

The marriage of a King of France needed to have a political purpose that brought his country diplomatic, trade, military or religious benefits.

Louis remained faithful to Maria Theresa during their first year of his marriage, but this fidelity did not last. The chief, and sometimes only, purpose of royal marriage was the provision of heirs. Beyond that, kings chose mistresses for their pleasure. French practice formalized the arrangement. The *maîtresse-en-titre*, the King's official mistress, held a recognized position at court. As such, she could acquire considerable power and wealth, as long as she remained in favour. Louis's first *maîtresse-en-titre* was the artless and adoring Louise de la Vallière. Louise was the stepdaughter of a French aristocrat, Jacques de Courtarvel, Marquis de Saint-Rémy, and this connection enabled her to enter royal circles.

Louise, aged 16, arrived at the court of Louis XIV in 1660 and was soon appointed a maid of honour to the English Princess Henrietta, who had recently married Philippe, Duc d'Orléans, the King's younger brother. Henrietta, sister of the English King Charles II, shared her rakish brother's taste for *amours*. After Henrietta's arrival at Louis's court in 1661, it was only a matter of time before she went to work on the young French monarch. Rumours quickly spread that an affair, and with it a full-blown scandal, was on its way.

The Infanta Maria Theresa of Spain, first wife of King Louis XIV. From her marriage in 1660 to her death in 1683, she remained the perfect consort — uninterested in politics, devout, providing heirs while turning a blind eye to Louis's love affairs.

Louise de la Vallière became Louis XIV's first mistress in 1661 and gave him four children before she was supplanted by the Marquise de Montesan in 1667. Afterwards Louise retired to a nunnery.

... And a suitable mistress

At that juncture, Louis's mother, Anne of Austria, stepped in and inserted Louise into the picture. Louise's task was to divert suspicion by making out that the young king was smitten by her rather than his sister-in-law. But an unexpected factor was involved: the innocent Louise was already in love with the king, who soon forgot about Henrietta and, instead, fell for her maid of honour. The haughty Henrietta was so enraged that she at once took up with the Comte de Guiche, her husband's favourite.

Louise's attraction for the king was something for which the proud, possessive Henrietta could never have provided. Outwardly, Louise was a very

Louise was a very plain Jane. She was mousy and retiring ... But she scored with the king where it most mattered. She was no artful, self-interested coquette. All Louise wanted was to love Louis, and Louis basked in her adoration.

plain Jane. She was mousy and retiring, whereas the beautiful Henrietta could enslave men with a glance. One of her legs was shorter than the other, and she had to wear special heels to prevent her limping. But she scored with the king where it most mattered. She was no artful, self-interested coquette. All Louise wanted was to love Louis, and Louis basked in her adoration.

Louis XIV and Louise de la Vallière had four children, the first born in 1663 and the last in 1667. Their relationship lasted for six years, but in 1661 almost foundered because of a fierce quarrel over Princess Henrietta. Despite their enmity, Louise remained loyal to Henrietta and refused to inform the king about Henrietta's liaison with the Comte de Guiche. Louis exploded in fury, and Louise was so frightened that she fled to a convent. Eventually, Louis learned of the affair with de Guiche after le Comte was threatened with exposure. In order to save her lover, Henrietta went to the king and told him everything. De Guiche was later exiled.

Princess Henrietta Anne, daughter of Charles I of England, was the wife of Louis XIV's brother Philip Duc d'Orléans.

A new favourite

Louise remained in place as royal mistress, but by 1666 she was falling from favour. The previous year King Louis had created her Duchesse de la Vallière and gave her the estate of Vaujours. It was a going-away present. This was not just a matter of Louis tiring of a long-term mistress, as kings tended to do. Louise was being undermined behind the scenes, by the venomous Françoise-Athénais, Marquise de Montespan, who was determined to replace her as *maîtresse-en-titre*. That position had far more prestige and offered far more money and advancement than her marriage to the Marquis de Montespan, a minor nobleman of only modest wealth.

The marquise planned her campaign carefully. Nothing dramatic. Nothing perceptible. Merely a series of apparently innocent moves that got her close

Françoise-Athénais, Marquise de Montespan, achieved her aim of making herself Louis XIV's mistress in 1668, after staging a campaign to ensnare him that was said to include sorcery and witchcraft.

TWO FRENCH ROYAL RAKES: LOUIS XIV AND LOUIS XV 51

RUMOURS OF THE DARK ARTS

The extraordinary hold the Marquise de Montespan exerted over Louis XIV gave rise to rumours that, even before she became his *maîtresse-en-titre*, she was using black magic, witchcraft and sorcery on him. Nothing was conclusively proved, but it was alleged that during her campaign to ensnare the king, the marquise purchased from the sorceress Catherine Monvoisin love powders containing obnoxious ingredients such as toad's spittle. She was also said to be involved in 'black' masses, which were held over her naked body. Later on, although no evidence was found against her, the marquise was again implicated when members of the aristocracy were, with others, put on trial for witchcraft and poisoning in 1675.

The king, it appears, was completely unaware of any of the rumours that his bewitchment had a darker source. He believed that in the marquise he had found his ideal companion, and lavished jewels, fine clothes and all manner of other luxuries on her. The king's money not only enabled the marquise to live in splendour and make substantial donations to her favourite charities, but also to obtain high positions for members of her family: her father, for example, became governor of Paris.

But talk of sorcery, poison and witchcraft did not go away. When Louis began to suffer from dizzy spells, fainting fits and bouts of uncontrollable shivering, rumour was soon claiming that the king's ardour was cooling and, in an effort to reignite it, the marquise was again plying him with noxious love powders. But

King Louis XIV never lost his appetite for sex. This made life difficult for his second wife, Françoise d'Aubigné, who wrote in her diary of 'painful occasions'.

the marquise, it seemed, chose another way. She decided that a gesture of piety was due. When she went to make confession of her many sins at Versailles, however, the priest, the Abbé Lécuyer, refused to hear it or to grant her absolution. Incandescent with rage, she complained to the king, only to learn that it was the Abbé's duty to refuse absolution to such an inveterate sinner. The marquise withdrew from the court and fasted to confirm her repentance. Louis, too, had been refused absolution in 1675 and went through a similar performance to prove his penitence.

THREE AFFAIRS

At last, in July 1676, the lovers were allowed to meet again. Soon after their reconciliation, the marquise was restored to her position as *maîtresse-en-titre* with all the privileges, such as precedence over duchesses, that went with it. Even so, she was aware that all was not well. Louis was having affairs with three other court ladies more or less simultaneously: one of them, it was rumoured, had given birth to a child by him.

The marquise reacted with predictable rage and also put it about that another of Louis's 'extra' mistresses, Madame de Ludre, suffered from a fearful skin ailment. She need not have bothered. De Ludre was already on the way out after Louis learned that she had appointed her own husband as messenger between herself and her royal lover.

enough to the King for him to notice her. First, the marquise became friendly with Philippe, Louis's younger brother. Next, she moved on to the queen, and put on a mask of piety and virtue which the devout Maria Theresa was bound to appreciate. After that, the marquise became close to Louise herself and, through Louise, to the king. Very little time passed

---

The Marquise could not have been more different from the diffident, devoted Louise. She was a formidable figure – arrogant, sensual, cruel and unremittingly vengeful against anyone who angered her.

---

before Louis noticed this witty, strikingly beautiful interloper. She attracted him so powerfully that, while Louise was giving birth to his son, the Comte de Vermondois, in 1667, the king was dallying with Montespan until early morning.

The Comte de Vermondois was Louise's last child by the king, although she remained at court until 1674, when the official separation of the Marquis and the Marquise de Montespan was announced. Louise's presence as the apparent *maîtresse-en-titre* was camouflage for the king's liaison with his new mistress. By this means, the jealous marquis, who had been attempting legal moves to get his wife back, was left with no real evidence of an affair. In order to maintain this charade, Louise was forced to attend the marquise like a servant, helping her with her toilette. In 1674, she was allowed to enter the convent of Sainte Marie de Chaillot and became a nun. Louise died in Paris in 1710. On hearing the news, King Louis commented that she had been 'dead' to him from the day she left.

By the time Louise de la Vallière escaped from her years of humiliation at court, the Marquise de Montespan had already given birth to the first five of her seven children by the king. The Marquise could not have been more different from the diffident, devoted Louise. She was a formidable figure – arrogant, sensual, cruel and unremittingly vengeful against anyone who angered her. She was a real challenge for Louis, defying him whenever the whim took her, giving as good as she got in violent quarrels, yet also bewitching him with her beauty and her charms.

Changing fortunes and changing attitudes

All the same, time was still running out for the marquise to score triumphs over all comers. By 1678, when her last child by Louis was born, she was almost 40 years of age and growing fat and frowsy. She was also being confronted by increasingly younger rivals such as Angélique de Fontanges, a beautiful but empty-headed maid of honour who had been instructed by her ambitious parents to become the king's mistress. The marquise found out, of course, but this time her fury failed to move Louis. Her time was up, but she went on living in her apartments at Versailles for some years. The king visited her there from time to time, but in 1691 the marquise retired to a convent with a large pension of 500,000 francs. She died in 1707. Angélique was discarded in her turn, as Louis tired of her.

This time, the successor to the King's favour was not some ambitious fortune-hunter, but a woman who had been around the court – and the king – for some time. Françoise Scarron, the widow of the writer Paul Scarron, first arrived at court in 1669, to look after and educate the marquise's first child by the king, who was born that year. Later, she also took charge of the six others who followed. Françoise was an exemplary nurse and governess, and the children quickly came to love her. Louis recognized

This is possibly a portrait of Marie Angélique de Scorraille de Russille, Duchesse de Fontanges, who in 1678 became Louis XIV's mistress.

Françoise's importance to his 'second' family by the marquise and, in 1674, gave her the money to purchase a house from the Duc de Maintenon. With this came a new title, Madame de Maintenon.

Even in the face of this generosity, it took Louis quite a while to appreciate her. At first, he looked on Françoise as a dull, difficult prude who was far too full of *bel esprit* – high moral tone. He knew that she disapproved of the licentious way he led his life and once said, 'To preserve one's honour, the first thing one must give up is pleasure.'

Yet, despite himself, the king could not help noticing how kind she was, how gentle and caring and how comely and pretty she looked, even at age 37. 'She knows how to love,' he remarked. 'It would be pleasant to be loved by her.'

> **He looked on Françoise as a dull, difficult prude who was far too full of *bel esprit* – high moral tone ... she disapproved of the licentious way he led his life ...**

Louis already knew Françoise well enough to realize that she would never consent to be his mistress. Morality and modesty would not permit it for, in her eyes, sex belonged to the marriage bed and only the marriage bed. The king was, by now, very much in love with Françoise, but could not accept the alternative to an illicit affair – a platonic relationship. The opportunity to solve this problem arrived in 1683, when Queen Maria Theresa died, probably of cancer, aged 44.

Louis summoned Françoise to his presence, and in his arbitrary way informed her that he meant to marry her morganatically. This meant that, as his wife and a commoner, she could not enjoy the honours and privileges usually due a royal consort. Françoise was

Madame de Maintenon was an unusual woman to find at the libidinous French court. During the 32 years that she was married to Louis XIV, she created a more dignified atmosphere at Versailles.

uninterested in honours and privileges, and married the king in secret some time in October 1683. The marriage lasted until Louis's death in 1715 and, during those 32 years, the high-minded Françoise managed, remarkably, to transform him from a licentious rake into a virtuous and faithful husband. Louis seemed to thrive on this new lifestyle and so did his libido which enabled him to make love to Françoise twice a day in 1710, when he was 72 years old.

Five years later, when Louis XIV was dying of gangrene, and his five-year-old greatgrandson was about to succeed him as King Louis XV, he told his courtiers: 'You are about to see one king to his grave and another in his cradle. Always bear in mind the memory of the one and the interests of the other.'

A new monarch

King Louis XIV, the mighty Sun King, was always going to be a hard act to follow, but for his greatgrandson even the attempt was impossible. Since 1711, the fifteenth Louis had been the 'last-chance' direct heir to the French throne after the deaths of all other males in the line of succession. As a result, he had been so coddled and spoiled that he grew up to be profoundly timid and indecisive. Although he dutifully performed the public role of imperious autocrat with all its pervading pomp, his own lifestyle choice was the quiet existence of a country gentlemen. Louis took little or no interest in affairs of state, became flummoxed when confronted with financial problems and, effectively, did nothing to promote the welfare of his realm or his people. As Louis's foreign minister, René-Louis de Voyer de Paulmy, Marquis d'Argenson, put it, the king 'opened his mouth, said little and thought not at all' when required to attend meetings of his ruling council.

Left: A portrait of King Louis XV. Louis, who became king when he was five, was the only survivor of a family tragedy in which his father, grandfather and all their other children died when an epidemic of smallpox swept through the royal household.

Louis XV greatly enjoyed the thrill of the hunt, but his overriding interest in life was the company of women. By this means, it was said, he sought to fill the gap left by the death of his mother, Marie-Adelaide of Savoy, in 1711, when Louis was less than two years old. The king's quest began in around 1725, shortly after he married his queen, Maria-Catherine Leszczynska of Poland. Within the year, she gave birth to twin girls, the first of her 10 children by Louis, but already the chase was on to find a mistress for the king.

He dallied for a while with an assortment of housemaids and other servant girls. After that, he went through all four of the de Mailly-Nesle sisters in succession.

Marie Anne de Mailly-Nesle was the youngest of four sisters, all of whom became successive mistresses to King Louis XV. She attempted to make the lazy, self-indulgent king more active, but died in 1744, aged 27.

It was early days, for Louis was only 15 years old when he married. He dallied for a while with an assortment of housemaids and other servant girls. After that, he went through all four of the de Mailly-Nesle sisters in succession. The most ambitious of the four was the youngest, who arrived on the royal scene in 1742. Marie-Anne wanted Louis to be a more active, involved monarch. She forced him to work harder at the business of government, see his ministers more often and attend to more and more detail of public affairs. This was torture for the indolent Louis.

King Louis XV's queen, Maria-Catherine Leszczynska, gave him 10 children, but four of his daughters and both of his sons predeceased him.

'Madame,' he protested. 'You are killing me!' The king was released from his torment after two years, when Marie-Anne died of pneumonia in 1744 aged only 27 years. Her successor was the beautiful, well-educated Jeanne Antoinette d'Etoiles, who initially lacked the basic qualification for the role of *maitress-en-titre:* connections with the aristocracy. Jeanne Antoinette, however, belonged to the more lowly bourgeoisie. Nevertheless, there was a prediction about Jeanne that gave her and her family high hopes of overcoming this difficulty. In 1730, at age nine, she was told by a fortune-teller that she would one day capture the heart of a king. After that, her family nicknamed her 'Reinette' – little queen – in anticipation of the exciting event.

The rise of Madame de Pompadour

The exciting event took place in February 1745, when the Dauphin Louis, heir to the French throne, married Princess Maria Teresa of Spain. Among the fêtes and celebrations, grand balls were held in Paris and Versailles where anyone who was suitably dressed was invited to attend. Jeanne Antoinette made a special point of attending a masked ball at Versailles, where she manoeuvred her way close to the king and engaged him in conversation, masks off. The signal was quickly understood. 'The handkerchief is thrown,' one of

Jeanne Antoinette Poisson, Madame de Pompadour, was the most able of all Louis XV's mistresses. Her 'reign' lasted 20 years and though not quite as powerful as some historians have made out, she took over much of the running of everyday royal business.

Louis's courtiers remarked in 'court-speak', meaning that an intimate relationship had begun.

A few days later, the king invited Jeanne Antoinette to meet him for a private supper at the Hotel de Ville in Paris. Before long, he was deeply in love with her and afterwards turned her into an aristocrat by giving her the title of marquise and later, Duchesse de Pompadour. Jeanne Antoinette lost no time exercising the power of a *maîtresse-en-titre*. She was not as politically active as some historians have believed, but her influence counted when it came to the advancement of her friends and relatives. For instance, she persuaded the king to champion the candidacy of her friend Voltaire, the brilliant writer and historian, for membership of the prestigious Académie Française.

Her most striking achievements, however, were in the social sphere, where she created a homely atmosphere for the king in which he revelled in the friendly, relaxed company of her family. She also coaxed Louis to interest himself in the theatre, listen to music or appreciate art and design, none of which had places at the trivial-minded, back-biting royal court. For the first time in his life, Louis XV was enjoying

> **Her most striking achievements, however, were in the social sphere, where she created a homely atmosphere for the king in which he revelled in the friendly, relaxed company of her family.**

himself and, if his snobbish court wanted to whisper enviously that his mistress had him in thrall, it scarcely bothered him.

There was, though, a dark lining to this silver cloud. Jeanne Antoinette did not enjoy good health, and she was in constant fear that she would not be able to keep up with the king's more lusty approach to sex. She began to consume vast quantities of aphrodisiacs – vanilla, truffles, celery – but all that did was to make her sick. Her condition was not helped by a series of miscarriages. Eventually, inevitably, Jeanne-Antoinette developed heart trouble, continual headaches, breathing difficulties and, in 1764, congestion of the lungs. She died, aged 42, on 15 April 1764 and was buried two days later in Paris.

As Jeanne Antoinette's health declined, it was likely that her sex life with Louis came to an end. He never ceased to love her, but kept other mistresses in the last few years before her death. He also returned to his servant girls and lodged them in a private brothel at the *Parc aux Cerfs* (Park of Deers), a small villa in Versailles. Louis sometimes visited the Parc disguised as a Polish nobleman, but one of the girls searched through her lover's pockets as he lay sleeping and discovered who he really was. The girl was hauled off to an insane asylum, a move that would certainly invalidate anything she said about the king.

The *Parc aux Cerfs* was the centrepiece of Louis's debauchery, which, by 1764, was profoundly affecting his popularity with his subjects. In 1744, he had been nicknamed *bien aimé* (well beloved) after recovering from a serious illness. Twenty years later

The Parc aux Cerfs near the royal palace at Versailles was Louis XV's bolt-hole where he could enjoy his energetic sex life in peace. The establishment was very efficiently run for him by Madame de Pompadour.

PHILIPPE, DUC D'ORLÉANS

LOUIS XIV'S 'HOMOSEXUAL' BROTHER

Philippe, Duc d'Orléans (1640–1701), may have been the younger brother of Louis XIV, but their mother Queen Anne treated them very differently. She guarded Louis's rights as king by deliberately making Philippe seem inferior, even ridiculous. That way, he could not challenge his brother's rule. Encouraged by his mother, Philippe pretended to be homosexual when he was, in fact, twice married and fathered several children. He also wore female dress, made up his face and chose handsome young courtiers as his favourites.

Louis was very fond of Philippe, who was known as 'Monsieur' at court, and continually showered him with gifts. Nonetheless, Louis continued his mother's work of distancing his young brother from the sources of power and influence in France. One way was to purchase the beautiful villa of St Cloud, which was

close, but not too close, to Versailles, where the business of government was conducted. Philippe was delighted with the villa and the opportunity it gave him to beautify its gardens. More important, however, was St Cloud's function in keeping Philippe away from the centre of royal power, and Louis deliberately saw to it that his brother played no part in French affairs. The king's attitude towards his brother was affectionate, but intensely patronizing.

'Now we are going to work,' he was reported to have told Monsieur before discussing royal business with his ministers. 'Go and amuse yourself, brother!'

King Louis XIV was very fond of his brother Philippe, Duc d'Orléans, but he did not consider him competent enough to be involved in state business and excluded him from councils with his ministers.

Marie Jeanne Bécu, Madame du Barry, was the last mistress of King Louis XV, who is shown standing by her bed. She made a tremendous impression when she was presented at court in 1769, and Louis, totally entranced, bedded her within a few weeks.

he had become 'well hated' for his weak government, his financial incompetence, the disasters France suffered in war and for the excesses of his sex life. But the girls at the Parc aux Cerfs were not as important as lurid tales of orgies made them appear. Rather, they provided Louis XV with a place to play while he waited for his next *maîtresse-en-titre* to emerge from the numerous hopefuls who crowded his court at Versailles.

Ambition realized

Among the women who aspired to the position occupied by the late Jeanne Antoinette was Marie Jeanne Bécu, the illegitimate daughter of Anne Bécu, a seamstress or cook. In 1758, aged 15, Marie Jeanne, a remarkably good-looking blonde, moved to Paris where she caught the eye of a philanderer, Jean du Barry. Du Barry soon realized that she was royal mistress material and, in 1768, provided her with the required noble title by marrying her to his brother Comte Guillaume. The new Comtesse du Barry was presented at court on 2 April 1769. She made a tremendous impression, with her extravagant gown and the diamonds that adorned her neck and ears.

The king was entranced, so much so that the delectable Jeanne quickly distracted him from his grief at the death of his queen, which took place on 25 June 1769. Even before the queen died, Louis had bedded his new mistress and next day remarked; 'I am delighted with … Jeanne. She is the only woman in France who has managed to make me forget that I am 60.'

'He is more in love than he has ever been,' commented the Duc de Croy, who had known Louis for many years. 'He seems to be rejuvenated and I have never seen him in better spirits, extremely good-humoured and far more outgoing.'

Jeanne achieved this transformation not only with her beauty, but, more importantly, through her charm and her ability to amuse the king while also giving him warmth and affection. In this, she was much like the late Duchesse de Pompadour, even though she lacked her predecessor's brains and talents. Like de Pompadour, she was at home in the world of the arts. Her *levées*, the gatherings where writers, artists, poets, dramatists and scholars flocked to enjoy her hospitality, became an established part of the intellectual scene. Ministers, financiers and bankers came to her for advice on their various projects. Jewellers regarded du Barry as their patron, for her love of jewels was well known. She was the only lady at court to wear jewels in mixed colours – rubies and emeralds or pink with grey pearls.

A nation revolts

King Louis was heedlessly extravagant, lavishing a fortune on his mistress at a time when public resentment was growing fast at the fundamental inequalities of French society. As a result, the Comtesse du Barry was in the popular firing line along with the king and the aristocracy. As he aged, Louis became more and more unpopular and was haunted by a fear of death and by guilt over his sexual transgressions. At such times, Louis kept away from du Barry. He paid frequent visits to a convent where his youngest daughter, Louise, had become a Carmelite nun. Louis believed that she had taken her vows in order to save his immortal soul and spent many hours with his daughter, praying for forgiveness.

Although the king always returned to du Barry, time was running out for both of them. In 1774, Louis contracted smallpox and, realizing he was dying, he sent du Barry away to the convent of Pont-au-Dames. Had she remained at Versailles, her 'immoral' presence would have prevented Louis receiving absolution. He died on 10 May.

The attack on the Bastille prison in Paris in 1789 and the release of its prisoners was the signal for the start of the French Revolution. It was, in fact, just a gesture, since there were few prisoners in the Bastille at the time.

THE MAN IN THE IRON MASK

The Man in the Iron Mask was one of Europe's great royal mysteries. First imprisoned in 1687, he was brought to Paris 11 years later and placed under close guard in the Bastille. No one knew who he was – nor were they meant to know. Rumour had it that he was a courtier who had fallen out of favour with Louis XIV, but there seemed to be more to it than mere disgrace. The anonymous man had to wear his mask all the time, and two musketeers stood close by in his prison cell, ready to kill him if he removed it.

He ate, slept and eventually, in 1703, died still wearing his mask. Some 50 years later, the famous French writer Voltaire speculated that the Man in the Iron Mask resembled someone very famous – Louis XIV himself. Among the many rumours surrounding the Man in the Iron Mask, this one gave rise to speculation that he was in fact Louis's twin brother, born a few minutes before him, and being kept confined in order to preserve the king's position.

The mysterious man in the iron mask who was imprisoned for 16 years, sparked off numerous conspiracy theories, a famous novel by Alexandre Dumas, published in 1848, and numerous movies. But his identity was never revealed.

A short while earlier, King Louis apparently remarked: *'Après moi le deluge.'* – 'After me, the deluge.' It was horrifically prescient. Five years after Louis's death, the French Revolution erupted, eventually sweeping away the monarchy and decimating the nobility and clergy. Thousands, including the reigning king and his queen, Louis XVI and Marie Antoinette, died by the guillotine in 1792–3 during the so-called Reign of Terror. One of them was the Comtesse du Barry.

Charged with treason and conspiracy, she was found guilty and condemned to death. On 8 December 1793, du Barry was taken through the streets of Paris in a tumbrel to the Place de la Revolution, where a guillotine was set up, waiting for her. She was panic-stricken and hysterical, screaming at the watching crowds to save her. She struggled with the executioners, but to no avail. They overcame her and she was laid on the scaffold. The knife blade sliced down and cut off her head. With the French Revolution, Louis XIV's famous dictum – *L'état c'est moi* – went into reverse. The king was no longer the state. Instead, the state was king.

In 1774, Louis contracted smallpox and ... sent du Barry away to the convent ... Had she remained at Versailles, her 'immoral' presence would have prevented Louis receiving absolution.

THE KING AND THE VAMP: LUDWIG I OF BAVARIA AND LOLA MONTEZ

Marie Dolores Eliza Rosanna Gilbert, alias Lola Montez (1818–1861), had all the qualifications required to be a femme fatale. She was dark-haired and blue-eyed, with a sensuous mouth and a voluptuous figure. There was also something quite mesmeric about her gaze. With this formidable equipment, Lola bewitched many men, including a king, Ludwig I of Bavaria (1786–1868).

✦

At their first meeting, in Munich in 1846, Lola barged her way into the royal presence and was asked by the king, who knew of her reputation, if her renowned beauty was really the work of Nature. Ludwig, aged 60, may have been deaf, but there was nothing wrong with his vision. He knew what he was looking at when Lola replied by tearing

Left: Ludwig I of Bavaria lost his heart and his throne to the *femme fatale* Lola Montez.
Above: King Ludwig was not the only man to be bowled over by Marie Dolores Elizabeth Rosanna Gilbert, alias Lola Montez.

open her bodice to show that, on at least two counts, Nature had done a fine job.

Despite her exotic name, which she devised for her short-lived stage career, Lola Montez was born in Ireland in 1818. Soon afterwards, her father, an English army officer, was transferred to India, and his family went with him. He does not seem to have survived long in India, where climate, epidemics and the excesses of expatriate life decimated Europeans. Her father died when Lola was still very young. Her mother, a very beautiful woman, promptly acquired a second husband, another English army officer.

A COQUETTE IS BORN

In 1836, Lola's mother, having shed her second husband, turned up in England from India escorted by a handsome young subaltern surnamed James. Lola was then a superbly well-equipped 19-year-old. Once Subaltern James set eyes on her, he had no chance. Neither did Lola's mother. James fell hopelessly in love and promptly eloped with Lola. He became the first of her many husbands when he married her in County Meath, Ireland, on 23 July 1837.

The Jameses settled for a while in Dublin, where the stunning Lola swiftly adapted to army social life. She seems to have behaved herself reasonably well, but her animal attraction still fired on all cylinders and the then Lord Lieutenant, Lord Normanby, was entranced as soon as he was introduced to her. Fortunately for Lady Normanby and the other army wives, Lola did not remain in Dublin for long. The city was, in any case, far too unglamorous for a girl brought up in the heady atmosphere of the East. To Lola's delight, her husband was posted back to India after a few months. The couple duly took up residence at Simla, the beautiful hill station that lay in the approaches to the Himalayan mountains.

Life in British India, for all its outward grandeur, could be very tedious and parochial, and Lola arrived in Simla like a firework illuminating a very humdrum scene. At the once-sedate parties, balls and social evenings Lola attended, there was a new and unaccustomed air of excitement. Lola had all the young officers agog in no time. Lola's husband, now Captain James, realized that Lola was too magnetic to other men to be the wife he wanted. He ran off with a less attractive woman who required less surveillance in defence of her reputation and his conjugal rights.

Naturally enough, Lola was mightily affronted, but worse than any ego-bruising she may have suffered was her new social status. As a deserted wife, she completely lost face and, by the brutal laws of expatriate society, became a pariah. The invitations dried up. She was snubbed in company. Lola could hardly stay in India under these circumstances; instead, she headed for Britain.

When Lola reached London, she found her mother had married for a third time and that her stepfather, a Mr Craigie, had decided to take his stepdaughter in hand. Craigie sent a Calvinist, a dour, probably immune character, to accompany Lola north to Perth where, he probably presumed, this wild young hoyden could be tamed. Craigie reckoned without Lola's resolve to do her own thing. She told her Calvinist minder exactly what he could do with dreary old Perth and the domineering Craigie and point blank refused to go. The Calvinist retired hurt, and Lola settled for a time in London, where, inevitably, she went through a string of lovers.

A social outcast

Not long afterwards, Captain James divorced Lola, or rather she believed he had done so. Where no other restraint had managed to hold Lola back, this one did. In the 1840s, and for well over a century afterwards, divorce labelled an ex-wife as a 'scarlet woman'. Lola dealt with this inconvenient turn of events in very

If she was going to be a social outcast, she might as well do the job properly and put herself beyond another social pale of her times by going on the stage.

practical fashion. If she was going to be a social outcast, she might as well do the job properly and put herself beyond another social pale of her times by going on the stage. Actresses were then regarded as little better than prostitutes, and the same went for dancers. Lola loved dancing and decided to specialize in the frankly sensual, unbridled dances performed in Andalusia in southern Spain. She was perfectly suited to the genre, with the dark looks, the curvaceous figure and, after several years of unbuttoned living, the alluring manner.

Marie James, as she was still called, lacked the exotic image required, so she adopted Lola as her first name and added Montez. There were, however, no long stints of 'resting', the frequent fate of newcomers to the world of theatre. Lola's exploits were already well known, not to say notorious, and she was able to attract a ready-made audience. This included the cream of society – Queen Adelaide, widow of King William IV; the Duchess of Kent, mother of the reigning queen, Victoria; and Victoria's uncle, the King of Hanover in Germany. At Her Majesty's Theatre in London, Lola was billed as Donna Lola Montez of the Teatro Real in Seville, but unfortunately one member of the audience, Lord Thomas Ranelagh, knew who she really was. Not long before, Lola had turned down

the lord's advances. In return, he saw to it that her first performance in London was also her last.

The rest of the audience was, at first, entranced by Lola's stage presence and not a little titillated by her suggestive movements. Until, that is, Lord Ranelagh called out: 'Why! It's Betty James!' and proceeded to hoot and boo her. His friends joined in. So did the audience, until Lola, unable to continue, fled the stage. She was so mortified that she left the country the next day.

Lola Montez found it easy to wow a whole crowd of men when she appeared onstage. To see her, it seems, was to fall madly in love with her. As a result, she left behind her a trail of would-be lovers and broken hearts.

Virtually destitute, Lola wandered Europe until, inevitably, a new lover came to the rescue. He was able to secure a dancing engagement for Lola in Warsaw, and the unsophisticated Poles went mad for her. The critics reached for their most colourful adjectives to describe Lola's performance and Lola herself. According to them, she was Venus, the Roman goddess of love, come to life. There were the shades of 16 different varieties of forget-me-not in her eyes. She upstaged the swan in the elegant whiteness of her neck.

Warsaw's new sensation naturally attracted eminent lovers, the sort who adorned their egos by seeking to possess the latest sex symbol. Lola's own ego was no

Prince Ivan Paskievich was another famous figure who fell for Lola Montez. This Russian military leader had taken part in the battle of Austerlitz in 1805, and was to command the siege of Silistria (pictured), a precursor to the Crimean War.

The next thing Lola knew, Paskievich had signed an order for her expulsion and she was unceremoniously dumped over the Polish frontier.

puny thing by now, and she could afford – or thought she could afford – to be choosy. This was how the 60-year-old Prince Ivan Paskievich, the Russian Viceroy of Poland, conceived a violent passion for Lola only to find that she was not interested. Paskievich possessed much more power to discredit Lola than Lord Ranelagh could have ever have hoped for. The next thing Lola knew, Paskievich had signed an order for her expulsion and she was unceremoniously dumped over the Polish frontier.

LUDWIG I, A BELOVED RULER

In 1846, when Lola came to Munich, Bavarians were not too concerned about the more oddball Wittelsbachs, as Ludwig I was obviously not one of them. In a reign of more than 20 years, he had unfailingly used his appreciation of the glories of classical Greece and Rome to grace the city of Munich with grand palaces, temples and museums. He made it a city of which every Bavarian could be proud and, despite the massive expense, his subjects loved him for it.

UNGUARDED FAMILY MAN

The man himself, by contrast, was unassuming. Unlike other rulers in Germany, which was then a collection of independent and semi-independent states, King Ludwig did not keep aloof from his subjects or regard non-royals as inferior to himself. Far from it. Ludwig loved to stroll unattended and unguarded along the streets of Munich, chatting to passers-by. He seemed to enjoy not being recognized and so passing for any other man in the street. In much the same vein, Ludwig preferred to live frugally and relished family life, a rare trait where too many other German royals were concerned.

Although King Ludwig I of Bavaria appears here in military dress, he was not personally aggressive, unlike some rulers in nineteenth-century Germany. Bavarians loved him for his kindness, modesty and warm-heartedness.

By the time she presented herself to the director of Munich's Royal Theatre for an audition, the word on the street had already marked her out as undesirable.

Lola set out for Paris, where she made her debut as a dancer in 1845. It was a humiliating failure. The French had far too much taste and artistic discernment to fall for the cavortings of an amateur, and Lola's performance went down in a barrage of hooting, booing and scathing reviews. Lola's next destination was Germany and on from there to Munich, capital of the Kingdom of Bavaria, where she found that tales of her escapades had already made her a celebrity. But reading sensational gossip and allegations of immorality did not mean that Lola was acceptable to the Bavarian powers-that-be. Family life counted for a great deal in Bavaria and, with that, the virtues of fidelity, chastity and, most vital of all, respectability. None of these was in Lola's curriculum. The cornerstone of all this righteousness was the Wittelsbach royal family, a gracious, artistic and, to the Bavarians, lovable crew whose often eccentric behaviour was accepted as part of their charm. At the centre of this family was the king, Ludwig I, revered for his programme of building and his apparent egalitarian attitude.

Lola Montez in a provocative pose, with a supposed 'come hither' look that enslaved virtually every man she met.

The king was not, of course, quite as too-good-to-be-true as his deeds and apparent frugality might suggest. Like other Wittelsbachs, whose family temperament was mercurial where it was not mad, Ludwig was a man of contrasts. He was liberal-minded, but could become very haughty if he thought his royal rights were being infringed. He was wise in many ways, yet gullible. He was an affectionate husband and father, yet he went through his quota of liaisons, and had no defence against a pretty face.

Not just a pretty face

As many men – and their wives or mistresses – had already discovered, Lola Montez was much, much more than a pretty face. As soon as officialdom learned of the presence in Munich of this outlandish adventuress, the knives were out. Lola was at once seen as a danger to the Bavarian realm and everyone in it. The Church seemed to believe that she was a destabilizing influence. Clerics did not hesitate to pile on the anti-Lola propaganda to this effect; by the time she presented herself to the director of Munich's Royal Theatre for an audition, the word on the street had already marked her out as undesirable.

Whether the rumours affected Herr Direktor's decision is not known. But he watched Lola dance, decided she was not good enough for his theatre and turned her down. The feisty Lola was not to be put off. Her scandal-filled life so far had shorn her of all the restraints that usually keep impudence in check, and her chutzpah was high. Foiled at the Royal Theatre, she decided to petition Ludwig I himself and went to his palace to demand an audience with him. It appears that once she

> **He spent whole afternoons in her boudoir, daily wrote her long, passionate verses and even neglected his once all-consuming interests in art, Italy and the classics.**

had displayed her magnificent breasts for the king's inspection, he was instantly hooked and soon gave her what she wanted – his permission to dance at the Royal Theatre. Ludwig was there to watch and fall even further under Lola's spell. Later, he told his ministers that he was 'bewitched' and, having seen Ludwig through several liaisons, they were in a good position to realize that this one was different – and dangerous.

Their fears were quickly confirmed. Before long, Ludwig seemed unable to keep away from Lola. He spent whole afternoons in her boudoir, daily wrote her long, passionate verses and even neglected his once all-consuming interests in art, Italy and the classics. Lola and the king always denied that their liaison was sexual and, given his age, some were willing to believe it. Others refused to credit that, if Europe's foremost vamp and the susceptible and amorous old king spent enough time together, nothing would happen.

An unhealthy obsession

Even more worrying, though, was Ludwig's habit of discussing state affairs with Lola. Lola's liberal views were as well known as her scandalous history, and that marked her out as a potential danger to the state.

Both men and women flocked to the fashionable salons of Europe whenever Lola Montez performed there. The public behaved in the same, wildly enthusiastic, way when she danced at the theatres.

Ludwig's sister, the Dowager Empress of Austria, wrote to Lola offering her a large sum of money to leave Bavaria and leave her brother alone. She refused, and tore up the letter.

Liberals were regarded as perilous to the established political and social order, and most especially to the rights and privileges of the absolute monarchs who dominated the royalty of Europe. Yet this was not all. With her Calvinist – that is, strictly Protestant – background, Lola was staunchly anti-Catholic. The Jesuits, the Catholic activists in Bavaria, were not going to stand for that. Jesuits had long ago proved themselves a fighting breed and, in declaring war on Lola, they did not care that Ludwig I also came into their line of fire. They began a whispering campaign against Lola, which reached the newspapers in the form of savage lampoons. The king, inevitably, was ridiculed at the same time.

The effect, however, was nil. Ludwig, far gone in infatuation, refused to part with Lola or believe any story against her, even if it were true. Mere months after their first meeting, Ludwig gave clear proof of Lola's hold over him by replacing his chief minister Abel with one of her supporters, Baron Schrenk. There was an immediate and vociferous outcry, and rumour began to hint darkly that, through the besotted

Right: Demonstrations took place across the German states in 1848, in a series of events known as the March revolution. This romanticized image shows rioters in Berlin, scene of some of the worst troubles, but there was unrest across the region.

king, Lola Montez would soon be ruling Bavaria. Several officials attempted to prise Ludwig from her grasp, but all failed. The Chief of the Bavarian Police was threatened with imprisonment for his protests about Lola's growing influence. Society ladies who deliberately snubbed her were answered when the king commissioned a portrait of Lola and ordered it to be hung in one of Munich's most important art galleries. Count Arco-Valley was so outraged that he removed the picture of his wife, which hung in the same gallery. Court officials entered the fray, only to be told by Ludwig that, far from setting Lola aside, he intended to make her a countess.

A cardinal threatened the king with excommunication, the direst penalty a Catholic could incur, but Ludwig took no notice. He went

Where Ludwig was weak, though, was in his perverse attachment to Lola, which allowed her to exercise controversial influence over him.

on spending most of his time with Lola and every afternoon could be seen walking to the magnificent mansion he had given her in Munich. Next, Ludwig's sister, the Dowager Empress of Austria, was persuaded by Jesuits to offer Lola £2000 to leave the country, but Lola was too clever to fall for bribery. She told the king about it. He became incensed and let it be known that the Dowager Empress's letter of offer had ended up on the fire. Ludwig carried out his threat and created Lola Countess of Landsfeld, Baroness Rosenthal and a canoness of the order of St Theresa.

The king was evidently resolved to champion Lola at all costs, but nevertheless had to overcome some hefty resistance before he could raise her to the peerage. First, Lola had to become a Bavarian citizen, but no minister would countersign her letters of naturalization, as required by the constitution. Then,

Lith Anst v. Ed Gust May in Frankfurt a M.

as one man, the Bavarian Cabinet threatened to resign unless Lola were sent away. Instead, the ministers found themselves sacked and replaced by a new, liberal Cabinet headed by a Protestant, who was only too willing to countersign the letters.

Revolutionary stirrings

Ironically, Lola's titles came to her at a time when royalty and nobility were starting to lose their grasp on power all over Europe. In 1848, ruling kings, dukes and other nobles were being threatened with riot and revolution if they refused to grant new, liberal constitutions: these enshrined popular rights, equality before the law, free speech and an end to economic deprivation. This was revolution indeed in a world where for centuries, royal rule and Church control had been absolute, and the only response was obedience, unquestioning and total. Many despots caved in and granted the required constitutions, then bided their time for a year or so, until they were able to retrieve their autocratic power.

Bavaria was not quite on the same footing, for its monarchy attracted popular goodwill and its monarch was much admired. Where Ludwig was weak, though, was in his perverse attachment to Lola, which allowed her to exercise controversial influence over him. Bavaria's revolution of 1848, therefore, was an effort to get rid of Lola rather than demote the king. Lola's enemies circulated stories designed to rouse superstitious fears, such as the tale which dubbed Lola a sorceress whose 'familiars' were huge black birds. Rumours that she was a spy gained currency and fired fresh controversy, much of it centred on Munich's university and its radical students.

There, as elsewhere, Lola had her supporters, but she also had vociferous opponents, some of whom got themselves very inebriated at the *Bierkeller* and afterwards surrounded her home, booing, shouting and bawling insults. Lola did not frighten easily. Instead of hiding herself indoors, she appeared on the balcony and showered the crowd with Champagne and chocolates. The uproar abated somewhat, more from surprise than anything else, and shortly afterwards

Left: The more mature Lola Montez, pictured holding a cigarette. Cigarettes were invented in 1832, but for a long time afterwards it was considered shocking for a woman to smoke, especially in public. But then, Lola made a career out of shocking people.

Ludwig I arrived. As he let himself in with his key, mounted police dispersed the students.

If Lola and Ludwig learned anything from this incident, it was not discretion. At around this time, a bust of Martin Luther, the original sixteenth-century Protestant, was placed in the Walhalla, one of Ludwig's country mansions. Bavaria's Protestants were delighted at this open concession to Lola's faith, but the Catholic clergy were purple-faced with fury. When Ludwig reshuffled his cabinet to weed out conservatives and replace them with radicals friendly to Lola, liberal-minded Bavarians were delighted. To the more traditional types, the nickname of the new

> **Ludwig I stood and watched her go. As the carriage drove off ... the mob rushed the doors of Lola's house and proceeded to rip the place apart for loot.**

cabinet – Lolaministerium – was an insult.

Fearing that Lola was now in physical danger, a group of her supporters at the University formed a bodyguard, the Alemannia, to protect her. They took to escorting Lola through the streets and guarding her house. Events soon proved that these precautions were very necessary. A band of Alemannia was, fortunately, present on 8 February 1848, when an angry demonstration in front of the University turned violent. Books and other missiles were thrown at Lola, and she was barraged with insults and threats. The uproar could easily have grown out of hand, but Lola went down into the street to answer her enemies face to face. When she threatened to have the University closed, which she presumably had the power to do, the mob made a rush for her. She was saved by the Alemannia, who closed around her.

Narrow escape

A pitched battle ensued as her enemies tried to break through the protective ring. Lola just managed to get away by running for shelter to a house in a nearby street, the Theatinerstrasse. She chose the wrong sanctuary. The family in the house refused to let her in. With the furious mob howling after her, she fled on to the Theatiner Church, where the doors shut behind her only just in time. Fortunately, a troop of cavalry galloped up as the mob was thundering at the doors, and chased them off.

Ludwig I was naturally appalled at these events, and next day he decreed the University closed. The offending students were ordered out of Munich within 24 hours. Ordinarily, Ludwig would have been obeyed, but with revolutionary fervour increasing all over Europe, the circumstances were not ordinary. The radicals were outraged at the king's decree, and a mob formed around the Residenz, the royal palace, demanding that Ludwig rescind it, and instead throw

A nineteenth-century illustration satirizing reactions to Lola's dance routines when she toured the eastern United States from 1851 to 1853. She also toured Australia in 1855.

Lola out of Bavaria. Barricades went up in the streets, citizens armed themselves, vigilantes grouped and Ludwig I now realized that in these archetypal ways, already perfected by French revolutionaries, Munich was about to rise up against him.

Ignominious retreat

At long last, through fear and the dread that his throne was tottering, Ludwig saw sense. He summoned his ministers, hoping they had a solution, but they simply confirmed his terror: only the royal signature on an order banishing Lola stood between Ludwig and the Wittelsbachs and disaster. Ludwig signed. The emergency had been so great that the order did not even give Lola decent time to prepare for departure: she had to go within the hour. Lola was stunned. She had been certain that the king would stand by her. Now she had time only to

> **After he relinquished his throne in 1848, Ludwig fared quite well. He remained in Bavaria and lived at the Wittelsbacher Palace.**

pack her jewels and a few necessities to the tune of curses and threats from a menacing rabble outside her house. Cavalry were sent to protect her as she emerged through her front door and stepped into a carriage. Somewhere in the crowd, incognito, Ludwig I stood and watched her go. As the carriage drove off, surrounded by horsemen, the mob rushed the doors of Lola's house and proceeded to rip the place apart for loot.

The king, already heartbroken, could not bear to see this place of lost happiness destroyed. Shouting out above the uproar, he ordered the pillage to stop. His presence rather than his words seemed to cool the frenzy, for recognizing him despite his disguise, people in the crowd started shouting: *'Heil Unsern König!'* – 'God save the King!' They pressed round him and, in the jostling, Ludwig either lost his balance and fell or was pushed. He managed to regain his feet, but was clearly dazed as he returned, unsteadily, to the Residenz, growing more and more bitter against his subjects for their ingratitude and the sacrifice they had forced on him.

The effect on him was significant. Ludwig neglected his family, lost interest in state affairs and brooded. In this unhealthy solitude, Ludwig's streak of Wittelsbach paranoia, which he possessed despite his basic normality, began to persuade him that maybe the stories about Lola had been true after all. Maybe she was a spy, a revolutionary in skirts, a tool of Giuseppe Mazzini, the Italian liberal republican, or of Lord Palmerston, the Whig foreign minister in Britain. Lola as a Prussian agent or a witch set on destroying the Wittelsbach dynasty were other possibilities that crossed King Ludwig's troubled mind.

Contrasting ends

After he relinquished his throne in 1848, Ludwig fared quite well. He remained in Bavaria and lived

A BITTER ABDICATION

When he sent Lola away, Ludwig had believed he was saving his throne, but the radicals, having tasted one triumph, were hellbent on another. Like revolutionaries all over Europe in 1848, they clamoured for liberal reforms and new popular rights. When Ludwig turned them down, the barricades went up once more and there was rioting near the Residenz. Suddenly, Ludwig realized that he had had enough and, on 21 March, he abdicated his throne in favour of his son, Maximilian. Ludwig's last act as king, the ultimate bitterness, was to sign documents withdrawing the rights of Bavarian citizenship from Lola Montez.

In 1848, King Ludwig was unable to stand the pressure of the Lola Affair and abdicated. Lola left Bavaria and as far as is known, Ludwig was careful to keep his distance from this woman who had ruined his life.

at the Wittelsbacher Palace. He was regularly seen at the opera and theatre, and had plenty of time for his enduring passion – Italy and its classical past. Now that he had been neutralized, the affection of his former subjects resurfaced and in 1862, when the old

In her 25-year career, Lola contravened almost every rule, trampled on all the mores and offended most traditions of society as her century knew them.

king's statue was erected in Munich, it was unveiled before an admiring crowd. Five years later, the ex-king went to Paris for a grand exhibition and was fêted by the French, for whom his sad, romantic story had great sentimental appeal.

Ludwig I provided Munich with many beautiful buildings, among them the splendid Basilica of St Boniface which he founded in 1835 to mark his silver wedding anniversary.

Ludwig died the following year, aged 82, on Leap Year Day 1868, at Nice in the south of France. Munich gave him a splendid funeral. For several days, Ludwig lay in state in the Glyptothek, one of his own neo-classical buildings, as thousands of Bavarians filed by his coffin. Afterwards, he was buried in the basilica of St Boniface, another great structure which his love of ancient architecture had inspired.

By that time, Lola Montez had been dead for seven years. Ludwig arranged for money to be sent to her, but this soon ran out and it seems that at no time between her dramatic departure from Munich and her death, aged 43, in 1861 did the ex-king attempt to make personal contact with her. There were good reasons for his reticence. Having lost face, his reputation, his throne and his family, who abandoned him in 1848, Ludwig may well have decided that the last shreds of his dignity had to be preserved against the woman who had ruined him.

Once her liaison with Ludwig was over, Lola reverted to type and became involved in a parade of scandals, some of which were new even for her. She discovered that Captain James, her first husband, had not divorced her, as she had believed, but just the same she went ahead with more marriages, which were, of course, bigamous. She soon abandoned her 'husbands' and went on to do the same to a long series of lovers, one of whom shot himself. Money ran short. She got into serious debt and her property was distrained after she went on the run from the bailiffs. At times, Lola was so hard up that she returned to the stage, to play herself in dramas about her adventures in Munich. Later, travelling the world as a professional dancer – to mixed success – there were records of fistfights and brawls between Lola and other actresses or dancers in the theatres where she occasionally performed.

Shamed and bemused

In this context, it was understandable that Ludwig preferred to distance himself from this outlandish woman. All the more so because, in her 25-year career, Lola contravened almost every rule, trampled on all the mores and offended most traditions of society as her century knew them. Along

the way, she left behind her a mass of wreckage – bemused, exploited or abandoned men, deserted wives and mistresses, outraged officials and clerics, exasperated creditors and, the most prestigious victim of them all, one sad and shamed old fellow who had once been a king.

A portrait of King Ludwig looking older and sadder in his mature years, when his life and reign were wrecked by his obsession with Lola.

CASTLES IN THE AIR: THE TRAGIC STORY OF LUDWIG II OF BAVARIA

Ludwig II of Bavaria (1845–1886) and his physician Dr Bernhard von Gudden had promised to return from their walk in the grounds of Castle Berg by eight o'clock on the evening of 13 June 1886. These walks were one of the few pleasurable features of a terrible situation, for Ludwig had inherited the madness that blighted the Wittelsbach royal family.

✦

Three days earlier, Ludwig had been declared unfit to rule, and a regent, his uncle Prince Luitpold, was appointed to govern in his place. Ludwig's initial reaction was violent and emotional. Afterwards, though, he calmed down and became quite malleable. When Doctor von Gudden suggested a light meal and bed, Ludwig quietly did as he was told. In fact, he behaved himself remarkably

Left: Ludwig II, grandson of the first King Ludwig, had a taste for fantasy which he expressed not only in his obsession with the operas of Richard Wagner but in the construction of extravagantly romantic castles such as Neuschwanstein.

well for the next three days, so well that von Gudden was fooled into believing that they could do without the guards who usually went with them on their walks. Eight o'clock came and went with no sign of the king or von Gudden. Von Gudden's assistant, Doctor Müller, became alarmed and ordered a search of the castle grounds. It revealed nothing. The search was extended, but more than two hours passed before Ludwig and von Gudden were found dead in the nearby Lake Starnburg. Both of them had drowned. Doctor Müller tried artificial respiration, but it was far too late. The king and von Gudden had been dead for nearly six hours.

Although nearly 41 years old when he died, Ludwig looked smooth-faced and young. His good looks were no longer tarnished by madness, as if the moment of death had wiped clean all the years of fearful imaginings known only to those who, like the king, had lost touch with reality. But there was no wiping away the horrifying fact that madness and the fear of madness had again been visited on the Wittelsbach

There was no wiping away the horrifying fact that madness and the fear of madness had again been visited on the Wittelsbach family.

family. This was an ongoing tragedy for the royal house of Bavaria. Ludwig's cousin Empress Elisabeth of Austria continually embarrassed her husband, the Emperor Franz Josef, with her abnormal behaviour. Her erratic traits emerged again in their son, the morose

This scene by Lake Starnberg, showing Schloss Berg and the elaborate palace gardens, depicts the last walk of King Ludwig II and his doctor, Bernhard von Gudden, before they were found dead at the lakeside.

King Maximilian II was the son of the ill-fated Ludwig I and succeeded to the throne of Bavaria on his father's abdication in 1848.

and suicidal Prince Rudolf. This was not all. Ludwig's younger brother and successor, Prince Otto. was also insane, and came to the throne in confinement, with keepers to monitor him day and night.

Disturbing early life

Tracking back to Ludwig's early life uncovered several pointers to the particular form his madness took. Born in 1845, Ludwig became Crown prince of Bavaria before he was three, on the abdication of his grandfather, King Ludwig I, in 1848. The position isolated him and planted in his child's mind an obsessive pride and a feeling of superiority. This was reinforced when servants in the royal household were ordered to bow in reverence to the young Ludwig.

When chided by his governess for stealing a purse from a shop, Ludwig maintained that, as future king, everything in Bavaria belonged to him.

He was also styled Royal Highness in a break with the tradition that this title was not accorded princes until they were 18 years of age and, presumably, old enough not to have their heads turned by it.

Ludwig always had to come first, whether it was in games with his brother Otto, who was three years younger, or in the order of precedence when entering a room in company. This extended to anywhere the boys might be. Ludwig once gave Otto a beating when he tried to precede his elder brother into a hothouse in the grounds of the royal palace at Berchtesgaden. After severe punishment from his father, King Maximilian II, Ludwig acquired another obsession: pathological hatred of Berchtesgaden. It was a pattern set for the rest of his disordered life. Any place connected to humiliation or any other unpalatable experience became instant anathema to him.

No moral compass

Even a simple sense of right and wrong seemed to be beyond Ludwig II. When chided by his governess, Fräulein Meilhaus, for stealing a purse from a shop, Ludwig maintained that, as future king, everything in Bavaria belonged to him. Meilhaus was unusual among the tutors and instructors whose task it was to turn Ludwig into a proper German prince. She treated him gently, with explanations rather than strictures, when his introverted temperament led him astray. She

was, in fact, virtually the only person close to him whom Ludwig did not either hate or fear.

Unfortunately, Meilhaus disappeared from Ludwig's life in 1854, when he was aged nine and was considered ready for more rigorous training. The purpose behind the 14-hour day now imposed on Ludwig was meant to forge a brave, self-confident, strong-willed prince worthy to inherit the Bavarian throne. Ludwig was in many ways an apt pupil and made sufficient progress in French and history to please his tutors. He also excelled at the tricky business of Ancient Greek translation and showed a strong talent for mathematics. These accomplishments were, however, a smokescreen covering Ludwig's secret inner life. He realized early on that he dared not reveal the excess of imagination, romanticism and fondness for art that were the mainsprings of his temperament. Surrounded by

A Wittelsbach family portrait. King Maximilian II and his wife, Queen Marie posed for this photograph with their sons, the future King Ludwig II (first on left) and Prince Otto (far right). Otto's insanity was more severe than his brother's.

A scene from *Das Rheingold* (1854), the first of Richard Wagner's four operas in *Der Ring des Nibelungen* (The Ring of the Nibelungs) cycle. Ludwig II was so enthralled by the operas' mythical world that he attempted to recreate it.

tutors intent on stiffening his spine, Ludwig took to active daydreaming to compensate.

What he dreamed of were the ancient Teutonic legends which the German composer Richard Wagner was then using for his mammoth operas. Ludwig revelled in Wagner's world of ancient pagan gods, valiant knights, mythical beasts and ferocious dragons. Wagner's music – huge, imposing, awash with dreamy melody and rich orchestral colour – meant little to Ludwig. It was the fabulous demi-world that Wagner brought to such spectacular life that really fascinated him. While a fantasy world was nothing unusual in early adolescence, for Ludwig, it was never just a stage in growing up that faded with

Below: The young Ludwig on horseback, from a painting by Theodore Dietz.

Prince Kraft wrote of Ludwig's 'brilliance, his physical skill and courage,' his elegant manner on horseback and knowledge of art and science.

maturity. To the violent end of his life, Ludwig never relinquished the fantasy.

In order to live undisturbed and undiscovered in this imaginary world, Ludwig assumed a carapace of outward normality. Physically, he had a great deal going for him. He was very handsome and impressively tall, and knew how to make an imposing appearance in public. In 1863, the year he came of age at 18, Ludwig was present when his great-uncle King Wilhelm IV of Prussia visited Munich, the Bavarian capital. Wilhelm's Adjutant-General, Prince Kraft, wrote of Ludwig's 'brilliance, his physical skill and courage,' and recorded admiration for the prince's elegant manner on horseback and knowledge of art and science. Even allowing for the sycophancy usually present in royal officials, Kraft's account glowed with appreciation of a fine, upstanding young prince whose future seemed golden.

Faraway manner

But Count Otto von Bismarck, the 'Iron Chancellor' of Prussia, was more perceptive. He sat next to Ludwig at dinner and noted the prince's dreaminess, and the faraway manner that made his conversation disjointed and also made it evident that, in thought, he was somewhere else entirely.

It was one thing for Ludwig to put up barriers between himself and men such as Bismarck or Prince Kraft; quite another when he encountered people who, unlike them, knew him as he really was. One of them was Prince Paul of Taxis, his aide-de-camp. Paul was an honest, pleasant young man and for any other prince would have made a friend worthy of trust, but only a friend. Ludwig's approach was much more intense and his attachment to Paul was passionate. He smothered his aide-de-camp with devotion and the need to share his innermost thoughts. Paul found all this overwhelming and kept away from Berchtesgaden by removing himself to a

country estate near Regensburg owned by his family.

Apart from his own experience, Prince Paul had proof of Ludwig's obsessive nature in an encounter with a young woodworker whom they met together while walking in mountain country. Paul saw a strong, healthy, good-looking peasant typical of the farmers and country people of the Watzmann valleys. Ludwig, by contrast, imagined a beautiful, romantic

Count Otto von Bismarck noted the prince's dreaminess, and the faraway manner that made his conversation disjointed.

figure, spoke of him as 'king of the mountains' and daydreamed that one day he might find unspoiled friendship among such peasants, far from the bitchery and conniving of the royal court. But the court was soon to close around him. In 1864, his father Maximilian died and Ludwig, not yet 19 years of age, came to the throne of Bavaria. Almost his first act as

Otto von Bismarck, the so-called Iron Chancellor of Prussia, noticed that Ludwig was strangely dreamy when he met the then 18-year-old in 1863.

WAGNER AND THE KING

Ludwig II's desire for Richard Wagner to be brought to court was a long quest, for Wagner was in hiding from his creditors, a usual state of affairs for him. The composer was eventually located in Zurich, Switzerland, and was invited to Munich by a royal messenger who handed him an effusive fan letter from Ludwig and a gold ring set with a ruby.

When Wagner reached Munich and met King Ludwig, he found himself treated as if he were the Messiah. Ludwig started by embracing him warmly, proclaimed him his 'Great Friend', then ordered a portrait made of Wagner to hang in his study beside those of two of his other heroes, William Shakespeare and Ludwig van Beethoven. Later, the king lavished thousands of florins on Wagner, gave him an annual allowance, bought him a substantial house in Munich, paid his remaining debts and forked out a hefty advance for his next opera – *Der Ring des Nibelungen* (The Ring of the Nibelungs). He even financed the composer's lavish tastes and paid for his large and costly entourage.

ENEMY OF THE PEOPLE

It could not last. The adoring young king was blind to the composer's true nature – grasping, egocentric and exploitative. But Bavarians were quick to see Wagner as a vampire bloodsucking their naive and overheated monarch. Wagner had barely settled into his new home in Munich before a press campaign began with the object of levering him out. The press was helped, unwittingly, by Wagner himself. One of King Ludwig's most pronounced obsessions was his desire to monopolize anyone he loved. Wagner was himself too highly charged and self-absorbed to realize the impact it would make when he sent for his pregnant mistress, Cosima von Bulow.

Wagner's many enemies saw at once what was going to happen. Gleefully, von Linfelder, the Bavarian court archivist, ran to tell Ludwig about Cosima and her unborn child. Instantly, the king cast Cosima as an obstacle between himself and his 'Great Friend' and indicated his displeasure by staying away from performances of Wagner's *The Flying Dutchman* and *Tannhauser* in 1865. Afterwards, he refused to grant the composer an audience.

Wagner failed to get the message. Instead, he targeted his enemies in the Bavarian government, and intrigued against Prime Minister Ludwig von der Pfordten, little realizing how much the king trusted and needed the politician or how dangerous it was to interfere with the royal dignity and the royal prerogatives. Pride in his royal birth and all it implied had been Ludwig's earliest obsession and proved to be his most enduring. It was unnatural and unhealthy,

> **The adoring young king was blind to the composer's true nature – grasping, egocentric and exploitative. But Bavarians were quick to see Wagner as a vampire bloodsucking their naïve and overheated monarch.**

like so much Ludwig did, but it was also fortunate, for it saved him from the sort of ruin Lola Montez had brought upon his grandfather King Ludwig I.

THREATENED RESIGNATION

Wagner's meddling trod this sensitive ground and Ludwig, for once, failed to rise to his hero's defence when the Prime Minister threatened to resign unless the composer was banished. Ludwig personally informed Wagner of this development and seems to have done so without emotional fireworks. Wagner and Cosima left Munich for Switzerland in December 1865 after some 20 months in the Bavarian capital.

Right: A meeting of musical minds. Richard Wagner (centre) with the composer and pianist Franz Liszt (right) and Liszt's daughter Cosima, also a pianist, who married Wagner.

The king slumped into a depression and in July 1866, after some seven months without Wagner, he threatened to abdicate.

king was to send for his great hero Richard Wagner. The eventual break with Wagner in 1865 (see box) hurt the king deeply. He was not made to withstand emotional shocks and, having been indulged and protected all his life, had no strength to overcome disappointment. He slumped into a depression and in July 1866, after some seven months without Wagner, he threatened to abdicate. Prince Paul of Taxis held him back from a final decision, appealing to Ludwig's ego by telling him that, as king, he was destined for greatness.

What use is an ex-king?

Paul had more practical reasons for his efforts at keeping Ludwig on the throne. Bavaria was then supporting Prussia in a war against Austria. The departure of the king for personal and emotional reasons would ruin the House of Wittelsbach as well as wreck Paul's own prospects and those of Richard Wagner. Wagner himself had been horrified at the prospect of losing his meal ticket: an ex-king was no use to him at all.

In August 1866, Wagner was working on *Die Meistersinger von Nürnberg* (The Mastersingers of Nuremberg). That month, during a visit to the composer's house at Lucerne, Switzerland, Prince Paul wrote to Ludwig telling him how Wagner longed to complete the work and how totally he relied on Ludwig for the purpose. It was, of course, emotional blackmail and Ludwig fell for it. There was no more talk of abdication, but the king remained severely depressed and was fast becoming subject to delusions.

Left: Richard Wagner by Giuseppe Tivoli. King Ludwig rescued Wagner from his many creditors and admired him inordinately, expecting total devotion in return. But when Wagner brought his then mistress, Cosima, to Bavaria, Ludwig's ardour cooled.

Elsa, seen here, was the heroine of Wagner's opera *Lohengrin*. The opera's first performance took place at Weimar in 1848. Wagner wrote both the music and the libretto.

Finally, on 7 October, Ludwig came clean and wrote to Sophie that, 'The wedding day was forced upon me, just as the day of the engagement was.'

Meanwhile, Ludovica, Duchess Maximilian Josef of Bavaria, had picked Ludwig for her young daughter Sophie Charlotte. Sophie, 19 years old, was a delightful girl, and well worth the Crown of Bavaria, which her ambitious mother was resolved she should wear. Ludwig already knew and at least liked Sophie, which made her unique among his female acquaintances: he usually preferred them to be much older than himself, or at least more mature.

Duty to marry

Despite his passion for beautiful males, there is no evidence that Ludwig put up a struggle against his engagement to Sophie. As an unmarried monarch, it was his duty to take a wife and secure the succession. So far, he had been let off this commitment because of his youth. At age 21, however, Ludwig's time for marriage had come and the official announcement was made on New Year's Day 1867.

At first, all seemed as it should be. The people of Bavaria warmly welcomed their future queen. Ludwig professed his love for Sophie and she for him. He even paid her the compliment of calling her Elsa, after the heroine of Wagner's *Lohengrin*. A new state wedding coach was ordered and a boudoir for Sophie was constructed in the royal apartments.

Privately, the couple exchanged correspondence of the most affectionate kind. 'A thousand inmost greetings from the bottom of my heart' and 'my heart is longing for you' were two of the ways in which Ludwig signed off when writing to his fiancée.

King Ludwig II with his fianceé Princess Sophie Charlotte of Liechtenstein. Ludwig came to regard the prospect of marriage with Sophie as 'the fearful thing', postponed the wedding twice and finally rejected her.

A FIANCÉE SUPPLANTED

Ludwig II had confined his real thoughts about marriage to Sophie Charlotte to his diary. 'Sophie got rid of,' he wrote on 8 October 1867. 'The gloomy picture fades ... now I live again after this torturing nightmare.' 'Thanks be to God, the fearful thing was not realized,' ran his diary entry for 28 November, when the twice-postponed wedding would have taken place. But Ludwig had no intention of lacking a love in his life. He had already provided it, unknown to Sophie or to Richard Wagner. In May 1867, the king had noticed Richard Hornig, a young groom at the royal stables. Hornig had all the qualifications for Ludwig's next grand passion. About five years older than the king, he was handsome, graceful, looked marvellous on horseback and, like all great Teutonic heroes, was a blue-eyed blonde.

In July 1867, Ludwig took Hornig off for a jaunt through one of the most beautiful and historic regions in Germany, the Thuringian forest, then proceeded to Paris, where they were entertained by the French Emperor Napoleon III and Empress Eugenie, and visited the Exposition at Versailles. By the time the king and the groom returned home to Bavaria, Hornig was firmly installed as 'Richard, Beloved of my Heart'.

There was, even so, a discordant note. Ludwig was still devoted to Wagner, in spite of everything that had occurred and felt no need to hide it. 'The god of my life, as you know, is Richard Wagner,' he wrote to Sophie in February 1867. Quite probably, Sophie had no reason to believe that this was anything more than the attachment of an artistic young man to a great genius. Nonetheless, by June 1867, two months before the wedding, set for 25 August, Ludwig's twenty-second birthday, Sophie was getting suspicious. For one thing, Ludwig was planning to bring Wagner back to Munich and became abnormally excited as the date for his return drew near. By August, Sophie's forebodings seemed confirmed as Ludwig started to show signs of wriggling out of the marriage. He postponed the August wedding date to October, then again to November. Finally, on 7 October, Ludwig came clean and wrote to Sophie that, 'The wedding day was forced upon me, just as the day of the engagement was.'

For all his emotional excesses, Ludwig was not a cruel man and he tried to let Sophie down lightly in a letter full of assurances of friendship and affection, if not love. He offered, too, to renew their engagement should Sophie fail to find another husband within the year. It was hardly a compliment to Sophie, but it showed generosity. Sophie was too beautiful and charming to remain available for long and, on 28 September 1868, she married a French husband, Ferdinand Philippe Marie, Duc d'Alençon.

At this stage, Ludwig's obsessions were about to scale fresh heights of fantasy. In 1869, he made plans to build the Neuschwangau, a new palace in southwestern Bavaria and one of the fantastic structures that later earned the popular title of 'castles in the air'. Another, the Linderhof Palace, was the only 'castle in the air' completed in Ludwig's lifetime, in 1878. The last, Herrenchiemsee, was meant to 'breathe the magnificence and imposing grandeur of Versailles' where, two centuries earlier, another of Ludwig's great heroes, King Louis XIV of France, had created the most splendid royal complex in Europe.

In debt to the tune of 14 million marks, Ludwig made plans for more palaces – one Chinese, another Byzantine – before death intervened to stop him.

The Herrenchiemsee featured a replica of the famous Hall of Mirrors at Versailles and cost so much that, by 1886, Ludwig was in debt to the tune of 14 million marks, almost three times his annual income. Undeterred, Ludwig made plans for more palaces – one Chinese, another Byzantine – before death

This painting of Siegfried and the Rhine Maidens by Ferdinand Leeke exemplifies the fantasy world of Richard Wagner's operas, a world which fascinated Ludwig and fed his obsession with Wagner.

intervened to stop him. Wagnerian themes were an inevitable feature of Ludwig's craze for castle building. Paintings of scenes from Wagner's operas covered the walls. The elves and fairies of Wagner's opera world, which Ludwig thought he saw flitting about the palace grounds, provided numerous decorations.

Escalating madness

All the while, Ludwig's madness was inexorably progressing. From his secret diaries, it is evident that the king was convinced that he was gradually losing control. He wrote of violent, involuntary physical movements, deteriorating eyesight, nightmares,

Left: Ludwig by Gabriel Schachinger, showing him in a stern martial pose. The impression given of a mighty warrior monarch was contrary to Ludwig's true character which was volatile and emotional.

sleeplessness, persistent headaches and a fearful guilt over some evil he discerned within himself, but could not quite identify.

Ludwig had good reason to fear being taken over by his own insanity. His brother Otto was already

From his secret diaries, it is evident that the king was convinced that he was gradually losing control.

subject to wild fits of physical violence and had to be guarded by keepers day and night. Otto's crazed mind sometimes persuaded him that disaster would follow if he took off his boots or went to bed. At other times, he made gargoyle faces, barked like a dog or was tormented by hallucinations. He then reverted to normal until the madness started all over again.

Desperately struggling to avert the same horrific fate, Ludwig resorted to cold baths to reduce

Prince Luitpold was the third son of Ludwig I of Bavaria. Like his father and his elder brother, Maximilian II, Luitpold escaped the curse of the Wittelsbach madness but had to serve as Regent for both his insane nephews, Ludwig II and Ludwig's brother Otto I.

excitability. He sought answers in numerology, mysticism and spiritualism. He recorded a solemn oath in his diary to 'refrain from all excitement for three months' or 'abstain from passionate embraces'. Perhaps it helped, if only for a while. Having consigned his most turbulent fantasies to his diary and purged himself through occult dabblings, Ludwig managed to retain an outer shell of normality. Nevertheless, the entries in his diary revealed how remorselessly Ludwig's mind was slipping away. He was increasingly obsessed with the idea of purity and with freeing himself from the dross of

Schloss Hohenschwangau in southwestern Bavaria, where Ludwig II grew up, was the official summer residence of the royal family. It was built in 1832–1837 by Ludwig's father, King Maximilian II, on the ruins of a twelfth century fortress.

his humanity. 'I will never cease [my efforts],' he wrote. 'I will never err.'

Quest for el dorado

Meanwhile, Prince Otto was growing worse, and his family was forced to admit he was incurable. Ludwig grew more terrified than ever: he was still seeing how his own symptoms more and more resembled those of his brother, who was officially declared insane in 1878. By 1879, Ludwig was starting to lose his battle to retain control. He decided that he must find El Dorado, the legendary country, or city, of gold tirelessly sought

by sixteenth-century Spanish conquistadors in South America, but never found. The king then suddenly lost interest in, and even consciousness of, El Dorado and anything that lay outside his own tortured world. Little by little, Ludwig withdrew into isolation. He dismissed his court officials, refused to see his ministers, sacked his personal staff and finally banished his valets, his dresser and his bedchamber servants. By the end of 1885, Ludwig had become a recluse.

Reluctantly, the Bavarian royal family and government were obliged for a second time to face up to a truth they had always shrunk from making public: Ludwig was mentally unfit to carry out his duties as king. Too many Wittelsbachs had gone mad, and the lunacy appeared on both sides of the family. The charade had to end. In June 1886, Prince Luitpold, Ludwig's uncle and second in line to the Bavarian throne after Prince Otto, ordered a formal investigation into the mental state of the king. Four doctors conferred on evidence already gathered by Dr von Gudden. Their diagnosis was never in doubt and, on 10 June, a government proclamation was posted in Munich announcing that Ludwig was incapable of ruling and establishing Luitpold as his regent.

Ludwig was not so far gone that he failed to understand what was happening. 'I can bear that they take the government from me,' he said. 'But not that they declare me insane.'

When news reached him at Hohenschwangau that court officials were coming to take him prisoner, he scribbled a hasty plea for aid to his cousin Prince Ludwig Ferdinand and dispatched a servant to deliver it. The servant failed to reach the prince, but in his frenzy to get away Ludwig hatched other plans. Hohenschwangau lay near the border with Austria, and Ludwig contemplated escaping from Bavaria by making a break for it into foreign, and therefore, safer territory. The king also had a counterproclamation drawn up, calling for support from his subjects.

But long before anyone could have made a move to rescue him, the king had been detained and placed under strict supervision in his private apartments. On 12 June, he was locked into the middle carriage of a

> ## Shortly after Ludwig's arrival at the castle, his attendants instantly suspected a suicide bid when the king demanded the key to the 61-metre high main tower.

convoy of three. The inside door handles had been removed, and he was not allowed out until the convoy reached the Castle Berg, some 80 kilometres (50 miles) and eight hours' travel away.

Suspected suicide bid

Shortly after Ludwig's arrival at the castle, his attendants instantly suspected a suicide bid when the king demanded the key to the 61-m (200-ft) high main tower. Ludwig's valet, a man called Mayr, pretended that the key had been mislaid and so fended off his master until Doctor von Gudden and his two assistants arrived. Meanwhile, Ludwig was on his way to the tower, and the doctor decided on an ambush. He placed warders armed with straitjackets along the corridor and staircase leading to the tower and sent Mayr to give Ludwig the key.

> ## When the bodies were examined, it was discovered that von Gudden had been badly beaten up, apparently in a vigorous fight for his life. By contrast, Ludwig was unmarked.

As the king approached, two warders leapt out, pinioned him and forced him into a straitjacket. Von Gudden appeared and suggested that Ludwig return to his apartments. Suddenly, the king calmed down. He went quietly, far too quietly, deceiving von Gudden

King Ludwig's physician, Dr. Bernhard von Gudden, paid with his life when he was fooled by his royal patient into leaving the usual guards behind on their last walk by Lake Starnberg.

MADNESS SUCCEEDS MADNESS

In confinement at Schloss Furstenreid, a royal castle near Munich, Prince Otto became king. He probably never knew that he had ascended the Wittelsbach throne. Certainly, he never truly ruled Bavaria. King Otto died in 1916, four years after the death of Prince Luitpold ended the 26-year regency he served for his nephews. He was succeded as regent by his son, Prince Ludwig Ferdinand.

For the Wittelsbachs, who never knew where the family madness would strike next or what it would do to its future victims, it was a traumatic situation none of them could escape. Eccentricity, 'abnormal' behaviour and even madness itself were one thing, but with Ludwig II, the family legacy, so notoriously unstable, had produced not only these afflictions, but suicide and murder as well. No wonder Prince Luitpold burst into tears and bitterly wept when he heard the news of Ludwig's death and the accession of another lunatic king, in the person of Prince Otto.

Otto I, Ludwig's mad brother who succeeded him in 1886, had already been declared insane 11 years earlier. He spent his entire reign of 27 years in confinement and under medical supervision.

into thinking that he had his royal patient under control. Next, Ludwig became upset after workmen, hired to prepare the castle windows for fitting with iron bars, set up a cacophony of hammering. Ludwig managed to get away from the noise by taking a short morning walk with Doctor von Gudden, but he soon became rattled once again when he saw a policeman walking ahead of him.

At this juncture, except for these two brief bouts of nerves, King Ludwig had been in a calm frame of mind for three days. Von Gudden regarded this as a hopeful sign and decided that, on their next walk, it would be safe for the policemen to stay behind. After dinner on the evening of 13 June 1886, the king and von Gudden set out once more, but this time they never came back, nor were they seen alive again. The unusual calm the mad king had assumed was simply

a cover to get von Gudden on his own and kill him before Ludwig killed himself.

Later, it became clear that this had been Ludwig's plan all along. When the bodies were medically examined, it was discovered that von Gudden had been badly beaten up, apparently in a vigorous fight for his life. His right eye was bruised blue; there were deep scratches on his nose and forehead. A nail on one finger of his right hand had been torn off. By contrast, Ludwig was unmarked.

The next night, 14 June, Ludwig's body was taken back to Munich, where he was dressed in sumptuous robes, a sword by his side. He lay in state on a flower-filled bier for three days, the blooms carefully arranged about his head to conceal the work of the surgeons who had performed an autopsy on him. On 17 June, Ludwig was buried with full state honours.

Ludwig's Linderhof Palace took 23 years to build at a cost reckoned to total just over £32.5 million. Ludwig had long admired the Palace of Versailles and reproduced in the Linderhof its most distinctive feature — the Hall of Mirrors.

VI

THE MAYERLING TRAGEDY

Early on the morning of 30 January 1889, Crown Prince Rudolf of Austria-Hungary was found dead, together with his young mistress, Baroness Maria Vetsera, in the royal hunting lodge at Mayerling, 10 miles (15km) from Vienna. Both had been shot. Maria had apparently died first and lay on the bed in the Crown Prince's bedroom, her body covered with roses. Having killed her, it seems, Rudolph had shot himself through the head, shattering his skull.

✦

Reaction to the Mayerling deaths was cataclysmic. The Crown Prince's father, Emperor Franz Josef, collapsed when he heard the news. His mother, Empress Elisabeth, was inconsolable. Grieving crowds thronging the streets of

Left: Crown Prince Rudolf was a liberal destined to inherit an absolute monarchy that was the antithesis of his beliefs.
Above: Baroness Maria Vetsera was a starry-eyed girl, entranced by a glamorous Crown Prince into a fatal romance.

Vienna went so far out of police control that the army had to be called in. One person was killed and several more injured before calm was restored.

What remained after that was a mystery – one that no one seemed able to solve. Why had a handsome, popular prince, heir to one of Europe's most powerful thrones, a man who had charm, intelligence, good looks and talent on his side, unexpectedly taken his own life at 30 years of age in so sombre and furtive a manner?

On the face of it, the handsome, charming Crown Prince Rudolf seemed the ideal prince and a worthy heir to the prestigious Austro-Hungarian throne.

Rudolph, however, was not at all the dazzling Prince Charming he appeared to be. The only son of Franz Josef and Elisabeth, he had inherited too much of his mother's melancholic nature and too little of his father's solidity. Add to those frustrating circumstances a miserable marriage and a sense of isolation and hopelessness, and the tragic Prince had all the makings of a man who to the outside world

The liberal journalist Moritz Szeps saw the maverick Rudolf as a great 'catch' in his efforts to promote radical ideas aimed at transforming the Austro-Hungarian Empire.

appeared to have everything, but in his own mind had nothing.

Progressive ideas

There was, for a start, no scope in the exalted royal environment for his advanced and progressive ideas. A liberal-minded prince more suited to be a constitutional monarch than a despot, Rudolph had a head full of exciting ideals about improving the lot of

---

Rudolph was not at all the dazzling Prince Charming. The only son of Franz Josef and Elisabeth, he had inherited too much of his mother's melancholic nature and too little of his father's solidity.

---

ordinary people and ruling by benign example.

His ideas found some expression, though no action, in his friendship with Moritz Szeps, a journalist who edited a radical newspaper, the Vienna *Morgenpost* (Morning Post). Rudolph contributed several articles to the *Morgenpost* anonymously. Szeps, naturally enough, regarded the Crown Prince as a great 'catch' for the liberal cause. So did a maverick within the royal family, Rudolph's cousin Archduke John Salvator of Tuscany. John Salvator's radical opinions went way beyond Rudolph's, to the point where he believed it valid for a man to strip himself of his titles, cast aside his privileges and live a commoner's life with a wife of his own free choice.

Right: The Emperor Franz Josef I of Austria-Hungary had absolute power over his subjects and expected his heir, Rudolf, to continue in the same way.

This, in fact, is precisely what John Salvator did after Rudolph's death. By 1888, he had already found the wife he wanted – a middle-class girl called Milli Stubel, who would never be acceptable to the royal family had he tried to make her an archduchess. John Salvator also proved bold enough to openly criticize the Emperor, his government and the Austrian army, for which Franz Josef had him banned from court. Banishment also served to break up the close friendship between Rudolph and John Salvator, who not surprisingly was considered a disruptive influence on the young prince.

Rudolph nevertheless contrived to see his cousin in secret, and discuss with him the ideas of the major liberal thinkers of the day. These encounters were a kind of sub-life in which Rudolph could give some rein to his deeply held political beliefs. All the same, it saddened him that they had to be clandestine and also that they possessed, of necessity, an element of self-interest. For the archduke, as for Moritz Szeps, the heir to the Austro-Hungarian throne could not be merely a fellow spirit, but a means to their own reforming ends.

Imposition of control

John Salvator certainly looked forward to a major role in affairs as and when Rudolph eventually became emperor, and Szeps had no hope of making radicalism reality without the support of a man in high places. Even so, as would-be liberals remaking a world of despots in a democratic image, Rudolph, John Salvator and Szeps all faced a monumental obstacle: the throne which Rudolph stood to inherit was ancient, well founded and extremely powerful. Led by Franz Josef, royal rule in Austria-Hungary was in the hands of men of repressive temperament. Their notion of government was the brutal suppression of all unrest and control by force and fear. To such men, liberals were a cancerous growth eating away at absolute royal authority. The emperor was nevertheless very conscious of how far apart he and Rudolph were, and for the sake of family peace the two of them never discussed politics.

Crown Princess Stephanie of Belgium, daughter of the Belgian King Leopold II, married Crown Prince Rudolf in 1881 after he bowed to family pressure to do his duty and take a wife.

Even so, Franz Josef believed that he could control his recalcitrant heir. He denied Rudolph a part in affairs of state, on the premise that where he had no knowledge, he had no influence. He also sought to shackle Rudolph domestically by finding him a 'suitable' wife, in this case the charmless but respectable Princess Stephanie, daughter of King Leopold II of Belgium. The wedding took place in 1881.

The fact that the marriage soon proved unhappy was not of great concern. A married Crown Prince who dabbled in superficial affairs on the side – as he was almost expected to do – was far less susceptible to outside influences than an unwed heir able to 'play the field'. Without a wife, Rudolph would also have fitted less conveniently into the social requirements of the imperial court, which was stiff with protocol, insistent on strict precedence and marked by that slavish deference so dear to the arrogant hearts of central European monarchs.

Anyone unable to prove a noble genealogy going back at least four generations was not permitted to attend at court, which largely accounted for its stuffy atmosphere. The haughty Princess Stephanie was, in fact, far better suited to such an environment than her husband. Rudolph found it choking, but he performed well enough and when in court circles could not be faulted on manners or protocol. The emperor naturally looked to his son to provide more male heirs to the imperial throne and, although the first child of Rudolph and Stephanie, born in 1883, was a daughter, it was expected that sons would follow and so cement the power of the Hapsburg royal family. In the event, no son was ever born, for it was doubtful that marital relations between the Crown Prince and his wife were very frequent after 1883 – if, that is, they existed at all.

This was hardly surprising when Stephanie was irascible, moody, jealous and disruptive, and pursued her husband with perpetual demands.

Stephanie and Rudolf were incompatible. The haughty, moody and demanding Stephanie could neither understand nor deal with Rudolf's melancholic nature.

The first child of Rudolph and Stephanie, born in 1883, was a daughter. It was expected that sons would follow and so cement the power of the Hapsburg royal family.

Stephanie grated particularly during Rudolph's periodic moods of depression, which were the fruit of his frustrations and his conviction that he was wasting himself in a hollow world that had no future, and certainly no liberal future. Like his mother, Elisabeth, he was plagued by a deep streak of melancholy and, when the mood was on him, a fearful sense of self-loathing. Stephanie was far too dense and unimaginative to understand what the problem was, and the rift occasioned by Rudolph's moods and her bad temper soon became permanent.

Cracks in the façade

The diligent gossips of Vienna quickly realized that the royal pair were chronically ill suited and saw clear evidence of the mismatch in Rudolph's frequent absences from the Austrian capital. They were far more frequent than his ceremonial duties or his obligations as an army officer required, and the rumour mongers were certain that, while Rudolph may not have had a girl in

> **It was understood that in royal circles, whatever went on behind the scenes, an impeccable front had to be maintained ... Stephanie had shattered that front and revealed a scandal: this made her more culpable than her errant husband.**

every port, his amours were plentiful in the provinces.

Unfortunately, Stephanie was just as certain and, unlike many royal wives of the time, did not have the tact to turn a blind eye to her husband's dalliances. She failed to realize, too, how little she had to worry about at this stage, for Rudolph's liaisons were usually short-lived and were more in the nature of brief snatches at oblivion than any quest for a serious relationship. This led her to create ructions at court in the autumn of 1888, when she made a public scene outside the house in Vienna where her husband was visiting the pretty Polish Countess Czewucka. The countess was little more than the latest fashionable flirt – she had scores of admirers – but Stephanie's action spilled a lot of beans. It was understood that in royal circles, whatever went on behind the scenes, an impeccable front had to be maintained. However hypocritical this attitude, Stephanie had shattered that front and revealed a scandal: in the ethos of the time, this made her more culpable than her errant husband.

The infuriated Franz Josef attempted to keep the scandal under wraps, but it soon leapt the bounds

Right: Maria Vetsera was infatuated with Rudolf long before she even met him and became his mistress. She fantasized about him, seeing him not just as 'Prince Charming' but the epitome of chivalry and all the noble virtues.

of court circles and became common talk in Vienna and beyond. A public display of unity was urgently required. This took place shortly afterwards, when Rudolph and Stephanie, both on their very best behaviour, attended a gala ball. The entire aristocracy of Vienna was there to see the royal 'face' restored and the occasion, richly dressed, lavishly victualled, was the sort of dazzling affair the Viennese accepted as a usual part of their social scene.

This was, after all, waltz-time Vienna, a city of legendary gaiety, with the lilting music of the Strauss family providing its theme tunes. When his mood switched away from depression and self-torture, Rudolph was very much part of this pleasure-loving world. His other, sunnier side was gregarious. He greatly enjoyed the theatre, social gatherings, salons, race meetings, concerts or riding in the Prater, the leisure complex of Vienna where the well-heeled paraded for the purpose of seeing and being seen.

A girlish infatuation

To catch a glimpse of the Crown Prince or, better still, to be acknowledged by him was the hope of every socially ambitious Viennese. A large number of them went to the Prater for this purpose alone. One of them was the 16-year-old Baroness Maria Vetsera, daughter of a minor Hungarian nobleman. As 16-year-olds will, Maria had developed a strong 'crush' on Rudolph after seeing him at the races in Vienna in April of 1888. Rudolph, for his part, was sufficiently struck by Maria's beauty to stare at her for several seconds.

This was quite enough to send the impressionable young girl into a tizzy of adoration. Maria had numerous admirers and usually created avid male interest, but from that moment on she could think of no one but the Crown Prince. To her, he was a shining knight endowed with all the chivalrous virtues, and an ideal man pluperfect in every possible way.

At this early stage, admiration from afar was all Maria wanted of the prince. Like any ardent 'fan', she quizzed her friends for titbits of news about him, following his movements in the court circular and nagging her mother into taking her to the theatre or

Crown Prince Rudolf (left) riding in an open carriage, covered up against the winter cold by a blanket.

opera driving in the Prater, all in hopes of fuelling her passion with a glimpse of her idol.

Maria knew that she could never entertain hopes of being formally introduced to Rudolph. She could not boast the lustrous ancestry that would have allowed her to be presented at court, although her mother was acquainted with both the emperor and the empress. The 'chance encounter' was a far surer bet and, in time, Maria's persistence paid off. Early in May 1888, a gala performance of William Shakespeare's *Hamlet* took place at Vienna's Burg Theatre, and Maria discovered the Crown Prince was going to be there. Maria persuaded her mother to accompany her – girls of Maria's class were not allowed out without a chaperone – and there, in the first interval of the play, she came face to face with her idol for the first time.

Rudolph's glance was openly admiring, and with it went a smile that made Maria blush furiously. Embarrassed, she fled to a small room nearby. Later

Left: Crown Prince Rudolph dressed in military uniform, with decorations. Generally, artists who painted royal personages glorified them, but in this picture Rudolf appeared like his true self — anxious, nervous and unhappy.

the same evening, Maria caught the prince's eye again. A few days later, while prowling the Prater in her mother's carriage, she saw him once more. As he rode past, he looked at her with evident interest and, on the return journey home, he rode past again and scrutinized her a second time.

Maria was now hopelessly in love with Rudolph, but she had no axe to grind as far as he was concerned. All she wanted was the chance to adore her prince and dream delightful hours away thinking about him. Though he did not yet know it, Rudolph had encountered the one and only person who sought nothing from him but the pleasure of his company. Maria mooned several months away in this ingenuous fashion until, in September 1888, the chance of closer acquaintance came along.

Romance furthered

One morning, Maria's mother returned home from shopping with a friend, Countess Larisch, who was Rudolph's first cousin. The countess, of course, had known the Crown Prince since childhood, and Maria lost no time pumping the visitor for details about him. Larisch, an astute woman of about 40 years old, did not taken long to realize the depth of Maria's ardour and took an early opportunity to let Rudolph know of his unknowing conquest.

Rudolph, intrigued, wanted to know the name of his admirer and, on being told, at once recalled the delectable teenager with the dark hair and ice-blue eyes who had caught his attention earlier in the season. Maria was almost delirious with joy when the countess afterwards brought her Rudolph's message of regard. Even so, she seems to have entertained no thought as yet of the next step: an actual meeting with the prince. Instead, Maria returned to her previous strategy of the 'chance encounter'.

Riding in the Prater, he not only noticed her, but also gave her a small but unmistakable bow.

When the encounter occurred, however, Rudolph proved to be more forthcoming than Maria had ever dared hope. Riding in the Prater, he not only noticed her, but also gave her a small but unmistakable bow. A few days later, on 21 October, a letter reached Maria which said all she had ever dreamt of, and more. In it, Rudolph invited her to meet him in the Prater next day. He had admired her for so long, he wrote, that now the time had come to make her acquaintance.

Maria's reply told the Crown Prince a great deal more than it actually said. She could not come to the Prater, she told him, because she had no chaperone. This, to Rudolph, was something quite new. He was accustomed to sophisticated women whose approaches were blatant and who were far less concerned with him than with the status they would gain from knowing him. Yet here was a girl with such a virginal sense of propriety that she would meet the heir to the throne only if she were accompanied. It was refreshing, even startling, and it came at a time when Rudolph badly needed just this sort of distraction.

Recently, the Crown Prince had received some very disturbing news. His cousin John Salvator was not content merely to talk over liberal principles. He

was planning nothing less than revolution, and the overthrow of Rudolph's father. John had even enlisted support in the Austrian army for his coup. Rudolph, who counted loyalty to his father's position as his priority, never mind their political differences, was both horrified and saddened. Talk of revolution had lost him his only friend, for John Salvator had been the one person to whom he could talk frankly. Now Rudolf began to doubt the strength of his beliefs. He could not contemplate treason against his father, and if he was content only to talk, not act, his ideals, he felt, must be very shallow.

Prescription for love

Imperial spies were everywhere, and fear that they might discover John Salvator's plans and that he might be implicated were Rudolph's next depressing thoughts. He was, in any case, beginning to feel the strain of spending most of his time with reactionary oafs at court and dealing with the tedious trivia of the vast bureaucracy that was the Austro-Hungarian Empire. The strain showed. The emperor had grown sufficiently alarmed at his son's pale face and gaunt appearance to have him examined by the imperial physician. He diagnosed what might today be called 'executive stress' and advised Rudolph to relax and rest. Rudolph's commitments made that impossible, but the young, innocent and even childlike Maria Vetsera could prove to be the next best thing.

As soon as he received Maria's reply, Rudolph wrote to Countess Larisch, demanding that she return to Vienna forthwith and introduce him to Maria. Larisch hastened back to the capital and soon performed the task for which she had been summoned. Chaperoned by the countess, Maria Vetsera came to the Hofburg, the imperial palace in Vienna, to come face to face with her hero. Both of them, it seems, found what they wanted in each other.

To Maria's starry-eyed gaze, the prince was more handsome and more courteous than even she had imagined. As for Rudolph, Maria was a beautiful delight and her extreme youth, obvious sincerity and modest charm were a wonder. Best of all, she was quite untarnished either by the sordid political world Rudolph was forced to inhabit or by the tedious social round that had, until now, been his only alternative. Susceptible as he was at the time, the disillusioned, world-weary Rudolph fell madly in love and was soon

... the disillusioned, world-weary Rudolph fell madly in love and was soon planning to divorce his sour-tempered wife and marry Maria.

planning to divorce his sour-tempered wife and marry Maria. Rudolph was well aware that he and Maria were being followed by palace agents whenever they met and, although he realized that this meant the liaison would soon reach the emperor's ears, he had become reckless enough not to care. All he cared about was Maria and the fact that he could not live without her.

Rudolph and Maria Vetsera became lovers on 13 January 1889, and the Prince was so wrapped up in this, his first serious affair, that he gave Maria a ring inscribed with the date to commemorate the event.

A sharp jolt back to reality was soon forthcoming. By 26 January, the emperor had in his possession a letter from Pope Leo XIII which revealed that Rudolph had written directly to the pontiff, asking him to permit the dissolution of his marriage to Stephanie. Such direct contact was a breach of protocol and told Franz Josef that the liaison with Maria that had prompted the request was going to be a serious problem. A divorce from Stephanie was out of the question, no matter how unhappy the marriage was. The stability of the Austro-Hungarian Empire, which relied on a united royal family, would not permit it.

No way out

It was then that Rudolph realized just how much he was in his father's power and how little courage he possessed to resist him. Franz Josef summoned his

The royal hunting lodge at Mayerling, where Rudolf and Maria Vetsera committed suicide, was set in an idyllic environment in the countryside around Vienna.

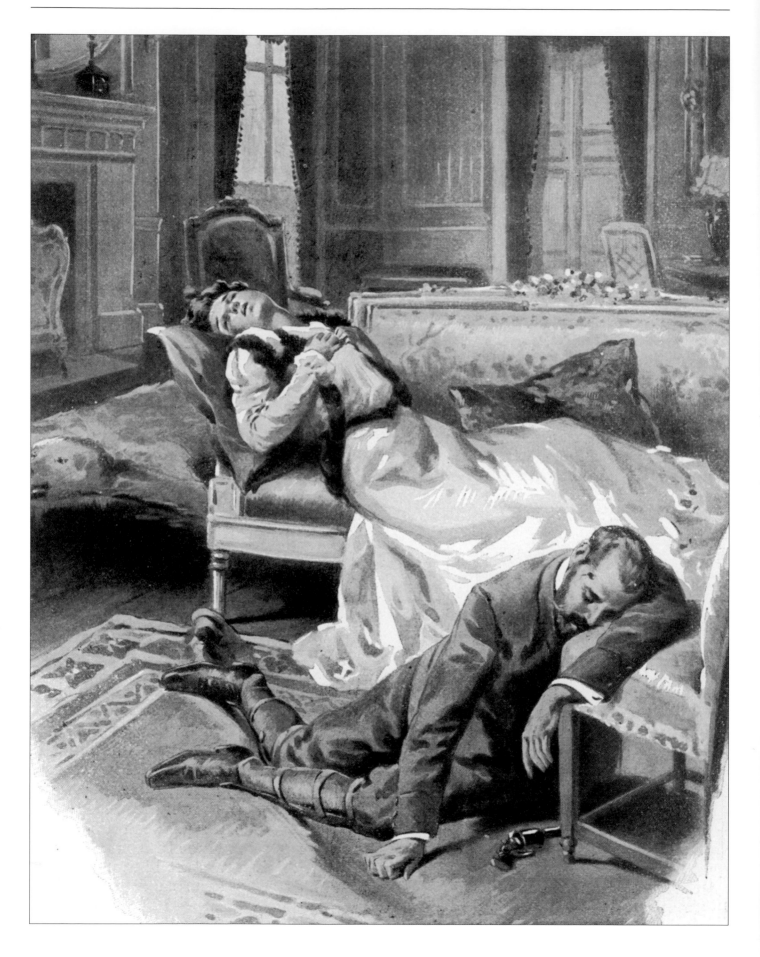

A dramatized illustration of the scene at Mayerling when the bodies of Rudolf and Maria Vetsera were discovered. Rudolf, in fact, was found dead in bed not draped over a chair.

son to appear before him, and demanded a promise that Rudolph would send Maria away. Thoroughly dejected, the Crown Prince complied, asking only that he might see her just once more. Having got what he wanted, the emperor agreed, little realising how shamed and hopeless his son felt as he left his presence.

Suicide Pact

Two days later, Crown Prince Rudolph left Vienna for Mayerling, ostensibly for some mid-winter hunting in the surrounding forest. Maria Vetsera was with him. On the afternoon of 29 January, the two of them took a long walk in the forest and there, it seems, Rudolph proposed a suicide pact. To him, it was the only way out of what he saw as his meaningless life.

The besotted Maria agreed. Most likely, she had no realistic concept of death, and doubtless thought only of herself and Rudolph mysteriously united in

It was then that Rudolph realized just how much he was in his father's power and how little courage he possessed to resist him.

perpetuity beyond the grave. That night, both of them wrote letters to their mothers. Rudolph asked Empress Elisabeth to see that he and Maria were buried together in a small nearby cemetery at Alland. The request was never granted.

That done, Rudolph bolted the door of the bedroom from the inside. Some time around dawn, when Maria was asleep, he fetched his revolver from a drawer and shot her behind the left ear. The range was point-blank. She died instantly. Rudolph's manservant Loschek

The body of Crown Prince Rudolph lies in state, partly disguised by a bandage over his head to hide the incisions made during an autopsy.

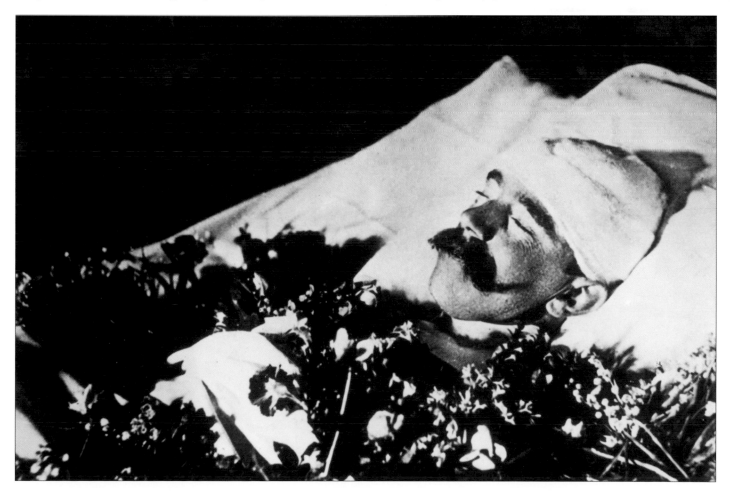

Above: Maria Vetsera was buried in the graveyard at Heiligenkreus in Lower Austria even though Rudolf had requested that they be interred together.

Suicide was regarded as a sin in the eyes of the Catholic Church. Consequently, a big cover-up was attempted to conceal the circumstances of Rudolf's death.

heard the noise. He leapt out of bed and rushed along the hallway to his master's room. The second shot rang out as he arrived, too late, outside the door.

Vatican cover-up

In the nineteenth century, suicide was regarded as a sin in the eyes of the Catholic Church. Consequently, a big cover-up was attempted to conceal the circumstances of Rudolf's death. Heart failure was the first official explanation, then a story was disseminated that he had been killed by conservative elements fearful of his liberal influence. Next, the Vatican issued a statement that Rudolph had been mentally unbalanced when he died. No one was really convinced and, eventually, the truth had to be admitted: Crown Prince Rudolf and Maria Vetsera had died in a suicide pact.

This, though, was not allowed to be the end of the story. Conspiracy theories had already sprung up and were proliferating even before the truth about the deaths of Rudolf and Maria Vetsera was reluctantly announced. Conspiracy theories never die and no official announcement, whether cover-up or truth, had the slightest effect on any of the many explanations surrounding the hunting lodge at Mayerling and the tragic events that happened there.

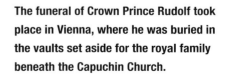

The funeral of Crown Prince Rudolf took place in Vienna, where he was buried in the vaults set aside for the royal family beneath the Capuchin Church.

EMPEROR MAXIMILIAN OF MEXICO

The Archduke Maximilian, younger brother of Emperor Franz Josef of Austria-Hungary (1832–1867), was the 'fall guy' in a scheme hatched in 1863 by the French Emperor Napoleon III. The idea was for Maximilian to retrieve money owed to France by the Mexican government. Napoleon's allies in Mexico, the Catholic Church and a group of wealthy landowners, had also been dispossessed of their land, cash and privileges by the liberal President of Mexico, Benito Juarez. They, too, wanted their money back. With the reluctant assent of Franz Josef, the landowners offered Maximilian the Mexican throne. He accepted. So far, so good – but there was a problem. Maximilian was a naive, starry-eyed idealist with a head full of utopian notions about banishing the poverty, squalor and disease that disfigured life for millions of disadvantaged people in Mexico and around the world.

HIGH-MINDED WIMP

Maximilian arrived in his 'empire' in 1864, accompanied by a substantial force of French troops and his wife Charlotte, daughter of the Belgian King Leopold I. Charlotte, too, had her head in the clouds. To her, Maximilian was an angel, whose destiny it was to serve and uplift humanity. But for his sponsors, Napoleon III and Franz Josef, Maximilian was a high-minded wimp who caused trouble from the start. He refused to restore Church property and privileges on the grounds that the Church belonged to the people. For the same reasons, Maximilian declined to let the landowners take back their lost estates and haciendas.

Next, Maximilian proceeded with utopian schemes such as a national theatre for Mexico and the creation of a world navy. He took to walking through the streets of Mexico City with minimal escort, engaging in friendly conversation with passers-by. He was so

obviously genuine that even Benito Juarez and his supporters found it hard to dislike him.

This did not mean that Juarez approved of Maximilian's assumption of power. Typically, on learning of Juarez's hostility, Maximilian invited him to Mexico City, thinking to offer the Mexican leader a place in his government. Juarez, of course, refused. Mayhem followed. Motley groups of bandits, some of them Juarez partisans, made the night and the roads dangerous. Juarez and his forces were still at large, awaiting their chance to fight and defeat the foreign intruders. The Americans then stepped in with demands that the French leave Mexico and take Maximilian with them. Maximilian refused at first, but as American pressure increased, he began to waver.

Charlotte refused to hear of giving up and sailed for Europe to seek help. She arrived in August 1866,

Maximilian, the starry-eyed idealist younger brother of Emperor Franz Josef of Austria-Hungary.

but soon discovered that nobody wanted to know. Napoleon III was facing fresh pressures from a rampant Germany on France's eastern frontier, and needed his troops at home. He was willing to abandon Maximilian in order to do so. Never very stable, Charlotte's mind gave way as fear, failure and stress finally snapped her sanity. When Maximilian learned of her condition, his first thought was to be with her. His second was to remain in Mexico, where, he believed, deserting his subjects would be cowardly and dishonourable. The same applied to abdication, which his brother urged on him.

HONOURABLE MARTYRDOM

By January 1867, French troops had withdrawn from Mexico and the armies of Benito Juarez were sweeping towards Mexico City. Maximilian still refused to cut and run. The most he would do was leave for Queretaro, northwest of Mexico City. He was still there when the Juarist forces arrived and captured him. Loath to execute him because he was so disconcertingly noble, the Mexicans tried persuading him to escape. Yet again, Maximilian refused. He seemed intent on martyrdom as the only honourable way out. All the Mexicans could do was to oblige.

On 19 June 1867, Maximilian was marched out of Queretaro to the nearby Hill of Bells. A firing squad awaited him. Taking a deep breath of the ice-fresh mountain air, Maximilian declared: 'What a glorious day! I have always wanted to die on such a day.' Seconds later, he was dead.

The news took 10 days to reach Europe. Nine months passed before her family dared tell Charlotte what had happened. She survived her husband by 40 years, which she spent mumbling to herself and gazing at pictures of Maximilian or smashing anything breakable and ripping up carpets, curtains and upholstery in violent fury. She died, still hopelessly insane, in 1927.

The French artist Edouard Manet produced four paintings and one lithograph depicting Maximilian's execution by firing squad which took place on 19 June 1867.

VII

MADNESS IN THE SPANISH ROYAL FAMILY

The madness of Queen Juana I of Castile (1479–1555) took many forms. Sometimes she crouched on the floor of her cell, unmoving. At other times, she backed into a corner, wild-eyed, as if trying to melt through the walls to escape the demons only she could see. She refused to eat if anyone were there to witness it. Instead, her food had to be left outside her door. She then darted out, snatched up the plate and retreated back to her cell. When she had finished, she carefully hid the plate under the bed, or flung it against the wall, laughing madly.

✦

Juana owed her frightening state of mind to her grandmother Isabel of Portugal, who introduced insanity into the Spanish royal family after 1447, when she became the second wife of King John II of Castile in north-central Spain. Her naturally melancholic

Left: Juana succeeded to her mother's throne after the deaths of her brother, Juan, and sister, Isabella.
Above: Queen Juana was the first victim of the madness introduced into the Spanish royal family by her grandmother.

disposition was exacerbated by the birth, in 1451, of her daughter Isabella, the future Queen of Castile. Afterwards, Isabel of Portugal shut herself away, sitting and staring into the distance for hours on end. Later, she progressed to hysterical tantrums and, in 1452, her daughter was taken from her and sent to be cared for by nuns at a convent in Avila. Isabel had already been deteriorating for some time. Her melancholia turned to full-scale insanity and, before long, she was unable to recognize anyone. She did not even know who she was.

In 1520, by the time Isabel's granddaughter Juana reached this same irretrievable depth of insanity, she had long been queen in name only. The real ruler of Spain and its gold- and silver-rich empire was Juana's son, Charles. Born in 1479, Juana was the third child of Queen Isabella I of Castile and King Ferdinand V of Aragon, and became her parents' heir after her elder sister, another Isabella, died in childbirth in 1498. Juana seemed ideal for her exalted position. She was a bright, attractive child, adept at languages. Like all proud parents, Ferdinand and Isabella showed her

Isabel of Portugal, the melancholy and eventually mad consort of King John II of Castile, blighted several generations of Spanish royals who inherited her insanity.

Juana was a bright, attractive child, adept at languages. She conversed in fluent Latin with clerics and performed with skill on the clavichord and guitar. But her outward gifts covered mercurial moods and an urge for solitude.

off at court, where she conversed in fluent Latin with clerics and performed with skill on the clavichord and guitar. But her outward gifts covered mercurial moods and an urge for solitude. One moment she was calm and dignified; the next, excitable.

An arranged marriage

Like most European princesses, Juana was headed for an arranged marriage. The young man picked for her by her parents – Philip, Count of Flanders, Duke of Burgundy and heir to his father, Maximilian of Austria, the Holy Roman Emperor – possessed the most dazzling prospects of any prince in Europe. Later on, Philip proved to be a disastrous choice, but that lay far in the future when the couple were betrothed in 1489: Philip was 11 years old at the time; Juana barely 10. A proxy wedding took place in 1496 and Juana, now aged 16, left for Flanders, accompanied by a magnificent fleet of ships numbering, it was said, up to 130 vessels. After a difficult, stormy journey, Juana disembarked in Flanders suffering from seasickness and a severe cold.

At least, though, the greeting she received was warm-hearted and Juana's entry into Antwerp was a triumph. Clad in shining cloth of gold, she rode through streets decorated with floral arches and reverberating with the greetings and singing of the crowds. A month later, on 19 October

Right: This illustration from Queen Juana's prayer book shows her (centre) with her parents, King Ferdinand of Aragon (left) and Queen Isabella of Castile (right).

Juana's husband, Philip the Handsome and Philip I of Spain, was a disaster for the Spanish royal family as he manipulated his insane wife for his own purposes.

Philip was 18 years old, golden-haired and marvellously handsome. Juana took in the sturdy physique, the shapely legs and Philip's air of boyish zest and fell in love at once.

1496, Juana and her entourage reached Lierre, now in Belgium, where she met Philip for the first time. The effect they had on each other was electrifying. Juana had never seen him before, but her first sight of Philip confirmed all the exciting stories she had heard about him. He was 18 years old, golden-haired and marvellously handsome. Juana took in the sturdy physique, the shapely legs and Philip's air of boyish zest and fell in love at once. But it was more than just love. It was lust at first sight, and it was mutual.

Blind infatuation

There were tedious official ceremonies to be performed, worthies to be greeted and nobles presented. But as soon as these chores were over, Juana and Philip buttonholed the nearest cleric, the Dean of Jaen, and ordered him to take their proxy marriage one step further and wed them then and there. The hasty ceremony had hardly finished before the couple vanished into one of the hotel rooms, flung off their clothes and made passionate love. Next day, a solemn church wedding officially completed the union that had already been so hotly consummated.

Juana was totally infatuated with Philip, and the spell never wore off. She went through the celebrations in honour of the wedding, which included a full-scale tournament, in a daze of desire for the beautiful creature whom the lottery of royal marriage had so unexpectedly dealt her. Philip appeared, at first, to be caught by the same hunger. What all this concealed, though, was that Philip and Juana were complete opposites. For Philip, the attraction was carnal, little more. Juana, however, wanted total possession – no mistresses, no separate lives, only absolute togetherness. She was too young and too completely consumed by the blaze of her ardour for Philip to realize that he could never give her what she wanted.

Long before he met Juana, Philip of Flanders had become accustomed to igniting nubile young women and already had at least one illegitimate child to prove it. Flemish society was intensely hedonistic and encouraged promiscuity. Almost every pleasure of the flesh was condoned. Extramarital affairs were common, and the registry of births overflowed with bastards. In this environment, not surprisingly, Philip saw no reason why his free-ranging way of life should be interrupted by marriage or why his personal advancement should be curtailed.

Rising Ambition

In 1498, Philip affronted his Spanish in-laws with an impudent bid for the Crown of Spain. He declared himself next in line to the thrones of Castile and Aragon. The claim had no legal foundation. Ferdinand

A portrait of King Ferdinand II of Aragon, Juana's father, by the painter known as the Master of the Legend of St Madeleine. Like his son-in-law Philip, Ferdinand exploited Juana for his own ends.

Philip the Handsome was the son of the Holy Roman Emperor Maximilian I and Mary of Burgundy.

It was not only Philip's crass claim to the throne that disturbed his parents-in-law. Less than two years after their marriage, Philip's love affairs were tormenting Juana with jealousy and began to corrode her personality as fixation wavered from passion to hate. Juana was so totally obsessed by her husband that she was unaware of important realities. France, for example, was Spain's great rival for supremacy in Europe. Yet Philip, the consort of the future Spanish queen, was a francophile, fed for years by the Flemish Council with pro-French propaganda. Philip, for all his glamour,

A view of Zaragoza, capital of the Kingdom of Aragon between the twelfth and fifteenth centuries, with the tower of the Church of St Magdalena (foreground) and the four towers of the Cathedral-Basilica del Nuestra Señora del Pilar (background).

and Isabella, appalled at Philip's rampant ambition, sidestepped him in 1499, by persuading the Cortes, the national legislative assembly of Spain, to confirm their grandson Miguel, the late Isabella's five-month-old son, as heir to their thrones. This, of course, superseded both Juana and Philip.

Philip was not thwarted for long. In 1500, little Miguel died and Juana was again named as her parents' heir. Now the law was on Philip's side, for the husband of a Queen Regnant could claim her title as his own, at least in her lifetime. Already, Philip had begun to found a new royal family. Juana gave birth to their first child, Elinor, in 1498, their second, Charles in 1500 and three more by 1505.

The law was on Philip's side, for the husband of a Queen Regnant could claim her title as his own, at least in her lifetime.

Philip's love affairs were tormenting Juana with jealousy and began to corrode her personality as fixation wavered from passion to hate.

was easily manipulated and made the perfect sponge to absorb these damaging political ideas.

As heir to the throne, it was vital that Juana wake up to the truth. The one man who could make her face facts was Juan de Fonseca, Bishop of Cordova, a long-time family friend who majored in tact and diplomacy. When he reached Brussels, Fonseca found Juana deeply depressed, prone to nervous fainting fits, isolated from court life and hedged in by spies. In this state, Juana was susceptible, and by the time Fonseca had finished with her she at last understood the pro-French and anti-Spanish nature of the Flemings and how they had influenced and moulded Philip to their ways.

Melancholy Zaragoza

Philip, who left Flanders with Juana for a visit to Spain in 1501, hated his wife's homeland and the melancholy pall that hung over it. He detested the moralistic spartan atmosphere and the sight of religious fanatics crying

Queen Isabella I of Castile was a reigning monarch in her own right. When she died in 1504, her throne passed to her daughter, Juana, and her husband, Ferdinand of Aragon, ceased to be consort.

out for remission of sins while flagellating themselves until the blood ran. The summer heat of Spain blazed like a furnace, raising clouds of shimmering dust that made it difficult to breathe. There was too little green, unlike Flanders – only stern mountains and half-desert terrain. Even the royal court was severe in tone. Philip came gaudily dressed in satin brocade, violet velvet and cloth of gold to meet his parents-in-law, while Ferdinand and Isabella sat like monk and nun in plain dark robes.

The official business of the visit to Spain was to persuade the Cortes of Aragon to recognize Juana and Philip as the official heirs of Ferdinand and Isabella. This proved difficult. Philip lapsed into a foul, sulking mood as the Cortes procrastinated, then made unpalatable conditions. Philip could be Consort only so long as Juana lived and, if her mother died and Ferdinand remarried, any son of this second union would supersede Philip. Philip might just have swallowed that one, but what he could not take was the next subject debated by the Cortes: raising funds for war with his beloved France. At that, Philip wanted nothing more to do with the Cortes or Spain, and told Ferdinand and Isabella that he and Juana, who was pregnant again, were going home to Flanders. His excuse was that he had been too long away from his northern realm.

The situation worsens

Adopting every persuasion they knew, Ferdinand and Isabella tried to make Philip change his mind. Their most cogent reason against Philip's decision was Juana's pregnancy, which would make a long and difficult journey in midwinter potentially dangerous for her and her unborn child. Isabella was

Adopting every persuasion they knew, Ferdinand and Isabella tried to make Philip change his mind.

gambling on Philip's love and concern for his wife, but she miscalculated. Philip was perfectly prepared to leave Juana behind in Spain and go home alone. Juana became hysterical when she learned of her husband's intentions, but no dramatics, no tears, no wailing, no begging – in fact, nothing – could make Philip set aside his plans. Philip left Spain on 19 December 1503. It took him more than a year to poodle his way through France, Switzerland, Bavaria and Savoy before he finally reached Brussels and home.

King Ferdinand II became king of Aragon in 1469, ten years after he married Isabella of Castile. On their marriage, Ferdinand became his wife's consort in Castile and she became his consort in Aragon.

Meanwhile in Spain, Juana lapsed into brooding silences as she contemplated how Philip had abandoned her. After the birth of her fourth child, Ferdinand, in early 1503, 15 months after Philip departed, she grew more frenzied. She cursed the clerics sent to calm her, flayed the servants with her fury, insulted her mother with language so foul that even the urbane Isabella was shocked. Juan de Fonseca came to the royal castle of La Mota, where Juana was staying, and tried to calm her down. But she threatened him with death or torture for foiling her attempts to leave Spain and return to Philip.

> **Philip had taken a new mistress. Juana went wild, searched out a pair of scissors and, seizing the woman by the hair, proceeded to scalp her.**

Fonseca retreated, horrified, but Juana came after him and he only just escaped before the castle gate closed behind him. Juana flung herself against the iron bars, yelling and screaming until exhaustion overtook her and she slid to the ground. There she remained all the freezing night long, apparently comatose. Eventually, Ferdinand and Isabella realized that Juana's sexual frenzy could be quenched only when she lay with Philip once again. They had to let her go.

Exchange of insults

Juana returned to Philip in April 1504, but their reunion did nothing to restore her senses. Philip had seen to that. He had taken a new mistress. Juana went wild, searched out a pair of scissors and, seizing the woman by the hair, proceeded to scalp her. The 'mistress' fled, bleeding and almost bald. Philip arrived. After exchanging insults with Juana, he hit her about the face. Even Juana was pulled up short by that. She subsided, retiring to bed for several days.

But she did not remain quiescent for long. Juana's retinue included a number of Moorish slaves, who had accompanied her when she first went to Flanders in 1496. These slaves seemed like devils with their dark, fierce faces scored by ritual marks and their skill with love potions and seductive perfumes. Philip decided

to get rid of them. Juana refused to let them leave, but Philip threw them out anyway. A savage argument ensued with Juana's full battery of insults and curses deployed. Philip, who was no slouch with swearwords, fought back in kind. In protest, Juana went on hunger strike. He let her starve and ignored her pleas when she began hammering on the floor of her bedroom, which was situated above his. After a while, Juana graduated to pounding the floor with a rock, then set about it with a knife. The assault lasted all night and next morning, when Philip finally came up to confront her, he found her exhausted but still defiant.

Increasing isolation

This was war and Juana's mother knew all about it as, herself worn out, she lay near death at the castle of La Mota, Queen Isabella died in late 1504, leaving behind a potentially disastrous situation. Juana was now Queen of Castile but, by her mother's express wish, Ferdinand was to be her regent. He would remain so if Juana turned out to be unable or unwilling to rule. Ferdinand did better than that. He made sure that his daughter would indeed prove unable because of her mental and emotional instability. That, of course, did away with Philip's chance to be king in Spain.

Philip, for his part, also wanted Juana out of the way so that he could claim the throne for himself. Juana's father and husband were, in effect, conspiring against her, each for his own nefarious reasons, and it was just a matter of time before one or other of them triumphed in the race to disinherit her. Philip struck first by forcing Juana, possibly by physical violence, to write a letter informing her father that she was coming to Spain with Philip to assume power in Castile. That done, Philip imprisoned her within the royal palace in Brussels and kept from her anyone who could report her plight to Ferdinand. Twelve soldiers guarded Juana's apartments day and night, and even her chaplain was not allowed to speak with her, except to say mass. Having neutralized Juana, Philip looked round for allies opposed to Ferdinand. He concluded treaties with the French king Louis XII and his own father, Maximilian of Austria, in which

Ferdinand and Isabella met Christopher Columbus (left) in 1486. Columbus visited several royal courts, seeking sponsorship for his plan to find a westward route to Asia. Isabella agreed to finance Columbus and on his voyage he discovered the Americas.

all three signatories vowed to prevent Ferdinand ruling in Castile.

Ferdinand was outmaneuvered, but there was one recourse left: remarriage, which might provide new sons to challenge Philip. In a move that also undercut Philip's new alliances, Ferdinand went to France, his old enemy, for his second bride and, in October 1505, his proxy wedding to Germaine, the French king's niece, was solemnized. Now it was Philip's turn to be outmaneuvered and this time, to his dismay, Juana refused to play his game. She declined publicly to condemn her father's second marriage, as Philip demanded. Slowly, as Philip and Ferdinand parried for control, the situation was moving towards civil war. It appeared imminent when Philip tired of long-distance sparring. Early in 1506, he embarked an army and, with Juana also on board, set sail for Spain. In response, Ferdinand called out the Aragonese militia and the artillery batteries at Medina

A portrait of Maximilian I, Queen Juana's father-in-law, who was known as Archduke Maximilian of Austria before his election as Holy Roman Emperor in 1493.

> **Juana declined publicly to condemn her father's second marriage, as Philip demanded. Slowly, as Philip and Ferdinand parried for control, the situation was moving towards civil war.**

del Campo to await what most presumed would be a Flemish invasion.

Guile and machinations

When Philip's fleet docked at Coruña in the northwestern corner of Spain, Ferdinand realized that his forces were greatly outnumbered and outgunned. He resorted to what he knew best: guile. Before long, news reached Philip that troop movements were under way in Andalucia to the south and Léon in the northwest, and that Ferdinand's army was slowly approaching his own. Any day now, Philip would be encircled. By 19 June 1506, Ferdinand's troops were only 10 kilometres away. The trap seemed about to close around Philip, but there was no fighting. Philip lost his nerve and agreed to negotiate with his father-in-law.

The result of their meeting was a pair of treaties, the first containing an agreement that Ferdinand would withdraw his troops from Castile. The second was a secret arrangement whereby Juana would never be permitted to rule. The ink on his signatures was barely dry before Ferdinand reneged and declared that he had agreed to the treaties under duress and that Juana was the rightful monarch of Castile after all.

Meanwhile, Philip thought he had won. Unaware of the old fox's reputation for cunning, Philip proceeded with plans to park Juana out of the way. But Juana was no longer easy prey. She had come to suspect that anything Philip said or did was in her worst interests and, besides, she very much wanted to be reconciled with her father, whom she adored. To accomplish this, she needed to escape. Her first two attempts failed, but

Juana the Mad was obsessed with her husband, Philip the Handsome, and consummated her marriage to him the first time they met, the day before their wedding took place officially in 1496.

her third bid to foil Philip, using a different tactic, was more successful.

When Philip demanded that the Cortes agree to putting his wife away as a mental incompetent, her cousin Fadrique Enriquez, Admiral of Castile, went to assess the state of her mind for himself. The

The Convent of Santa Clara at Tordesillas where Juana was confined from 1509 to her death in 1555.

> ### The ink on his signatures was barely dry before Ferdinand reneged and declared that he had agreed to the treaties under duress.

cousins spent 10 hours together; Juana was calm, perfectly in control of herself and the admiral found her conversation both intelligent and astute. No way, he told Philip later, would he connive at any scheme to have Juana pronounced unfit. The admiral defended her so forcefully that the Cortes threw out Philip's proposal. Frustrated and furious, he moved his army on to Burgos in northern Spain. It was here that fate intervened and provided the perfect, if tragic, solution to the problem of Philip the Handsome, scourge of the royal house of Spain.

On 17 September 1506, Philip played a hard game of pelota with one of his men and ended up covered in sweat and ragingly thirsty. He drank a pitcher of water while standing where a cold mountain wind would, he hoped, cool him down. Philip began to feel ill that same night and woke next morning with a temperature. Three days later, he was coughing blood. His throat swelled up and, by 24 September, black and red spots had appeared all over his body. He lapsed into a coma, and died two days later. It was three hours before Juana, who was once again pregnant, would permit his courtiers to dress the corpse and prepare it for burial. After that, she draped herself in black and sat dazed and unresponsive in her apartments.

A morbid procession

When, eventually, Juana came out of her trance, she had only one thought in mind: she must take Philip's body south to Granada for burial. A grisly procession set out in the freezing winter fog, with Juana walking behind the hearse. She managed 61 kilometres (38 miles) across hard mountain terrain before exhaustion and the imminent birth of her child forced her to halt at Torquemada in central Spain. There, early in 1507, Juana gave birth to her sixth child, her daughter Catalina.

Every day, a funeral service was performed in front of the altar in the local church, and all day and all night Juana's courtiers stood guard around the catafalque. In April 1507, after plague struck Torquemada, Juana gave orders to leave. The procession took to the road once more and came to its next halt, in a miserable little village called Hornillos. By now, Philip had been dead for seven months, plenty of time for gossip to create lurid tales about Juana's behaviour. It was said that she believed Philip would come back to life after a monk told her of a corpse that had revived after 14 years. Most gruesome were the stories telling how Juana had the coffin opened almost daily and made love with the remains.

The truth was that Juana had the coffin opened four times in all, but she did little more than gaze at what remained of her husband. Philip was still unburied in late August 1507, when Juana set out from Hornillos for her long-awaited reunion with her father. When she saw him at last, she fell to her knees and attempted to kiss his feet. Apparently shocked by his daughter's haggard, ravaged appearance, he burst into tears.

Final descent into madness

The touching moment of emotion did not mean that Ferdinand was going to play the caring father. At some time during the long conversation that followed, it seems that Ferdinand persuaded Juana to hand over Castile, its government and its revenues. At long last, Ferdinand had everything he wanted. It only remained for him to get Juana out of the way now that he no longer needed her.

A grisly procession set out in the freezing winter fog, with Juana walking behind the hearse.

This truth took a long time to dawn on Juana. All deference was paid to her as Queen of Castile. Even Germaine, her father's second wife, paid homage to her. But then, Juana began to notice that her new courtiers, appointed by Ferdinand, owed allegiance to him rather than to her, and acted more like spies than attendants. In the spring of 1508, Ferdinand showed a glimpse of his hand. He began to press Juana to marry again. The English king Henry VII had asked for her, and it occurred to Juana that Henry's distant realm would conveniently remove her from Spain. Juana refused and Ferdinand finally lost patience.

He was about to set off on an expedition to Cordova in southern Spain to deal with a rebel aristocrat and, he claimed, he wanted Juana to stay somewhere safe in his absence. Ferdinand's idea of somewhere safe was the dank, menacing, prison-like castle of Tordesillas. Juana begged her father not to put her there and, after a tussle, Ferdinand gave in, but took revenge by removing Juana's five-year-old son, another Ferdinand.

Peculiar behaviour

When her father and her son had gone, Juana lapsed into a stupor and her mind, long poised on the edge of madness, began to give way. Her behaviour grew more and more peculiar. She refused to wash or change her clothes. She passed water almost constantly. By early 1509, when Ferdinand returned from Cordova,

King Charles I of Spain, who bypassed his mad mother, Juana, to succeed to the thrones of Castile and Aragon in 1516. Three years later he succeeded his paternal grandfather Maximilian as the Holy Roman Emperor Charles V.

were few humiliations Juana did not suffer. She fought back in her usual ways – refusing to eat, go to bed, wash or dress – but there is some evidence that she was beaten to make her more tractable. Her father visited her twice – in October 1509 and November 1510. On the second occasion, he brought with him a group of nobles opposed to his takeover of Castile, and took Juana by surprise. The doors to her apartments suddenly opened and, there, the nobles were aghast to see the shrunken, bedraggled Queen of Castile dressed in grubby rags, looking ravaged and smelling worse, in surroundings of utter squalor. Ferdinand never did anything by halves. He had brought the nobles to see the wreckage of his daughter and to see for themselves that Juana was a totally lost cause.

Ferdinand died in 1516, and Juana succeeded him as nominal queen of his realm of Aragon. The new double crown of Castile and Aragon meant nothing to her. Her elder son, Charles, proved no less malevolent than his father and grandfather before him. The prize he had to inherit – all of Spain and Spanish America and half of Europe – overcame filial conscience. But Charles would succeed to this vast swathe of territory and its immense riches only if his mother stepped down in his favour. It was not difficult to persuade her. Juana was now so far gone into madness that she gave in meekly and agreed that Charles should rule on her behalf.

Having got what he wanted, Charles kept Juana closely confined and concealed her under an impenetrable pall of secrecy. Juana was not permitted to see anyone from the outside world and, on Charles's orders, was made to keep to her room, preferably in bed. When she heard mass, it was not in the castle chapel, but in the room next to her own.

there were plenty of witnesses to attest to her descent into madness. Ferdinand ordered that Juana be taken under heavy guard to the castle of Tordesillas. Philip's coffin went with her and so did her daughter Catalina, now two years old.

Locked away in the castle, her final prison, there

The nobles were aghast to see the shrunken, bedraggled Queen of Castile dressed in grubby rags, looking ravaged and smelling worse, in surroundings of utter squalor.

A PITIFUL FIGURE

Despite her utterly wretched condition, Juana was able to contemplate escape and received her chance after news of her confinement at Tordesillas got out in 1519. Rebels opposed to Charles's heavy taxation marched to the castle and managed to get into the courtyard. This gave Juana the opportunity to break out of her cell and watch the rebels clamouring for her as their rightful queen. But she was too confused to realize what was going on. She stared at her would-be champions with glazed, vacant eyes, then allowed herself to be taken back to the castle and locked up. This time, though, she was put into a pitch-dark, windowless cell. She was let out occasionally, once in 1525, when her daughter Catalina left the castle on her way to marry King John III of Portugal. Juana watched the procession wind away towards the horizon through windows heavily barred to prevent her throwing herself out.

Juana mouldered at the Castle of Tordesillas for another 30 years, falling deeper and deeper into fantasy and the horrible imaginings that fill unhinged minds. She died in 1555, aged 76, after spending two-thirds of her life in confinement. Juana was buried in the royal chapel at Granada next to Philip, whose grotesque odyssey ended in 1525, when he was interred there some 20 years after his death. Juana's parents were similarly paired nearby. As with Philip, their effigies took the customary pose of piety and dignity. Juana's image was different. The sculptor who carved it scored into the marble the lines and hollows that had ravaged her face in real life and, in posthumous consolation, placed in her hands the royal sceptre, the symbol of authority she was never allowed to possess.

The tomb of Philip the Handsome and Juana the Mad in the Royal Chapel, Granada. Juana, who died in 1555, outlived Philip by more than 50 years.

VIII

MORE MADNESS IN SPAIN

Madness in the Spanish royal family, which began in the fifteenth century with Isabel of Portugal, spread through subsequent generations, sparing some, but striking others with destructive force. Add to that one further factor – frequent intermarriage, a device for preserving Habsburg family power in Spain – and the stage was set for a sequence of horrors unmatched by any other dynasty in Europe. They appeared most spectacularly in Don Carlos (1545–1568), and, generations later, in King Carlos II of Spain (1661–1700).

✦

Don Carlos was a fearful example of the damage wrought by interbreeding, which disabled him in almost every possible way. His parents were first cousins twice over. Two of his great-grandmothers were sisters: one was Queen Juana, who was still alive,

Left: Carlos II of Spain was just sane enough to recognize the symptoms of the madness which afflicted him, although he believed the cause was sorcery. His sixteenth-century ancestor, Don Carlos (above), suffered similarly and died tragically young.

far gone in fantasy and fearful imaginings, in her squalid cell at the castle of Tordesillas, when Don Carlos was born in 1547. The birth was so arduous that his mother, the 18-year-old Princess Maria Manuela, survived for only four days following it.

Physically, the infant Carlos was a monster, a hunchback with his right leg shorter than his left. He was mentally retarded and unable to speak until he was five years of age. Even then, some deformation of his mouth may have prevented him from pronouncing the letters 'l' and 'r', which made it difficult to understand what he was saying. The problem increased when he developed a pronounced stutter. This, in its turn, led to frustrations that fed his violent tendencies. Even as a baby, he was subject to outbursts of sadistic violence which included biting the breasts of his wet nurses so hard that three of them nearly died.

An untenable position

Despite his alarming physical and mental state, the fact remained that Don Carlos was his father's only male heir. This position had to be formally acknowledged. But Philip postponed the official ceremony, hoping against hope that his son's condition would improve. There was no improvement. Then, in 1555, Philip's father, Charles, abdicated and Philip succeeded him as King of Spain in the following year. Carlos, for all his manifest disabilities and frightening behaviour, was now one step away from the throne and there could be no more delay. He was officially recognized as Spain's future king and, as he was required to produce his own heirs to the throne, he duly took his place in the royal marriage market.

> **A pronounced stutter led to frustrations that fed Don Carlos's violent tendencies. Even as a baby, he was subject to outbursts of violence which included biting the breasts of his wet nurses so hard that three of them nearly died.**

Several potential candidates were suggested, including Queen Elizabeth I of England, who was considerably older than Carlos, by 14 years. Marriage to either of two further candidates, Carlos's aunt Joanna, Princess Dowager of Portugal, and his cousin Archduchess Anna of Austria, would have been incestuous. The last thing the Spanish royal family

The melancholy, taciturn King Philip II came to the throne of Spain in 1556, after his father, Charles V, abdicated. Philip's severely disabled son, Don Carlos, was the great tragedy in his life.

A PENCHANT FOR TORTURE

On the premise that lack of male company and the absence of what would now be termed suitable 'role models' were having an adverse effect on him, Don Carlos was removed from the exclusively feminine company of nurses and governesses when he was aged seven. This served only to make his propensity for cruelty and violence even worse. By the time he was nine years old, Carlos had taken to torturing little girls and servants. He became worse still after he was aged 13. He maimed the horses in the royal stables so severely that 20 of them had to destroyed. Carlos was also fond of spiking small animals on spits and roasting them alive: his favourites were hares.

One of the characteristics of the mad Don Carlos was extreme sadism. His father, King Philip II, hoped that he would somehow be cured, but it never happened. It was rumoured that Philip engineered Carlos's death in 1568.

DON CARLO SPANA

This portrait of Don Carlos disguised the truth about him. The hump on Carlos's back is effectively disguised by his cloak and the black background of the painting, but the shapely legs were far from the truth: one of Carlos' legs was shorter than the other.

needed was more interbreeding, and it was fortunate that all the unions proposed for Carlos failed to transpire. In the event, Carlos never married. It was just as well, for he spelled enough disaster for his family without reproducing himself.

Carlos's numerous shortfalls included an aversion to learning. His interests stopped at wine, women and the food that lost him his thin boyhood physique and transformed him into an overweight adult. In the forlorn hope that higher education might break through his indifference to learning, Carlos was sent to attend lectures at the University of Alcala de Henares in 1562. Carlos had no interest in lectures, but while at the Alcala he fell madly in love with the daughter of one of the university's servants. Then, one day Carlos was running down insufficiently lit stairs when he stumbled and fell. He was found lying unconscious with a gaping wound in his head. It became infected, and subsequently his head swelled to such an enormous size that he became temporarily blind.

Anxious father

King Philip, meanwhile, was consumed with anxiety and the fear that he was about to lose his one and only male heir. He hurried to the Alcala and prayed for his son's recovery day and night.

> He was found lying unconscious with a gaping wound in his head. It became infected, and subsequently his head swelled to such an enormous size that he became temporarily blind.

Philip threw out the official physicians who had proved useless and turned to 'quacks' who were even worse: their 'cures' were not far removed from those of witch doctors and magicians. Eventually, when Don Carlos was running a high fever and the situation was desperate, Philip called in a group of Franciscan friars who owned a relic, the mummified body of the Blessed Friar Diego, who had died about a century earlier.

The Friars placed the body in Carlos's bed and that night, it appears, the prince dreamed of Friar Diego. From then on, his fever gradually reduced, his pulse became steadier and, after two months, he was able to walk a short distance. But the crisis was not over. The fall and its aftermath had clearly done even

Carlos never married. It was just as well, for he spelled enough disaster for his family without reproducing himself.

more damage to Don Carlos's disordered brain. He would spend hours sitting in silence, then start talking gibberish. Even more alarming, he became more violent than before.

Without provocation, Carlos assaulted servants and high court officials, and nearly threw one of them out of a palace window. A shoemaker who made a pair of boots Carlos did not like was forced to cut them up and eat them. Carlos was intrigued by weapons of all kinds and once used his sword to threaten the powerful and imposing Fernando Alvarez de Toledo, Third Duke of Alba. The duke was equal to the challenge. He roughly seized Carlos by the arm and removed the weapon from his hand.

Worsening violence

This far, it had been possible to keep Carlos's strange behaviour a secret. But as he sank deeper and deeper into madness, secrecy became impossible. With his rages, his arrogance and his sudden bouts of violence, Carlos was proving too much for his father – or anyone else – to handle. Towards the end of December 1567, Carlos stepped irretrievably too far over the line between what Philip would and would not tolerate when he told his confessor that he 'wanted to kill

a man'. He meant his father. This, of course, was treason. Either the confidentiality of the confessional was broken or Carlos told someone else, but, whatever way the news reached him, Philip soon learned what his son had said. King Philip had been away in the Spanish Netherlands, but on 17 January 1568, when he returned to Spain, he took immediate action.

That night, Carlos was relaxing in his room, surrounded by a mass of weapons, when the door to his room burst open. There, in the doorway, stood three men – King Philip, his adviser and his confessor. Carlos immediately took fright, and apparently fell to his knees in front of his father and begged him

This portrait of King Philip II, the father of Don Carlos, shows him surrounded by the six coats of arms that symbolized the Spanish territories.

to end his life there and then. When the king refused, Carlos tried to throw himself into the fire that was burning in the grate nearby. He was forcibly held back from the flames.

Carlos immediately took fright, and apparently fell to his knees in front of his father and begged him to end his life there and then.

Poisonous diamonds

Don Carlos was imprisoned in strict confinement in the tower of Arévelo castle, near Madrid. The only light in his tiny cell came from a window set high up in one wall. From then on, King Philip pretended his son did not exist. No one was allowed to mention his name, enquire as to his whereabouts or say prayers for him in church.

As the months passed, Carlos became more and more crazed. He went on hunger strike and had to be force-fed with soup to keep him alive. Believing that diamonds were poisonous, he swallowed a diamond ring in an attempt at suicide. Finally, on 9 July 1568, Carlos's imprisonment was legalized by charging him with treason for plotting to kill his father. Carlos was not allowed counsel to defend him, and the sentence was pronounced as death. It was a formality. Philip had no intention of executing his son, but he did drop

Medical knowledge in the seventeenth century was unable to diagnose, let alone treat, the causes of insanity. Exorcism by a priest was all that could be done, although the tragic King Carlos II, shown here, kneeling, failed to benefit from it.

strong hints that if the precautions taken with his diet were relaxed, and he was allowed to indulge his natural inclination to stuff food, the eventual result would be excesses leading to his death.

The taciturn Philip shut himself away, to sit brooding for days on end. Meanwhile, in close confinement, his son's condition rapidly worsened. He developed a high fever and vomited incessantly. Ice was poured onto the floor of his cell to cool him down, and Carlos's clothes were stripped off so that he could lie in it. For days on end, Carlos refused to eat anything but fruit. He asked for pastry, but when a huge spiced cake was brought to him, he ate it all, then doused it by drinking more than 10 litres of water. Soon afterwards, he became violently sick. On 24 July 1568, Don Carlos died, aged 23. A cryptic announcement was made that he had 'died of his own excesses', but rumours were soon spreading that the cause of death was slow poison mixed in with Carlos's food.

Fast-forward a century

King Philip had to wait a further 10 years for another son, the future Philip III, to succeed him. But again he was courting danger, for the mother of the third Philip was Anna of Austria, once a candidate to marry Don Carlos, and King Philip's niece. Worse still, the dangers of interbreeding were compounded even further after Philip IV, son and successor of Philip III, also married his niece, Maria Anna.

The son of Philip IV and Maria Anna succeeded to the Spanish throne as King Carlos II in 1665 when he was four years of age. He was soon nicknamed *El Hechizaldo*, 'the Bewitched'.

The son of Philip IV and Maria Anna succeeded to the Spanish throne as King Carlos II in 1665 when he was four years of age. He was soon nicknamed *El Hechizaldo*, 'the Bewitched'. His fearful mental and physical state was ascribed to sorcery, and Carlos himself was convinced of it. 'Many people tell me I am bewitched,' he said. 'I well believe it, such are the things I experience and suffer.'

The young King Carlos II of Spain dressed, as children were in the 17th century and afterwards, as a miniature adult.

In an effort to cure him, Carlos was exorcized. The priests involved were ordered to close-question the 'devils' that 'possessed' him, but they refused to make an appearance, and the effort was abandoned.

Physical deformities

Almost everything that could be wrong with the unfortunate Carlos *was* wrong. For a start, he had a

IMPOTENCE AND DEATH

As he grew, however crookedly, to manhood, Carlos II had to face up to a new disability: he was not thought capable of siring a child. Carlos's impotence was said to have been apparent when he was born. Nevertheless, in 1679, he married his first wife, Marie Louise of France, who was, understandably, not best pleased when her uncle King Louis XIV told her of the match that had been made for her. After several years of trying, Marie Louise told the French ambassador to Spain that she was not a virgin any more, but did not believe that she would ever have children. The ambassador somehow got hold of a pair of Carlos's drawers and had them examined for traces of sperm, but the physicians who carried out the tests were unable to agree about their findings.

RAPID DEGENERATION

Marie Louise died, still childless, in 1689, and three months later Carlos remarried. His second wife, Maria Anna, belonged to the fertile Neuburg Line of the Wittelsbach royal family, later to become notorious for its own eccentricities and insanity. Maria Anna's fertility was not in doubt, though, but just to make sure she was exorcised to promote her childbearing chances. Even then, there were to be no children, nor did there seem to be hope of any, for within a few years Carlos was degenerating rapidly. In 1696, at age 35, his hair and teeth had fallen out, and his eyesight was deteriorating. In 1698, he suffered three epileptic fits and became deaf. He was lame and suffered bouts of dizziness. All his physicians could do was place the steaming entrails of animals on his stomach to keep him warm. King Carlos, a wreck of a man if ever there was one, died in 1700, aged 39.

The bizarre-looking Carlos II of Spain dressed in the robes of the Most Illustrious Order of the Golden Fleece, a chivalric order which had been founded in 1430. He was the last Habsburg monarch to wear the robes.

huge, misshapen head. There was also a pre-existing characteristic of his family – an unusually large, jutting jaw known as the 'Habsburg lip'. In Carlos's case, the lip was so exaggerated that the upper and lower rows of his teeth did not meet and he was unable to chew his food. Carlos's tongue was excessively large and protruded from his mouth; this made it difficult for anyone to understand what he said. He drooled continuously. His legs were so weak that he was unable to stand or walk, and frequently fell down in

Philip V, the first Bourbon King of Spain. Though not as severely afflicted by the family madness as some of his relations, Philip was eccentric and suffered from melancholia and hallucinations.

Congenital syphilis was another ingredient of Carlos's disastrous genetic cocktail, the probable result of the visits his father paid to brothels in Madrid.

the attempt. His overprotective family would not allow him to walk unaided until he was almost full grown. Similarly, Carlos did not feed himself until he was aged five or six: instead, he was fed by wet nurses. He

was considered so frail that he was not required to keep clean or even have his hair combed.

As if all this were not enough, the inherited hormonal disease acromegaly may have been added to Carlos's numerous afflictions. Caused by excessive amounts of hormones, particularly growth hormones, this rare but severe disease produced overlarge hands and feet, and weak muscles, among other symptoms. Congenital syphilis was another ingredient of Carlos's disastrous genetic cocktail, the probable result of the visits his father, King Philip IV, paid to brothels in Madrid.

> ## To compound these already fearful genetic prospects, Philip V's mother, Maria Anna of Bavaria was a Wittelsbach and hence from a family whose instability had been passed down to her over several centuries.

Carlos was also mentally retarded, though not so severely that he was unaware of his disabilities. He was deeply superstitious. His apparent lack of intellect seems to have been due less to a defective brain and more to his lack of an education. The royal family, it appears, feared to put him under undue strain and preferred to leave him barely able to read or write. Little wonder that Carlos II was unable to comprehend the world in which he lived. What knowledge he possessed derived from superstition, which exercised a strong hold over him.

A new line, but no respite

Carlos II was the last of the Spanish Habsburgs. His death in 1700 without a son to succeed him was the signal for an outbreak of faction fighting and, in 1701, a full-scale war. The War of the Spanish Succession, the struggle to decide who would be the next King of Spain, came to an end in 1713, with victory for another powerful European family, the Bourbons of France. Tragically, though, Philip V, the first Bourbon king of Spain, brought another disastrous legacy to his new throne, for interbreeding was endemic in his

> ## ... for Philip's Wittelsbach melancholia came so close to madness that he was unable to rule effectively or, indeed, rule at all.

family background, too. Philip V was a grandson of King Louis XIV and his Spanish Habsburg wife, Maria Theresa, who were double first cousins. Maria Theresa was also a daughter of Philip IV and so a direct descendant six generations on from the mad Queen Juana of Spain. To compound these already fearful genetic prospects, Philip V's mother, Maria Anna of Bavaria was a Wittelsbach and hence from a family whose instability had been passed down to her over several centuries.

Fortunately, Philip V remained stable enough for long enough to hold the Spanish throne for all but seven months of 46 years. The seven months occurred in 1724, four years after Philip, who was a deeply devout man, had made a solemn vow to renounce the world and his throne with it. 'Thank God I am no longer king,' he declared after he abdicated on 14 January 1724. 'The remainder of my days I shall apply myself to the service of God and to solitude.'

The expectation was premature. Philip's son Luis I succeeded him, but the following August he died of smallpox and his father was, with difficulty, persuaded to resume his reign.

Eccentricity and insanity

Despite the length of that reign, a distinct achievement for such a crazy mixed-up family, Philip V's tenure of the Spanish throne was punctuated by lapses marked, at best, by eccentricity and, at worst, by full-blown insanity. Sometimes, it came to the worst, for Philip's Wittelsbach melancholia came so close to madness that he was unable to rule effectively or, indeed, rule at all. He himself doubted that he was fit to be a king. At such times, Philip retreated into prolonged periods of

Philip V of Spain (first from left) with his second wife, Elizabeth Farnese (third from left) and their son and heir the future Ferdinand VI (fourth from left).

solitude and displayed most, if not all, the symptoms of a recluse. Company was anathema to him. He was suspicious and trusted no one. He had little self-confidence or self-esteem. His ancestor King Philip II had possessed many of these same characteristics two centuries before him.

A ravaged ruler

Philip V suffered his first really serious attack in 1717, when he was all but overcome by deep melancholia that verged on hysteria and provoked horrible imaginings. Philip said he felt as if a raging fire was consuming his innards like a shaft of sunlight piercing him through and through. He was convinced, too, that he was dying in mortal sin and shut himself away in his apartments. The only visitor allowed in from the outside was his confessor. The confessor had his work cut out, for Philip was sure that he was being made to suffer by divine punishment for his personal inadequacies. A more scientific explanation was that

> **Philip's moods ranged rapidly from lethargic to madly excited and back again. He was delusional and believed that he could not walk because his feet were of different sizes.**

these delusions were typical of manic depression.

Although he was sufficiently recovered to return to his public duties by 1718, Philip's sufferings had exacted their toll. Although he was only 35 years old, he looked as if he was well advanced into extreme old age. He was bent over with a shrunken body and, according to the French writer Louis de Rouvroi, Duc de Saint-Simon, he walked in a strange way with 'his knees more than one foot apart'. Saint-Simon went on: '… his words were so drawled, his expression so vacuous, that I was quite unnerved.'

Ten years later, when he suffered another attack of manic depression, Philip's moods ranged rapidly

King Ferdinand VI was neurotic, melancholic and lived in constant fear of sudden death. He was also subject to violent rages.

from lethargic to madly excited and back again. He physically attacked his doctors and his second wife, Queen Elizabeth of Parma, leaving her black and blue with bruising. Philip was delusional and believed that he could not walk because his feet were of different sizes. He refused to be shaved or have his toenails cut. Eight months passed before his son and heir, Ferdinand, managed to persuade him to let his barber shave him.

Spain grinds to a halt

In 1732, Philip retired to bed, and declined to get up. He ate his meals in bed, but refused to change his clothes or shave. He also refused to speak to anyone except Queen Elizabeth and Ferdinand because, he let it be known, he was dead. Neither would Philip agree to see his ministers or sign documents. With this, government in Spain virtually ground to a halt. Fortunately, Philip recovered in 1733, after some seven months.

Six more years went by before Philip succumbed yet again. This time, it manifested itself in fearful howlings that echoed through the apartments and corridors of his palace. His ministers and courtiers had to work hard to prevent the news getting out that the King of Spain had once more lost his mind.

There was, though, another side to Philip V, and a paradoxical one. His Bourbon ancestry had given him a voracious appetite for sex. At the same time, his scrupulous morality prevented him from doing as other monarchs did and take a mistress. He continually moved between the confessional and his queen's bedroom, and his demands on his first wife, Marie Louise of Savoy, were excessive. In 1714, she died, worn out, at the age of 26, and a near-hysterical Philip had to be forcibly removed from her deathbed.

Philip retired distraught to his palace of Medina Coeli in Andalucia. He wept loud, long and copiously, for he needed sex to live as much as he needed air to breathe. After eight months, Philip married again, and had seven children by his second wife, Elizabeth of Parma, to add to the four borne him by the unfortunate Marie Louise. Eventually, though, the hurly-burly of Philip's life caught up with him. On 9 July 1746, he suffered a stroke and died. He was 63 years of age.

Unfortunately, Philip's third surviving son and successor, Ferdinand VI, was fully equipped for yet

another round of royal madness. Ferdinand was born in 1713 and succeeded to the Spanish throne at age 33. Initially, the future seemed brighter for the Bourbons, who had suffered so much anguish and embarrassment over Philip V. At first, Ferdinand ruled as a benign monarch, eager to care for his subjects and improve their lives. He gave vast sums to charity and in 1750 withdrew taxes due when Andalusia was stricken with drought.

Grandeur and show

Ferdinand was a keen patron of the arts and sciences, founding the San Fernando academy of fine arts in Madrid and building three royal astronomical observatories. His favourite relaxation was the opera with his wife, Maria Teresa Barbara, and he delighted in sailing downriver in a luxurious barge equipped with a plush red velvet pavilion trimmed with silver. The fleet of boats accompanying the royal barge was made in the shapes of peacocks or deer. Luxury all the way was the watchword, for Barbara loved grandeur and outward show. She, too, loved music and opera, and was a talented harpsichordist. During a river voyage, she accompanied songs sung by the great castrato counter-tenor Farinelli, who was a great favourite at the Spanish court.

> **Like Ferdinand, the queen came from a mentally unstable background and shared with him a deep fear of sudden death and a neurotic, melancholic nature.**

Ferdinand's public face made him deservedly popular with his subjects, and the splendour of his public appearances assured them of his high status among the great monarchs of Europe. Yet beneath all the glitz and grandeur, and the royal *bonhomie*, there was a dark underside to the Spanish Bourbons. Like Ferdinand, the queen, who belonged to the Braganza family of Portugal, came from a mentally unstable

Both Ferdinand VI and his wife Barbara loved lavish royal show. In this 1756 painting, they are shown with members of their court in the gardens of the palace of Aranjuez, near Madrid.

AN END TO THE MADNESS

With King Ferdinand VI, the long and tragic tale of royal insanity, melancholia and instability came to an end. There had, though, been a chance that the sequence might have continued. Ferdinand was succeeded by his half-brother, King Carlos III, who escaped the curse of royal insanity, but after him the family problem resurfaced. The heir to Carlos III's throne by birth was his elder son Don Felipe, who was mentally retarded or, as some physicians classed him, an imbecile. He was also epileptic. This was enough for the direct line of royal descent to be diverted to a more suitable heir. Felipe was passed over in favour of his younger brother, who succeeded to their father's throne as King Carlos IV in 1788. It had taken almost 300 years, but the Spaniards had learned a vital lesson at last: absolute monarchs, like the kings of Spain, might be chosen by God, but earthly realities must sometimes supervene.

King Carlos III, an enlightened despot who succeeded his half brother Ferdinand VI in 1758, escaped the legacy of madness that had blighted the Habsburg and Bourbon royal families.

background and shared with him a deep fear of sudden death and a neurotic, melancholic nature.

Barbara could be outgoing and vivacious, but Ferdinand, whose mental problems were more intense,

> ## He asked for poison, which was, of course, refused, then tried to stab himself with scissors or make a rope to hang himself out of knotted napkins and curtains.

turned out to be another Philip V – only worse. He was neurotic and suspicious by nature and was subject to sudden violent rages. He went about in the daily fear that he would fall victim to sudden death. Without warning, he would be consumed by violent fits of rage. Longing for solitude, Ferdinand would withdraw to a monastery where his ministers could not reach him. Like his father, he signed no documents and refused to speak. As time went on, his rages, which drove him to bang his head against the wall, grew increasingly violent. Afterwards, Ferdinand collapsed to the floor and for several hours lay motionless where he fell. He was convinced that, if he lay down, he would die, but then changed his mind and refused to leave his bed for days on end.

Between these episodes, the king could be quite lucid and pleasant, but he finally sank into irretrievable insanity in 1758, when Queen Barbara, whom he adored, died. If anyone

suggested to him that he remarry, he flew into a frenzy. He refused to wash, shave or dress. He went without sleep for 10 nights at a stretch. He attacked members of his entourage without warning: his most frequent weapon was his own excrement. Ferdinand refused to eat anything but soup, but then refused all food. He suffered such severe weight loss that he shrank to little more than a skeleton covered in skin. Several times he attempted suicide. He asked for poison, which was, of course, refused, then tried to stab himself with scissors or make a rope to hang himself out of knotted napkins and curtains. Before long, Ferdinand was suffering from convulsions, and it was in one of these fits that he died on 10 August 1759, aged 46.

Like her husband, Barbara, Ferdinand VI's queen came from a mentally deranged family. the Braganzas of Portugal. Her death in 1758 pushed Ferdinand over the edge into total insanity.

FOUL PLAY AND ELEPHANT HUNTING

Towards the end of his life, General Francisco Franco, who'd held dictatorial rule over Spain since 1939, chose Juan Carlos, grandson of the exiled King Alfonso XIII (reigned 1886–1931), as his successor. Franco believed that Juan Carlos would continue his authoritarian rule, but following the General's death in 1975, Juan Carlos began to dismantle the legacy of Franco's regime and introduce reforms to transform Spain into a democracy. In 1978, a new constitution was approved, creating a constitutional monarchy.

Three years later, members of the Guardia Civil (Civil Guard) seized the parliamentary chamber in an attempted coup. They claimed that they had the

support of the king, but his appearance on television, dressed in the uniform of the Captain-General of the Spanish armed forces and restating his belief in the constitutional monarchy, helped thwart the efforts to reinstate a dictatorship. Not only did the coup fail, but it helped consolidate Juan Carlos's position: before the coup support for the monarchy had been limited, but Juan Carlos's handling of the affair helped increase its popularity.

Throughout the 1980s and 1990s, Juan Carlos was one of the world's most popular constitutional monarchs, but in the new millennium his appeal began to wane, particularly at home. With Spain deep in economic recession in 2012 and unemployment at 23 per cent (and almost 50 per cent among young adults), it was regarded as glaringly out of touch for the king to go elephant-hunting in Botswana. While

Juan Carlos (right), honorary president of the Spanish branch of the World Wide Fund for Nature (WWF), poses in front of a dead elephant on his hunting trip to Botswana in 2012.

In 2016, Princess Cristina became the first member of the Spanish royal family in modern times to go on trial.

the trip was not part of Juan Carlos's official duties and was paid for by a friend, the national newspaper *El País* estimated that the total cost of the trip was €44,000, about twice the average annual salary in Spain at the time.

In addition, a petition was launched calling for the king to resign as honorary president of the Spanish branch of the World Wide Fund for Nature (WWF). Within months, the WWF-Spain had voted 226 to 13 to remove the king from his role. He later apologised for the trip.

HANDBALLER FOR THE HIGH JUMP

In the same year, a corruption scandal began to emerge involving Juan Carlos's daughter, Princess Cristina, and her husband, former team handball player Iñaki Urdangarín. Urdangarín was accused of embezzlement, perverting the course of justice, falsification and money laundering through his organisation, the Nóos Institute, a non-profit company that allegedly charged inflated prices to regional governments for leisure-related events.

Despite Urdangarín's efforts to limit the damage, by the following year the investigation had been broadened to include Cristina, and in 2014 it was announced that she would stand trial for tax fraud. Cristina was half-owner of Aizoon, officially a property company set up with her husband but which was allegedly used as a means to channel Nóos funds. The

scandal led to Cristina and Urdangarín being sidelined by the royal family.

In fact, eyebrows had already been raised regarding the couple's financial dealings when in 2004 they bought an apartment in Barcelona for, allegedly, €6 million. With Cristina earning around €90,000 a year from her job at savings bank La Caixa and little known about the size of Urdangarín's income following the end of his handball career, questions were asked about how they had afforded the property. It was later admitted that Juan Carlos had lent his daughter €1.2 million to secure the mortgage on the property.

Amidst this, and with questions being raised about the source of the king's own private wealth, in June 2014 Juan Carlos announced that he was abdicating the throne in favour of his 46-year-old son Felipe. In a reference to the English crown, the 76-year-old king said: 'I don't want my son to grow old waiting like Prince Charles.'

Notably, neither Cristina nor Urdangarín were present at Felipe's coronation, nor has Felipe since offered any public support to his sister. In 2015, Cristina was deprived of her title Duchess of Palma de Mallorca, meaning also that Urdangarín now lost his aristocratic status. In what has been seen as an effort to clean up the image of the monarchy in Spain, Felipe promised on his accession an 'honest and transparent monarchy' and in his inaugural speech pledged that 'the crown must constantly earn citizens' appreciation, respect and trust'.

The legal proceedings against Cristina, Urdangarín and others were long and drawn out. In March 2016, Cristina appeared in court, denying being an accessory to tax evasion and knowledge of her husband's activities. She said that her husband handled the couple's finances, and that she did not know why some large personal expenses were charged to a credit card of a company that the couple owned.

In February 2017 she was found not guilty, but Urdangarín was convicted and sentenced to six years and three months in prison.

QUEEN CHRISTINA OF SWEDEN: A QUESTION OF GENDER

The gender of Queen Christina of Sweden (1626–1689) was in doubt after she was born at Stockholm castle, the fourth and only surviving child of King Gustavus Adolphus II and his wife, Queen Maria Eleonora. At birth she was greeted as male, but it was afterwards realized that a mistake had been made. How that mistake came about was – and still is – a mystery.

◆

It is possible that Christina was born with some malformation of the genitals that made her appear to be male. Whatever the reason, Christina's sex remained ambiguous throughout her life and later led

Left and above: Queen Christina of Sweden, heir to the hero-King Gustavus Adolphus II Vasa, was brought up as the prince her father had wanted. She hated being feminine, disliked women and made a point of dressing, gesturing and swearing like men.

to claims that she was a hermaphrodite, part-male/ part-female, a bisexual or a full-blown lesbian. She was certainly masculine in appearance and manner, sitting, riding, walking, talking, gesturing and swearing as men did. She was also a misogynist.

Despised her own sex
'As a young girl,' Christina later wrote, 'I had an overwhelming aversion to everything that women

155

do and say. I couldn't bear their tight-fitting, fussy clothes. I took no care of my complexion or my figure or the rest of my appearance…. I despised everything belonging to my sex.'

In distancing herself from the 'feminine' side of life, Christina did not content herself with being a tomboy. As a young child, she studied for 12 hours a day, six days a week. She claimed that she needed no more than four hours of sleep before getting up at four in the morning to start her day's work. By age 15, Christina could speak and write five languages – French, German, Italian, Spanish and Latin, the lingua franca of her time. She read intensively and took as her heroes the great men of ancient history, such as Alexander the Great and Julius Caesar. Any time left

Christina's father, Gustavus Adolphus, was a much admired warrior-king and was known as the Lion of the North.

over from study was spent in vigorous exercise and Christina's favourite sports, riding and hunting bears.

A determined nature

Her father had specifically ordered that Christina receive this rigorous and far-reaching education, even though it was usually confined to princes. Christina took to it with zest. With her formidable intellect and abundant physical energy, she relished the challenge.

> **Her father had specifically ordered that Christina receive this rigorous and far-reaching education, even though it was usually confined to princes. Christina took to it with zest.**

She cared nothing for the idea that she was 'abnormal' for her interest in 'non-feminine' subjects such as literature, politics and statecraft, philosophy, history and, for her the most intriguing, the ancient world.

Gustavus Adolphus was killed aged 38 while leading a cavalry charge at the battle of Lutzen during the Thirty Years' War.

It was just as well that she was so determined to go her own, natural way, for the circumstances of her early life demanded that Christina mature quickly and cope with the responsibility of succeeding to the Swedish throne at a very early age. In 1632, her father, King Gustavus, was killed in battle during the Thirty Years' War and, with this, Christina, aged five, became Queen of Sweden. Her mother, Maria Eleonora, who tended to be hysterical, went into paroxysms of mourning at her husband's untimely death. She clung obsessively to Christina and forced her to share a life given over to grief and the manifestations of that grief.

The royal apartments were dark with black curtains and hangings; the windows were covered over so that no daylight could filter in. Priests intoned prayers and sermons all day and all night. Maria Eleonora insisted that her daughter sleep in her bedchamber, where a casket containing her dead father's heart was kept.

Christina never forgot this macabre experience, which held her in thrall to her unstable mother for three years. Later, it helped to create in Christina a disenchantment with Lutheranism, the official religion of Sweden, which, to her, was steeped in gloom and an obsession with sin. Already, at age nine, she was not only questioning the credentials of Lutheranism, but also, as she wrote later, thinking for herself and making her own decisions. While still a child, she proved capable of handling royal duties with a self-assurance that was well beyond her years. She also acquired a regal personality and a grand manner that inspired respect among her courtiers and ministers.

Although King Gustavus Adolphus had appointed five regents to handle the day-to-day business of government, Christina was already attending council meetings at age 13, and acquainting herself with the royal role in government. More than that, she was firmly convinced that she had been appointed by God to rule Sweden and to do so not as a reigning queen, but as a king. Christina even dreamed of leading her troops into battle, as her father had done.

The expected path

Although Christina was so precocious and clearly averse to everything labelled 'feminine', she was still expected to marry and produce heirs, while her husband would either rule alongside her or instead of her. Plans for Christina's marriage were already in place in 1630, when she was only four years old. Her proposed husband – her first cousin Friedrich Wilhelm – was aged 11. The match fell through and, two years later, so did the next, with Archduke Ulrich, son of King Christian IV of Denmark, who was some 15 years older than Christina. As she later revealed, however, Christina was not all that keen on marrying anyone, and she refused to contemplate sharing her royal rights with a husband.

In her portraits, Queen Christina was often shown in feminine dress wearing a female hairstyle. In reality, she preferred male dress, complete with a sword by her side and a short haircut.

> **Christina was not all that keen on marrying anyone, and she refused to contemplate sharing her royal rights with a husband.**

Nevertheless, when she was 16 years old, she developed a powerful 'crush' on her splendidly handsome, dark-eyed cousin Karl Gustav, son of Johann Kasimir, Count Palatine of Zweibrücken-Kleeburg. Karl Gustav and Christine had been close childhood friends, but when friendship turned to romance it was, for her, more of a sentimental adventure than a love affair. Christina, it seems, enjoyed the secret meetings, the passionate notes written in code and the declarations of 'eternal love' and 'faithfulness unto death', but she took care not to get too seriously involved and she made no promises.

Consequently, in 1644, when she turned 18, the age of majority, and her Regency Council was disbanded, there were no signs of an impending royal marriage. Karl Gustav lived in hopes for another five years, but the prize offered him in 1649 was not the queen's hand, but an extraordinary advancement:

Karl Gustav on horseback in a military pose greatly favoured by seventeenth century painters. Charles was Christina's cousin and succeeded her as king after she abdicated the throne in 1654.

Christina announced that she was making Karl Gustav the official heir to her throne.. The connotations were, of course, unmistakable. After making her announcement to a shocked Rikstag, Christina rammed home the lesson in strong terms.

'I am telling you now,' she told the Swedish parliament, 'it is impossible for me to marry. I am absolutely certain about it.... My character is simply not suited to marriage. I have prayed God fervently that my inclination might change, but I simply cannot marry.'

Unsuitable Liasons

Playing the field, however, was still an option for Christina, who from time to time created scandals with her outlandish conduct. In 1645, for example, she began keeping company with colourful adventurers and even fell in love with one of them, Count Magnus Gabriel de la Gardie. Part French, part Swedish, Magnus was a handsome charmer whose father had once been a favourite of King Gustav

> **'I am telling you now,' she told the Swedish parliament, 'it is impossible for me to marry. I am absolutely certain about it.'**

Adolph. He was, nevertheless, a man on the make, and the rumours that the queen was madly in love with him increased his attraction. Magnus became Colonel of the Queen's Guard and Ambassador Extraordinary

to France. He departed for Paris in a special gold and silver carriage, accompanied by a 300-strong retinue and a lavish expense account that helped to make him rich in only a couple of years. Gardie, however, matched his royal mistress for headlong extravagance, and the queen had to go on rescuing him from debt until their relationship ended in 1651.

Meanwhile, Christina seems to have moved on and into another, highly controversial liaison. She formed a close attachment to one of her ladies-in-waiting, the pretty Ebba Sparre, whom the Queen called 'Belle'. Belle was Christina's opposite – timid where the Queen was outspoken, with no intellectual interests, and the diffident, 'feminine' ways which Christina disliked, but accepted in a relationship where she was evidently the stronger partner. Christina and Belle frequently slept in the same bed. The queen embarrassed the strait-laced English ambassador Bulstrode Whitelocke when she told him that Belle's 'inside' was ' as beautiful as her outside'. The ambassador was so shocked that his ears turned red.

Although controversial, indulging favourites and taking up sexually deviant practices were not usually serious enough to imperil thrones or monarchs. Nor were some of Christina's other activities, such as selling noble titles to solve a financial crisis or maintaining an extravagant lifestyle. What was not so easily accommodated was Christina's long-standing attraction for Roman Catholicism, which was illegal in Lutheran Sweden. Nevertheless, by 1651, she was already planning to convert, knowing full well that as a Catholic she could not remain Queen of Sweden. Instead, she would have to abdicate. The Rikstag went into uproar when Christina announced her decision, but no amount of nagging, begging or pleading succeeded in making her change her mind.

Once across the border and into Denmark following her abdication, Christina took on the identity of one of her companions – Count Christophe von Donha, who

was about 27 years old, the same age as the ex-queen. She exchanged her skirts for trousers and, in this male disguise, headed west, making for Rome. She rarely wore female dress after that, but often appeared with her hair cut short and a sword at her side.

A new life in costume

At the end of 1654, after passing through Germany and into the Spanish Netherlands, Christina was

A QUEEN ABDICATES

The abdication ceremony took place on 6 June 1654 in the grand hall of Uppsala Castle; however, when Christina commanded that the crown be removed from her head, no one came forward to perform the task. At length, though, two of her courtiers took the crown and laid it on a velvet cushion. After that, her ceremonial robes were removed and set aside, until all she wore was a simple white dress. Christina's appointed heir was crowned King Karl X Gustav the same morning. A few days later, Christina was gone, racing towards the Danish border on horseback, with no official farewells, no ceremony and no regrets. She was accompanied by only four attendants. Ebba 'Belle' Sparre, the only person Christina was sorry to leave behind, was not one of them.

received into the Catholic Church at a private ceremony in Brussels. Her new Catholic status was subsequently confirmed at Innsbruck, in Austria, where she was formally accepted into the Catholic communion. After that, Christina took the second name of Alexandra, probably as a compliment to the pope, Alexander VII.

Christina formed a close attachment to one of her ladies-in-waiting, the pretty Ebba Sparre, and frequently slept in the same bed.

The one-time Queen of Sweden was a splendid 'catch' for the Roman Catholic Church, which was still struggling to reassert itself after the schism caused by the Protestant breakaway more than a century

The building of Uppsala Castle, north of Stockholm, began in 1549 and was later the scene of several important royal events. One of these was the announcement in 1654 that Queen Christina intended to abdicate the throne of Sweden.

before. Celebrations for the event were high-profile, including bells ringing and cannon firing, which greatly pleased the ex-queen, who was extremely vain and thrived on veneration. Afterwards, her journey to Rome resembled the Triumphs of the ancient Roman emperors. On the way, Christina's love of luxury and extravagant show was continuously satisfied. A gilded barge was provided to take her across the River Po near Ferrari. Once within the territory of the Papal States, she travelled in a new carriage specially sent by Pope Alexander. Alexander also provided two beds, with canopies and matching armchairs, a splendid set of table silver and a top chef, Luigi Fedele, who was famous for his imaginative use of spices.

> **At the end of 1654, after passing through Germany and into the Spanish Netherlands, Christina was received into the Catholic Church at a private ceremony in Brussels.**

On 10 December, Christina arrived in Rome and was received by the Pope in private audience. It was unusual for a woman to be allowed to spend the night in the precincts of the Vatican, but the Pope conferred a singular honour on the former queen by having prepared a suite of beautiful rooms at the top of the Tower of the Winds. The rooms, which afforded a magnificent view of the city, were decorated in satin, brocade, lace and embroidery. Frescoes were painted on all the walls.

Renaissance home

After a few days in the Vatican, Christina moved to a more permanent place, the Palazzo Farnese, one of the loveliest palaces in Rome, partly designed by Michelangelo and a gorgeous example of Renaissance architecture. The rooms were furnished with magnificent paintings, sculptures and tapestries, and there was a painted gallery built in imitation of the Sistine Chapel, as decorated by Michelangelo.

Christina achieved her long-held wish to convert to Roman Catholicism in 1655 and is seen here, being blessed by the pope, Alexander VII.

Unfortunately, with her often coarse manners, Christina could be an embarrassing guest. For example, at the Palazzo Farnese, she revealed parts of the body usually kept hidden for reasons of modesty: this was done by removing strategically placed fig leaves and carefully arranged draperies from some of the paintings. When taxed about it, Christina declared that she was not going to be confined by 'rules made for priests'.

A step too far

With irreverent attitudes such as this, Christina was soon the subject of gossip, which thrived on her activities and her power to shock. As a woman, she was supposed to be modest, diffident and pure. Christina was frequently rude, pushy and ambitious. As a Catholic, Christina was expected to be submissive to God and His Church, and spurn the carnal and other ribald temptations of the devil. Instead, Christina frequented the theatre and its often bawdy entertainments, and relished the forbidden pleasures of the flesh, which she enjoyed with a parade of lovers.

One of them, allegedly, was her Master of Horse, the Marchese Gian-Rinaldo Monaldeschi, a minor Italian nobleman, who was the sort of rough-mannered rogue Christina appreciated. But he was untrustworthy and the ex-queen suspected – and accused – him of betraying to the Pope plans

> **She revealed parts of the body usually kept hidden for reasons of modesty... When taxed about it, Christina declared that she was not going to be confined by 'rules made for priests'.**

which she made in 1656 to seize the Kingdom of Naples with military backing from France. Naples, which was then a Spanish possession, had a dual purpose for Christina. The kingdom could have served as a replacement for the royal power she had relinquished in Sweden, which she now sorely missed. Naples could also help to solve her perennial financial problems. The Swedish treasury paid her an allowance, but Christina often found it difficult to extract the monies due. The real problem, though, was that the payments could never keep up with the former queen's luxurious lifestyle. Consequently, Christina had to live on loans and gifts, or was forced to pawn the silver plate, jewellery and other valuables she had brought with her from Sweden.

Mondaleschi's betrayal ruined her chances in Naples, but Christina waited to extract her revenge until she was in France, where she went to confer with her French allies about their joint Neapolitan adventure. The former queen was staying at Fontainebleau, near Paris, on 10 February 1657 when, on her orders,

This painting by the artist Niclas Lafrensen (1737–1807) portrays a seated Christina of Sweden joking with 'Belle' as they visit the sick French scholar Claude Saumaise.

Christina gives the order for Monaldeschi to be murdered in this painting by Eugène Delacroix (1798–1863). The case fascinated artists and playwrights in the ensuing centuries.

Monaldeschi was done to death by members of her entourage. He took more than 15 minutes to die, from sword thrusts to his stomach, head and throat.

The French were profoundly shocked by the gruesome murder and even more by Christina's heartless behaviour. She justified the killing as a punishment an absolute monarch, which she still believed herself to be, had the right to impose on a member of her retinue. No one was impressed. The ex-queen was soon shunned by Paris high society, the royal court and the Church, and Pope Alexander made it clear that he did not want her back in Rome. Christina went back anyway. She arrived in mid-May 1658, only to find herself as ostracized there, as she had been in Paris. Pope Alexander, alarmed at her return, sent Christina a message to leave forthwith,

The former queen was staying at Fontainebleau, near Paris, on 10 February 1657 when, on her orders, Monaldeschi was done to death by members of her entourage.

though in time he relented. All the same, the relationship between them was always wary.

A final bid for royal power

Christina was not yet done with outrageous adventures. She made one last bid to retrieve royal power in 1668, when she attempted to acquire the crown of Lithuania-Poland, then the most extensive country in Europe. The Polish monarchy was

elective and Christina had a good case, for the Swedish House of Vasa, to which she belonged, had already provided several monarchs for Poland. Realistically, though, she had little chance of success. She was a woman, when the Poles wanted to be ruled by a man. In 1668, she was 42 years old, unmarried and likely to remain so, with no heirs of her own, and a murky reputation that included the Monaldeschi scandal. The successful candidate, Michael Korybut Wisniowiecki, who became King of Lithuania-Poland in 1669, had better credentials and he was, most importantly, Polish by descent from the Jagiello dynasty, which had ruled Lithuania-Poland between 1386 and 1572.

After this last tilt at royal power, Christina returned to her intellectual interests. She studied astronomy, had an observatory built in the Palazzo Riario and staffed it with two live-in astronomers. She sponsored archaeological 'digs' and, in 1670–1, began writing a book of maxims. She also went into the theatre business, employed a company of actors and staged several successful plays which became renowned for their bawdy content. This was followed by the Tordinona, one of the

Left: Christina (centre) meets French philosopher and mathematician René Descartes (pointing at document), one of the greatest minds of the seventeenth century.

Pope Innocent XI, the prudish pope, who after 1676 closed down the bawdy theatres which Christina liked to attend.

first public opera houses in Rome, and academies of literature and philosophy. Before long, the Palazzo Riario became a focus of cultural and intellectual activity in Rome. But not everyone approved. Some of the more conservative popes seemed to believe that theatres and sin were synonymous. Christina's and other theatres, bawdy and otherwise, were closed down after 1676, when a new, more prudish pope, Innocent XI, was elected.

Peace in death

Christina had another brush with Innocent after she became attracted to Quietism, a contemplative form of Christian mysticism. In 1687, this became a dangerous interest when it was banned by the Catholic Church after its chief proponent, Miguel de Molinos, was convicted of heresy.

The passive, retiring nature of Quietism seemed an odd match for the turbulence of Christina's life and the furious energy and egotism that typified her nature. Yet, after she died of a fever in Rome on 19 April 1689, Quietist influence was evident in the instructions she left for her funeral: it was to be 'a private affair, without undue ceremony' and 'no

A TRUE FRIEND

Fortunately, Christina made a much truer friend than some of those in her past in Cardinal Decio Azzolino, her priest, whom she first met in 1656. Azzolino, who had a passionate but platonic relationship with the former queen, remained loyal to her through all her tribulations and was responsible for much of the improvement in her public relations. It was Azzolino who found her a charming Renaissance-style villa, the

Palazzo Riario, when most aristocratic landlords in Rome wanted nothing to do with her. He went on to regularize Christina's everyday life, ejecting the ruffianly hangers-on and other sycophants who had accumulated around her. Instead, Azzolini hired reliable servants and staff, many of them his own relatives who, with his keen eye always on them, were less likely to take undue advantage of the former queen.

pomp or exhibiting of the body or other vanity'. A further request was more like the imperious Christina, the queen with an overwhelming sense of her own greatness: she asked for three new chaplains to be specially appointed at St Peter's in Rome, with the task of saying 20,000 masses for the repose of her soul.

The heartbroken Cardinal Azzolino, who was himself dying, had kept vigil at Christina's bedside during her last night. But though well aware that she wanted no fuss at her funeral, he could not bring himself to let her go quietly. Instead, Azzolino proposed a public event, one that would see Christina into the next world in a grand manner befitting her royal status. The Pope gave his permission, and Christina's embalmed corpse lay in state at the Palazzo Riario, dressed in a white satin gown embroidered with flowers and an ermine-trimmed purple cloak decorated with gold coins. On her head, she wore a small silver crown, and she held a silver sceptre in her hand. A silver mask covered her face. She looked magnificent, just as the grieving Azzolino had intended.

This 18th century engraving inaccurately portrays Christina in the fashions of a century after her death, but it does illustrate her interest in science and passion for intellectual activity.

Reverent monks

Carmelite monks stood on guard as the local populace moved past Christina's coffin in silent awe and reverence. After four days, she was taken to the Church of Santa Maria in Vallicella, near Rome. There, by the light of 300 torches, a requiem was said for her, in the presence of hundreds of monks and other churchmen, together with the entire College of Cardinals. Only Azzolino, who was too weak to attend, was absent.

Afterwards, watched by cardinals, diplomats, scholars and artists, Christina was buried in the great Basilica of St Peter's, a rare honour for a woman and unique for a woman who had once been a reigning queen. Azzolino, who died seven weeks after her, had understood very well what Christina's love of grandeur and reverence needed. This was why the show he put on for her was a perfect fit for her requirements and a fitting farewell.

KING ERIK XIV VASA OF SWEDEN (1533–1577)

King Erik XIV Vasa married his mistress Karin Mansdotter, the commoner daughter of a jailer in 1567. The following year Karin was made a member of the aristocracy and was crowned queen.

Erik XIV Vasa, who became King of Sweden in 1560, was educated as a true Renaissance prince, the ideal polymath of his times. Erik studied geography, history and political thought. He played the lute, wrote his own music and spoke several languages. Erik also possessed a trait, however, that was the exact opposite of scholarship – his barbaric streak. His father, King Gustav I Vasa, was on a similarly out-of-control-wavelength: he was subject to violent, manic rages. This mixture of sophistication and wildness produced a curious mentality: Erik was determined to make Sweden the dominant power in the Baltic region of northeast Europe, yet he felt disadvantaged by his descent from a family of the minor Swedish nobility.

This gave him an inferiority complex and planted in him the fear that another, similar, noble family would supplant his own. As a result, Erik became paranoid and suspected every noble at his court of plotting against him. Erik had bizarre ideas of what constituted plotting. Anyone fell under suspicion if he cleared his throat, whispered or coughed. In addition, Erik patrolled the corridors of his palace, sword in hand, looking for any smartly dressed courtier, pageboy or servant who, to his disordered mind, was intent on seducing the ladies of his court.

ECCENTRIC FANTASIST

By 1567, Erik was becoming more and more eccentric and unable to sort fantasy from reality. He suddenly ordered the arrest of several aristocrats and condemned them to death. He imprisoned Svante Sture and his son Nils, who belonged to a family that had once ruled Norway, and stabbed Nils to death in his cell at Uppsala Castle. Later, after Nils's father died, Erik was overcome with remorse and arranged for both the Stures to be given magnificent funerals.

Eventually, in 1569, Erik was deposed and put on trial for his crimes. He was found guilty, and imprisoned with his wife, Karin, and their children, while his half-brother, John, took his place as king. While in prison, Erik was in constant fear of assassination and ultimately, in 1577, his fears came true. He was murdered by poison mixed in with a dish of pea soup – although a public announcement made it known that he died 'after a long illness'.

HAEMOPHILIA: THE ROYAL DISEASE

When haemophilia made its first appearance in the British royal family, it was as if the tenth biblical plague had struck the House of Hanover. If anything, haemophilia was worse than the killing of the first born visited by Jehovah on the Ancient Egyptians, for this deadly condition, in which the blood fails to clot normally, could strike younger sons as well, and lie hidden in the genes of daughters, ready to be passed on to their children.

✦

Haemophilia lay low for some time in the family of Queen Victoria and her husband, Prince Albert of Saxe-Coburg-Gotha, and advanced to be recognized only in their fourth and last son, Leopold, who was born in 1853. Leopold

Left: Tsar Nicholas II of Russia with his haemophiliac son, the Tsarevich Alexis. Above: The British Queen Victoria (seated, centre) with her family. Many of Victoria's descendants were affected by haemophilia.

was diagnosed with haemophilia three years later. His brothers Edward, Prince of Wales (born 1841), Prince Alfred (born 1844) and Prince Arthur (born 1850) had all escaped the affliction. Unknown to anyone until after they married, however, three of Victoria's five daughters – Vicky, Alice and Beatrice – were carriers of the disease. All three married European princes, with the result that haemophilia was carried into several European royal houses and many of their children and grandchildren suffered cruelly because of it.

Prince Leopold, the fourth and youngest son of Queen Victoria and Prince Albert, believed that his haemophilia had ruined his life.

A devastating legacy

Leopold's haemophilia was all the more worrying because its origin was unknown. There was no history of the disease in Victoria's family, nor in Prince Albert's, and the medical knowledge of the time was insufficient to explain the mystery. It was possible, though, that the problem arose spontaneously. Queen Victoria may have inherited the defective gene for haemophilia from one of her parents, probably her father, Edward, Duke of Kent, the fourth son of King George III. Later research revealed that the gene and its mutation in the X chromosome occurred more frequently in older fathers: the Duke was 51 when the future Queen Victoria was born in 1819.

The fearful legacy of haemophilia soon became apparent, for it could make an otherwise mild

> **Leopold was intellectually brilliant, with an active, questing mind that made his frail health a great frustration to him. In order to lead the normal life he craved, Leopold had to take risks.**

childhood illness fatal. This is what nearly happened in 1861 when Prince Leopold caught measles. So did Prince Arthur and Princess Beatrice, but, whereas they fought off the infection and were not so badly affected, Leopold nearly died. The eight-year-old prince managed to survive through his own powers of recovery which, this time, proved equal to the task.

Massive haemorrhage

But it was not always so. Prince Leopold had several narrow escapes before he was finally carried off by a massive haemorrhage in 1884, 10 days before his thirty-first birthday. What killed him was a second injury to his knee, which occurred within a few weeks. His end came swiftly, in 24 hours. Anyone else might have had a bruised knee and a limp for a while, but would have thought nothing of it. Leopold, on the other hand, had to be constantly aware of the danger in which he stood and considered that haemophilia had ruined his life.

Had he been a dullard, without much zest for life, his problems might have been less. But like his father Prince Albert, Leopold was intellectually brilliant, with an active, questing mind that made his frail health a great frustration to him. In order to lead the normal life he craved, Leopold had to take risks. He also needed to defy his strong-minded mother. Despite Victoria's repeated attempts to smother him in overprotection, Leopold managed to escape to university, took part in public life and married and had children. Victoria was gratified, but surprised, for she had imagined that haemophilia would make it impossible for Leopold to father a family.

Right: The melancholy and depressive Tsarina Alexandra of Russia, seen here with her son the Tsarevich Alexis, made herself ill with guilt because she had 'given' him haemophilia.

Even royal families ... were not immune, so that Vicky and Alice, mourning their young sons, could view haemophilia as yet another threat to survival among many others.

For a haemophiliac, Leopold's achievements were a significant success. All the same, he was always aware of the reality that overshadowed them. He even told his sister Alice, Grand Duchess of Hesse-Darmstadt, that the death in 1873 of her three-year-old son in an accident was a blessing in disguise: the child, Frederick William, was another haemophiliac. Leopold told Alice that his death after falling out of a window had spared him a life of suffering and misery.

Seven years earlier, in 1866, Alice's elder sister Vicky, Crown Princess of Prussia, had also lost a son, Sigismund, when he was under two years old. Another son, Waldemar, Vicky's youngest, died aged 11 in 1879. Both these deaths were caused by infections – meningitis and diphtheria – but the fact that both boys were suspected haemophiliacs could well have hastened their demise.

Not that death in infancy or childhood was unusual at this time. It was one of the grimmer realities of nineteenth-century life that one or more children in large families would die prematurely – from accident, disease (especially infectious disease) or as a result of unsanitary living conditions. This was accepted as a sorrowful fact of everyday life. Even royal families, who presumably lived in the best conditions, were not immune, so that Vicky and Alice, mourning their young sons, could view haemophilia as yet another threat to survival among many others. For royal families, however, haemophilia was no ordinary disease, for its intrusion into their bloodlines could mean dynastic disaster.

A continuing curse

The wider implications of this disaster did not become clear until after Alice, Vicky and Queen Victoria were dead, and the next generation of royal daughters had children of their own. Haemophilia cursed the royal houses of Hohenzollern (through Vicky) and of Hesse-Darmstadt (through Alice). Next, it appeared with destructive force in the Bourbon dynasty of Spain and the Romanov ruling house in Russia, after one of Queen Victoria's granddaughters married the Russian Tsar Nicholas II and another wed the youthful King Alfonso XIII of Spain.

Nicholas's wife was Princess Alexandra of Hesse-Darmstadt, the fourth daughter of Princess Alice. Nicholas and Alexandra married in 1894, just over three weeks after Nicholas became Tsar of all the Russias. Both were aware that Alice had been a carrier for haemophilia and that Alexandra's sister Irene had given birth to a haemophiliac son, Prince Waldemar, in 1889. Remarkably, Waldemar lived into his fifties, dying in 1945. But another of Irene's three sons, the haemophiliac Heinrich, was not so lucky. He died aged four in 1904, after he fell and struck his head.

The fact that Alexis suffered from haemophilia became apparent six weeks after his birth, when he began to bleed from his navel: the bleeding went on for three days before it stopped.

Ten years of marriage passed before Nicholas and Alexandra were themselves confronted with the terrible legacy ill fortune had planted in her family. Their first four children were daughters, but the fifth was their only son, the Tsarevich Alexis, born in 1904. The fact that Alexis suffered from haemophilia became apparent six weeks after his birth, when he began to bleed from his navel: the bleeding went on for three days before it stopped. Later on, Alexis suffered unusual bruising whenever he fell or tripped because of bleeding beneath the skin, as well as the appalling agonies of internal bleeding or bleeding in the joints from casual injuries.

Nicholas and Alexandra were distraught. This, though, was not only a family tragedy. A diseased royal heir was the worst thing that could have happened in Russia, for Nicholas's hold on his throne was tenuous as popular unrest and demands for a Duma,

Alexandra became spellbound by Rasputin and was soon dependent on him for her son's life, which he subsequently 'saved' more than once.

or Parliament, and more representative government steadily undermined his autocratic rule. Alexandra, who tended to be morose and pessimistic, took to praying desperately for hours on end. She was wracked with guilt, knowing that she had transmitted the disease to her son. She began to suffer heart problems and developed sciatica, together with a whole range of symptoms which today might be termed 'psychosomatic'.

In her state of extreme, even obsessive, anxiety, Alexandra became overprotective. Two sailors were employed to follow the Tsarevich everywhere and prevent him from hurting himself, and his haemophilia was kept a dread family secret. Doctors, servants, members of the imperial household and anyone else who might know or guess what was wrong were all forbidden to talk. Just the same, there were rumours, for it proved impossible to keep the secret when Alexis nearly died from a nosebleed or a minor fall required him to stay in bed for weeks on end.

Rasputin and the Romanovs

Then, in 1905, a holy man, or *starets*, from Siberia named Grigori Rasputin arrived at the royal court in St Petersburg. A *starets* was supposed to have extraordinary healing powers, achieving cures by prayer, and it was not unusual for aristocratic families to keep one of these peasant mystics in their household for use as and when their skills were required. For Alexandra, Rasputin was the answer to her prayers, for he seemed to have the ability to cure the Tsarevich, even when his haemophilia threatened to kill him and his doctors had given up. In 1905, the Tsarevich Alexis was

The *starets* or holy man Grigori Rasputin who achieved extraordinary power over the Tsarina Alexandra after he apparently enabled Alexis to recover from bouts of bleeding.

seriously ill and wracked with pain from a swollen leg. Overnight, Rasputin restored the boy to full health, although no one saw or could even guess how he had achieved this 'miracle'.

Rasputin in charge

From then on, Nicholas and Alexandra were Rasputin's devoted disciples and, where the imperial household was obliged to address the Tsar and

The Tsar and Tsarina and their children, their servants and even their little dog were killed at Ekaterinburg in Siberia on 17 July 1918.

Tsarina with excessive reverence, they allowed him unprecedented freedom of speech and conduct in their presence. Alexandra became spellbound by Rasputin and was soon dependent on him for her son's life, which he subsequently 'saved' more than once. From there, Rasputin moved easily into a position where he was exercising political influence at court and handing out plum positions to his cronies. After Russia entered World War I in 1914, Nicholas departed for the front, leaving Alexandra in charge. Or so he thought. Before long, Rasputin was dominating the Tsarina to the point where he was virtually running the country.

This was too much for some younger members of the Romanov imperial family whose influence Rasputin had supplanted. In 1916, a group led by the Romanov Prince Felix Yousoupoff poisoned, shot, clubbed and finally drowned Rasputin in the River Neva at St Petersburg. Nicholas and Alexandra were horrified. Alexandra now believed that, with Rasputin dead, her link with God had been severed and her son had been abandoned. Russia, she was sure, was now doomed – and the Romanov family with it.

This was not one of Alexandra's morbid fantasies. On 15 March 1917, less than three months after Rasputin's death, Tsar Nicholas was forced to abdicate when Russian troops mutinied, hunger riots broke out and a new provisional government under Alexander Kerensky took power in St Petersburg. Seven months after that, Kerensky was overthrown by the Communist Bolsheviks under Vladimir Lenin and, with that, the fate of the Romanovs was sealed. Imprisoned in the grimly named House of Special Purpose at Ekaterinburg in Siberia, the entire family was shot dead by a Bolshevik firing squad on 17 July 1918. Ironically, the last to die was the Tsarevich Alexis.

Haemophilia in spain

Around the time the ill-fated Alexis was born, the scenario of haemophilia was becoming better understood. There was still no cure, of course, nor any certain treatment, but the hereditary pattern was now recognized. Consequently, in 1905, when the nineteen-year-old King Alfonso XIII of Spain arrived in England seeking a bride, he was warned that several eligible English princesses might carry the curse of the bleeding disease.

Alfonso's fancy ranged over Princess Patricia, daughter of Prince Arthur; Beatrice of Saxe-Coburg, Prince Alfred's daughter; and Princess Victoria Eugenie, daughter of Queen Victoria's last child, Princess Beatrice of Battenberg. Beatrice of Saxe-Coburg and Patricia were almost certainly not carriers of the haemophelia gene, as their fathers were free

of the disease. Unfortunately for Alfonso, he chose Victoria-Eugenie, known as Ena, who had received the carrier characteristics from her mother. There was certain evidence that Ena's mother, Beatrice, was a carrier; her son, another Leopold, suffered from haemophilia and later died of it, aged 33, in 1922.

Irresponsible alfonso

With this evidence before him, Alfonso knew perfectly well the chance he was taking in marrying Ena. He was warned by his own Foreign Minister, by his family, by Ena's mother, by King Edward VII, Ena's uncle, and by Ena herself. He listened to all of them, but failed to hear. Alfonso possessed the hot blood of the Bourbons and the arrogant insouciance of youth, and he wanted the curvaceous Ena with a fierce passion. He reckoned, quite irresponsibly, that if they had a sufficient number of children some of them at least would escape the bleeding disease.

> **... the scenario of haemophilia was becoming better understood. There was still no cure, of course, nor any certain treatment, but the hereditary pattern was now recognized.**

Alfonso was able to deceive himself for only a short time. He rapidly changed his attitude and his marriage to Ena, which took place in Madrid in 1906, headed for disaster when their first son, Alfonsito, was born in 1907. When the time came for the infant prince to be circumcised – a practice long ago introduced into the Spanish court by Jewish doctors – the surgeons found to their dismay that the child bled profusely for several hours. There was no doubt that it was haemophilia, and Alfonso descended into an abyss of depression and despair. He blamed Ena, he blamed his mother-in-law, Beatrice, but he also blamed himself for being led on by his foolhardy lust for his English bride.

This, though, did not prevent the king from trying again. In 1908, Ena gave birth to another son, Jaime, who was perfectly healthy. At this, Alfonso rallied somewhat and persuaded himself that Alfonsito would somehow recover from his illness, just as

A MARRIAGE DESTROYED

After eight years of marriage, in which Ena had borne seven children, the royal Bourbon house of Spain had only one fully healthy heir, Don Juan, who was born in 1913 and eventually became the father of the present Spanish king, Juan Carlos. Of the others, three had been haemophiliacs and Don Jaime became deaf and dumb after an attack of mastoiditis in 1911, when he was three years of age. This appalling family experience ruined the relationship between the King and Ena. He turned to his mistresses and the healthy children they bore him; she to good works and charity. In 1931, after King Alfonso was forced to abdicate in the face of demands for more democratic rule in Spain, he lost no time in obtaining a judicial separation.

The marriage of Alfonso and Ena went down in the flames of mutual recrimination and charges of adultery that, on Alfonso's side, were certainly true. Curiously, Ena kept up hopes of a reconciliation for some years, but it never transpired, even though the deaths of their two surviving haemophiliac sons gave them opportunities.

Princess Victoria Eugenie of Battenberg, known as Ena, was a grand daughter of Queen Victoria. She received the gene for haemophilia from her mother, Princess Beatrice, and like Beatrice, was herself a carrier of the disease.

Alfonso XIII, who was born as King of Spain, refused to listen when Beatrice, Victoria Eugenie and several others warned him about the dangers of haemophilia.

Prince Albert had once hoped would happen with Prince Leopold.

Like Leopold, Alfonsito, Prince of Asturias, was bright and intelligent, and his father, full of hope, enrolled him in the First Royal Regiment of the Spanish army and made plans for his training as the future King of Spain. But however much Alfonso fooled himself over his eldest son and heir, the shock of haemophilia in his family had drastically altered his attitude to his wife. Hatred, bitterness and fury consumed Alfonso when his mood, always mercurial, swung towards the morbid thought that the Prince of Asturias would not live to inherit his crown. The birth of his next son, after a daughter was born in 1909, confirmed Alfonso's darkest imaginings. The boy, who arrived in 1910, was stillborn, but he was also another haemophiliac. So was the last child of Alfonso and Ena, Gonzalo, who was born in 1914, a year after another daughter, Maria Christina.

An attempt at normalcy
Like their erstwhile great-uncle, the English Prince Leopold, Alfonsito and Gonzalo insisted on leading active lives and, once their father's abdication released them from royal restraint, both went their own way. Gonzalo, who appeared to suffer from a less virulent form of haemophilia than his older brother, entered the University of Louvain in 1934 to study engineering. Then, one day in August 1934, while Gonzalo was out driving with his sister Beatrice, their car swerved to avoid an oncoming cyclist and crashed into a wall. Brother and sister suffered only slight injuries, but soon afterwards Gonzalo began to bleed. He died two days later, aged only 20.

Alfonsito, meanwhile, had been sent to a clinic in Switzerland once the family was exiled from Spain. It proved impossible to keep him there, despite the risks he would run in trying to lead a normal life. In 1933, Alfonsito, then 26 years old, fell in love with a fellow patient at the clinic and, despite his father's disapproval, insisted on marrying her. Ten days before the wedding in June 1933, Alfonsito was forced to renounce his rights to the Spanish throne. Alfonsito's wife, a grandly named Cuban girl called Edelmira

Left: Alfonsito, Prince of Asturias, the first child of King Alfonso XIII and Queen Ena, as Victoria Eugenie was known in Spain, was the first victim of haemophilia in the Spanish royal family.

Sampedro-Ocejo y Robato, was not considered to be a fitting consort for a young prince whose father still had hopes of retrieving his Crown.

The newlyweds left for the United States, where Alfonsito planned to indulge his lifelong interest in farming. Instead, he indulged the full Spanish royal taste for promiscuity and, by 1937, his marriage had perished. The same year, Alfonsito married another Cuban, but the union ended after only six months.

> In August 1934, while Gonzalo was out driving with his sister Beatrice, their car crashed into a wall. Gonzalo began to bleed. He died two days later, aged only 20.

With all the desperation of a young man cramming life with experience before his time ran out, Alfonsito embarked on a series of passionate love affairs which finally led to a liaison with Mildred Gaydon, a Miami nightclub hostess. Once again, Alfonsito's thoughts turned to marriage; however, one night in September 1938, he was driving Mildred home when he crashed his car. After being rushed to hospital, Alfonsito took several days to bleed to death. He was 31 years old.

A glimmer of hope
The chronicle of ruined lives and hopes in the Spanish royal family which haemophilia had authored could never have had a happy ending. But at least its tentacles did not reach as far as King Alfonso feared. For years, he felt duty bound to warn would-be suitors with an eye on his daughters Beatrice and Maria Christina that they might be transmitters of the deadly disease. Many, not surprisingly, were put off by the warning because the story of the girls' haemophiliac brothers was now common knowledge.

Beatrice and Maria Christina, both attractive, with a fine sense of fashion and deservedly popular on the European social circuit, were made to feel like pariahs, condemned through no fault of their own to the wastage of spinsterhood. In time, though, King Alfonso relented and, rather late in the day for princesses, the sisters were allowed to marry. In 1935, when she was 26, Beatrice married Prince Alexander Torlonioa of Civitella-Cesi. Maria Christina, 27, wed Enrico Marone-Cinzano, a member of the famous vermouth company. For her sake, he was created Count Marone, and the Spanish princess became his second wife and first Countess Marone in 1940. Both girls had children, but none inherited haemophilia. Nor did the other grandchildren of King Alfonso and Queen Ena.

Haemophilia had nevertheless clocked up a fearsome record of depredation. It affected, in all, some 16 of Queen Victoria's descendants in three generations, ruined two royal families, shortened several lives, made miserable many more and, perhaps most insidious of all, created a climate of fear pervading royal families who did not, and could never, know where the dread disease was going to strike next.

Beatrice and Maria Christina, both attractive, with a fine sense of fashion and deservedly popular on the European social circuit, were made to feel like pariahs, condemned through no fault of their own to the wastage of spinsterhood.

Queen Ena (centre) with her daughters Beatrice (left) and Maria Christina (third from left). After their long-delayed marriages, however, neither Beatrice nor Maria Christina passed on haemophilia to their children.

A BRIEF HISTORY OF HAEMOPHILIA

Haemophilia, a condition confined to males, was first scientifically observed and described in 1803 by an American physician, John Conrad Otto, of Philadelphia. The disease had been known since biblical times as a mysterious malady which caused profuse bleeding from even the most trivial cause. Cases had been recorded of boys bleeding uncontrollably if their gums were rubbed too roughly. A minor cut could kill. A boy could die from grazing his knee in the rough and tumble of childhood games. A bruise to the knee, joint or elbow might set off serious internal bleeding.

CRIPPLING DISEASE

Early death was very likely, but even if a haemophiliac survived he would endure agonies of pain before the blood at last coagulated and the bleeding ceased. The process might take a minimum of 30 minutes, or could last several hours. In a normal male, the blood would clot in wounds after five minutes or, in more serious cases, in up to 15. But severe bleeding was only part of the horror of haemophilia. The condition so damaged the body's systems that few haemophiliacs escaped crippling joint disease, such as arthritis, or another danger, anaemia: both laid them open to infections that, but for their weakened state, they might have been able to resist.

Morphine could be used to mitigate the pain, but it was addictive, and virtually the only other relief was for the sufferer to pass out when the agony became too much to bear. What was missing was a scientific therapy, but that was out of reach until the mid-twentieth century. In the 1930s, egg white, peanut flour and snake venom were suggested as potential treatments for haemophilia, but the real, successful breakthrough had to wait until the cause of haemophilia was discovered some 20 years later.

In haemophiliacs, it was found, there was a mutation in one of the X chromosomes of their genetic make-up; this caused a deficiency of the clotting agent Factor VIII, which was also known as anti-haemophilic globulin. Although haemophilia was, and still remains, incurable, this discovery made it possible, after 1955, to control the disease with intravenous Factor VIII.

The coffin of Prince Leopold, Duke of Albany, the haemophiliac son of Queen Victoria, lying in a room at the Villa Nevada, Cannes, in France, festooned with wreaths.

KINGS AND COMMUNISTS: CAROL II OF ROMANIA

His cousin, the British King George V, called King Carol II (1893–1953) 'an unmitigated cad'. He was twice thrown out of his kingdom, made lurid headlines in the newspapers with his scandalous escapades and three marriages – and yet he ended up largely forgotten and in exile, with only two members of his family in attendance at his funeral.

✦

From the start there was little chance that King Carol II of Romania would turn out to be ordinary. Carol was too much like his mother, Marie, a granddaughter of the English Queen Victoria and a passionate creature much given to dramatic gestures. The strong-minded Marie never hesitated

Left and above: King Carol II of Romania was a nasty piece of work but extremely attractive to women. His escapades made lurid newspaper headlines across Europe.

to shock and, only five years after Carol was born in 1893, she embarked on a series of affairs and romances that lasted to the end of her life.

Carol's father, Crown Prince Ferdinand of Romania, could not have been more different. Shy, self-effacing and malleable, he lived under the thumb of his uncle King Carol I. Unlike Marie, who was not afraid to clash with the formidable king, Ferdinand allowed his uncle to order his life from waking to bedtime. He followed to the letter King Carol's decreed regime of study, performed to order on state occasions and never agitated for the social life that his uncle denied him.

Carol's mother, Queen Marie, was a granddaughter of Queen Victoria and, like her son, revelled in outrageous behaviour. Her lovers were legion.

It was hard, even cruel, but the received wisdom at the court of King Carol I was that 'Der Onkel', as he was usually called in awed tones, always knew best. In fact, what Der Onkel knew best was the relentless creed of discipline, obedience to authority and devotion to duty he brought with him from his native Germany when he was elected King of Romania in 1866. As king, the former Karl Eitel, Prince of Hohenzollern-Sigmaringen, took it as his right to impose his iron grip not only on Ferdinand, but also Ferdinand's son. It started in the nursery, where the king chose for the younger Carol an English nanny, Mary Green, who was a formidable example of that draconian breed, and went on to the martinet tutors in charge of steering young Carol through a punishing schedule of study.

Mercurial and secretive

Carol soon soaked up the many frictions of his home environment – the weakness of his father, Marie's restlessness, his domineering great-uncle, the atmosphere of tension and intrigue in a household packed with the king's spies and suppressed fury at his mother's many lovers. As a result, the 'extremely amiable' outgoing boy Queen Marie had called Carol as a small child became wilful, mercurial, secretive and much given to depressions.

Fortunately, in 1913, Carol was able to enjoy some relief from this poisonous atmosphere after his mother suggested, and the king agreed, that he should attend the military academy in Potsdam. Carol took readily to military training and even seemed to enjoy the strict Prussian-style routine that prevailed there. He became liable to army service after World War I began in 1914. Two months later, in October 1914, old King Carol died, so that in 1916, when Romania entered the war against Germany, Carol's father, now King Ferdinand, made the decision.

Secret marriage

As Crown prince and heir to the throne, Carol was kept well away from the fighting – in Bucharest, the Romanian capital, where he fell in love with Iona Lambrino, known as Zizi, a Romanian aristocrat whose family were frequent visitors at court. He

Right: Carol with his first wife Iona Lambrino, known as Zizi. The marriage was morganatic: when Carol became king, Zizi would not be queen. But the union did not last that long, anyway.

wanted to marry her, but his way was barred by law: after Carol I had been elected king in 1881, it was forbidden for members of the royal family to marry Romanians.

Carol, however, played cunning. He took Zizi across the Russian border and married her in secret. The clandestine wedding took place at an Orthodox Church near Odessa on 31 August 1918. That done, he sent his father a telegram announcing the marriage. In Bucharest, there was consternation. King Ferdinand wept and pleaded with his ministers for time to see Carol and maybe prise him away from Zizi. Ferdinand began by sentencing his son to 75 days' imprisonment at Horaitza, a monastery in the mountains near Bicaz. To save royal face, no mention was made of the marriage. Instead, it was announced that the punishment was for leaving his army command and crossing the Russian border without permission.

> **Carol took Zizi across the Russian border and married her in secret. The clandestine wedding took place near Odessa on 31 August 1918. That done, he sent his father a telegram announcing the marriage.**

But before his prison sentence could be anything more than an empty gesture, Carol had to be persuaded or pressurized into returning to Romania. With Zizi, Carol was tempted on board a train at the Russian border and was soon back in Bucharest. From that moment on, Carol was barraged with demands to give up his wife. At first, he resisted, but in the end Carol became sufficiently worn down to cave in. On 20 September 1918, three weeks after the marriage, he finally agreed to an annulment. The situation seemed resolved, but the time for sighs of relief was short.

Renewed controversy

The controversy quickly burst back to life when Zizi announced that she was pregnant. The news propelled Carol out of his complaisance and he burned with a new zeal, this time to stand by Zizi, even at the cost of

giving up his right to the throne. Carol also underlined his resolve by making two attempts to disable himself – once by throwing himself under his horse; once by shooting himself in the leg. This, though, was not the time for heroics.

In 1919, Romania was being threatened by its neighbours Czechoslovakia, Hungary, Poland and Yugoslavia. An heir apparent who, like Carol, was prepared to desert his dynasty and his country put both at risk at a potentially perilous time. Romania's political problems succeeded, however, where his father had failed. Neighbouring Hungary fell under the power of communist revolutionaries and the Romanians, highly agitated at this development, invaded Hungary to keep the communists away from their frontier. Carol, still an army officer, was obliged to leave Zizi and join his regiment.

Carol's parents exploited this opportunity to the full. They made sure that military orders kept their son well away from Bucharest and his wife. For the next six months, Carol was confined to one army camp after another, while pressure was again exerted to make him come to heel.

Capitulation and remarriage

Gradually, Carol's resistance crumbled until at last, at Christmas 1919, he sent Zizi what she called a 'letter of rupture and abandonment'. The letter reached her two weeks before her child, a son named Carol Mircea, was born on 8 January 1920. Carol made no attempt to see his son. It was evident that he was putting his illegal and therefore nonexistent marriage to Zizi out of his mind when he agreed to an arranged marriage with Princess Helen of Greece. The impulsive Carol asked Helen to marry him only a week after first meeting her in Switzerland. His mother, Queen Marie, was overjoyed. She looked on Helen as Carol's saviour, fondly believing that a good, properly royal marriage meant lifelong rehabilitation.

The marriage of Carol and Helen, which took place in Athens on 10 March 1921, proved to be nothing of the sort. The couple had little in common, and the premature birth of their only child, Michael, the following 25 October, exhausted Helen before any relationship had time to form. Helen soon became homesick for Greece and, in early 1922, took young Michael on a visit to Athens. She stayed away for four months.

Carol married a more acceptable wife, Helen of Greece, in 1921. Their only child, Michael (right) was born seven months later. Michael was to be the last king of Romania.

While she was there, her father, King Constantine, was driven into exile, and the rest of her family were being hounded by the Greek revolutionaries. When, finally, Helen returned to Romania, she brought her mother and her youngest sisters with her as royal refugees. Before long, it was not lost on Carol that his wife had grown some distance away from him. Carol had been unfaithful more than once, even while 'married' to Zizi Lambrino, and this time the most likely reason for Helen's coolness was the gossip that Carol's latest liaison, with Eleana Lupescu, was no passing fancy.

Discretion had never been one of Carol's virtues, and he did not hesitate to flaunt his new infatuation.

As a result, Lupescu's character, ancestry and personal history were soon to become common gossip and newspaper sensation. The coverage was, of course, salacious and hostile.

Magnetic personality

 Red-haired and green-eyed, Eleana Lupescu, later known as Magda, was born in 1899, the daughter of a Jewish pharmacist in Jassy. When Carol met her, she was still the wife of a Romanian army officer, Lieutenant Ion Tampeanu. Tampeanu later divorced Lupescu for adultery. Lupescu was a familiar peril

Eleana Lupescu, known as Magda, was the great love of Carol's life. They met in 1923 and remained together for 30 years, until Carol died in 1953.

for those beleaguered wives who had to struggle to keep hold of straying husbands. She was neither beautiful nor charming, yet possessed powerful sexual attraction and a magnetic personality that could easily overwhelm susceptible males. Carol, of course, was extremely susceptible. He was inevitably hooked and, before long, Lupescu was being vilified as his 'Jewish whore'. With this, Carol's enemies were handed the perfect opportunity to topple him.

Carol's indiscretions had not only been sexual, but political as well. He alienated the Liberal Party, which came to power in Romania in 1922, by threatening that, when he became king, he would outlaw the party and exile the Liberal Prime Minister, Ion Bratianu. And not only Bratianu, but also his brother-in-law and supporter, Barbu Stirbey, Queen Marie's most enduring lover and reportedly the father of her last child, Mircea.

An opportunity missed

It was an unwise move for Carol to lay his cards so openly on the table before a cunning politician such as Bratianu, who hit back in more subtle and more invidious fashion. Jews were greatly hated in Romania and, probably engineered by Bratianu, there was an upsurge of anti-Semitic feeling against Magda Lupescu and, through her, against Carol. Carol also found himself excluded from the Regency Council when his parents went abroad on a goodwill tour in 1924. Usually, he would have headed the council. Next, Bratianu accused his Air Minister of taking bribes over the acquisition of new machines for the Romanian Air Force. This directly implicated Carol, who was Inspector-General of the Air Force. Even though a subsequent inquiry exonerated the hapless minister and his associates, there was no antidote for the poison, once it was sown.

Within a short time, the entire Romanian establishment, orchestrated by Bratianu, was opposed to Carol. The end came in November 1925, when Carol was sent to England to represent Romania at the funeral of his great-aunt, Queen Alexandra, the widow of King Edward VII. He had no intention of leaving Lupescu behind and so risk losing her. Instead, he arranged for Lupescu to leave Romania for Paris. Instead of returning home after the funeral, he headed for the French capital, picked up Lupescu and moved on to Italy.

This was disturbing enough, but the real bombshell burst later in December, when Carol wrote to his father from Venice, shedding his army commission, his status as Crown prince and his membership of the Romanian royal family. He even asked King Ferdinand to give him a new name.

A new life and a new heir

Pressure to return, reconsider and recant descended on Carol in full force, but, for once, with Lupescu's support, he was well placed to resist all blandishments. At last, it dawned on all concerned that Carol was not going to be persuaded. Not long afterwards, on 20 July 1927, King Ferdinand died and his demise was widely ascribed to a 'broken heart'. Carol's five-year-old son Michael succeeded him, with his uncle Prince Nicolas as regent. Carol, meanwhile, was living in Paris, having taken a new name, Caraiman. He was happy with Lupescu and with the freedom he now enjoyed to indulge his interests in philately, music and fast cars. Nevertheless, Carol hankered after Romania and remained alert for any sign that might give him a chance to return home.

Lupescu was neither beautiful nor charming, yet possessed powerful sexual attraction and a magnetic personality that could easily overwhelm susceptible males.

The chance came after Ion Bratianu died in 1927 and the Liberal Party lost its motive power. The following year, on 10 November, Bratianu's successor, Juliu Maniu, leader of the National Peasant Party, which was sympathetic to Carol, took office as Prime Minister. But before Carol could return, Maniu needed to make sure that his power base was sufficiently secure. This was why another 18 months passed before Carol could board an aircraft in Munich and land at Bucharest's Bancasa airport on 6 June 1930, to be greeted by intense rejoicing throughout Romania. At last feeling secure in his support, Carol made it clear that he had not returned, as Maniu had

Ion Bratianu, who became Liberal Prime Minister in Romania in 1922, was daggers drawn with Carol who threatened that when he became king, he would exile Bratianu.

Romanian wife, Jeanne, in April 1937. With stunning hypocrisy, Carol punished Nicolas for a 'crime' which he himself had already committed: Jeanne was a Romanian, like Zizi Lambrino, but Carol told his

> **Carol wrote to his father from Venice, shedding his army commission, his status as Crown prince and his membership of the Romanian royal family.**

brother that he could not recognize his marriage, stripped him of his title and threw him out.

Magda Lupescu returned to Romania soon after Carol, probably by August 1930, and was installed in a splendid house in Bucharest's most fashionable suburb. Carol spent a fortune on his mistress, decking her out in the finest jewels, specially made for her in Antwerp and elsewhere. He visited Lupescu every evening, but had the grace not to give offence on official occasions, which he did not allow her to attend. Lupescu, however, was not made for a back-seat existence. In time, she gathered her own informal court about her, entertaining industrialists – especially arms manufacturers – and, curiously, mixing together her Jewish friends with fascists. Carol doted on his mistress, who was indeed extraordinary in taming a man who, until then, had womanized as naturally as he breathed.

An active ruler

As sovereign, though, Carol proved to be much more than a king of dalliance and self-indulgence. To keep vital foreign investment continuing, Romania had to be perceived as a country under strong rule. Carol was perfectly capable of exercising firm but not too despotic control, and among his initiatives were the revival of the Romanian oilfields, a rapid increase in the manufacturing industry, the promotion of scientific studies and the nationwide airlines and the fostering of Romanian music, literature and art.

supposed, to be co-opted onto the Regency Council. Carol meant to be king with full royal rights and that meant autocratic rights.

Exacting revenge

For the first time in his life, Carol, now 36, was free to do as he chose and what he chose to do first was exact revenge for past wrongs. His principal victim was his mother, Queen Marie. He had never forgiven Marie for her part in destroying his first marriage. Now, he placed spies in her household. Her income was cut and she was banned from attending state functions.

Eventually, to escape Carol's depredations, Marie went travelling outside Romania until, in 1938, she returned home to die. She almost failed to make it. Marie was in a Dresden sanitarium after years of ill health when she realized that her end was nigh. But Carol refused to send an aircraft for her, and Marie had to make the journey by train. She survived to reach Bucharest and the Pelisor Palace on 18 July, but died there the same evening.

Carol was not finished yet. His vengeance also took in his brother Nicolas, whom he exiled with his

Only a few years after Carol's return, his country was culturally and industrially in better shape than it had ever been. But this was the 1930s, the decade of dictators in Germany, Italy, Portugal and Spain, and Romania was not going to be left alone to enjoy its revival for long. Germany under the Nazis was already spreading tentacles across Europe, soon after Adolf Hitler seized absolute power in Germany in 1934. Hitler's plans for Romania were to make it increasingly dependent on Germany through trade links, particularly the trade in oil. The Nazis also fostered ideological ties with Romania in the form of the Iron Guard, an extreme right-wing element that the Nazis financed.

He had never forgiven Marie for her part in destroying his first marriage. Now, he placed spies in her household. Her income was cut and she was banned from attending state functions.

Like Hitler, the Iron Guard and its leader Ion Antonescu were dedicated to wiping out Jewish influence and, with it, all Romanian Jews: Magda Lupescu was top of the list. The Iron Guard's links with the Nazis remained clandestine for some time, and King Carol did not become aware of them until late 1937. To counter the Iron Guard and its Nazi backers, Carol and his Prime Minister Nicolas Titulescu sought new trade links with Britain and France, and friendlier relations with states such as Czechoslovakia, which could act as geographical buffers between Romania and Germany.

Carol also took steps to weaken the Iron Guard by decimating its leadership. Corneliu Codrianu, who founded the Iron Guard in 1927, together with his associates, was put on trial for treason and imprisoned. In 1938, they were shot dead while trying

Carol's mother, Queen Marie, was a seemingly ageless, fashionable woman. This 1926 picture shows her with the bobbed hairstyle adopted by women in the 1920s.

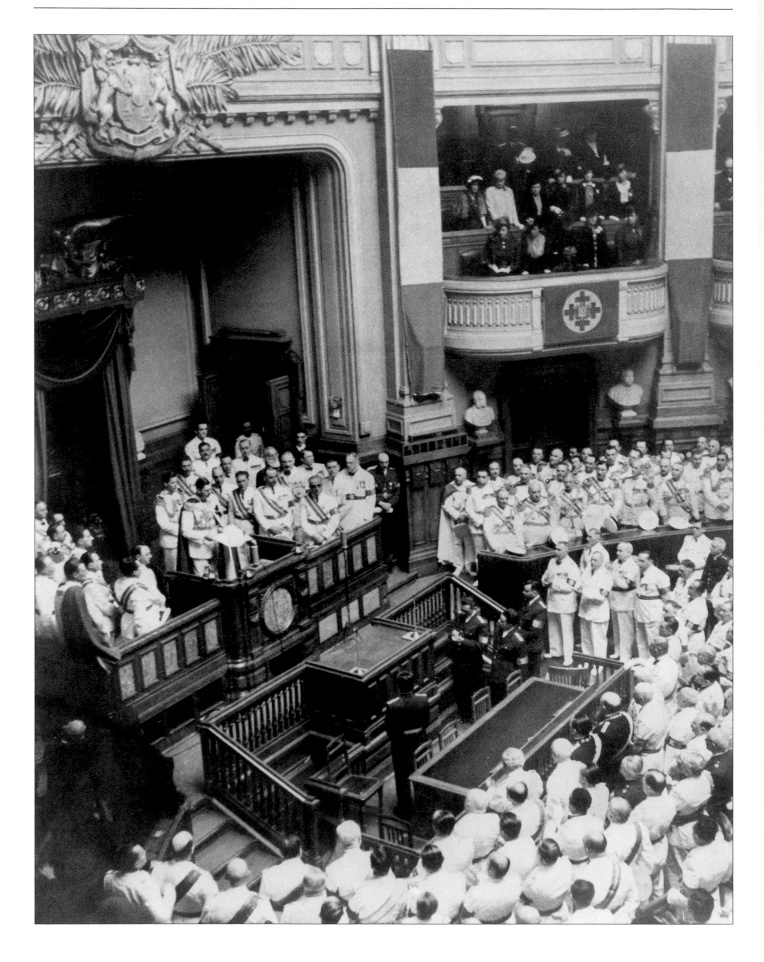

to escape, or so it was given out. In reality, Codrianu and his followers were strangled by their guards.

A new figure rises to power
Eventually, inside a rapidly shrinking Romania, there emerged the inevitable 'strong man' who claimed to have the power to save the country. He was General Ion Antonescu, who had Nazi sympathies but wanted a fascist Romania independent of German control. When he proposed to provide just that, but wanted absolute power to do it, the embattled Carol was, unfortunately, tempted. In accepting Antonescu's terms, he turned himself into a figurehead, and a figurehead Antonescu lost no time in throwing overboard.

A scene of splendour at the inauguration of the new Romanian government under Prime Minister Armand Calinescu in 1939, nine years after Carol's return from exile.

Carol appointed General Ion Antonescu Prime Minister on 4 September 1940. Almost immediately, Antonescu forced Carol to abdicate and leave Romania.

Carol was perfectly capable of exercising firm control, and among his initiatives were the revival of the Romanian oilfields, a rapid increase in the manufacturing industry, the promotion of scientific studies and the nationwide airlines and the fostering of Romanian music, literature and art.

THE FOLLY OF APPEASEMENT

Unfortunately, French and British reaction to the Nazi threat was far less muscular than Romania's. They turned instead to appeasement, a craven policy that ultimately led to the outbreak of World War II in Europe on 3 September 1939. The shock waves soon reached Romania. On 21 September, Carol's trusty Prime Minister Armand Calinescu was ambushed and murdered, together with his bodyguards. The culprits were, of course, members of the Iron Guard. Six months later, in May/June 1940, the war brought the major part of continental Europe under Nazi occupation. At that, Russia seized Romanian Bessarabia and Germany, together with Bulgaria and Hungary, poached even more territory.

Antonescu is shown making a speech, surrounded by his Nazi-backed Iron Guard, an extreme right-wing, paramilitary force originally founded in 1927.

> **The Nazis also fostered ideological ties with Romania in the form of the Iron Guard, an extreme right-wing element that the Nazis financed.**

The strong man assumed power on 4 September 1940 and at once, Carol was faced with anti-royalist demonstrations and popular demands to abdicate. Completely outmaneuvered, Carol stepped down on 5 September; the following day, his son, 16-year-old Michael, who had been demoted when his father returned to claim the Crown in 1930, became king for a second time. On 8 September, with Magda Lupescu and a small entourage, Carol was bundled out of Romania on a train that did not stop until it crossed the border with Yugoslavia. On the way, members of the Iron Guard attempted an ambush and several shots were fired at the carriages, but no one was hurt.

Life in exile

Carol and Lupescu became nomads, moving from Yugoslavia to Switzerland, on to France, Spain and Portugal, then across the Atlantic to Mexico and Brazil. In Latin America, Carol felt more assured

December 1941: Michael I, the youthful King of Romania, with General Antonescu as they study the progress of Romanian troops in the Soviet Union. Nazi Germany had invaded the USSR six months earlier.

that his 'Jewish' mistress was safe than would have been the case in Nazi-dominated Europe. At the same time, a base across the Atlantic was handy for keeping in touch with influential war leaders. This, Carol believed, was vital to prevent him sinking into oblivion, after his ignominious exit from Romania. The ex-king set up a court in exile with former officials

Magda Lupescu (left) and ex-King Carol (second from left) in a carriage driving through Hamilton, Bermuda, in 1941 with Carol's Royal Chamberlain Ernest Urdarianu (third from left).

who had remained loyal to him and never let a chance go by of keeping the world in mind of his existence. He kept contact with the United States ambassadors in Havana and Mexico City, wrote to US President Franklin Roosevelt and to his cousin King George VI in England, outlining his plan for a National Council for Free Romania.

But, to Carol's dismay, the British, who were already hosting other royal and government exiles from occupied Albania, Czechoslovakia, France, the Netherlands, Norway and Poland, declined to

add Romania to the list. The letter that reached the ex-king from Buckingham Palace was couched in terms of exemplary politeness. But the answer was still no. The US State Department reacted in the same way.

Hopes for return dashed

Despite being spurned, Carol never lost hope that the British and Americans would win the war and allow him to return to Romania. In 1944, the ex-king had the satisfaction of seeing his son Michael gather enough support to arrest Antonescu for war crimes. Found guilty, Antonescu was executed in 1946. This, though, did not bring salvation for Carol. Even before the war ended in 1945, King Michael was faced with an even greater challenge – a takeover masterminded by Communist Russia. A communist government was imposed on him, and the Romanian Democratic Popular Republic was declared. By 1947, Michael, too, was an ex-king and went into exile early in 1948.

Now, Carol had little or nothing to hope for and, by mid-1947, it seemed that what little he had managed

Carol and Lupescu became nomads, moving from Yugoslavia to Switzerland, on to France, Spain and Portugal, then across the Atlantic to Mexico and Brazil.

Carol and Magda pictured just after their wedding on 5 July 1947. Although she looks well, Magda was desperately ill with anaemia. It was a surprise to many that she ever recovered.

to retain was about to be taken from him. Magda Lupescu, it appeared, was dying. In what Carol saw as a last loving gesture, he married her on 5 July and gave her the title of Her Royal Highness Princess Eleana of Romania. But although the new princess seemed far gone in anaemia and depression at the time, she recovered with the help of blood transfusions and ultimately outlived Carol by 24 years.

KING PETER II OF YUGOSLAVIA

King Peter II of Yugoslavia (1923–1970) was another royal exile, forced out of his kingdom after his country was invaded by the forces of Nazi Germany in 1941. Only 17 years of age at the time, Peter had exercised full royal powers for only 10 days before he went on the run and eventually arrived in England as a refugee. But while other royals retired sadly but gracefully into exile, Peter never accepted the situation. Instead, he became obsessed with the forlorn hope of regaining his throne, regaling anyone and everyone with the tragedies of his life and the

beauties of Yugoslavia. His wife, Princess Alexandra of Greece, whose family had long experience as royals in exile, attempted to persuade him that retrieving his throne was a lost cause. Eventually, the issue came decisively between them and the marriage broke up.

DRINK AND DOOMED PLOTS

Afterwards, in 1965, Peter moved to the United States, where he tried but always failed to make a new life for himself, first as a consultant, then as a

King Peter II of Yugoslavia reigned for only 10 days before he was forced out by a Nazi invasion in 1941. Here is the 17-year-old ex-King (left) with US President Franklin Roosevelt.

financier. He sought solace in drink and attempts to gather together a band of royalist Yugoslavs to back his efforts to retrieve his Crown. They soon dwindled away. Frustration and resentment ate away at him. He never forgave wartime British Prime Minister Winston Churchill for backing Marshal Tito, his Communist rival in Yugoslavia, rather than himself. Believing that the British had cynically betrayed him, the ex-king hatched plots against Tito, who took over in Yugoslavia after World War II. But all of them were doomed.

By his mid-forties, Peter was an old, tired man, bloated by drink, worn down by self-pity and broken by failure. In 1970, he died of liver failure, aged only 47 and an all-but-forgotten figure. Peter's lack of standing among the monarchs and ex-monarchs of Europe was poignantly illustrated when press interest, such as it was, centred on the fact that Peter was the only monarch ever to die in the United States.

> **By his mid-forties, Peter was an old, tired man, bloated by drink, worn down by self-pity and broken by failure. In 1970, he died of liver failure, aged only 47 and an all-but-forgotten figure.**

Other royals in exile after World War II adjusted to their fate because they were able to adapt to alternative ways of life. But Peter II was never meant to be a businessman, an executive or a consultant. As he himself confessed, he was suited only to be a king and, with a mere 10 days in 1941 as the only time he held real royal power, he had scant experience even of that.

When she was strong enough, the newlyweds left Rio de Janeiro in Brazil and settled in Estoril, the fashionable coastal resort near Lisbon in Portugal. There, in 1949, to scotch rumours that they were about to divorce, Carol and Lupescu went through a religious wedding ceremony at which she appeared a dazzling bride. Carol, by contrast, looked pale and drawn, and far from well. Four years later, he began to suffer chest pains and, after a particularly bad attack on 3 April 1953, a doctor was called. By the time the doctor arrived, Carol seemed better; however, when the doctor turned to leave, another, swifter heart attack suddenly killed Carol. He was 59.

> **The news of Carol's death made only modest copy in the press that had once gorged itself on his headline-making escapades. The one-time king was past history, and the world had no more use for his high-profile type of monarch.**

Almost ignored in death

Through his paternal grandmother, Carol was related to the erstwhile royal family of Portugal, who had lost their throne in 1910. Consequently, he was given full royal honours at his funeral and was buried in the Pantheon reserved for the Portuguese kings. His widow was there, shrouded in black from head to foot. She wept throughout the ceremony. Of Carol's immediate family, only his nephew Prince Alexander of Yugoslavia, yet another royal exile, and Carol's estranged brother, Prince Nicolas, attended the funeral. Everyone else, including Michael, found reasons for staying away.

The news of Carol's death made only modest copy in the press that had once gorged itself on his headline-making escapades. The one-time king was past history, and the world had no more use for his high-profile type of monarch. For a man such as Carol, who had lived on controversy and its attendant publicity, that was a fate much more ignominious than the death in exile which, at the end, was all he could expect.

XII

THE NETHERLANDS: A ROYAL FAMILY IN TROUBLE

The Dutch have experienced problems with their monarchy ever since Queen Wilhelmina of the Netherlands married Prince Hendrick of Mecklenburg-Shwerin in 1901. Since then, the ruling dynasty, the Royal House of Orange-Nassau, has thrown up a long series of difficulties, stemming from one or other of two main sources.

◆

One problem was the tendency of Dutch monarchs to abdicate when the going got rough. The other derived from the marriages of three successive reigning queens – Wilhelmina, her

Left: Queen Wilhelmina of the Netherlands taking the oath of the constitution at the new church in Amsterdam on 1 August 1898. Above: Princess Juliana, who became Queen in 1948, seen before her accession with her controversial husband Prince Bernhardt.

daughter Juliana and Juliana's daughter Beatrix – to Germans whose nationality alone provoked alarm and enmity among their subjects.

The abdicating habit began with the first Dutch monarch, Willem I, who declared himself king in 1815 only to find, in time, that his royal powers were limited by a liberal constitution. Unable to live with the popular rights, free speech and democracy which liberal rule required, Willem, a natural autocrat, abdicated in 1840. His grandson, Willem III, who became king nine years later, was a chip off the same royal block and struggled hard against the same restraints. He was constantly trying to escape liberal controls, and threatened abdication several times. But Willem III never got away: he was talked out of it by his strong-minded Russian mother, Queen Anna Pavlovna, and ended up reigning in the Netherlands for 50 years.

Uneasy alliances

Wilhelmina, his 10-year-old daughter and only surviving heir, succeeded him as queen regnant on his death in 1890. This introduced new trouble: the discontented male consort. Wilhelmina's husband,

Prince Bernhardt, pictured here in military uniform, was a daredevil risk-taker and womaniser but did a great deal of work for the Netherlands.

Prince Hendrik, disliked being a royal consort, hated having to walk one step behind his wife and was, as he put it, thoroughly bored with being a mere decoration. Hendrik had no real power in the Netherlands, and it did their marriage little good when Wilhelmina saw to it that it stayed that way.

> **Wilhelmina's husband, Prince Hendrik, disliked being a royal consort, hated having to walk one step behind his wife and was, as he put it, thoroughly bored with being a mere decoration.**

Still, the policy of keeping Hendrick on a leash may well have commended itself to Wilhelmina's subjects. Hendrick's homeland, Germany, was the rising power in Europe, and the neighbouring Netherlands was, at best, wary of its ambitious and expansionist neighbour. This long-lasting perception turned to real fear after 1933, when the Nazis and their leader Adolf Hitler seized power and turned Germany into a racist totalitarian state ruled by terror and repression that soon became a threat to the peace of Europe and the world.

Dutch fear of Germany and Germans was strong enough by 1937 to provoke serious objections to the prospect of Juliana, Wilhelmina's heir, marrying a German husband, Prince Bernhardt of the Lippe-Biesterfeld. Despite the objections, the marriage took place in The Hague on 7 January 1937.

A playboy and a hero

Bernhardt had his attractions, as a dashing 'man about town' with an exciting though often dangerous lifestyle. He was a reckless driver who crashed several cars in his time, and he often injured himself quite seriously. He loved big-game hunting, boating and flying, and was almost killed in high-speed accidents. A prince as reckless as this had a certain daredevil glamour which was augmented by the loyalty to the Netherlands which he displayed during World War II. Bernhardt helped to organize Dutch resistance to the Nazi occupation, saw action with the British Royal Air Force, carried out reconnaissance missions over Europe and, in 1945, took part in arranging the German surrender in the Netherlands.

After the war, the initial enmity the Dutch had shown Bernhardt had turned to admiration, and he was now regarded as a hero. But rather unfairly, he still carried his playboy label and regularly made the gossip columns in the newspapers with his jet-setting lifestyle, his extramarital affairs, his lavish partying and his shady friends who included Juan Péron, the Argentine President and his wife, Eva.

Attention diverted

Bernhardt never entirely shed this fly-by-night reputation, but in 1947 he moved out of the scandal spotlight for a time. Attention was beamed instead on Juliana and her unorthodox methods of trying to cure the eye problems of her youngest daughter, Princess Marina Christina, usually known as Marijke. Marikje, born in 1947, was the fourth daughter of Juliana and Bernhardt, after Beatrix (1938), Irene (1939) and Margriet (1943). At birth, Marijke had cataracts over both eyes, after her mother caught German measles during pregnancy. World-class physicians and surgeons were called in, but the most they could do was restore blurred vision to one eye.

> ## At birth, Marijke had cataracts over both eyes, after her mother caught German measles during pregnancy.

Juliana and Bernhardt were distraught, but hope of a full cure was restored after the couple encountered Greet Hofmans, a faith healer who claimed to be a representative of God. Hofmans told Juliana that, with sufficient prayer and belief, God would give little Marijke her sight. Juliana, who believed in miracles and astrology, and had a penchant for the supernatural, became convinced of the faith healer's powers. When the child was brought in to meet Hofmans, the healer fell to her knees and prayed long and fervently. Afterwards, she told Juliana: 'God will give the child sight in two years, if we pray hard enough.'

Juliana and even Bernhardt, who had reservations

Princess Marikje, the youngest daughter of Queen Juliana, who was born with severe eye problems.

about Hofmans, were impressed. The faith healer moved into the Soestdijk Palace near Amsterdam. Every day, the entire royal family attended prayer sessions at the palace. But, before long, Bernhardt began to suspect that his wife was becoming unduly dependent on the faith healer. He realized that Hofmans would always promise a dazzling future. 'You will be the greatest queen (the country) has ever had,' she told Juliana. But this future would transpire only as long as Juliana prayed fervently enough and listened to God, which, of course, meant listening to Greet Hofmans. After that, Bernhardt resolved to get rid of the faith healer. Juliana, of course, would not hear of it.

Queen Wilhelmina (foreground, left) at the bombed out ruins of the Dutch church at Austin Friars in London on 10 May 1941, the first anniversary of the Nazi German invasion of the Netherlands. She was accompanied by her son-in-law, Prince Bernhardt (saluting).

Misplaced faith

The situation became even more serious in 1948, when Wilhelmina abdicated and Juliana became queen. Now Juliana possessed the powers of a sovereign and, though they were limited by law, a measure of political muscle as well. To the worried Bernhardt, this gave much more room for Greet Hofmans to influence his impressionable wife.

Bernhardt's fears soon came true as Hofmans extended her activities to giving the new queen political advice. This was too much for Bernhardt. In 1950, he ordered Hofmans's belongings removed from the Soestdijk Palace, where she had been living for the past nine years.

But this was by no means the end of Hofmans' royal connection. The faith healer went on to

Wilhelmina abdicated the Dutch throne after a reign of 58 years. This photograph, taken on 2 September 1948, four days before the formal abdication, shows crowds in front of the royal palace in Amsterdam to cheer Wilhelmina as she appeared on the balcony.

hold meetings where she propounded the virtues of pacifism and mysticism, and the need to make contact with creatures from outer space. Juliana and her mother, ex-queen Wilhelmina, attended several of these meetings and were strongly influenced by them. This became clear when several of Juliana's fellow 'believers', such as Baron von Heeckeren van Molecatan, who became the Queen's private secretary, were given important positions at court.

To add another layer of unease, this was the Cold War era. This made the Hofmans affair even more alarming when Juliana's public speeches began to reflect the faith healer's pacifist ideas: Juliana advocated Dutch disarmament and the disbanding of the Dutch armed forces. Alarm bells rang in Washington and other Western capitals at the prospect of the Netherlands, tiny though it was, providing a hole in the defences the United States

and the West were striving to maintain against the spread of communism.

By this time, Bernhardt and Juliana were on opposite sides over the Hofmans affair, and their disagreement was so serious that it was starting to affect their marriage. This placed Bernhardt in a dangerous position. He owed everything – his public posts, his titles, his business connections and much more – to remaining married to the Queen of the Netherlands.

Usually, protocol demanded that no story of this kind reached the Dutch media. But in 1956, in a desperate move, the prince leaked news about the Hofmans affair to the German magazine *Der Spiegel*. The story spread from there to the world's press. The respectful Dutch media sat on the revelations for a while, but eventually could keep silent no longer. Now, Juliana's subjects, too, learned about the weird goings-on behind the royal scenes.

Juliana advocated Dutch disarmament and the disbanding of the Dutch armed forces. Alarm bells rang in Washington and other Western capitals

The publicity unleashed by *Der Spiegel* had been so embarrassing that powerful political and business figures, who had a lot to lose unless the Hofmans affair was solved, exerted heavy pressure on Juliana to send the faith healer away or abdicate or face being forced to resign. This was stern stuff, but thankfully it made the queen pause and think again. So did the fact that Hofmans had failed to cure Marikje's eye troubles. Juliana agreed that the faith healer's contacts with the court and the royal family should be severed, and purged her household of Hofmans supporters. After that, Greet Hofmans faded away and died in obscurity in 1968. By then, new medical treatments had vastly improved Marijke's sight until she was able to lead a normal life.

Further ructions

Meanwhile, Juliana and Bernhardt had been through another serious problem with another of their daughters, Princess Irene. In 1963, news broke that Irene had secretly converted to Catholicism and was engaged to Prince Carlos Hugo of Bourbon Parma, heir to Xavier, Duke of Parma, a pretender to the Spanish throne.

The new Queen Juliana with Prince Bernhardt on their way to her inauguration ceremony after her mother's abdication, 6 September 1948.

For the fiercely Protestant Dutch and their queen, Irene's conversion was bad enough, but there was more. Prince Carlos Hugo was a supporter of General Francisco Franco, the fascist dictator who had ruled Spain since the end of its Civil War in 1939. Franco, in his turn, was detested by the Dutch for supporting Nazi Germany during World War II.

> **For the fiercely Protestant Dutch and their queen, Irene's conversion was bad enough. Queen Juliana became desperate to prevent Carlos Hugo's marriage to her daughter.**

Princess Irene, second daughter of Queen Juliana, with Prince Carlos Hugo of Bourbon-Parma. Juliana strongly opposed their marriage which nevertheless took place on 29 April 1964.

Against this background, Carlos Hugo meant big trouble for Queen Juliana, who became desperate to prevent his marriage to her daughter. Irene, however, proved to be extremely stubborn and also had no qualms about deceiving her mother. Juliana sent one of her secretaries to Madrid to see the princess and to Juliana's relief reported that the engagement was off and that Irene was returning to the Netherlands. Juliana's relief was short-lived. When the aircraft supposedly flying her daughter home arrived, Irene was not among the passengers. Juliana and Bernhardt resolved to go to Madrid themselves and make their daughter see sense, but Dutch hatred of all things Spanish was so great that the government vowed to resign to a man if the queen were to set foot in Spain. Juliana returned home deeply distressed and in tears. Meanwhile, in Madrid, Irene went into hiding, first at a convent, then afterwards in rooms near Carlos Hugo's apartment. Both suspected that they were under some sort of covert surveillance, which included tapping their telephones. They resorted to standing at windows exchanging hand signals. Back in the Netherlands, resistance to the marriage remained as fierce as ever, but early in 1964 a breakthrough appeared imminent when Irene indicated that she was ready to come home.

No compromise

Hopes rose that the impasse would be resolved, but they were false hopes. When Prince Bernhardt flew to Madrid and brought Irene and Carlos Hugo back to the Netherlands, it was soon plain that the young couple was in no mood to compromise. If anything, their impudence knew no bounds. In a heated six-hour exchange at the Soestdijk Palace, they made it plain that they expected a lavish Roman Catholic wedding in the Protestant Nieuwe Kerk in Amsterdam, with all members of Europe's royal families invited. Juliana, utterly taken aback, told the couple in no uncertain terms that she would never sanction the wedding and that, if one did take place, it could mean the end of the royal House of Orange-Nassau.

> **Juliana, utterly taken aback, told the couple in no uncertain terms that she would never sanction the wedding and that, if one did take place, it could mean the end of the royal House of Orange-Nassau.**

Juliana was by no means overstating the case, for a full-blown constitutional crisis was certainly in prospect unless a way out was found. Until now, Irene, who was second in line to the Dutch throne after her elder sister, Beatrix, had been anxious to preserve her rights of succession. Only if she renounced those rights, Irene was told, would she

> **Irene's reaction was defiant. With Carlos Hugo, she went to Rome where the couple had an audience with Pope Paul VI.**

be able to marry Carlos Hugo and at the same time preserve the monarchy.

Irene's reaction was defiant. With Carlos Hugo, she went to Rome where the couple had an audience with Pope Paul VI. As a public statement of her intransigence, this was hard to beat. All the same, Irene managed it. Soon after returning from Rome, she was scheduled to make an official visit to Mexico with her mother, but she failed to turn up at Schiphol Airport. The departure was delayed, but still no Irene. Juliana, badly shaken by this public humiliation at her daughter's hands, had no option but to fly to Mexico alone.

Irene was not finished yet. She publicly supported the claim of Carlos Hugo and his father to the Spanish throne and was photographed attending a rally staged by the Falangist party of General Franco. Irene had attracted some sympathy in the Netherlands as a young woman being thwarted in love, but the sentimental Romeo-and-Juliet image faded away after she openly sided with the fascist Franco and his right-wing rule in Spain.

Yet another controversial marriage

Back in the early 1960s, the Dutch had little respite from controversy before another royal marriage caused another uproar. In July 1966, Queen Juliana broadcast on television and radio the news that Princess Beatrix, the heir to the throne, was engaged to the diplomat Claus-Georg von Amsberg.

'I assure you,' Juliana told her people. 'It is a good thing.'

As far as Juliana's subjects were concerned, it was very far from being a 'good thing'. Claus von Amsberg, an aristocrat who had met Beatrix on a Swiss skiing holiday, would be the third German in succession to marry into the Dutch royal family. More than that, he had been a member of the Hitler Youth and the Wehrmacht, the German Army.

MARRIAGE AT A PRICE

Irene and Carlos Hugo were married in Rome on 29 April 1964. No member of her family was present at the ceremony, and all important members of European royalty stayed away. As the marriage had not been sanctioned by the Netherlands Estates-General, or Parliament, as required by law, Irene automatically lost her rights of succession to the throne. She had already agreed to live with her husband outside the Netherlands, which many Dutch people agreed, sadly, was just as well.

Ultimately, this painful experience proved to be all for nothing. Irene and Carlos Hugo divorced in 1981, and Irene returned to the Netherlands with their four children. The dramatic events of 1964 were not forgotten, however, and, when Irene's book *Dialogue with Nature* was published in 1995, the Dutch media could not resist a 'dig' at its author by publicizing those passages that revealed her conversations with trees and dolphins.

Princess Irene and Carlos Hugo were married at the Basilica of Santa Maria Maggiore in Rome. The Dutch royal family was not present. They are pictured here in their car shortly after the controversial ceremony.

Crown Princess Beatrice, heir to the Dutch throne, and the West German diplomat Claus von Amsberg, at their wedding on 10 March 1966. Like her sister Irene, though for different reasons, Beatrix's marriage was controversial.

Inevitably, it was not long before demonstrations and protests against the marriage erupted onto the streets. There were anti-Claus marches and rallies. Furious crowds chanted, 'Claus raus! Claus raus!' ('Claus out! Claus out!') Orange-coloured swastikas appeared on buildings and billboards, and were chalked on pavements and walls, and even on the walls of the royal palace in Amsterdam, daubed there by an audacious protester who managed to get through the security cordon. More worrying still, cries of 'Up the Republic!' were heard in some places, indicating that a vociferous section of the public, albeit a probable minority, was tiring of monarchy.

There was little real danger of a republic, but, according to a public opinion poll taken soon after the engagement was announced, support for the monarchy dropped from 86 to 74 per cent. The newspaper *Nieuwe Courant*, published in Rotterdam,

A LESS-THAN-SERENE WEDDING DAY

In spite of all the problems and protests, the marriage of Princess Beatrix and Claus von Amsberg took place in Amsterdam on 10 March 1966. But it turned out to be one of the most disorderly weddings in royal history. Most European royals and nobles, apprised in advance of serious trouble, stayed away, and their caution proved justified. The wedding day started with a protest march on the royal palace, followed by street fighting between protesters and police, and several arrests. It continued with a smoke bomb that was rolled underneath the wedding carriage and exploded. The carriage was also struck by a dead

There were boycotts and anti-German demonstrations in Amsterdam on Beatrix's wedding day. Smoke bombs were thrown, one of them into the path of the golden coach carrying the newlyweds.

chicken with a Nazi swastika painted on its body. Stink bombs and more smoke bombs were flung at the procession until a column of acrid smoke rose some 50 feet (15 metres) into the air.

Rabbis, remembering the sufferings of Dutch Jews during World War II – thousands were sent to die in the Nazi concentration camps – boycotted the event. So, too, did the members of Amsterdam city council and several government employees. The police who were supposedly charged with keeping the peace beat several protesters to the ground, in a display so savage that the Burgomaster of Amsterdam and the Chief of Police were afterwards dismissed from their posts. But much, if not quite all, was forgiven a year later, in 1967, when Beatrix gave birth to the first of her three sons, Willem-Alexander, who became the first surviving male heir to the Dutch throne in 116 years.

commented: 'Can a German put flowers at our memorials for heroes he fought against?' A group of six prominent Resistance fighters who had fought the German invaders during World War II publicly denounced the marriage of Beatrix and Claus as 'unbearable'. A monthly magazine *De Gide* suggested that, like her sister Irene, Beatrix should abdicate her rights to the throne.

Averting another succession crisis

Beatrix, who was ambitious and not a little impatient for her mother to abdicate so that she could become queen, would never have agreed to that. But Juliana, who was not as keen on the marriage as she gave out, had her own plan to avoid such a situation, by preventing the marriage taking place at all. Juliana made contact with the West German foreign minister, Claus's superior in the diplomatic service, and asked him to have Claus transferred to somewhere outside Europe. Juliana's plan failed after the strong-minded Beatrix heard

The newspaper *Nieuwe Courant*, published in Rotterdam, commented: 'Can a German put flowers at our memorials for heroes he fought against?'

of it and went on a three-day hunger strike that so alarmed her mother that she gave up.

Instead, in a complete turnaround, Juliana decided to commend Claus von Amsberg to her subjects by arranging for him to appear at a televised press conference with Beatrix. This was a significant

In March 1954, Prince Bernhardt (left) visited Maxwell Air Base in Alabama, USA, where he met Dean C. Strother, Deputy Commander of the Air University. Bernhardt had an interest in buying aircraft for the Dutch air force.

concession by the House of Orange-Nassau, which had hitherto shrunk from exposing themselves to media scrutiny. But 38-year-old Claus had not been a diplomat for nothing, and his 'stage presence' was perfect. Slim, handsome and elegant, he appeared on screen as a modest man, very much in love with Beatrix, regretful about the Nazi past of his youth, and aiming above all to win the acceptance of the Dutch people.

> # Claus's personal wartime record in Soviet Russia and East Germany was checked and nothing incriminating was found.

This last was easier said than done. Claus won over many viewers and others who believed he should have a fair chance to prove himself. But there were still many who could not be mollified – not even when Claus's personal wartime record in Soviet Russia and East Germany was checked and nothing incriminating was found. All the same, the protesters made their point quite forcefully. Anti-royal pamphlets were thrown onto the deck of a ship taking Beatrix and Claus on a tour of Amsterdam's canals. Despite a nationwide appeal, less than US$20,000 (£9790) was raised for a wedding present from a populace that soon afterwards contributed almost 18 times that much for the relief of famine in India. Even Claus's mother, Julie, Baroness von dem Bussche-Haddenhausen, was targeted, and received letters signed 'with hate'.

A scandal too far

While the drama of Beatrix's marriage grabbed national and world headlines, yet another controversy for the House of Orange-Nassau was brewing in the background. Serious though the others were, this one eclipsed them all and proved to be one scandal too far for Juliana and Bernhardt.

Although he was in his mid-sixties by the time Beatrix married, Prince Bernhardt was still essentially the fast-living, jet-setting man about town he had been since his youth. He was no gadabout wastrel, though: Bernhardt worked long and hard to promote the Netherlands economy and did it so successfully that he rarely

returned home from abroad without obtaining overseas contracts for Dutch companies and corporations.

Sailing close to the wind

Nevertheless, Bernhardt sometimes sailed too close to the wind. His travels around the world on official, charity or private business afforded him a wide-ranging social life which included ties with disreputable entrepreneurs and other wheeler-dealers Foreign travel also gave Bernhardt opportunities for extramarital affairs. Queen Juliana was not a strong-minded, outspoken woman like her mother, Wilhelmina, or her daughters, Beatrix and Irene. She was more comfortable in the dreamy world of mystic religion and was not the sort to deal effectively with an errant husband. This, though, did not mean that Juliana was unaware of what Bernhardt was up to. For one thing,

Prince Bernhardt photographed on 2 July 1979, when he was already in trouble over his suspect deals with the Lockheed Corporation.

she knew all about his liaison with Helène Grinda, known as the 'Paris Poupette', who gave birth to Bernhardt's daughter Alexia in 1967, 13 years after he fathered another girl, Alicia, with another mistress.

One of the Prince's biggest business contacts was the American Lockheed Corporation, the military aircraft of which he had been urging the Netherlands government to buy since the early 1950s. But somewhere along the line, proper business relations strayed into malpractice and, in around 1959,

**Proper business relations strayed into malpractice ...
In return, Bernhardt would 'improve the climate'
in the Netherlands on Lockheed's behalf.**

Juliana (centre) with Prince Bernhardt on her left, makes a specch on 30 April 1980, the day her daughter (left) became Queen.

through a Swiss lawyer, Lockheed proposed to pay the prince one million US dollars (£490,770), spread over the following three years. In return, Bernhardt would 'improve the climate' in the Netherlands on Lockheed's behalf.

Juliana stands by her man

The arrangement remained confidential for some 16 years, until rumours about what was, effectively, a very large bribe began to circulate at the end of 1975. Bernhardt at once denied any wrongdoing, claiming that a man in his exalted position was 'above such things'. The time was long past, however, when royalty could place itself above the law and get away with it. If found guilty of taking bribes, Bernhardt faced prison, prince or no prince. He was fortunate, though, that Juliana saw it as her duty to stand by him. She threatened to abdicate if Bernhardt were not exonerated.

The accusations deepen

Neither government nor people wanted Juliana to go; however, despite denials, the accusations against Bernhardt kept on coming from Lockheed operatives and others who had known the prince over the years. Another bribe allegedly received by the prince from Lockheed, in 1968, was for US$100,000 (£49,077), which was paid to a certain 'Victor Baarn'. Lockheed claimed that Victor Baarn was Prince Bernhardt under an assumed name. Among further allegations, Bernhardt was said to have given the Argentine dictator Juan Péron US$1,000,000 (£490,770) as part of a deal in which Argentina ordered Dutch railway equipment.

> **Juliana had ... been queen for almost 30 years and was approaching 70 years of age. These facts meant that she could abdicate with honour instead of in a blaze of adverse publicity.**

All these stories were given headline coverage by the European media, together with revelations about Bernhardt's affairs. One of these alleged that Bernhardt had mistresses in Tanzania and the Ivory Coast in Africa, as well as in Mexico. It was alleged, too, that he had bought an expensive apartment in Paris for Helène Grinda and that he threw lavish parties with call girls for his friends.

Bernhardt's personal and business lives were unravelling fast. Ultimately, he was saved by a special government commission, which published its findings on 26 August 1976. The commission concluded that Prince Bernhardt, acting in the belief that his position was unassailable, had been careless when he entered into 'transactions which were bound to create the impression that he was susceptible to favours'.

Bernhardt's position was boosted by a vote in the States-General of 149 to 2 in favour of not prosecuting him and also by the fact that Juliana did not, in the event, abdicate in the wake of the Lockheed scandal. But Bernhardt's escape from prosecution had its price. He was obliged to resign from all his official, military, charitable and business posts, give up wearing his many uniforms – a lifelong pleasure of his – and, effectively, retire from national and international life.

A new queen

Although Juliana had chosen not to give up the throne in 1976, by then she had been queen for almost 30 years and was approaching 70 years of age. These facts meant that she could abdicate with honour instead of in a blaze of adverse publicity. Juliana signed the Act of Abdication on 30 April 1980, the day she turned 71 years of age. Afterwards, she reverted to her original title of princess.

Beatrix succeeded her mother, so realizing her own long-awaited ambition. Prince Claus was now the queen's consort. But, like Prince Hendrik, the consort of Queen Wilhelmina, Claus eventually became discontented with his secondary position. He particularly resented the fact that it placed him behind his own sons in the royal order of precedence. Claus began to suffer from depression, which continued for many years before his death in 2002.

Juliana and Bernhardt, who both died two years later, spent their remaining years in charity work, which doubtless afforded them a much-needed time of quiet after the many storms of their 67-year marriage. For Bernhardt, the contrast was total. In the Netherlands, as in other European monarchies, there was no traditional role on offer for the consorts of reigning queens. Instead, they had to make their own way. Bernhardt's way had taken him to impressive heights – politically, militarily, financially, internationally. In his time, he was arguably the mightiest of male consorts. But Bernhardt's way had a fatal flaw ...

'He thought he was a ninetheenth-century prince,' one Dutch politician commented. 'That he could do whatever he wanted, that he was above the law.'

Having reigned for 33 years exactly, Queen Beatrix herself abdicated on 30 April 2013, at the age of 75, and was succeeded by her son Willem-Alexander.

Queen Beatrix attending the Queen's Day celebrations on 30 April 2002, the anniversary of her accession and also her official birthday.

XIII

KING LEOPOLD II AND THE BELGIAN CONGO

In the late nineteenth century, Africa, the 'Dark Continent', was one of the great unknowns of world geography. Unknown, that is, to Europeans who suspected, rightly, that its unexplored interior was a treasure house of untapped mineral and other commercial wealth. In particular, for the major imperial powers – Britain, France, the Netherlands, Spain and Portugal – Africa meant more trade, more wealth and more territory to add to their already extensive empires.

✦

The so-called Scramble for Africa that resulted saw the rival empires carve up the greater part of the continent between them. But virtually unknown for more than 20 years, the Scramble also saw the greatest humanitarian crisis – one that verged on genocide – ever to come out of nineteenth-century

Africa. The culprit was not a major player, but a king: Leopold II of Belgium, who ruled one of the smallest countries in Europe.

Visions of empire

Belgium was a newcomer nation that became independent only in 1830. Nevertheless, King Leopold was not content to let his realm, with an area of only around 30,500km² (11,800 sq miles), remain among the small fry of Europe. He wanted to match the big imperial powers with a colony of his own.

Left: King Leopold II of Belgium. Leopold was the major villain of the European Scramble for Africa.
Above: A much earlier photograph of Leopold, the second king of Belgium, a newcomer nation created in 1830.

221

At the personal level, Leopold was well equipped to bulldoze his way through all obstacles to his ambition. He was tenacious and stubborn, and never took no for an answer. He cared little for personal popularity. Admittedly, Leopold had a surface charm, but beneath it he was vindictive and cunning. Above all, he was dangerous when let loose to work out his ambitions unrestrained, guided by nothing more than his autocratic will to succeed.

When Leopold became king in 1865, there were still many blank spaces on the map of Africa, and the French and Germans were busy filling them – in the Sahara, along the border with Nigeria and at the mouth of the Congo (Zaire) River. Non-Europeans were getting in on the act, too: the Sultan of Zanzibar and the Khedive of Egypt were together planning to carve out a huge Muslim empire in central Africa. Leopold followed these developments very closely

and promoted his own colonizing schemes in 1875, with plans to send Belgian settlers to Mozambique in east Africa, the island of Borneo in the Malay Archipelago and the Philippine islands. All these ventures failed, however, not least because the territories in question were already occupied by the Portuguese, the Dutch and the Spaniards, respectively. None of them was keen to have Belgians or anyone else poaching their preserves.

The chief focus of Leopold's interest was the Congo, a vast area of central Africa more than 75 times the size of Belgium. Sited in a huge depression of the African plateau, the potential wealth of the Congo was immense. Among the prizes there for the taking were rubber, industrial diamonds, gold, silver, copper and other valuable metals. Large areas of this enormous treasure house were still unclaimed in 1876, when Leopold revealed his plan for establishing a Belgian foothold in Africa. The king summoned Baron Auguste Lambermont, a civil servant at the Ministry of Foreign Affairs, to his palace and told him: I would like to do something in Africa. You know exactly what the explorers have done there and together we shall see what we can make of it with a peaceful humanitarian objective – my only concern and aim.

Among the prizes there for the taking were rubber, industrial diamonds, gold, silver, copper and other valuable metals.

A share of the cake

Leopold s real objective was very different. Peaceful humanitarianism was the last thing on his mind. In 1876, when he convened a Geographical Conference in Brussels, ostensibly for the purpose of exploring and 'civilizing' Africa, he deliberately concealed his true intentions from the delegates.

'Needless to say,' Leopold told them, 'in bringing you to Brussels, I was in no way motivated by selfish designs. No, gentlemen, if Belgium is small, she is also happy and contented with her lot.'

Except for the British, who saw through him at once, the delegates – representatives of foreign governments, explorers, philanthropists, business entrepreneurs – became convinced of Leopold's altruism and hailed him as the leader of Europe's humanitarian mission in Africa. But far from lacking colonial ambition, as he pretended, the king was a brutal opportunist who wrote: I do not want to

The Belgian Congo was a phenomenally rich territory. This photograph was taken in around 1905 showing a dredge sampling the waters of the Congo River for gold.

miss the [chance] of our obtaining a share in this magnificent African cake.'

The slicing of the cake took place at the Conference convened in Berlin on 15 November 1884, but not without controversy. So much self-interest was in play that, inevitably, proceedings were marked by rival claims to the most advantageous areas of Africa. One

thing soon became clear, though: none of the major colonial powers wanted any of the others to claim an area large enough to give them a dominant interest. The greatest of these areas was the Congo, where Leopold had created for himself an exemplary image as the champion of law, order and civilization – to make sure that the prize would be his when the time

The African continent was carved up between several Europe countries aiming to create or enlarge their empires. This is a scene from Nigeria, showing representatives of local tribes meeting with British officials after Britain appropriated the region in 1885.

Leopold took the name King-Sovereign of the Congo Free State and began by taking the initiatives expected of an enlightened nineteenth-century ruler. By 1889, he had a railway built to create a modern system of communications through what was effectively near-impenetrable mountain and jungle.

As ever the humanitarian overtones were deceptive. Leopold's real purpose was to promote profits.

In 1889–90, he hosted an anti-slavery conference in Brussels designed to destroy the slave trade. The conference was attended by Britain, France, Germany and other imperialist powers, and Leopold proposed that all of them construct a series of forts in their various territories. These would put a stop to raids by 'Arab' slavers and serve as bases for pursuing caravans carrying slaves into the interior.

Leopold claims his prize

It looked good, as Leopold meant it to look, but as ever the humanitarian overtones were deceptive. Leopold s real purpose was to promote profits. For example, decrees issued by Leopold in 1891 and 1892 effectively turned the ivory and rubber trades into a state monopoly. This, in turn, dispossessed the Congolese living in and around the forests in the Ubangi-Uele river basins where they hunted elephants for ivory and tapped the rubber trees. This was now forbidden, unless they handed over their produce to the Belgian authorities. At the same time, all trading was banned in the Uele valley, damaging if not destroying the livelihood of the native Congolese.

Abuse and exploitation

While the native inhabitants struggled to survive, exports of rubber from the Congo Free State rose from less than 250 metric tons in 1893 to 6000 metric tons by 1901. Economically, the Free State seemed to be thriving. But socially it was a disaster. Behind

came. The time came on 25 February 1885, when the Berlin Act was signed and the Congo was allocated to Leopold, as the only neutral involved in the Conference. When he was mentioned by name, the delegates rose to their feet and cheered in an outburst of approval. It was an emotional moment. Leopold s triumph was complete.

Two Congolese rubber workers weigh their loads as Belgian officials watch. Native workers could be severely punished if they failed to reach set targets.

these soaring trade figures, shocking tales of abuse and savage exploitation were coming out of the Congo. After 1891, numerous letters and reports reached the British Colonial Office in London recounting how Belgian authorities were cruelly misusing Africans. Witnesses spoke of floggings, torture, forced labour, hostage-taking, imprisonment in chains, and several deaths in consequence. There were, too, fearful tales of other inhuman treatment and even the massacre of entire Congolese villages.

This, though, was by no means the end of it. Missionaries in the Congo weighed in with their own evidence of cruelty towards the natives, and the looting by State soldiers of their homes and property. These stories were emblazoned across newspaper headlines and received particular attention in *The Times*, Britain's most renowned and respected newspaper.

Henry Morton Stanley warned King Leopold of the deleterious effect the horror stories were having in Britain. 'The [British] are such believers in what they see in print,' he told the king. King Leopold appeared to take the lesson to heart.

'If there are abuses in the Congo, we must stop them,' he wrote to Baron Edmond van Eetvelde,

Right: Henry Morton Stanley was a journalist-turned-explorer who helped King Leopold develop the Congo. Here he is shown dressed for his most famous exploit: finding explorer Dr David Livingstone.

KING LEOPOLD THE HYPOCHONDRIAC

King Leopold II was something of a hypochondriac and went to extreme lengths to preserve his health: his self-protection went so far that he had a waterproof cover made for his beard so that, if it got wet in the rain, he would not catch a cold. If anyone sneezed near him, he almost panicked at the prospect of catching something. Some of Leopold s aides-de-camp soon learned how to play on his fear of illness to their advantage, securing a day or two off duty by pretending to have a cold: Leopold forbade them to come near him or his court until they had recovered.

The elderly King Leopold was a health and fitness fanatic. For his aides, the way to get a holiday from his service was to pretend to be ill, preferably with something catching.

> ## Leopold set up a Commission for the Protection of Natives, the task of which was to advise of any malpractices that came to their attention.

the Secretary of State in the Congo. 'If they are perpetuated, they will bring about the collapse of the State.'

A cynical smokescreen

Leopold set up a Commission for the Protection of Natives, the task of which was to advise of any malpractices that came to their attention. This, though, seemed to be yet another of Leopold s smokescreens, for the new Commission was organized in a way that virtually guaranteed it could not work. Its members, all missionaries, were sited hundreds of kilometres apart so that contact between them, never easy in the best of times, was greatly compromised. In addition, the Commission s powers were limited: it had no right

to demand information, even though it was dealing with the very officials who had every reason to conceal it. Unsurprisingly, the Commission achieved little, if anything, of note, and the abuses continued.

Some of the worst examples of maltreatment came about because of the quota system applied to rubber production, the most vital component of the Congolese economy. If the native inhabitants did not produce as much rubber as they should, vicious punishments – floggings, beatings, mutilation, even the murder of family members – were applied to make them do better.

One missionary, the Reverend John Harris, wrote a truly harrowing account in 1905, describing how brutally underproduction was punished. He wrote:

'The people from Esanga [south of the Congo River] told how, on one occasion, because 49 instead of 50 baskets of rubber were brought in, some [of them] were imprisoned and sentries were sent to punish the people... all had harrowing stories to tell of the brutal murder of near relatives. Some they had seen shot before their eyes; in other cases, they had fled into the

In 1865, when Leopold became king of Belgium there were many blanks in the map of Africa. By 1884 large areas had been filled in by European colonization.

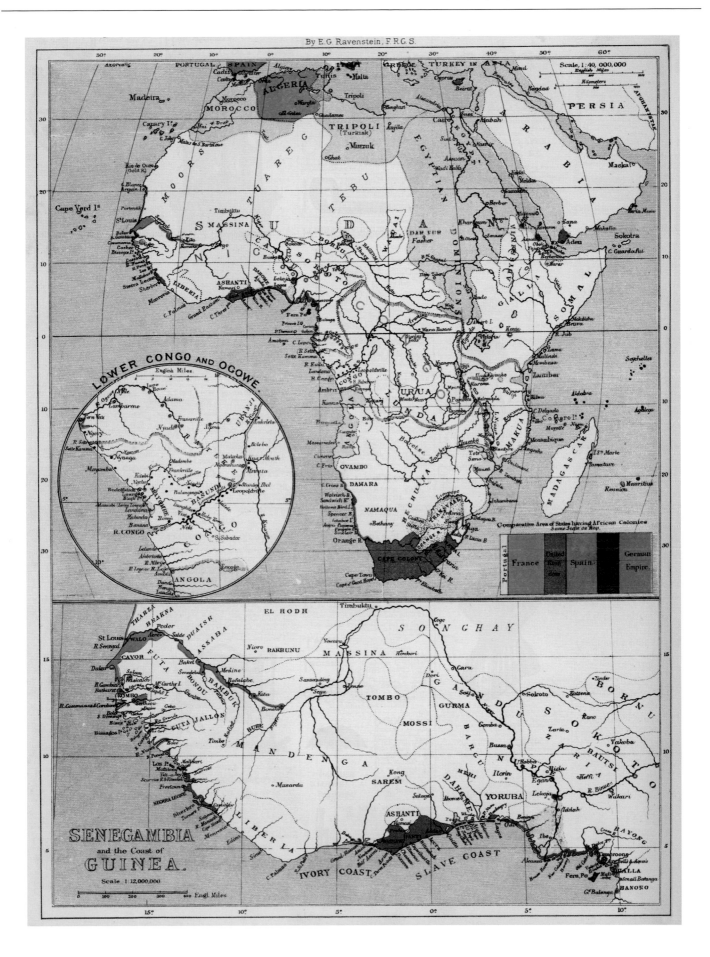

By E.G. Ravenstein, F.R.G.S.

Scale 1:40,000,000

LOWER CONGO AND OGOWE.

Comparative Area of States having African Colonies
Same Scale as Map.

Portugal | France | United Kingdom | Spain | German Empire.

SENEGAMBIA
and the Coast of
GUINEA.

Scale 1:12,000,000

In 1904, Sir Roger Casement (first left) who worked for the British consular service reported atrocities being committed in the Belgian Congo. Here he is with Congolese men who are holding the severed hands of men killed by Congo 'Free State' troops.

bush to save themselves and, when they returned, had found the dead bodies of their relatives lying about.

'While the men were in the forest trying to get rubber, their wives were outraged, ill treated and stolen from them by the sentries. In the light of all they have suffered at the hands of their oppressors, one wonders they do not hate the very sight of white men. We missionaries sometimes feel that our message of salvation [through Christ] must seem like a mockery to them.'

The uproar that first arose in Britain when news of the Congolese atrocities broke spread to Germany where, in 1899, a damning report was published in a Cologne newspaper, the *Kölnische Zeitung*. In this

report, Achille Fiévez, commandant in Sultanate of Zemio, a Free State protectorate, was charged with no fewer than 1308 mutilations, most of them the severing of hands.

> **they had fled into the bush to save themselves and, when they returned, had found the dead bodies of their relatives lying about.**

A barrage of criticism

By this time, at the turn of the twentieth century, Leopold found himself under fire from virtually all sides as a man responsible for some of the most fearful atrocities it was possible to commit. Not all of it was true. There were exaggerations, outright lies or highly

It was reckoned that, since the advent of the Free State in 1885, the population of the Congo had declined by 70 per cent, from around 30 million to 9 million.

King Leopold, who had posed as a benefactor of the Congolese, was universally condemned for the near-genocide he permitted in the Congo.

coloured speculation. Nevertheless, the valid evidence was sufficient to establish the fact that an appallingly savage state of affairs had developed in the Congo, where innocent people were being maltreated and murdered in the name of commercial profit. The scale of these abuses was appalling. It was reckoned that, since the advent of the Free State in 1885, the population of the Congo had declined by 70 per cent, from around 30 million to 9 million. With this, the mask of good intentions, humanitarian concern and civilizing purpose which King Leopold had cultivated for so many years at last fell away.

Atrocity and abuse

When charges of atrocity and abuse were first laid against the Congo Free State around the turn of the twentieth century, Leopold felt deeply hurt. As the attacks escalated to nearly worldwide proportions, however, he thought he could see the reason behind them: he believed it was a British plot, backed by King Edward VII and powered by malicious jealousy, all of it designed to destroy the Congo Free State and, with it, the great achievement of his life and effort.

This conspiracy theory intensified in Leopold's mind in 1903, when Sir Roger Casement, British consul to the Congo, was sent to the Free State to investigate the situation. Casement discovered a litany of horrors, including one young man whose

KING LEOPOLD III (1901–1983)

On 16 July 1951, the unpopular King Leopold III of Belgium (third from left), signed an instrument of abdication in favour of his son, Baudouin (far right).

The sons of hero-kings have always had a hard time matching the renown of their fathers, and King Leopold III, who succeeded to the throne of Belgium in 1934, was certainly one of them. His father, Albert I, had made himself a national hero in Belgium during World War I. As his son and successor, Leopold III never managed to live up to his father s shining example. Instead, his reign was marked by painful controversies. The last of them cost him his throne.

In 1926, Leopold married the beautiful Princess Astrid of Sweden. Astrid was instantly popular in Belgium, for her informality, her grace and her refusal to follow strict royal protocol and so hold herself aloof from the adoring masses who flocked to her every public appearance. Leopold and Astrid had a daughter and two sons, and were expecting a fourth child in 1935. On 29 August of that year, Leopold was driving along a narrow, winding road near their villa on the shores of Lake Lucerne in Switzerland. Without warning, he suddenly lost control of his car. The vehicle veered off the road and plunged down a ravine before crashing into the lake. Astrid, aged 29, was killed and her unborn child with her.

The effect on the people of Belgium was comparable to the response in 1997 to the death of Diana, Princess of Wales, who was also killed prematurely in a car crash. The mourning crowds were inconsolable in their grief as Astrid was buried in the royal vault at the Church of our Lady in Laeken. Her tomb became a focus of pilgrimage for many years afterwards. In a sense, the Belgians never stopped grieving for Astrid and laid the blame for her death on her husband. Leopold became seriously unpopular in Belgium and was never able to repair his reputation.

The Belgians never forgave Leopold III after his beautiful Swedish wife, Queen Astrid, was killed in 1935 in a car accident while he was at the wheel.

ACCUSED OF COWARDICE

This hostility came home to roost after the forces of Nazi Germany invaded Belgium in 1940, soon after the commencement of World War II. The Belgian army was totally outmatched by the German Blitzkrieg – lightning war – but they nevertheless managed to keep the invaders at bay for more than two weeks. The Belgians were prevented from fighting to the finish by King Leopold, who realized that his people were likely to be slaughtered and their towns and villages pulverized if the hostilities continued. Leopold capitulated to the invaders and, although he refused to cooperate with them, he was still accused of cowardice and treason by British Prime Minister Winston Churchill and Churchill's French counterpart, Paul Reynaud.

The mud stuck. The Belgians were convinced that Leopold had betrayed them, and their attitude was reflected by his government ministers, who fled to London to escape the invaders. There, they set up a government-in-exile, but refused to accept Leopold s rights as their king.

Leopold spent the rest of the war as a prisoner of the Germans. Then, on 11 September 1941, he created yet another controversy, this time by marrying again. His second wife, Liliane Baels, afterwards created Princess Liliane, became a hated figure in Belgium, where her marriage was regarded as an affront to the late, still lamented Astrid.

The war ended in 1945, but Leopold did not immediately resume his reign in Belgium. The Germans had moved the king and his family to a fort in Saxony in 1944; a few months before hostilities ended, they were moved again, this time to Salzburg in Austria. After being liberated by the US Army, the king chose not to return to Belgium immediately. Instead, he removed to Switzerland, where he remained for the next six years until his position in Belgium was sorted out.

In 1946, a special Commission of Enquiry found Leopold not guilty of treason, but his loyalty to his country remained in doubt and the intense bitterness against him failed to diminish. In 1950, a referendum was held to decide whether the Belgians wanted their king back or not. The results looked hopeful: around 57 per cent of Belgians voted for him to return, but the story was quite different after Leopold arrived home. He was greeted with strikes and vociferous protests in which several demonstrators were killed. Civil war seemed about to break out between Leopold s supporters and his enemies. Rather than divide the country and damage the monarchy, Leopold decided to abdicate in favour of his eldest son, Baudouin, who succeeded to the throne on 16 July 1951. Leopold died in 1983, aged 82.

hands had been beaten off with the butt ends of rifles against a tree . In another village, three small children, a youth and an old woman had had their right hands cut off at the wrist.

'I visited two large villages in the interior,' Casement reported. I found that fully half the population now consisted of refugees...I saw and questioned several groups of these people...They went on to declare, when asked why they had fled [their district] that they had endured such ill treatment at the hands of the government soldiers...that life had become intolerable, that nothing had remained for them at home but to be killed for failure to bring in a certain amount of rubber, or to die from starvation or exposure in their attempts to satisfy the demands made upon them ...'

Casement had intended to probe further into the interior of the Congo, but by November 1903,

six months after his arrival, he had seen and heard enough. He returned to Britain to present his report to the Foreign Office.

With the Casement report, another similar opinion from Evelyn Baring, 1st Earl of Cromer, who also visited Free State territory in 1903, and the conclusions of a British commission of inquiry in 1905, the evidence against Leopold was piled too high for him to be saved by any denials, protests or obfuscations.

The government intervenes

This far, the Belgian government had remained in the wings. But the scandal of the Congo and the

This document, signed by King Leopold II in 1906, ended his control of the Congo and allowed the Belgian government to annex the territory that he believed was his private possession.

1860 — 1908

exploitation and maltreatment that had taken place there were so abominable that it could no longer afford to stand aside. There was talk of removing the Congo from the king s jurisdiction and annexing it to Belgium if he could not or would not introduce fundamental humanitarian reforms to put the situation right. No one seriously believed that the autocratic Leopold would backtrack as far as this, if at all. It would not be an easy task to prise his private colony from his grasp, as Leopold registered a furious reaction to a motion passed in the Belgian parliament in 1906 to examine the legal framework for annexation

'My rights over the Congo cannot be shared,' the king announced. They are the fruit of my own labours the adversaries of the Congo are pressing for immediate annexation. These persons no doubt hope that a change of regime would effectively sabotage the work now in progress and would enable them to reap some rich booty from the wreckage.'

Leopold had underestimated his liberal-minded enemies in the Belgian parliament. They wanted him out of the Congo forthwith. A similar debate in the British Parliament four months later reached the same conclusion and for the same reasons. There had been no real sign that any reforms were going to be introduced in the Congo or that the condition of the native inhabitants would in any way be mitigated. Then, on 13 December 1906, Leopold suddenly changed tack and announced that he was in favour of annexation and wanted it to take place soon.

The scandal of the Congo and the exploitation and maltreatment that had taken place there were so abominable that it could no longer afford to stand aside.

This sudden about-turn was largely due to news that the United States might soon intervene in the Congo affair. Leopold had always valued the approval and support of the United States, and, in an effort to make sure of it, he invited American millionaires, such as Daniel Guggenheim, to invest money in the development of a stretch of territory covering more

than one million hectares at the mouth of the River Kasai, a tributary of the Congo River. By this means, Leopold hoped to tie up the wealth of the Free State in foreign companies, invest in those companies and, through them, retain control of the Congo s money supply. If, however, the Americans were to side with his European enemies, it would destroy Leopold's plan.

Leopold loses his hold

The plan failed anyway. Once again, Leopold had underestimated the strength of the opposition to his Congo policy. The Americans, like the British and also the Germans, were horrified at the cruelties and abuses that had taken place in the Congo and refused to support Leopold. With this powerful united front ranged against him, Leopold knew the end when he saw it. On 14 December 1906, the Belgian Prime Minister, Baron Beernaert Smet de Naeyer, announced that his government was now committed to the annexation of the Congo. For a while, Leopold kept up the fiction that only he had rights over the Congo, but it was a fantasy that soon faded when, on 18 October 1908, he was obliged to sign the Treaty of Cession which finally took the Congo away from him and made it a Belgian colony.

Belgium was now the imperial power Leopold had wanted it to be, but the price, for him, was a new status as a pariah. He was detested by the Congolese and spurned by his government and people, by public opinion abroad and by his fellow monarchs and their ministers, diplomats and parliaments. On a personal level, Leopold was also estranged from his wife and two of his three daughters.

Only one person in the world, it seemed, wanted to know the King of the Belgians. Blanche Delacroix, who became Leopold's mistress in 1900 and later gave birth to his two sons, brought him some happiness, but their affair also incurred resentment among the Catholic Belgians, whose strict morality had no room for irregular liaisons.

Despised even in death

Leopold was nearly 75 years of age when he lost the Congo Free State. It was a traumatic experience that he did not survive for long. In early December 1909, he became seriously ill with an intestinal blockage. No drugs or other treatment succeeded in shifting it and Leopold realized that he was dying. He

Belgium was now the imperial power Leopold had wanted it to be, but the price, for him, was a new status as a pariah. He was detested by the Congolese and spurned by his government and people.

summoned his priest, Father Coorean and married his mistress Blanche Delacroix, whom he had created Baroness de Vaughan. A few days later, Leopold died and Blanche, who had stayed with him to the end, was led away in floods of tears.

A month before his death, Leopold had given instructions that his funeral should be a simple affair, without pomp or show, and no procession following his cortège. It was feared, though, that a humble burial would be interpreted as an insult to the dead king and a last cruel barb from his successor, his nephew Albert, and his government.

Instead, Leopold's wishes were ignored. He lay in state for two days at the royal palace in Brussels and was afterwards given the full state funeral that was appropriate for his high position. All the same, the hostility and disgust Leopold had aroused played its part in the ceremony. His enemies among the crowd watching his funeral procession were determined to have the last word. Some onlookers booed as his cortège passed by, and others, it was said, spat at his coffin. No one could have been more detested than that.

Leopold II was so detested by his subjects in Belgium that some of them booed and spat at his coffin during his funeral procession in 1909. This illustration shows him on his deathbed.

KING ALBERT II AND HIS ILLEGITIMATE DAUGHTER

For at least half a century after the scandals and controversies surrounding King Leopold III, the Belgian royal family carefully cultivated a respectable, even staid, image that made them too dull for sensational media interest.

Then, in October 1999, a sex scandal broke with a story that King Albert II had sired an illegitimate daughter, born in 1968. There was widespread television coverage and, in Britain, *The Times* splashed the news across its front page.

'This is an earthquake for royalty,' one newspaper editor commented. 'For the first time in our history, the Belgian media has looked through the keyhole of the royal palace.'

If it were an earthquake, then the Belgian royal family did their best to fend off the aftershocks and prevent too many media revelations. Nevertheless, the press did discover enough to identify Albert's illegitimate daughter as Delphine Boel, a sculptor and artist living in London's Portobello Road. Delphine's mother, the Belgian aristocrat Baroness Sybille de Selys Longchamps, married a wealthy industrialist after Delphine's birth when her rumoured royal father was heir to his brother, the late King Baudouin. Albert succeeded him in 1993.

After the first burst of publicity, however, everyone involved – Baroness Sybille, Delphine and the Belgian royal palace press office – remained very close-mouthed about the affair. The palace dismissed the story as 'malevolent gossip' and Albert denied that Delphine was his daughter. There has been no formal proof, and no paternity test has ever been carried out, but in recent years Delphine has sought to be acknowledged by Albert as his daughter.

Delphine Boel (right) the illegitimate daughter of King Albert II of Belgium, on a shopping trip with her mother the Baroness Sybille de Selys Longchamps (left) in 1999.

THE GRIMALDIS OF MONACO

**The Grimaldis of Monaco – Prince Rainier III, his wife, the former Hollywood film
star Grace Kelly, and their three children – formed another royal family
who have kept rumour mongers and the popular press well fed with salacious
gossip, innuendo and sensation.**

◆

When it was not the romantic adventures of Rainier and Grace, it was the antics of their two daughters, Caroline and Stephanie, both of whom became pregnant first and married afterwards. Either that or the spotlight was on their brother Albert, the present ruler of the tiny Mediterranean principality, whose sexual orientation was considered suspect as he aged, but remained unwed.

**Left and above: Prince Rainier and actress Grace Kelly at her
parents' home after their engagement was announced on 5
January 1956. Kelly gave up her successful Hollywood film career
when she married Rainier in 1956.**

The irony of the Grimaldi story derives from the convincing but false snow-white image that Hollywood manufactured for the beautiful blonde Grace Kelly, who was a star turn of Tinseltown during the 1950s. She was presented as a virginal Roman Catholic who was far too scrupulous to 'play around' and a young woman who avoided all the temptations, sexual and otherwise, offered by the glamorous movie capital. Before Grace married Prince Rainier in a so-called 'fairytale' wedding in Monaco, her record was apparently checked for any scandals, affairs or less than respectable boyfriends. Anything untoward might have ruined Grace's chance of marrying Rainier: as a reigning prince, he could not afford a wife, the future mother of his heirs, who had a suspect past. But nothing incriminating was discovered, or so it was reported, and the wedding duly took place in Monaco on 19 April 1956.

The truth beneath the image

Subsequently, the report turned out to be one of the greatest cover-ups of all time. The truth about Grace's life before Rainier came from an incontrovertible source – her mother, Margaret Kelly, who provided the press with the low-down on her daughter's affairs. So many lovers were involved that there was enough information for a 10-part series, entitled 'My Daughter Grace Kelly – Her Life and Romances', which appeared in newspapers right across America. There was no shortage of famous names: the cast list for the series included almost every male star in Hollywood, married

> **Her mother, Margaret Kelly, provided the press with the low-down on her daughter's affairs. There was no shortage of famous names: the list included almost every male star in Hollywood, married or single...**

or single, who made films there in the early 1950s.

Gary Cooper, Bing Crosby, William Holden, Ray Milland, Frank Sinatra and David Niven were among them. So was Clark Gable, whom Grace seduced during the making of the film *Mogambo* in 1952. 'What else do you do when you're alone with Clark Gable in Africa?' she reputedly commented. Cary Grant had an on-again, off-again affair with Grace for seven years. Alfred Hitchcock, the renowned director of Hollywood thrillers, was also in love with Grace. He lived a mile away from her home in Laurel Canyon, Los Angeles, and provided himself with a powerful telescope so that he could see Grace undress next to a window left open for the purpose.

Other 'dubious' characters were also listed as Grace's lovers. One was the French film star Jean-Pierre Aumont, who, Grace came to suspect, wanted to promote his own career by appearing with her in

THE NEED FOR HEIRS

Rainier was in the United States when Margaret Kelly's revelations appeared in the American press. He arrived late in 1955, ostensibly to have a medical check-up. In reality, Rainier wanted to see Grace and meet her family. It was already well known that the 32-year-old prince was looking for a suitable wife for political as well as personal reasons: if he failed to marry and died without a legitimate heir, Monaco would be absorbed by France in accordance with a treaty signed in 1918. This was a fate that Rainier believed it was his duty to prevent. He had hoped to marry the French model and actress Gisèle Pascal, but was forced to break with her on learning that a physical examination showed she was unable to bear children. The diagnosis proved incorrect when Pascal gave birth to a child in 1962. Rainier was heartbroken, but by then it was too late. Rainier had already been married to Grace Kelly for five years.

'sensational' paparazzi-style photographs. Another was the fashion designer Oleg Cassini. Shortly after they first met in 1955, Grace and Cassini announced their decision to marry and were obviously in a hurry to do so. It transpired that the reason for their haste was that Grace was pregnant. Grace's parents did not approve of Cassini, who was 16 years older than their daughter and had already been married and divorced twice. Grace bowed to parental pressure and, instead of marrying Cassini, she had an abortion. Afterwards, Cassini always refused to talk about it. 'It's too delicate a matter,' he would say. 'Let people think what they want to think.'

The hunt for a suitable bride

In 1955, there were several names on Rainier's list of potential brides, but Rainier believed that Grace Kelly filled the bill best – for her looks, her elegance, her fame and her fertility, which was proved by a routine test.

Right: Grace Kelly dancing with the singer and film star Bing Crosby in her last Hollywood film, *High Society*. Crosby was allegedly one of Grace's numerous lovers.

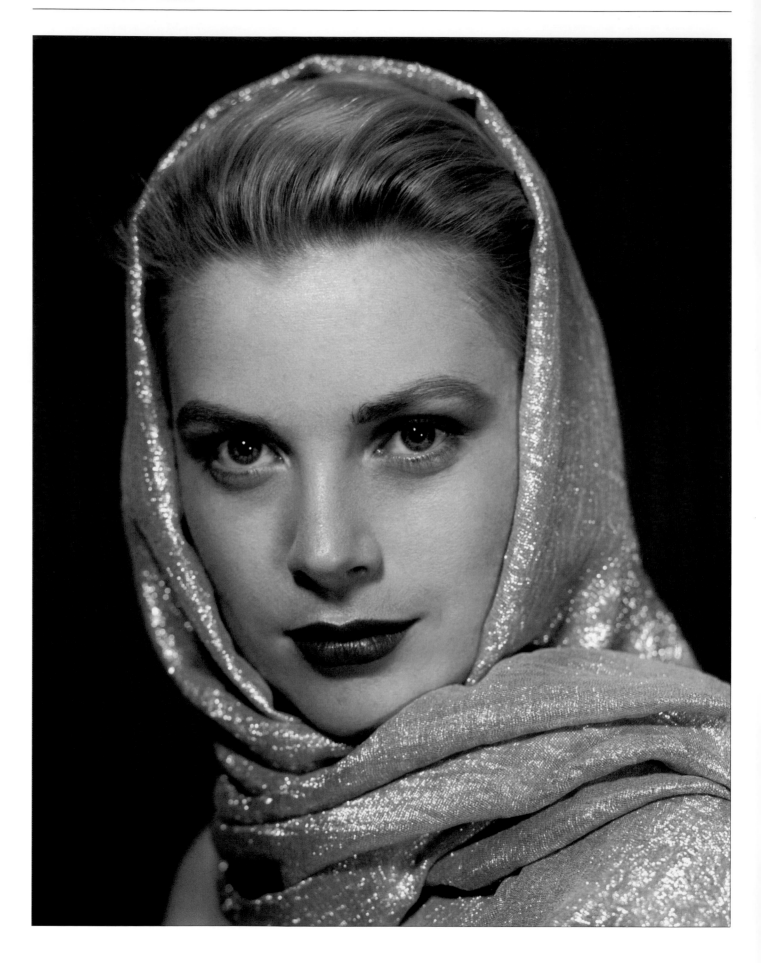

Rainier and Grace first met in September 1955, when she was attending the Cannes Film Festival. Rainier was surprised that, instead of the hard-faced glamour queen he expected, Grace was a pleasant, ladylike young woman with excellent manners, but without the demanding temperament usually associated with film stars. His opinion was confirmed by their meetings in the United States, including several days which Rainier spent on the film set where Grace was making her last movie, *High Society*. Besides Grace, the film starred two of her former lovers, Bing Crosby and Frank Sinatra, but it seems that Rainier had been so completely taken in by Grace's virginal 'made in Hollywood' persona that he noticed nothing to suggest

---

MGM could do nothing to prevent the Kelly series appearing In American newspapers, but it did manage to get hold of all the copies intended for Europe. The articles were heavily edited to excise any coverage of sexual or other misdemeanours.

---

that they were more than her fellow film stars.

Jack Kelly, Grace's tough, outspoken father proved harder to take. Basically, Grace's parents did not approve of Rainier, who, though royal, they considered not quite good enough for their daughter. Jack also believed that Rainier was after Grace's money and later went ballistic when the prince asked for a dowry of US$2,000,000. In addition, Jack Kelly was under the impression that Rainier was Prince of Morocco, not Monaco, and became alarmed at the thought that Grace meant to marry a man from this Muslim country in northwest Africa.

'I don't want any broken-down prince who's head of a country that nobody ever heard of marrying my

On the face of it, Grace Kelly lived up to the reputation for purity which her studio, MGM, had created for her. But the face of it was deceptive.

daughter.' was how Jack Kelly put it. He eventually calmed down and paid the $2,000,000 dowry because a royal, even a 'broken-down prince', went one better as a son-in-law than had been managed by other socially ambitious families in the snobbish world of American high society.

A hasty cover-up

Of course, Margaret Kelly's series of articles might have wrecked the whole arrangement and, even though he was not directly involved, the publicity placed Rainer too close for comfort to a potential scandal. He soon departed the United States, heading for Monaco and leaving Grace, her family and Metro-Goldwyn-Mayer, her studio, to try to repair the damage. This was achieved by some fast thinking on the part of MGM executives, who fortunately did not have to contend with international television and radio, computer links, Internet websites and other means of rapidly spreading scandalous news around the world. MGM could do nothing to prevent the Kelly series appearing in American newspapers, but it did manage to get hold of all the copies intended for Europe. The articles were heavily edited to excise any coverage of sexual or other misdemeanours. They were then dispatched across the Atlantic to convince European newspaper readers that Prince Rainier's bride was as she should be: *virgo intacta*.

The arrival of children

Any fallout from this close shave with the truth vanished shortly after the wedding, when it was announced that Princess Grace of Monaco was expecting her first child. The Monagesques celebrated as never before, as an heir for Prince Rainier meant freedom from French laws and, above all, French taxes. The couple's first daughter, Princess Caroline, was born on 23 January 1957, and was followed on 14 March of the ensuing year by a son, Prince Albert. In two years, Rainier and Grace had managed to produce 'an heir and a spare', and the first purpose of their marriage was accomplished. So were other, social, purposes. The former film star became president of the Red Cross of Monaco and the Garden Club of Monaco, and created the Princess Grace Foundation, which worked to involve young people in the creative arts and set up scholarships for suitable students.

Grace gave birth to a third child, Princess Stephanie, on 1 February 1965, but by then, it appears, her marriage to Rainier was already in trouble and had been for some time. In 1960, when Grace went home to Philadelphia to be with her father, who was dying of stomach cancer, Rainier was seen out on dates with one of her ladies-in-waiting. When Grace returned, she demanded to know what had been going on. Rainier denied everything. The lady-in-waiting was dismissed, but that was not enough for Grace. She invited a former film star lover, Cary Grant, to Monaco, and saw to it that photographers were at the airport to see the two of them kissing. From the shots that appeared in the newspapers, it seemed clear that Grace was doing much more than welcoming an old friend. Rainier fired back and banned cinemas in Monaco from screening the 1955 film *To Catch a Thief*, which featured Grace and Grant in love scenes.

> **Grace invited a former film star lover, Cary Grant, to Monaco, and saw to it that photographers were at the airport to see the two of them kissing. From the shots that appeared in the newspapers, it seemed clear that Grace was doing much more than welcoming an old friend.**

After this, the marriage of Rainier and Grace gradually became a game of scoring points, one over the other, to show which of them had the upper hand. Grace had become extremely popular and greatly loved in Monaco. Rainier began to feel that he was playing second fiddle and grew jealous. Friends noticed that he tended to push her into the background, where before he had consulted her on matters to do with the government of Monaco.

A marriage unravelled

A spate of rumours arose, suggesting that the 'fairytale marriage' was on the rocks. Rainier and Grace were sleeping in separate bedrooms. There was talk of 'his

and hers' love affairs. The children, it appeared, took up so much of Grace's time and attention that she had little or none left for Rainier. He resented this. It was true, though, that Grace began to spend more and more time away from Monaco on visits to her family or to Paris with the children. Before long, Grace's trips to Paris were no longer just visits: she was living in the French capital for long periods of time while Rainier remained in Monaco and made a life of his own there. It seems that in Paris, Grace, now in her late forties, was 'supplied' with young men around 10 or 15 years younger than herself.

Paris was not the only place to find these 'toy boys', as Grace's friends called her youthful lovers. While in New York, Grace met a Swedish actor named Per Mattson, 33, who was at once invited to her hotel room and, apparently, remained there until 5 a.m. next morning.

After little more than 20 years of marriage, the relationship between Rainier and Grace had unravelled so far that communication between them was virtually nonexistent. Grace had become a saddened figure, drinking too much, eating too much and growing fat. In the spring of 1978, she was staying at an Oxfordshire farmhouse owned by the English author Gwen Robyns, where the two of them were co-writing Grace's *Book of Flowers*. To Robyns's amazement, Grace made a startling relevation. 'I have begun to feel quite sad being married to Rainier,' she said. 'It's not what I'd hoped for.' Asked why she felt that way, Grace replied, 'He's not really interested in me.'

A united front

There was, though, one situation where Rainier and Grace, so distant in other ways, worked as a team, and that was where their children were involved. In 1978, the couple were faced with the sort of situation all parents dread: their elder daughter, Caroline, now aged 21, wanted to marry a man who, her parents were convinced, would be disastrous for her. Caroline had always been a 'wild child', headstrong and rebellious. She smoked in public, drank heavily and was frequently pictured in nightclubs and bars with rock stars or raffish young men of dubious respectability. Rainier and Grace scanned the royal families of

Right: Rainier and Grace with their 14-month old daughter Stephanie in 1966. Stephanie was their third child, following Princess Caroline, born in 1957 and Prince Albert, born 1958.

Europe, desperate to find a prince capable of reining in their wayward daughter. Charles, Prince of Wales, was one suggestion, but he was not interested. Unsurprisingly, as Caroline was obviously too hot to handle. Nor was anyone else.

Playboy banker

Caroline, meanwhile, had been making her own arrangements. She had fallen for a Paris *boulevardier*, the wealthy playboy banker Philippe Junot, whom she met in 1976. Junot, 17 years older than Caroline, was still 'playing the field' at age 36. In addition to womanizing on a grand scale, he was interested in fast cars and racehorses, the typical pastimes of the pleasure-seeker. Rainier and Grace were aghast. They tried separating the couple by sending Caroline to the United States. But out of sight was not out of mind. Junot followed and the romance resumed. Next, Grace delivered an ultimatum: 'Leave or marry this man who is not for you!' she told Caroline. The effect was nil. Then Caroline was pictured – topless – on a yacht with Junot. Imagining, correctly as it turned out, that Caroline and Junot were already sleeping together, her parents finally gave up in despair. Rainier confessed to Grace that he was heartbroken. 'I know this marriage will end in tears,' he said.

Rainier and Grace scanned the royal families of Europe, desperate to find a prince capable of reining in their wayward daughter.

And so it did. Married on 28 June 1978, Caroline and Junot were divorced just over two years later. The trouble had started on their honeymoon in the Polynesian Islands, after Caroline discovered that her new husband had invited press photographers to join them. Junot intended to sell the pictures to the world press, which was avid to print them. The trouble continued when it became clear that Junot had no intention of letting his marriage get in the way of the 'good time' he had been enjoying for years. The paparazzi photographers were soon nosing out the haunts where they could take pictures of Junot romancing other women. Before long, Caroline was having assignations of her own and, again, the paparazzi were there to provide the pictures. Husband and wife accused each other of adultery, and the marriage finally ended in mutual recrimination on 9 October 1980.

Grace's sudden death

Some two years later, on 14 September 1982, Princess Grace died, aged 52, after suffering a cerebral haemorrhage. She was driving back to Monaco along a winding mountain road that led from the royal retreat at Roc Angel. Grace's younger daughter, Stephanie, aged 17, was with her when she lost control of their car. It left the road and plunged more than 30 metres down the mountainside. Stephanie was injured, but

survived, although in later years the long-term effects of shock and grief seem to have increased the 'wild child' tendency she shared with her elder sister.

Despite the chill that had lain over their marriage for some years, Rainier was devastated at the unexpected death of his wife.

'My life will never be the same again,' he said. 'Without Grace, none of it matters to me now. It's all meaningless. My God, it's all meaningless.' And he hid his face in his hands and wept. He never really recovered and 20 years later confessed that he still felt the same about Grace's death as when he had first learned of it.

In 1978, Princess Caroline, 21, married the first of her three husbands, the playboy Philippe Junot, 38. The marriage did not last long. The couple were divorced in 1980.

Rainier, who survived Grace by 23 years, aged rapidly after she died, becoming a white-haired old man before he reached the age of 60. He never remarried, nor was he ever likely to.

The princess marries again

In contrast to her father, Caroline *did* marry again, on 29 December 1983. Her second husband, Stefano Casiraghi, was the heir to an Italian oil fortune.

Casiraghi was three years younger than Caroline, but he was a strong personality who, at long last, managed to keep the princess in order. Caroline was already pregnant when she married Casiraghi, a fact which pained her conventionally minded father. After the Philippe Junot fiasco, however, it was a relief for Rainier to know that here was a husband who truly cared for his daughter. It was said of Casiraghi, who was created Duke of Monaco after the marriage, that Caroline felt 'safe' with him. He was certainly the love of her life. But tragedy was not yet done with the

Prince Rainier, shown at Princess Grace's funeral in 1982, never recovered from the shock and pain of losing her and aged rapidly in the years that followed.

Grimaldi family, who were said to be subject to a curse that meant they would never have long marriages.

On 3 October 1990, close on seven years after he had married Caroline, Casiraghi, a world powerboat champion, was taking part in a race near Cap Ferrat when his boat foundered and sank. Casiraghi, aged 30, was killed. Caroline, who had left for a visit to Paris the previous day, became distraught when she heard the news. She returned to Monaco immediately. Rainier was scarcely less affected: he collapsed in tears and virtually went into shock on hearing of the death of the son-in-law he had come to regard as a son.

Caroline mourned her young husband for many years, but she still had three young children to care for. Years later, she explained how she faced up to the task.

Despite the chill that had lain over their marriage for some years, Rainier was devastated at the unexpected death of his wife.

'Strength comes when you're in a very narrow valley and have no way of turning back,' Caroline explained. 'You just have to choose to live your life. I had to go on.'

Stephanie now the 'wild child'

Caroline, by now aged 33, had obviously matured well beyond the tempestuous rebel she had been in her youth. Her sister Stephanie, however, eight years younger, was misbehaving in ways that made the Caroline controversies seem mild. Stephanie had been profoundly affected by her mother's death. The broken bones she suffered healed soon enough, but the emotional trauma remained. She was, after all, in the car with Grace when it crashed, and subsequent rumour suggested that she had been driving. This made her appear guilty, something that Stephanie resented, yet at the same time seemed to believe.

Like many people who escape

Stefano Casiraghi, Princess Caroline's second husband, was a successful businessman and sportsman. The couple, who married on 29 December 1983, had three children. Casiraghi was killed in 1990 in a boating accident.

Tragedy was not yet done with the Grimaldi family, who were said to be subject to a curse that meant they would never have long marriages.

death in dramatic circumstances while others die, Stephanie seemed to lose all sense of self-preservation – a process usually known as 'living life to the full'. She did not bother about her own wellbeing or the feelings of her family, and became unmindful of the future.

She frequently appeared drunk in public. She took drugs. She dated several 'undesirable' young men and, in 1985, signed a modelling contract with a model agency in Paris and another in the United States. Rainier was in despair. He took the old-fashioned view that princesses should not stoop to modelling, but Stephanie went ahead anyway, and posed for fashion pictures that appeared *Vogue, Rolling Stone, Elle* and other international publications.

Next, complaining of the pressures that went with her new job, Stephanie checked in to the Belvedere Clinic in Paris, which specialized in detoxifying its clients.

Rainier, Caroline and her brother,

Princess Caroline, photographed on 20 March 2004, attending the Rose Ball a charity event, in Monte Carlo. In 1999 she had married again: her third husband was Prince Ernst of Hanover.

Albert, descended on her and persuaded her to give up modelling.

Stephanie went on to design swimwear, then became a recording artist. Her single, entitled 'Irresistible', scored immense success in Europe, especially in France, where more than a million copies were sold. The recording fully exploited Stephanie's 'bad girl' image and went with a video that Rainier considered 'provocative'. What it also exploited, of course, was Stephanie's royal status, something which, ironically, she was trying to shed. She went on trying, causing shock waves with her personal life. In 1987, while on holiday in Mauritius, she was photographed topless while embracing her current boyfriend, Mario Oliver, a convicted rapist.

Princess Stephanie tried several times to separate herself from her royal status and make a life of her own. One of her attempts was becoming a pop music star: here she is on 14 October 1985 recording a song called *Irresistible*.

The two of them were soon living together in Hollywood, in a mansion in Benedict Canyon. Stephanie had marriage in mind, but as soon as he heard of it Rainier put his foot down at last. He threatened to deprive Stephanie of her royal title if she dared to marry Mario. As things turned out, Rainier need not have bothered. By mid-1988, Stephanie's romance with Mario was over, and all she had to remember him by were his initials tattooed on her bottom. The initials were removed the painful way, by laser surgery.

Running off to join the circus

Far from being cured of her excesses following the failure of her marriage to Daniel Ducruet (see box), Stephanie went on as she had begun. In 1998, she

Princess Stephanie, aged 25, photographed in 1990 when she was still creating one scandal after another with her outrageous behaviour.

> **Like many people who escape death in dramatic circumstances while others die, Stephanie seemed to lose all sense of self-preservation – a process usually known as 'living life to the full'.**

gave birth to her third child, a daughter, again out of wedlock. She refused to reveal who the father was, but gossip and suspicion picked out Jean-Raymond Gottlieb, another security guard at Rainier's palace. In 2000, Stephanie announced a fresh romance; the new man in her life was Franco Knie, who co-owned the popular Circus Knie. Stephanie met Franco while on royal duty, presenting him with the Silver Clown Award for the Best Animal Trainer at the Circus Festival. The twice-married Franco, 47 years old, left his wife for Stephanie. For a year, the princess lived in a trailer with Franco and her three children, following the Circus Knie from one engagement to the next. Stephanie even allowed her elder daughter, Pauline, aged six, to perform with elephants in the circus ring while her eight-year-old brother Louis learned to be a juggler.

Final acceptance

Stephanie had long wished to live her life as someone other than a Princess of Monaco, and her year with the Circus Knie gave her the chance. But as so often with Stephanie, it did not last long. By 2002, her affair with Franco was at an end. For a while, she remained in the circus world by marrying one of the Circus Knie acrobats, Adans Lopez Perez, in 2003. This marriage also foundered and, after it ended in 2004, Stephanie returned home to live in Monaco. She was now aged 37 and, after some 20 years of trying to escape her royalty, it seems that she had at last accepted it. Rather late in the day, but very welcome to her long-suffering father, Rainier, she was prepared to settle down, do her duty and leave her 'wild child' image far behind.

'I've stopped trying to change the game, stopped trying to change people,' Stephanie admitted. 'You build your own way in life with everything that is thrown at you, and make what you can from it.... I don't look back any more and I don't have any regrets.'

THE PRINCESS AND THE BODYGUARD

Stephanie's two liaisons following her abortive relationship with Mario Oliver, one of them to a man who had been jailed for fraud, were similarly brief. She then met Daniel Ducruet, a palace guard hired by Rainier to guard his son, Albert. Ducruet was a tall, dark-haired and handsome athlete and bodybuilder, covered in tattoos. He had been previously married and, in 1991, had a son by a former girfriend. The

same year, Rainier chose him to guard Stephanie during her tour to publicize her record album.

It was not a good idea. Stephanie and Ducruet began an affair and she gave birth to two children, in 1992 and 1994. Significantly, neither Rainier nor Caroline, nor her brother, Albert, visited her in hospital on either occasion. But they were there when Stephanie and Ducruet married in 1995. For a while, the couple seemed happy, and Stephanie declared in an interview, 'He really loves me for myself. He has proved to me that I am the one who counts.' Her family had some hope that Stephanie, now 30 years old, was starting to settle down at last.

The hope was brief. In 1996, Ducruet was photographed enjoying a poolside 'sex romp' with Muriel 'Fifi' Houteman at Villefranche-sur-Mer. Ducruet claimed that he had been entrapped by Houteman – who had been Miss Bare Breasts of Belgium in 1995 – one of her lovers and a photographer. They had 'spiked' his drink with drugs, making it that much easier for Miss Bare Breasts to seduce him.

'My mistake has destroyed me!' Ducruet declared. 'I curse the day I met her,' he said of Houteman, but neither remorse nor the suspended prison sentences later handed down to the three conspirators was able to save him. Stephanie at once filed for divorce and the marriage ended before the year was out.

Daniel Ducruet, a tall, handsome athlete, was hired by Prince Rainier as Stephanie's bodyguard. He later became the father of her two children, born in 1992 and 1994. Stephanie and Ducruet married in 1995, but divorced the following year.

The good son

Prince Albert, Rainier's only son and heir, had always been a total contrast to his sisters, with their riotous behaviour and flamboyant social life. Albert was the 'good boy', pleasant, polite, widely touted as the most eligible bachelor in Europe, but seemingly uninterested in girls or the high life, and therefore hardly worth space in the gossip columns. The one thing about Albert that sparked press interest was his persistent failure to marry.

By 2002, when Albert was 44 and still showed no signs of taking a wife, Rainier decided he must secure the succession or risk Monaco returning to the jurisdiction of France. In that year, the Principality's constitution was changed to name Caroline as her brother's heir and, after her, her three children by her second marriage to Stefan Casiraghi and her then three-year-old daughter by her third marriage, in 1999, to Prince Ernst August V of Hanover.

Stephanie with her second husband, Adans Lopez Perez, circus acrobat. Married in 2003, the couple divorced in 2004.

Three years later, on 6 April 2005, Prince Rainier died, aged 81, and his son succeeded him as His Serene Highness Prince Albert II of Monaco. Almost at once, Albert made public two secrets he had been keeping for several years: he revealed that he had two children. The first was a daughter, born in 1991 to an American waitress, Tamara Rotolo. His other child was a son born in 2003 to Nicole Coste, a flight attendant who met Albert on an Air France flight in 1997. Neither of these children was eligible to succeed to the throne of Monaco, as both were illegitimate.

Then, in 2011, the 53-year-old monarch married 33-year-old Charlene Wittstock, a former Olympic swimmer for South Africa. In 2014, she gave birth to twins Jacques and Gabriella. Jacques is now first in line to the throne.

A happy ending?

With the unspectacular Albert in charge and his once untameable sisters calmed down and more mature, the time when Monaco was persistently embarrassed by its royal family could be at an end. For the Grimaldis, Albert's reign could also add a happy ending after so much trauma and tragedy in a 'fairytale' gone wrong.

The Grimaldi family on Monaco's National Day, 19 November, in 2006. The picture shows (left to right) Princess Caroline, her third husband Prince Ernst of Hanover, her brother Prince Albert, her elder son Andrea Casiraghi, and Princess Stephanie.

THE KINGS &
QUEENS OF ENGLAND

MAP OF GREAT BRITAIN
AND ASSOCIATED PLACES IN EUROPE

ATLANTIC OCEAN

NORTH SEA

Fort William
Balmoral Castle
Glencoe
SCOTLAND
Inveraray
Dunbar
Edinburgh

NORTHERN IRELAND

REPUBLIC OF IRELAND

R. Boyne

Middleham

Lancaster
York
Pontefract
Wakefield

Llantrisant
Anglesey
Conwy
Caernarfon
ENGLAND
Chester
Lincoln
Derby
Nottingham
Sandringham House
WALES
Leicester
Worcester
Warwick
Naseby
Brampton
Evesham
Althrop House
Framlingham
Edgehill
Milford Haven
Hereford
Tewkesbury
Gloucester
Oxford
St. Albans
Hoddeston
Berkeley
Stoke
Barnet
Bristol
Richmond
London
Windsor
Hampton Court
Taunton
Winchester
Dover
Devonshire
New Forest
Brighton
Calais
Cornwall
Portsmouth
Torbay
Isle of Wight

IRISH SEA

ENGLISH CHANNEL

Rouen
Falaise
Paris
Normandy
Brittany
Le Mans
Chinon
Poitou
Angoulême
Aquitaine

KEY TO THE SYMBOLS
USED THROUGHOUT THIS BOOK

The family trees at the start of each chapter show the relationships between persons mentioned in the text and are not intended to be comprehensive. The dates given for each monarch denote the period of their reign. The following symbols are used:

The Normans		Illegitimate	
The Plantagenets		Heir who did not succeed	
The Tudors		Crown won in battle	
The Stuarts		Usurper	
The Hanoverians		Abdicated	
The House of Saxe-Coburg-Gotha		Murdered	
The Windsors		Died in battle	
		Executed	

INTRODUCTION

✦

The British royal family is considered by many to be the most prestigious in the world.

Yet its sensational and often lurid past contains deeds so dark and dastardly that they were covered up and remained secret for centuries.

Over the last thousand years or so, many of the kings and queens of England have played their part in betrayals, regicides, plots, treason, atrocities, and revolts. The English throne has been usurped four times. There have been five pretenders to the crown, two of them impostors. Four kings have been forcibly deposed. All were subsequently murdered. One of them was publicly executed.

Kings and queens of England have been responsible for thousands of executions and deaths. Tudor king Henry VIII set out to exterminate every surviving member of the Plantagenets, the dynasty that preceded his own. And Henry's daughter, Queen Mary I, burned 300 Protestants at the stake.

English royalty was a regular target for conspiracies and assassination attempts. Queen Elizabeth I was at constant risk from plotters who wanted to kill her and replace her with her cousin, Mary, Queen of Scots. The Gunpowder Plot of 1605 was a Catholic conspiracy to blow up King James I, his government and the Houses of Parliament.

Two kings of England went mad. One was kidnapped, and another was mercilessly bullied by his own nobles. King Henry VIII, who married six times, hounded his first wife, Catherine of Aragon, to her death in 1536. Later, he executed his second and fifth wives.

While King George IV was Prince of Wales and heir to the throne, he incurred so many debts that he had

Henry VIII, shown here with Pope Leo X, was a sincere Roman Catholic, but that did not stop him from breaking his ties with Rome when the pope would not grant him a divorce.

to be bailed out – twice – by Parliament. His father, King George III, derived little pleasure from his family of 15 children, many of whom were enveloped in scandal. Two of his offspring were suspected of incest, and his sons provided him with an army of illegitimate grandchildren.

Queen Victoria and her husband, Prince Albert, tried to raise the moral standards of royalty, but they were frustrated by their eldest son, the future King Edward VII, who enjoyed nothing more than drinking, gambling and womanizing to excess.

In 1936 King Edward VIII nearly wrecked the monarchy when he abdicated to marry the unsuitable, twice-divorced Wallis Simpson. More recently, the royal family has been rocked to its foundations by the Charles and Diana scandals.

This book pulls no punches in telling the whole shameful story of royal deeds that were never intended to be revealed.

A detail from the invitation to the fireworks display held to celebrate the coronation of King Edward VII in 1902.

CONSPIRATORS AND CONQUERORS
A DIRTY BUSINESS

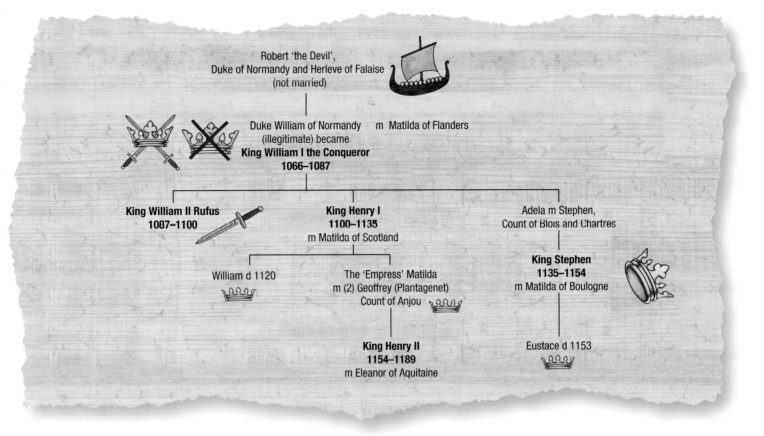

Robert 'the Devil',
Duke of Normandy and Herleve of Falaise
(not married)

Duke William of Normandy m Matilda of Flanders
(illegitimate) became
King William I the Conqueror
1066–1087

King William II Rufus   **King Henry I**   Adela m Stephen,
1087–1100   **1100–1135**   Count of Blois and Chartres
    m Matilda of Scotland

    King Stephen
William d 1120   The 'Empress' Matilda   **1135–1154**
    m (2) Geoffrey (Plantagenet)   m Matilda of Boulogne
    Count of Anjou

    King Henry II   Eustace d 1153
    1154–1189
    m Eleanor of Aquitaine

Exactly what happened in the New Forest in southern England on 2 August 1100, remains a mystery, despite the fact that it was broad daylight and there were several eyewitnesses.

◆

On that morning King William II, nicknamed Rufus for his red hair, red face, and violent temper, ate an early breakfast and set off for the forest, equipped with bows and arrows for a day's hunting. His close friend Walter Tirel went with him.

Once inside the forest, the royal hunting party spread out in search of prey. Tirel remained with the king and soon the beaters accompanying the hunt drove a herd of stags toward the pair. King William shot at them but missed. According to a witness named Knighton, the king shouted to Tirel: 'Draw, draw your bow for the devil's sake or it will be the worse for you!' It has long been accepted that Tirel did as he was told, but his arrow ricocheted off a tree, missing the stag and striking the king in the chest.

The English chronicler and historian William of Malmesbury, writing a few years later, described what happened next.

A late fifteenth-century portrayal of the death of William II. The King is shown lying on the ground with the fatal arrow in his chest at the top left of the picture.

An account of King William II's death from 'A Chronicle of England', published between 1300 and 1325. William sits on a bench, an arrow in his chest, but still, curiously enough, very much alive.

'On receiving the wound, the king uttered not a word; but breaking off the shaft of the weapon where it projected from his body, fell upon the wound, by which he accelerated his death.'

Horrified, Tirel rushed to the king, but he was dead. Now Tirel's only concern was to escape. He leapt onto his horse and spurred it on through the dense forest, galloping furiously without stopping until he reached the English Channel and crossed to France. From there, Tirel vehemently denied killing the king and continued to deny it for the rest of his life.

A royal death foretold

When news of the king's death spread, many people in Europe claimed they had experienced premonitions of the event. In Belgium, Abbot Hugh of Cluny revealed he had received a warning on the night of August 1 that the king of England would die the next day. A monk told that on 2 August, while his eyes were closed during prayer, he had had a vision of a man holding a piece of paper bearing the message 'King William is dead'. When the monk opened his eyes, the vision disappeared.

The circumstances of the king's death remained shrouded in secrecy. Tirel, the prime suspect, was never punished in any way, and most people were inclined to believe his denials. Yet no further investigations into the death took place, nor was any evidence ever submitted. So the death of King William II went down in history as a tragic accident.

A murder in the family

The story quickly spread that the king's death was really a murder that had been disguised as an accident. The disrespectful way in which the king's body was handled after the fatal hunt seems to point to a murder plot. A lowly charcoal burner named Purkiss was ordered to remove the corpse. Purkiss placed the king on a wooden cart and covered him with an old work cloth. Then he trundled the cart to Winchester Cathedral where William was hastily buried by the monks. This was certainly no funeral fit for a king.

Motives for murder

While Tirel was generally presumed innocent, there were several suspects who might indeed have wanted

King William dead. The king had never married, and the heirs to the throne were his two brothers: Duke Robert of Normandy, known as Curthose for his short

When news of the king's death spread, many people in Europe claimed they had experienced premonitions of the event.

legs, and Prince Henry, known as Beauclerc because he could read and write. Of the two, Henry was the more likely culprit. He had been one of the hunting party and had probably witnessed the king's death.

As he had been present at the grisly scene, Henry had had the opportunity to act quickly and grab what he most wanted – the throne of England – before Robert, or anyone else, could stop him. He wasted no time mourning his dead brother. Instead, he went straight to Winchester, where he seized the royal treasure, then raced the 60 miles to London and had himself crowned king. It was all over within three days. By 5 August, Henry was England's new sovereign.

Resentful and greedy, Henry had plenty of reasons for having wanted the king dead. When his father, King William I the Conqueror, had died in 1087, Henry had been overlooked and received neither titles nor land. Robert Curthose, on the other hand, was awarded the family duchy of Normandy, in France, and William was placed on the throne of England. All

Archers, seen here in a reenactment, were the 'artillery' of medieval armies. They could fire a barrage which filled the air with a mass of deadly barbs that could fell knights in chainmail – and kill their horses, too.

FACT *or* **FICTION**

A CULT KILLING?

MANY CHURCHMEN BELIEVED that William, who was upheld as a Christian king, was really a pagan – a practitioner of sorcery and witchcraft. In medieval times people were terrified of witchcraft, so much so that the *Anglo-Saxon Chronicle* dared not even hint at such inflammatory gossip. This was all due to William's grandfather, Robert, Duke of Normandy. The duke's father, it was believed, was the devil. That is why the duke was nicknamed Robert the Devil, making King William II the great-grandson of the devil.

EVIDENCE OF BLASPHEMY

He certainly acted in a devilish manner. He was a blasphemer and often swore 'by the devil'. Nor had he any respect for the Church. When he attended services, he spent his time doodling or gossiping with his courtiers. William was also homosexual. This was considered a scandalous sin in the eleventh century. One chronicler described William's 'camp' court in scathing terms:

'…then there was flowing hair and extravagant dress, and was invented the fashion of shoes with curved points; then the model for young men was to rival women in delicacy of person, to mind their gait, to walk with loose gesture and half naked….'

In 1094, Anselm, the Archbishop of Canterbury, publicly accused King William of sodomy and other 'unnatural sins of the flesh.' Most people tended to side with Anselm, who was later made a saint. With this in mind, it was easy to believe that the 'devil' king was indeed a secret pagan.

Centuries later, this belief formed part of a theory that William II was killed by a pagan cult that practiced royal sacrifice. In her book *The Witch Cult in Western Europe*, published in 1921, Margaret Alice Murray wrote that this cult was widespread throughout pre-Christian Europe. According to the author, the Norman family itself belonged to a cult that demanded the ritual killing of the monarch for the good of the community.

This seems in line with King William's strange behavior on the night before his death. He behaved as if he knew that he was going to be the target of a cult killing. On the evening of 1 August 1100, the king ate and drank more than usual and slept badly.

AN UNWELCOME GIFT

Next morning, William was given a surprise gift of six newly made arrows. He gave two of them to Walter Tirel, saying cryptically: 'Walter, take good care to carry out the orders I gave you.' Some have suggested that Tirel, too, belonged to the pagan cult. A monk named Serlo warned the king not to go hunting that day, but William ignored his advice. Minutes after he reached the forest, he was dead.

Sensational gossip about William's death continued for many years. In 1107, the tower of Winchester Cathedral collapsed. The fact that William was buried there was blamed for the disaster. God, it was said, had cursed the king for his many sins.

The twelfth century was a very superstitious time, in which the remains of holy men were believed to have supernatural powers. This 15th-century chronicle shows Norman knights at prayer before the relics of Saint Valery.

ROUGH JUSTICE

HENRY'S CRUELTY WAS LEGENDARY throughout the country. For instance, in 1118, he demonstrated his idea of justice when he refused to execute one Herbert, a treasurer in the royal household. Herbert had been plotting against Henry, but the king was fond of Herbert so, instead of executing him, he had him blinded and castrated. With a king capable of such rough justice, even powerful men such as the landowning barons thought it best to defer to his wishes.

A representation of King Henry I. Though more refined and educated than other Normans, he was just as brutal.

Henry received was £5,000 in silver. Although this was a huge amount of money in the eleventh century, it was not nearly enough for a cunning, hard-nosed prince who felt he had been wronged.

Robert Curthose was also suspected of wanting the king dead, but it is unlikely that he was involved in the affair. Robert dearly wished to rule England and had been deeply disappointed when his father chose William to succeed him on the English throne. After all, Robert was the elder brother. Twice Robert

---

Other than the Norman royal family there were many ordinary people who would have been glad to see King William II dead. They had good reason. The Norman conquest of England after 1066 had been a savage business.

---

had tried to seize the kingdom – at the start of King William II's reign in 1087, and again in 1088 – and twice he had failed.

But William the Conqueror had had good reason for passing Robert over. William had won his crown at the battle of Hastings in 1066, and from then on ruled England by force. He considered Robert weak and

easily led. It would have been easy for his stronger-willed barons to get the better of him – and that was the last thing William the Conqueror had in mind. The Conqueror wanted a brute like himself to succeed him. That brute was not Robert. It was William.

Ultimately the wily Henry I found it easy to outwit Robert. At the time of William II's death in the New Forest, Robert had been halfway across the world in the Holy Land, fighting in the crusades. He returned to find his younger brother well and truly in the saddle. Besides claiming the throne, Henry had married Matilda, daughter of King Malcolm III of Scotland, who would soon be pregnant with their first child, the heir to Henry's throne.

There was no place for Robert at court, and eventually Henry imprisoned him for life until his death in 1134 at the age of 81. Robert never tried to escape, and spent his time learning Welsh and writing poetry.

Justice for the people

Other than the Norman royal family there were many ordinary people who would have been glad to see King William II dead. They had good reason. The Norman conquest of England after 1066 had been a savage business. Anyone who resisted Norman rule was cruelly punished. In the rebellious north of England,

Hand-to-hand fighting, as seen in this reenactment, was a bloody and barbarous business. Although Norman soldiers wore the chainmail, helmets and kite-shaped shields shown here, they were not immune to the blows of swords and axes.

for instance, Normans burned crops and destroyed hundreds of villages. They slaughtered cattle and sheep, and killed inhabitants by the thousands. Only when the whole area was laid waste were the Normans satisfied.

Normans were just as brutal about the rights they claimed to English forests. Throughout history local peasants had relied on the forests to gather wood for their fires and kill animals for food. Now, anyone who entered the forests faced appalling punishments. Poachers who shot deer had both hands cut off; even if they merely disturbed the deer they were blinded. And intruders who played music to draw the deer out into the open suffered the same fate. This, though, did not stop the peasants, who continued to enter the forest illegally. So it is possible that the arrow that killed King William II in 1100 was fired by a trespasser hidden among the trees.

Perversion, blasphemy and pagan sacrifice

The list of King William's enemies did not end there. The English Church hated him, too. Churchmen wrote

This nineteenth-century engraving of King William II Rufus bears a close resemblance to the picture of King Stephen on page 19. Neither picture was a contemporary portrait and no one really knows what either of these kings looked like.

the chronicles and histories of the time, and took every opportunity to give William a bad 'press'. This was the entry for the year 1100 in the most famous of all the medieval histories – the *Anglo-Saxon Chronicle*:

'He was very harsh and fierce with his men, his land and all his neighbours and very much feared. He was ever agreeable to evil men's advice, and through his own greed, he was ever vexing this nation with force and with unjust taxes. Therefore in his days all justice declined ... he was to nearly all his people hateful, and abominable to God.'

Divine retribution

William was not the only royal in his family to suffer. People believed that King Henry I and the entire Norman dynasty were also cursed by God. This seemed to be confirmed when Henry suffered the worst disaster that could befall a medieval monarch.

In medieval times, a king was required to be a warrior. This was why he needed male heirs to succeed him. Henry had sired around 25 children by eight or more mistresses. But they were illegitimate and there-

fore could not inherit the English throne.

So it was a terrible blow for Henry when his only legitimate son, Prince William, drowned in the English Channel on 25 November 1120. Henry's courtiers did not dare tell him for two days. When they did, he fainted from shock.

That left Henry's daughter Matilda as his only legitimate heir. This was a great problem for the king. The twelfth century was dominated by men and war, and women were regarded as unsuitable to reign as queens. Henry's first wife, Matilda, was dead, so he remarried, hoping to have more sons. But Henry, now 53, was unable to father more children. So the king resolved that his only heir Matilda would, after all, reign.

Although she was only 19, Matilda was very much like her father. She was intelligent, forceful, well-educated and self-confident. She was also highly disagreeable. Henry felt sure that Matilda could continue his policy of strong-arm rule. But the decision was not his alone. Matilda had to be accepted by the country's powerful barons. The barons of England and Normandy were semi-independent, with their own private armies, fortified castles, and extensive landholdings. These were powerful men who were not afraid to voice their opinions to the king.

Henry realized that the barons were much too pig-headed to welcome the idea of a woman reigning over them, but he was desperate. So he commanded the nobles to swear an oath before God accepting Matilda as his rightful successor. Henry made them swear four times – in 1127, 1128, 1131, and 1133. Although the barons resented being forced to take the oath, they were only too well aware that Henry was not a man to be refused.

Matilda is betrayed

The barons, however, were just biding their time. As soon as King Henry died in 1135, they went back on

King Henry I lost Prince William, his one and only surviving son and heir, when the White Ship sank in the English Channel in 1120. The tragic story was told in this manuscript produced two centuries later, in 1321.

Cui successit Henricus frater
eius 7 regnauit annis xxxvi
hic erat pastor ferax 7 custos
nemor fuit 7 sapiens 7 stre
nuus dux normannie que
euersinus ambrosius Leonem iusticie
in historia Regum nomauit ffecit et eni
iusticium 7 iusticiam in terra Duxit et
uxorem generosam 7 optimam de
nobili genere anglorum 7 Britonum p
quam multum sibi confederauit Reg
num scilicet filiam principis sui Albã
nie uita 7 moribz ornatam sororem
scilicet Alexandri principis sui scocie
7 dauitis scocie qui postea fuit princeps
Albanie. Cui uero Rex Henricus pfa
tus sedit honorem de huntingdon
cum matilda cognata sua que erat
uxor prius principis simonis de seenliz
comitis de huntingdon 7 norhamp
ton cum custodia puerorum suorum et dic
concordes ad inuicem deinde effecti
fuerunt qua prestus Alexander ven
sichiuit filium suum hereditario coronam
7 monarchiam tocius Regni predic
sicut uerus heres 7 iustus de iure boni
Regis Edwardi ultimi. Alexr et diu
sup omnia dilexit et scdm ecclesiam in
multas p loca ffecit et bonu in cultu
tocius multum et deseruit uocabretur
matild Regina optima Obiit uo
predictus Henricus in normannia
apud Lyons. sepultus enim fuit
in anglia apud Redinges in Alba
thia quam construxerat. matilda
uero Regina predicta sepulta fuit
in anglia apud Westmonasteriu
cuius animae ppicietur deus.

Henricus primus genuit:

Willm
qui periit
in mari

Ricm
qui periit
in mari

Matil
dam im
peatrice

Richardum
q obiit

Henrica
Regis se
cundi

their oaths, but not because Matilda was a woman. The barons knew she was more than a match for them and that they would never be able to get the better of her. They had their eyes on a far more malleable candidate.

The effects on England were devastating. Towns and villages were pillaged by both sides. Refugees wandered the countryside.

Stephen de Blois, Matilda's first cousin, was a gentleman. He was kind-hearted, good-natured, and tolerant. In other words, he was a promising soft touch. This did not mean, though, that Stephen lacked cunning. As soon as he heard that his uncle, Henry I, was dead, he left France for England. Within three weeks he had raised enough support for his claim to the throne among barons, government officials, and the Church. He also seized the royal treasure. On December 22, 1135, Stephen had himself crowned king.

The result was civil war, because Stephen was a usurper with no legal right to the throne. Also, Matilda had her supporters among the barons who believed in her legal succession. They soon lined up against Stephen but they had to wait for Matilda. She finally brought her army across the Channel to England from Normandy in 1139.

The civil war was a miserable affair. Neither Stephen nor Matilda was strong enough to win a final victory. So, the war ended as a succession of long sieges of castles and other strongholds. The effects on England were devastating. Towns and villages were pillaged by both sides. Refugees wandered the countryside, seeking shelter in monasteries and

In December 1142, Empress Matilda and four of her knights escaped from confinement in Oxford Castle wearing white robes to disguise themselves against the thick snow. King Stephen's guards were too busy carousing to notice them.

nunneries. Trade slumped and the barons took advantage of the anarchy caused by the civil war to raid, rob, and rape. A contemporary chronicler, Henry of Huntingdon, described the scenes of suffering:

'There was universal turmoil and desolation. Some, for whom their country had lost its charms, chose rather to make their abode in foreign lands; others drew to the churches for protection, and constructing mean hovels in their precincts, passed their days in fear and trouble.

'Food being scarce, for there was a dreadful famine throughout England, some of the people disgustingly devoured the flesh of dogs and horses; others appeased their insatiable hunger with the garbage of uncooked herbs and roots.... There were seen famous cities deserted and depopulated by the death of the inhabitants of every age and sex, and fields white for the harvest... but none to gather it, all having been struck down by the famine. Thus the whole aspect of England presented a scene of calamity and sorrow, misery and oppression....

'These unhappy spectacles, these lamentable tragedies...were common throughout England.... The kingdom, which was once the abode of joy, tranquillity, and peace, was everywhere changed into a seat of war and slaughter, and devastation and woe.'

Henry Plantagenet: a new hope for England

The obnoxious Matilda cared nothing for the sorry plight of the population. In June 1141, while she was in London preparing for her coronation, she demanded huge sums of money from the citizens. But the civil war had ruined them and they could not pay.

When officials and bishops tried to explain the situation, Matilda cursed and swore at them. Very soon, London had had enough. A raging mob burst in on Matilda's pre-coronation banquet at Westminster. They drove her out of the city. She never returned.

The civil war dragged on, but Matilda's chances of success were fading. In 1148, she finally gave up and returned to Normandy. King Stephen, it seemed, had won. But within five years, fate gave a bitter twist to his success. His eldest son and heir Eustace died suddenly in 1153. His wife, Queen Matilda, had died the year before. Losing his wife and son was too much

This strong, determined-looking king, dressed in armour, is King Stephen. The portrait is somewhat flattering: the soft, gentlemanly and sensitive Stephen wasn't nearly as resolute as the picture makes him appear.

for Stephen. Although he had other sons, he was too heartbroken to groom them for the throne. Instead, in 1153, he made a deal with Matilda and her 20-year-old son, Henry Plantagenet. Henry was named as Stephen's successor on the condition that he allow Stephen to remain king in England while he lived.

But Henry did not have to wait long. Less than a year later, on October 25, 1154, Stephen, the last of the Norman kings, died. Now, Henry Plantagenet became the first monarch of the new Plantagenet dynasty.

Henry was a lot like his mother – hot-tempered, masterful, and stubborn. He was also like a time bomb waiting to go off. What followed was the most vicious royal family quarrel England had ever seen. And it was a fight to the death.

2
UNHOLY ALLIANCES

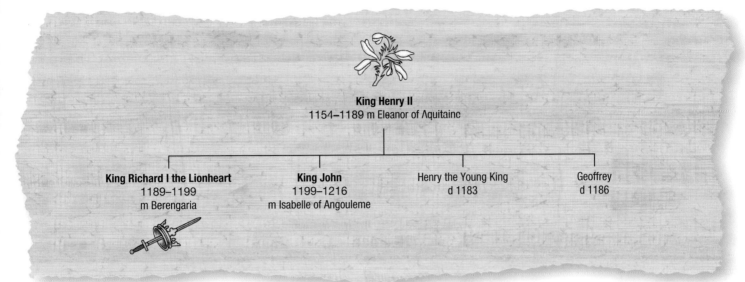

King Henry II
1154–1189 m Eleanor of Aquitaine

King Richard I the Lionheart
1189–1199
m Berengaria

King John
1199–1216
m Isabelle of Angouleme

Henry the Young King
d 1183

Geoffrey
d 1186

When Henry II became King of England in 1154, he was just 21 years old. But he was neither an ordinary man, nor an ordinary king. Despite his youth, he had a natural air of command. He was greatly admired and also greatly feared.

◆

Yet 35 years later, Henry was a worn out, sick old man. He died deserted by his family and his barons, and humiliated by his great rival, the king of France. The monk chronicler Gerald of Wales wrote that Henry was 'without ring, sceptre, crown and nearly everything which is fitting for royal funeral rites.'

How could such a brilliant monarch, one of England's greatest, come to such a miserable end? It all came down to a single, fatal flaw: Henry's ferocious temperament. First of all, his fiery nature involved him in the most sensational murder of his time. Later, it made his family and his nobles conspire together to destroy him.

Canterbury Cathedral, the scene of the murder of Archbishop Thomas Becket on 29 December 1170. Henry II was thought to have ordered his knights to kill Becket.

A passionate pairing

Henry II was not only King of England. He also ruled Normandy, Anjou, Maine, Touraine and Poitou in France. When he married Eleanor, a former queen consort of France, in 1152, he acquired his new wife's own territory, Aquitaine, the largest duchy in France. Together, these lands made up the Angevin Empire. It stretched from England's northern border with Scotland down to the Pyrenees mountains in southwest France. No monarch of England ever came to the throne with a more splendid inheritance.

The marriage of Henry II and Eleanor of Aquitaine was a marriage of two dynamic personalities. Sooner or later, a violent clash between them was inevitable. Eleanor was not a traditional royal wife. She was heiress to Aquitaine in her own right, and the former wife of King Louis VII of France. She

ELEANOR OF AQUITAINE: A SCANDALOUS QUEEN

ELEANOR'S FIERCE INDEPENDENCE and wayward nature led, naturally, to accusations of immorality. One of her courtiers, named Andrew, seems to have cashed in on Eleanor's reputation in a piece of salacious fiction that he wrote in 1186. Andrew's *De Amore or The Art of Courtly Love*, was set against the background of Eleanor's court at Poitiers between 1167 and 1173. Here, according to Andrew, Eleanor and Marie de Champagne, one of her two daughters by King Louis VII, were the focus of a cult that practiced adultery.

Eleanor's real love life was hardly less sensational. Gossip linked her with her father-in-law, Geoffrey d'Anjou, and with her own uncle, Raymond de Poitiers, the crusader Prince of Antioch. Eleanor's affair with Raymond was supposed to have taken place when she accompanied King Louis on the second crusade to the Holy Land, where Christians and Muslims waged war over Christ's birthplace between 1147 and 1149. The smears, however, went even further than this.

'She carried herself not very holily,' wrote Sir Richard Baker in *A Chronicle of the Kings of England*, published in 1643, 'but led a licentious life; and, which is the worst kind of licentiousness, in carnal familiarity with a (Muslim) Turk.'

Beautiful, charismatic and clever, Eleanor of Aquitaine was too sexy to meet with the approval of the prudish clerics of her day.

had tasted power long before she married Henry, who was ten years her junior.

None of these credentials equipped Eleanor to conform to the 'ideal' consort of her time – the type of wife who stayed in the background while her husband took the limelight, or was expected to put up with her husband taking mistresses. Sometimes, in such circumstances, the wife and mistress actually became friends.

Eleanor was most decidedly not that sort of woman.

A page from a medieval history of England showing (clockwise from top left) King Henry II, Richard I the Lionheart, King Henry III and King John. Each is holding a representation of a church with which he is associated.

She was strong-minded, self-confident and very independent. She objected fiercely to King Henry's numerous affairs and to his two known illegitimate children. When Rosamund Clifford, considered by some to be the great love of Henry's life, died suddenly in 1176, it was hinted that Eleanor had had her poisoned. Whatever the truth of the matter, Eleanor seems to have paid back her husband in kind by taking lovers of her own.

Hot-headed and unkempt

Henry II was not a regular medieval king, either. In the twelfth century, kings needed to be visibly impressive. Henry was hardly that. He had no interest

King Henry II and Thomas Becket, once personal friends, argued fiercely about the rights of the Pope over the Church in England. In this medieval manuscript, their hand movements represent their diametrically opposed opinions.

in the outward show and fashionable finery that surrounded other kings. Known as 'Curtmantle' or 'short coat', he was squat, square and freckle-faced. He often appeared unkempt and even grubby, and thought nothing of appearing at court straight from riding his horse, his clothes and boots covered in mud.

In a religious age, Henry cared nothing for religion. He frequently missed church services, and when he did attend, he spent his time sketching and chatting with his courtiers. All the same, beneath this rough and casual exterior, Henry II had a personality that hit people between the eyes. He was stubborn, autocratic and a powerhouse of energy, just like his mother.

But also like his mother, his temper was terrifying to witness. When in a rage, Henry went completely over the top: his pale eyes became fiery and bloodshot and he would literally tear his clothes apart, fall to the floor and chew the carpet. Luckily for him, in medieval times, 'carpets' were made of loose straw.

Anyone who crossed King Henry II was taking a huge risk. The one man who did so, not once but many times, set the scene for an epic tragedy. Henry appointed Thomas Becket as Chancellor of England at the start of his reign in 1154. Although Becket was 15 years older than Henry, the two men were close friends. They went hunting, gaming and hawking

> **When Becket appeared in court, dramatically carrying a large cross, he claimed that, as a churchman, the secular judges had no right to try him.... Even for Becket, this was going too far.**

together. Henry gave Becket so many estates and royal grants that Becket became a very wealthy man.

Excess and extravagance

Unlike the king, Becket had a taste for the high life. When Henry sent him on an embassy to Paris in 1158, Becket took with him 250 servants, 8 wagons full of provisions and expensive plates, and a wardrobe of 24 different outfits. In England, Becket kept a personal household of some 700 knights and employed 52 clerks to manage his estates. Devoted to the finest foods, he once ate a dish of eels that cost 100 shillings – at the time a phenomenal price for a meal.

Friends become foes

Henry came to trust Becket absolutely. In 1162, Becket became the most important churchman in England when he was appointed Archbishop of Canterbury. But this was more than just the latest in a long line of royal gifts. Ever since the time of William the Conqueror, the kings of England had tried to diminish the power of the Pope over their realm. Making Becket Archbishop of Canterbury was Henry's

way of putting in place a man who would fend off the Pope's demands. But if this was what Henry believed Becket would do for him, he was completely wrong.

Instead, a complete change came over Becket. He at once resigned as chancellor. He abandoned the good life and all its pleasures, giving away his expensive wardrobe, his fine plates and exquisite furniture. Instead, he devoted himself to study, prayer and acts of charity.

The fact that Henry's luxury-loving friend had become an ascetic was startling enough. But Becket's conversion went deeper than outward show. Instead of backing up Henry in dealings with the Pope, he obstructed the king at every turn.

Accusations and insults

The crunch came when the king demanded that clerks found guilty of crimes in the independent church courts should be handed over to the ordinary, secular courts for punishment. Becket turned this down flat. His relations with Henry, already strained, turned from friendship to black hatred. Henry hit out at Becket by fabricating various criminal charges against him. These included embezzling public funds while serving as chancellor.

When Becket appeared in court, dramatically carrying a large cross, he claimed that, as a churchman, the secular judges had no right to try him. He also appealed directly to the Pope for assistance.

Even for Becket, this was going too far. In 1164, realizing his life was in danger he fled to Sens in France.

Becket's exile lasted six years. During that time, the king of France and the Pope managed to patch things up between the former friends-turned implacable enemies. This allowed Becket to return to England on 1

An engraving of a twelfth century crown, which was meant to fit across the wearer's brow. It might have been worn in battle over the king's head armour in order to identify him to his soldiers – and his enemies!

MURDER IN THE CATHEDRAL

At around 5:00 p.m. on 29 December 1170, Henry's four knights marched into Canterbury Cathedral where they found Becket at prayer before the altar. In front of a large, frightened crowd of worshippers, they demanded that he cancel the excommunications. Becket ordered them to leave, in no uncertain terms.

Nearby, a young monk, Edward Grim, was watching the scene from behind the altar. Later, he wrote the following account of everything he saw and heard on that tragic evening.

'"You shall die!" the knights threatened Becket, only to receive the answer: "I am ready to die for my Lord that in my blood the Church may obtain liberty and peace."'

'Then,' wrote Edward Grim, 'they laid sacrilegious hands on him, pulling and dragging him that they may kill him outside the church, or carry him away a prisoner…. But when he could not be forced away…one of them pressed on him and clung to him more

Archbishop Thomas Becket was unarmed and at prayer when King Henry's four knights burst into Canterbury Cathedral and attacked him as he prayed at the altar.

closely. Him he pushed off...crying, "Touch me not, Reginald; you owe me fealty and subjection! You and your accomplices act like madmen!"

'The knight, fired with a terrible rage...waved his sword over (Becket's) head. "No faith," he cried, "nor subjection do I owe you against my fealty to my lord the king."

'Then (Becket), seeing the hour at hand which should put an end to this miserable life...inclined his neck as one who prays and, joining his hands, he lifted them up and commended his cause and that of the Church to God.... Scarce had he said the words than the wicked knight, fearing lest he should be rescued by the people and escape alive, leapt upon him suddenly and with his sword struck him on the head, cutting off the top of the crown.... (Becket) received a second blow on the head, but stood firm. At the third blow, he fell on his knees and elbows...saying in a low voice: "For the name of Jesus and the protection of the Church, I am ready to embrace death."

'Then the third knight inflicted a terrible wound as he lay (on the ground) by which the sword was broken against the stones and the crown, which was large, was separated from the head.... (Another) knight...put his foot on the neck of the priest and, horrible to say, scattered his brain and blood over the stones, calling out to the others: "Let us away, knights. He will rise no more".'

The 'meddlesome priest', his skull hacked to pieces, his brains splattered on the cathedral floor, was dead. But Henry was still not rid of him. Becket dead became just as irksome for the king as Becket alive.

The scene of the crime can still be seen today, at the altar in Canterbury Cathedral, Kent. Becket's death was known as The Martyrdom, since he was regarded as a martyr who died for the Church.

The murder caused anger and outrage throughout Christian Europe. In 1173, Becket was made a saint and a martyr. Canterbury became a place of pilgrimage and the cathedral a shrine to the murdered archbishop.

came to crowning English monarchs. As archbishop – even a disgraced archbishop – Becket's rights had been usurped. He was not prepared to let the insult pass. Instead, he excommunicated the Archbishop of York and the six bishops involved in the Young King's coronation.

Henry was in Normandy that Christmas, and when the news reached him he flew into one of his terrifying rages, shouting:

'What miserable drones and traitors have I nourished and promoted in my household who let their lord be treated with such shameful contempt by a low-born clerk? Will no one rid me of this meddlesome priest?'

Four of Henry's knights, Hugh de Moreville, William de Tracey, Reginald FitzUrse and Richard le Breton, took Henry at his word. They crossed to England, arrived at Canterbury whereupon they stormed into the cathedral, fully armed, and slaughtered Thomas Becket.

Far from being rewarded for their deed, the four knights were disgraced. They were forced to do penance by fasting. Then they were banished to the Holy Land. But the greatest display of remorse had to come from the king. Soon after the murder, Henry went to Ireland and laid low for a year or more. But the Angevin Empire could not, of course, be properly ruled by a fugitive, so eventually King Henry had to return to England and face the music.

December 1170. But deep down his quarrel with the king was not resolved. Once home, Becket proved even more recklessly defiant than before.

Defiance leads to death

On 14 June 1170, Henry's eldest surviving son, eight-year-old Prince Henry, had been crowned by the Archbishop of York and became known as the Young King. The crowning of an heir in his father's lifetime was a failsafe device: it was meant to deter powerful rivals and would-be usurpers. What King Henry had forgotten, or more likely ignored, was the fact that archbishops of Canterbury had a monopoly when it

Canterbury Cathedral became a place of pilgrimage after the murder of Thomas Becket. Becket's shrine was visited by thousands of pilgrims, until it was destroyed by King Henry VIII in the sixteenth century as an unwelcome reminder of how a subject had defied a king.

King Henry II was made to suffer for the murder of Thomas Becket. Here he is pictured doing penance at Becket's tomb in Canterbury, a public demonstration of remorse demanded of him by the Pope.

A king is humbled

His punishments were grave, but they were not too damaging, except perhaps to the royal ego. Henry was not excommunicated, though he was banned from entering a church. This would hardly have troubled Henry, who was not particularly religious anyway. In addition, his lands in France were laid under interdict: this meant the protection of the Church no longer applied there. So any rival could invade them. And if that happened, Henry could not seek aid from the Pope. But there was more to come.

On 12 July 1174, King Henry walked barefoot through the streets of Canterbury dressed in sackcloth, the traditional garb of humility. He prayed at the cathedral and was afterwards scourged by 80 monks, who beat him with branches. Sore, bleeding and half-naked, the king spent the following night in the freezing crypt where Thomas Becket was buried. Only after this was Henry given a pardon for the sin he had committed.

Unfortunately, King Henry did not learn very much from the Becket affair. He certainly made no attempt to tame his temper or to think before speaking. Far from it. Three years after Becket's murder, his fiery nature led him into another, much more damaging, quarrel. This time, it led to disaster.

Apple of the king's eye

In 1169, at Montmirail, some 40 miles (64km) east of Paris, King Henry shared out his vast empire between three of his four surviving sons. Prince Henry, heir to the throne and now aged 14, would have England and Normandy. Richard, 12, the future King Richard the Lionheart, received his mother's Duchy of Aquitaine. The fourth surviving son, Geoffrey, aged 11, was to have Brittany in France. The youngest, John, received no lands, for he was only two years old when the

---

Henry was not going to get away with handing out empty promises. In 1173, his sons' resentment boiled over into open rebellion.

---

arrangements were made. But this was not due to any lack of fatherly affection.

John, who was given the nickname of 'Lackland', was Henry's best-loved child. The king made several efforts to provide for him. These efforts included marriage to a wealthy French heiress, but it never came about. In 1177, when John was aged 10, Henry made him Lord of Ireland. Eight years later, John visited Ireland. But he spent his time frittering away his father's money on luxury living, and annoyed the Irish by poking fun at them.

Family feud

As for Henry's other sons, they fully anticipated ruling the lands they had been given. They also expected to receive the revenues their lands produced. But King Henry had never intended his sons to have any real power in his lifetime. They were simply figureheads. All power and revenues remained in their father's hands.

But Henry was not going to be able to get away with handing out empty promises. In 1173, his sons' resentment boiled over into open rebellion. Queen Eleanor, who had grudges of her own against the king, was their chief ally. Henry's sons also found

many malcontents to join them, including barons in both England and Normandy who chafed under King Henry's control. But by far their most important supporter was King Louis VII of France, their mother's former husband.

Louis coveted Henry's Angevin lands and was only too pleased to help his rival's sons destabilize their father's power. Not this time, however. In 1173, King Henry had sufficient military punch to put down the family rebellion and it came to nothing.

Even before the actual rebellion, Queen Eleanor had realized what a dangerous game she was playing. She tried to slip away across the English Channel to Chinon, in Anjou, disguised as a man. But she was recognized and brought back to England. Henry placed her under house arrest at Winchester, where she remained for the next 16 years.

The seal of King Henry II, showing him seated on his throne, sword in one hand and in the other the orb that was an indication of his royal authority. Royal seals on documents and charters showed they had royal sanction and were therefore legal.

Philip, the robber king

Once the rebellion was over, King Henry was arguably more generous towards his sons than they deserved: he forgave them and presented the Young King and Prince Richard with castles and revenues. This gesture, he hoped, would prevent them from rebelling again.

But the family disputes were not over. King Louis of France died in 1180 and was succeeded by his much more capable and far more dangerous son, King Philip II Augustus. Together with his father's throne, Philip inherited his father's plans to poach the Angevin lands. The Young King and Geoffrey were ready-made stooges for Philip's wiles, but the French king's plans were stymied when both of them died prematurely. The Young King died of dysentery and fever in 1183. Geoffrey, who had a passion for tournaments, was killed in 1186 while fighting in the lists.

Only two of Henry's four legitimate sons were left. John remained faithful to his father, but Richard was

Henry II was heartbroken when he learned that his son John had betrayed him by joining his brother Richard in open rebellion. This picture shows the moment when the king, hand clutched to his heart, received the news.

nursing a new grudge: the king planned to give John certain castles in France which Richard claimed as his own. Even worse, King Henry refused to recognize Richard as heir to the English throne, even though, with the death of the Young King, he had become the eldest surviving son.

This was how Philip got a second chance in his bid to destroy the Plantagenets and their Angevin Empire. No one knows if Richard knew about Philip's secret agenda. But he made no bones about joining the French king in a last all-out assault on his father in 1189.

The king's premonition

King Henry had known all along that this was going to happen. Before the death of the Young King in 1183, he had commissioned a painting and ordered it to be displayed in the royal chamber of Winchester Palace. The painting showed four eaglets attacking a

A silver penny minted in the reign of King Henry II. The king's portrait, together with his sceptre, the symbol of his power, is on the obverse (left). The lettering on the reverse (right), shows that the coin was minted in London.

Sick at heart and already ill with a fever, Henry died five days later. As he lay dying, he cursed his sons for their treachery. Only Geoffrey, his illegitimate son, was there at his bedside.

---

parent bird. The fourth eaglet was poised to peck out the parent's eyes.

'The four eaglets', the king explained 'are my four sons who cease not to persecute me even unto death. The youngest of them, whom I now embrace with so much affection, will sometime in the end insult me more grievously and more dangerously than any of the others.'

The King's prediction came true when Prince John deserted his father and joined forces with Richard: the castles his father planned to give him were not grand enough for John's ambitions. The news broke Henry's

heart. After that, the end came quickly.

Richard and King Philip stormed across the territories of the Angevin Empire in northern France, capturing each of the king's strongholds, one after the other. At the same time, almost all the barons of Maine, Touraine and Anjou deserted Henry. Driven out of Le Mans, where he had been born, Henry fled to Chinon in Anjou and took refuge in his castle. His enemies pursued him even there. On 4 July 1189, they made humiliating demands on Henry. There was no way he could resist them.

Guillaume le Breton, King Philip's chaplain and biographer wrote:

'He resigned himself wholly to the counsel and will of Philip, King of France, in such a way that whatever the King of France should provide or adjudge, the King of England would carry out in every way and without contradiction.'

A broken man

Sick at heart and already ill with a fever, Henry died five days later. As he lay dying, he cursed his sons for their treachery. Only Geoffrey, his illegitimate son by Rosamund Clifford, was there at his bedside. This was how the chronicler Gerald of Wales described the last painful days of King Henry II:

'For as branches lopped from the stem of a tree cannot reunite,' he wrote 'so the tree stripped of its boughs, a treasonable outrage, is shorn both of its dignity and gracefulness.'

3

CRUSADING KINGS AND TROUBLESOME BARONS

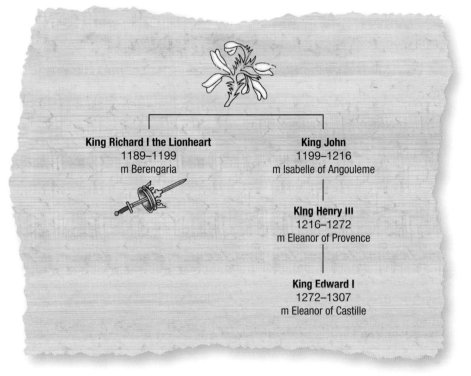

King Richard I the Lionheart
1189–1199
m Berengaria

King John
1199–1216
m Isabelle of Angouleme

King Henry III
1216–1272
m Eleanor of Provence

King Edward I
1272–1307
m Eleanor of Castille

When he learned of his father's death, the first thing the new king, Richard I, did was to go and pay his last respects to the parent he had betrayed. He didn't waste much time on it. Some said Richard knelt beside his father's body only for as long as it took to recite the Lord's Prayer.

◆

Next, Richard freed his mother, Queen Eleanor, from imprisonment at Winchester. Richard's coronation took place in September 1189. After that, he returned to Aquitaine. Leaving England set the pattern for Richard's reign.

Richard was already a celebrated warrior, so much

Although he shamefully neglected his kingdom of England, Richard the Lionheart has long been admired as a great and valiant warrior monarch. This statue stands in Old Palace Yard, close by the Houses of Parliament in London.

so that he was nicknamed the Lionheart. He certainly stands as the ultimate fighting king of medieval times. But he had no interest in fighting to defend England. Apart from crusades, Richard's main aim in life was defending his beloved Duchy of Aquitaine against the French king, Philip II.

Philip was not Richard's only dangerous enemy. Richard's younger brother, John, aimed to seize England during several of Richard's frequent absences. The chronicler Richard of Devizes once described John as 'a flighty, habitual traitor'. John had no

This picture, painted between 1475 and 1500, shows the coronation of King Richard I, which took place in London on 30 September 1189. Barons, bishops and monks took part in the coronation procession.

reservations about betraying his brother, just as he had betrayed his father.

Even so, Richard was fond of John. He arranged a marriage for him with a wealthy heiress, Isabel of Gloucester, and gave him huge estates in England. This, though, was not good enough for John, who had his heart set on becoming regent of England when

> **Richard gave the Muslims a thrashing and was hailed as an even greater hero than before. But while in the Holy Land, Richard insulted a fellow crusader, Duke Leopold of Austria. Leopold swore vengeance....**

Richard left on a crusade. Instead, Richard chose his mother, Eleanor of Aquitaine, to look after his kingdom. John also expected to be named as Richard's heir. But that prize went instead to four-year-old Prince Arthur of Brittany, son of their late brother Geoffrey. As time would tell, John would deal with Prince Arthur in his own ruthless way.

Embarking on crusades to fight Muslims in the Holy Land was phenomenally expensive. To raise much-needed funds, King Richard virtually put England up for sale. He sold earldoms, lordships, sheriffdoms, castles, lands, estates, entire towns and anything else convertible into ready cash. He even planned to sell the capital, London. But, so he complained, he could not find anyone rich enough to buy it.

At last, in July of 1190, Richard set out for the Holy Land with a fleet of more than 100 ships and 8,000 men, intending to return within three years. But that was not to be.

Royal blunder

In military terms, the Third Crusade was a success. Richard gave the Muslims a thrashing and was hailed as an even greater hero than before. But while in the Holy Land, Richard made a crucial error. He insulted a fellow crusader, Duke Leopold of Austria. Leopold swore vengeance and spotted his chance when Richard was on his way home by sea in 1192. Richard's ship sank near Venice. From there, Richard was forced to complete his journey overland. In Vienna, Austria, Duke Leopold was waiting for him.

Many stories went around about how Richard slipped up, enabling Leopold to capture him. One had it that Richard tried to pass himself off as a kitchen

This picture, from the *Luttrell Psalter* (1300–1340) shows King Richard and Saladin jousting at a tournament. Saladin is portrayed with a fearsome blue face. The picture is fanciful: in real life, Richard and Saladin never met at a tournament.

A BITTER END

NO ONE KNOWS FOR CERTAIN what happened to Prince Arthur once he had been incarcerated in King John's castle in Rouen. But the annals of Margam Abbey in Glamorgan, Wales, contain a gruesome version of his final fate:

'... King John kept (Arthur) alive in prison for some time. At length, in the castle of Rouen, after dinner on the Thursday before Easter (3 April 1203) when he was drunk and possessed by the devil, he slew him with his own hand, and, tying a heavy stone to the body, cast it into the (River) Seine. It was discovered by a fisherman in his net... (and) taken for secret burial.'

Prince Arthur, who had a better claim to the English throne, was wasting his time pleading for his life with King John. John couldn't afford to let him live.

hand, but forgot to remove an expensive ring that no kitchen hand could possibly have owned.

The king's ransom

Once Leopold got his hands on Richard, he went for a quick profit. He 'sold' Richard to Emperor Henry VI of Germany. With this valuable 'property' in his possession, the emperor demanded a huge ransom. To make the most out of his rare acquisition, Henry put Richard up for auction. One of the main bidders was Richard himself. The others were King Philip and the faithless Prince John: John had allied himself to the French king as part of his latest scheme – to take Richard's lands in France.

This was an auction Richard had to win. If he had lost, King Philip would have had his wicked way with the Angevin lands in France. And Prince John would get his greedy hands on England. Fortunately, Richard was able to outbid his rivals. The ransom was set at 150,000 marks of silver.

Once again, England was milked dry to raise this immense sum of money. Every possible money-raising device was used Church gold and silver plate were seized and sold. A whole year's wool crop was taken from ranches run by two Cistercian monasteries, and a hefty 25 per cent tax was levied on all incomes.

Big brother walks free

Richard was finally freed after 16 months, on 4 February 1194. He arrived in England about six weeks later.

Prince John had been informed that Richard was on his way. King Philip warned him: 'Look to yourself, the devil is loosed'. As soon as he heard Richard was coming home, John fled to Philip's court for protection. He was terrified of what would happen when his brother found him. Luckily for him, Richard did not punish John too severely. He took away John's lands for a time, but only to teach him a lesson, and they were soon restored.

A picture illustrating Richard's imprisonment in Austria, painted in 1200, the year after his death. Richard appears twice, in the middle holding a glove, and looking thoroughly fed up at a window, on the left.

RUTHLESS REVENGE

Maybe it was no coincidence that the de Briouze family were the patrons of Margam Abbey, where Arthur had disappeared. They soon found themselves next in line for John's revenge. William de Briouze had borrowed large sums of money from John, but he had failed to pay him back. Now John not only demanded immediate repayment, but ordered de Briouze and his wife, Matilda, to hand over their two sons as hostages for their father's debts. Matilda refused, courageously telling King John to his face that a man who had murdered his own nephew was not fit to have charge of her children.

From then on, the full weight of royal vengeance fell on the de Briouze family. William's castles were confiscated and his lands were seized. Worst of all, Matilda and her children were imprisoned in Windsor Castle: despite offers of ransom, John left them there to starve to death. After this, William de Briouze was a broken man. He fled to France, where he died in 1211.

'Think no more of it, John', Richard told him, 'You are only a child who has had evil counsel.' Yet John was no child – he was 27 years old at the time.

Although he forgave and indulged him, Richard did not trust his younger brother. He gave him no powers in England when Richard once more left for France on 12 May 1194. Richard never returned. King Philip was

> **John's second marriage was controversial from the start. Isabella had already set her heart on another man – Hugh de Lusignan.**

still preying on the Angevin lands, and Richard spent the last five years of his life fighting to keep him at bay. In 1199, he was badly wounded during the siege of Chalus Castle in Limousin. The wound became septic and killed him.

John's dream comes true

When news of his brother's death reached him, Prince John was in Brittany. He acted fast and returned to England at once. John spent the next few weeks gathering support from the barons and the clergy. That done, he had himself crowned king at Westminster Abbey on 27 May 1199. Next, John prepared to provide his throne with heirs. He divorced his childless wife, Isabella of Gloucester, and married another Isabella, 12-year-old heiress to Angoulême in France.

A reluctant bride

John's second marriage was controversial from the start. Isabella had already set her heart on another man – Hugh de Lusignan. Hugh loved Isabella in return and the couple were betrothed. But Isabella's ambitious family had other ideas. They saw great advantage for themselves in having her as queen of England. If that meant Isabella had to give up the love of her life, well, so be it. Isabella dutifully married King John, who was 20 years her senior, at Bordeaux Cathedral on 24 August 1200.

Hugh de Lusignan was furious and complained to King Philip. Philip, of course, was only too pleased to beat the king of England with this particular stick. He demanded that the king explain himself. John, meanwhile, attempted his own solution. He tried to appease Hugh de Lusignan by offering his own illegitimate daughter, Joan. Hugh declined. In 1202, John refused to appear before Philip, as ordered. This gave the French king the excuse he needed to confiscate all John's lands in France. For the moment, though, Hugh de Lusignan had lost his Isabella.

John's luck holds

For John, there still remained the problem of his nephew, Prince Arthur of Brittany. As the son of

John's elder brother, the late Geoffrey, Arthur had a better claim to the English throne. King Philip, always on the lookout for ways to cause trouble for John, supported Arthur's claim. So did the barons of Anjou, Maine and Touraine. This was powerful

King John is shown paying homage to King Philip of France for his French lands. Although he was King of England, John was the vassal of the French monarch, and regular homage reinforced his fealty to his lord.

opposition, but then John had a stroke of luck.

While in France in the summer of 1202, fighting to regain the lost Angevin lands, he managed to capture more than 250 knights during his siege of Mirabeau Castle in Aquitaine. One of them was Arthur of Brittany.

Arthur was imprisoned at a castle in Falaise belonging to John's chamberlain, Hubert de Burgh. John supposedly wanted Arthur blinded and castrated, but Hubert de Burgh would not hear of it. De Burgh

REGAL PROFILES

UNSCRUPULOUS AND IMMORAL

ALONG WITH NUMEROUS OTHER BAD HABITS, John also went in for sexual blackmail. He made a habit of seducing the wives, sisters and daughters of his barons, and then demanding hush money to keep the affairs quiet. The families of his victims had no choice but to pay up: if they refused, their family dignity was at stake.

John's queen, Isabella of Angoulême, was naturally resentful. She tried paying her husband back in kind by taking lovers of her own. John soon brought her up short, however. He had her lovers killed and draped their bodies over her bed.

King John was the most reviled and detested monarch England ever had – the complete villain, in total contrast to his valiant brother Richard the Lionheart.

was not alone in his disdain for the king's plan. Another great magnate, William de Briouze, fourth Baron Briouze, also refused to countenance so callous a retribution.

John was not going to let the baron get away with such treachery. He marked down William de Briouze and his family for future punishment. As for Arthur, he was transferred to one of John's own castles, at Rouen. Once there, the king could do what he liked with him. Soon afterwards, Prince Arthur disappeared from history.

A slur on the king

By his ruthless and cruel treatment of the de Briouze family and others, John had fully alerted his barons to the fact that he was a dangerous tyrant. Even then,

In this illustration, King Henry III is flanked by two bishops who have just placed a crown on his head. This is possibly meant to illustrate Henry's coronation, although at the time, he was a young boy, not a grown man.

John might have saved himself had he proved to be that medieval ideal – a successful warrior king. Instead, he lost the Angevin lands in France to a triumphant King Philip in 1204. The magnificent Angevin Empire was gone forever. With this loss, the barons coined another nickname for John: 'Softsword'. It was the worst insult the barons could have dreamed up.

John, in turn, became intensely suspicious of anyone with power in the land. He even pursued barons who remained loyal to him, forcing some to become royal debtors by imposing huge sums in return for new titles. His victims, of course, could not refuse. Geoffrey de Mandeville, for example, was obliged to offer 20,000 marks for the earldom of Gloucester: part of the deal was that Geoffrey took John's former wife, Isabella of Gloucester, off the king's hands.

The king's bloodthirsty activities were taking a toll on his supporters. His treatment of the barons eventually became too much for them, and they rebelled. At Runnymede on 15 June 1215, the barons forced John to sign the Magna Carta. This was not a declaration of democratic liberties, as is often thought, but a statement of the barons' rights and privileges.

Victory for France

However, breaking his word came all too easily for King John. He reneged almost at once. Civil war ensued. Surprisingly enough for 'Softsword', John was soon winning. In desperation, some barons turned traitor: they invited Louis Capet, the son of King Philip of France, to bring an army to England. Louis Capet was to remove King John from the throne and take his place.

Louis arrived at Dover, on the south coast of England, on 14 May 1216. Twelve days later he reached London, where his forces captured two important strongholds: the White Tower, at the Tower of London, and Westminster Palace. That done, Louis was hailed as King of England by his army. But in Rome, the Pope had other ideas. Louis had broken rules by attacking a rightful Christian king. As punishment, the Pope excommunicated Louis and placed his lands in France under interdict.

Meanwhile, John was gathering support all over England. If there was one thing the English detested, it

REGAL PROFILES

A DELUDED BRAT

NO ONE KNEW IT at the time, but the child-king Henry III would prove just as troubling as his father. He was a spoiled brat with very disturbing ideas. The most disquieting was that kings were absolute rulers, who were appointed by God and were God's representatives on earth. Their every command had to be automatically obeyed.

Henry was a great one for royal show and was thrilled by royal ceremonies. But beneath this grand exterior, Henry had a deeply suspicious and fearful mind. He was, at heart, a coward. And, after the way the barons had treated his father, King John, he was sure they were all brutes. This is where King Henry III started to make disastrous mistakes.

King John's son and successor, King Henry III, didn't understand how to be an acceptable monarch in medieval England.

A charter issued by King John, dated 9 May 1215, carrying the royal seal. The same design was often used for seals in successive reigns. The royal seal validated the document to which it was attached and was therefore a protection against forgery and fraud.

was a foreigner attempting to snatch the throne. They would rather be ruled by a home-grown king like John, however unsatisfactory he was.

A child takes the throne

Then, quite suddenly, John died of dysentery on 18 October 1216. He was succeeded by his nine-year-old son, who became King Henry III. Now that the barons had a rightful king with no track record of dark deeds and dirty doings, their support for Louis Capet began to fall away.

But England was still in crisis, and Henry III's coronation was a hasty, hole-in-the-wall affair. The child-king, mother Queen Isabella and the royal family had fled to England's west country after Louis Capet reached London. This was why the ceremony took place in Gloucester Cathedral on 28 October 1216, ten days after John's death. It was a coronation without a crown: instead, Henry had to make do with his mother's torque, a small twisted gold necklace.

Regent saves the day

The situation in England was still very dangerous. Fortunately, William the Marshal, who was appointed King Henry's regent, was a splendid fighter. He soon dealt with Louis Capet. The French prince was forced to sign a peace agreement in London on 12 September 1217. By 1219, William the Marshal had the barons under control and order was restored. Only then, when she knew her son was safe on the throne, did Queen Isabella return to France. There, in 1220, she at long last married Hugh de Lusignan. Their long-delayed marriage was a happy one, and they had nine children.

Henry's views on the status of kings were ill-considered and unrealistic. He did not seem to understand that English kings had never been absolute rulers: there was always some assembly – the Anglo-Saxon Witangemot, the barons, ultimately Parliament – which took it as their right to 'advise' the monarch. Challenging such a right was something even kings could not get away with. As long as he remained under age, Henry's views on kingship did not matter too much. But he failed to outgrow them once he took on his full royal role in 1227.

Conflict of interest

There were serious differences between the interests of the king and those of his barons. Henry loved all things French. His barons had little interest beyond the shores of England. Henry dreamed of regaining the lost Angevin lands and even extending the empire eastward into Germany. The barons could not have cared less.

At court, where the barons believed they should

Des Roches, who had served King John, believed that royal power should be unrestricted and encouraged King Henry to become a despot.

---

have a major influence, they were vastly outnumbered by the French. Henry took a French wife, Eleanor of Provence, in 1236 and filled his court with her relatives. There was always a warm welcome, too, for the king's Lusignan half-brothers, the sons of his mother Isabella by her second marriage. But worst of all by far, King Henry ignored his barons and surrounded himself with French advisers.

One was Peter des Roches, who had served King John. Des Roches believed that royal power should be unrestricted and encouraged King Henry to become a despot. Another influential adviser was William of Savoy, Queen Eleanor's uncle, who became important in the royal council. Even the Archbishop of Canterbury was a Frenchman – Boniface of Savoy, another of the Queen's uncles.

King hatches wild scheme

But then King Henry himself wrecked the whole situation, and gave the barons their chance to get their own back. The king was fond of ambitious, crazy schemes, and in 1254 he ran into big trouble. He had made a deal with the Pope to conquer the Mediterranean

> ## De Montfort was a Frenchman who had inherited an English earldom through his mother. He was every inch a brutal, macho, self-seeking baron. But he possessed a personality that overwhelmed lesser men.

island of Sicily: after that, Henry had planned to make his second son, Prince Edmund, king. To fund this plan, the Pope gave permission for King Henry to exact heavy taxes from his subjects. Henry's barons were furious. They had no interest in the King's mad plan. They refused to pay. The Church refused, too. The ordinary people were struggling with bad weather, failed harvests and famine, so they could not pay either.

Henry was unable to raise the funds agreed upon. There were rumblings from the Pope, and the king was threatened with excommunication. But with the king in trouble, a far greater threat came from a great council convened by the barons. In 1258, they drew up a long-term plan called the Provisions of Oxford. This was intended to banish French members from Henry's court.

Under the Provisions, the most important government posts were to go to Englishmen. The royal revenues were to be paid directly into the Exchequer: this was to prevent King Henry from frittering funds away on his French admirers. Among the most important provisions was the setting up of a 15-man baronial council to 'advise' the king. It was actually intended to control him.

The barons in this nineteenth-century engraving look respectful as they bow to King Henry, but what they're really doing is making their demands. This is why Henry, standing (left) with a crown on his head, looks so wary.

The king is captured

Henry was caught off guard. The royal treasury was almost empty. His subjects were starving. Their mood was turning ugly. He was left with only one course of action – give in. So Henry duly signed the Provisions of Oxford. This kept the barons happy for a time. But at once, Henry started to look for ways to renege.

Henry had to wait awhile for the chance to go back on his word. It came in 1264, when the barons, always vicious rivals, began to quarrel among themselves. But when Henry renounced the Provisions of Oxford, they set their rivalries aside. War followed, and extreme humiliation for King Henry. At the battle of Lewes in Sussex on 14 May 1264, the king and his son and heir, Prince Edward, were taken prisoner. They fell into the hands of the barons' charismatic leader, Simon de Montfort, Earl of Leicester.

Ironically, de Montfort was a Frenchman who had inherited an English earldom through his mother in 1230. He was every inch a brutal, macho, self-seeking baron. But he possessed a magnetic personality that overwhelmed lesser men. He was also a brilliant military leader of the Richard the Lionheart class.

Henry had been so impressed with Simon that in 1238 he had been allowed to marry the king's sister, Princess Eleanor. But Simon was not the sort of man to bow and scrape to his royal brother-in-law. Far from it. Simon had little time for the cowardly king. He once told Henry he should be locked up because of his feeble military abilities. Nor was Simon afraid to exploit his grand position to the fullest. He was impudent enough to use the king's name without permission to secure loans. He almost ended up in the Tower of London for such acts.

King's humiliation is complete

But when Henry reneged on the Provisions of Oxford, it was too much for Simon de Montfort. As far as he was concerned, breaking an oath was more than just blasphemy – it was an insult to God.

Thus Simon treated Henry III with even more contempt after the battle of Lewes. The king was not only Simon's prisoner, he was Simon's hostage and puppet.

Nor was Simon above intimidating Henry. He forced him to sign certain laws, orders and other documents. In 1265, he also convened a Parliament – something only the king could normally do – and made Henry submit to its demands. No king of England had ever suffered such humiliation, not even King John.

The son shines brightly

King Henry's son, Prince Edward, was kept prisoner along with his father. Edward, aged 25, was much more gutsy than Henry. He was not afraid of the mighty Simon de Montfort. Edward knew, too, that many barons were chafing under Simon's rule. They

DEEDS
of
POWER

MERCILESS UNTIL THE END

WHEN THE PAID KILLERS found Simon de Montfort, they showed him no mercy. They hacked him through the neck, and once on the ground, he was mutilated horribly. His body was torn to pieces. Having dealt with their leader, Edward was determined de Montfort's supporters should not get away. As they fled into a nearby church, they too were pursued and ruthlessly cut down by the same hit squad.

A monk who was hiding in the church at the time left an account of what he saw:

'The choir... and the inside walls and the cross and the statues and the altar were sprayed with the blood of the wounded and the dead, so that from the bodies that were around the high altar a stream of blood ran down into the crypt.'

Prince Edward (right), protects his aging father, King Henry III, during the battle of Evesham in which Simon de Montfort was killed.

The South Nave Aisle of London's Westminster Abbey, photographed in 1912. After he regained his throne in 1265, Henry III left political affairs to his son, Prince Edward. Instead, Henry spent the last seven years of his reign working on the restoration of the Abbey.

He was watched by guards, including Simon's son, Henry de Montfort. Another of the guards, Thomas de Clare, seems to have been involved in the plot. Edward was riding side by side with Henry de Montfort when, by a given signal, he edged away. Then he spurred his horse and galloped off. Thomas de Clare followed. Though chased by other guards, they managed to make their escape.

Now that Edward was free, the discontented barons had a leader. A few weeks later, led by Edward, the forces of the king met Simon's army at Evesham in Worcestershire. Edward organized a hit squad to seek out Simon de Montfort and kill both him and his followers.

After this overwhelming and bloody victory, King Henry was restored to his throne. He immediately revoked all the documents Simon had forced him to sign. But at last he had learned his lesson. In the seven years until his death from a stroke in 1272, Henry concentrated on completing a new Westminster Abbey, leaving the government of England to Prince Edward.

objected fiercely to the way he was feathering his family nest while the king was in his power.

First, though, Prince Edward had to escape. His opportunity came on 18 May 1265, while he was out riding near Hereford in the west of England.

As the Battle of Evesham demonstrated, Edward was not in the least like his father. Forceful and brutal, he was willing to shed blood in buckets to get his own way. But as King Edward I after 1272, he was also the strong, dominant royal leader England had been lacking for more than 80 years. The downside was that Edward I was a hard act to follow. The son who had to follow him in 1307 was not up to the job. Yet another scandalous reign loomed over England. And the new king, Edward II, was going to suffer for it in the most ghastly way his enemies could devise.

LOVERS, LAND AND TREASON

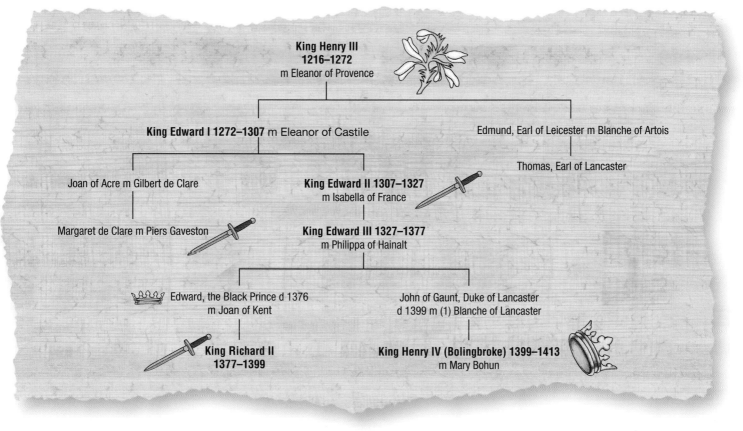

King Henry III
1216–1272
m Eleanor of Provence

King Edward I 1272–1307 m Eleanor of Castile

Edmund, Earl of Leicester m Blanche of Artois

Thomas, Earl of Lancaster

Joan of Acre m Gilbert de Clare

King Edward II 1307–1327
m Isabella of France

Margaret de Clare m Piers Gaveston

King Edward III 1327–1377
m Philippa of Hainalt

Edward, the Black Prince d 1376
m Joan of Kent

John of Gaunt, Duke of Lancaster
d 1399 m (1) Blanche of Lancaster

King Richard II
1377–1399

King Henry IV (Bolingbroke) 1399–1413
m Mary Bohun

Edward II was undoubtedly a disaster on two legs. Long before he became king in 1307, his courtiers and officials knew all about his curious habits and strange interests.

◆

Edward enjoyed menial pursuits. He liked nothing better than digging and thatching, very undignified work for an heir to the throne. The barons were thoroughly scandalized. For them, it was bad enough that Edward was no good at proper royal activities – like jousting in tournaments and making war. But a king who enjoyed grubbing around in the earth like a peasant was just too much.

On 28 February 1308, Edward II and his wife Isabella were crowned king and queen at Westminster, London, by the Bishop of Winchester.

The king in love

This was not the worst of it. Edward II was a blatant homosexual. Except for his wife, Queen Isabella and her ladies-in-waiting, Edward banned women from his court. He was much more interested in beautiful young men like his beloved 'Perot' – Piers Gaveston, a Gascon knight who became his closest companion. No one doubted that Edward and Gaveston were lovers. They had known each other since they were children. Gaveston was good looking and physically attractive. Unlike Edward, he excelled at jousting tournaments. He made a habit of challenging barons to matches and beat them all. What's more, he insulted them by poking fun and assigning them rude nicknames. They hated him.

While King Edward I was still alive, father and son had violent public quarrels over Gaveston. Twice, the old king threw Gaveston out of England, and forbade him to return. But once his father was dead and he became king, there was no holding back King Edward II. He immediately recalled Gaveston to England and showered him with gifts. He made him Earl of Cornwall and lord of the rich estates that went with the title.

Marriages a sham

Gaveston married Edward's niece, Margaret Clare, a rich heiress in her own right. But Margaret's marriage was no more fulfilling than Isabella's. Their husbands were besotted with each other and the wives had to take a back seat.

King Edward was warned often enough that he was playing a dangerous game. But he was stubborn, always wanted his own way, and paid no attention. Secure, so he thought, in the love of the king, Gaveston himself became unbearable.

'He lorded it over (the barons) like a second king,

Brute force and threats came naturally to Thomas of Lancaster and his fellow barons. In 1308, they resorted to both. Like his grandfather, Henry III, Edward was at heart a coward.

---

to whom all were subject and none equal ', wrote the monk of Malmesbury. 'For Piers accounted no one his fellow, save the king alone.... His arrogance was intolerable to the barons and a prime cause of hatred and rancour.'

King and lover delight to shock

Edward took every opportunity to show off his lover. The greatest performance of all was at his coronation in 1308, where a major role was bestowed upon Gaveston: he carried the crown and another precious piece of regalia, the sword of Saint Edward. So splendidly dressed was he that it was said he appeared more like the Roman god Mars than a mere mortal.

At the feast that followed, Gaveston sat next to the king in the place Isabella should have occupied. Even more shocking, the king and his lover repeatedly fondled each other at the table while the guests watched, open-mouthed.

Isabella was only 12 years old when she came to England to marry King Edward II. It was a dynastic marriage, meant to ally England with France. But for Isabella, a homosexual husband was not part of the deal. Nor did she expect to see Gaveston wearing rings and jewels that her father had given Edward as wedding presents. So it wasn't long before the child bride was writing to her father complaining she was 'the most miserable wife in the world'.

Barons demand Gaveston's exile

Queen Isabella was too young to do anything about her wretched situation. But the barons had no intention of sitting helplessly on the sidelines. They planned to get rid of Gaveston. Fortunately, the barons had among them the leader they needed to oppose King Edward and bring Gaveston down: Thomas, Earl of Lancaster, Leicester, Derby, Lincoln and Salisbury, and lord of extensive lands in the north of England. Thomas was King Edward's first cousin. He was vicious, greedy, ambitious and self-serving. And he hated Edward with a passion.

Brute force and threats came naturally to Thomas of Lancaster and his fellow barons. In 1308, they resorted to both. Like his grandfather, Henry III, Edward was at heart a coward. He caved in to the barons' demands.

Gaveston was again forced to leave England. But he soon returned, and the barons had to turn up the pressure. On 27 September 1311, the barons warned Edward that if he did not get rid of Gaveston the result would be civil war. Once again, Edward caved in. Gaveston left for France, but again he came back, this time within three months, at Christmas, 1311.

The end of the affair

Eventually the barons acknowledged that exile was not working. Gaveston would always find some way to sneak back to his lover. And the infatuated king would always welcome him, quite literally, with open arms.

The English barons were sick of Piers Gaveston, who was stopping them from exerting influence over King Edward II. Once they made Gaveston their prisoner, he was doomed. He was summarily killed, without trial.

The barons knew what they must do. On 9 June 1312, they had Gaveston kidnapped and imprisoned in Warwick Castle. The castle belonged to Thomas of Lancaster. Ten days later, Gaveston was marched out, barefoot, to nearby Blacklow Hill. There, two of Thomas's men impaled him on their swords and hacked off his head.

King Edward was distraught. He wept and lamented over his murdered lover. But killing Gaveston was not the barons' only intention. They were determined to grab top positions in the king's government. So, in 1311, they forced Edward to agree to a set of ordinances. Edward was forbidden to leave

England without the barons' permission. He must stop appointing ministers and officials. He had to summon Parliament at least once a year. Parliament would control the king's finances. It was a straitjacket: the purpose was to prevent another Piers Gaveston from monopolizing the king.

Two new companions

Edward chafed and fumed over these restraints. All the same, for nine or ten years, he more or less behaved himself. He had had to. Thomas of Lancaster, now the real ruler of England, was watching everything he did. Then, in about 1320, the king's love life started to heat up again. He managed to sneak two new close friends into his court – a father and son, both named Hugh Despenser.

It was the Gaveston business all over again. The Despensers snapped up gifts, estates and money. Hugh

Thomas of Lancaster wanted to ensure Gaveston was dead and ordered one of the Welshmen who had killed him to show him Gaveston's severed head. After this, a Dominican friar took it to show King Edward.

Despenser the son acquired a rich wife who was one of the heiresses to the earldom of Gloucester. Between them, the Despensers kept the king to themselves. Presumably, both were his new homosexual lovers.

Just how damaging these men's power over the king became was revealed by the French chronicler, Jean Froissart:

'...Hugh Despenser told King Edward that the barons had formed an alliance against him and would remove him from the throne if he was not careful. Swayed by [Despenser's] subtle arguments, the king had all these barons seized at a Parliament at which they were assembled. Twenty-two of the greatest... were beheaded, immediately and without trial.... '

But the barons who survived this slaughter were undaunted. They were still gunning for the Despensers. They went to the king and in July 1321, demanded that father and son be exiled. King Edward was thoroughly cowed. The barons got their way, only to find history repeating itself. Within a few months, Hugh Despenser the son was back in the arms of the king. Hugh Despenser the father also returned to England. Edward welcomed him back with a great gift: he made him Earl of Winchester.

This portrait of Queen Isabella, wife of Edward II, is very deceptive. Here, she looks sweet, good natured and gracious. In real life, Isabella was the vicious mastermind behind the downfall and death of her husband.

DEEDS *of* POWER

HARSH JUSTICE

THE ELDER DESPENSER was first to be captured. He was taken to Bristol in southwest England. There, he was stripped naked and a crown of nettles placed on his head.

Next, on 24 November 1326, in front of a large crowd, Despenser was dragged

This fourteenth century manuscript illustration shows the fires being lit. Sir Hugh Despenser is mutilated, hung, drawn and quartered.

by four horses to a gallows 50 feet (15m) high. Queen Isabella was there, watching, as her arch-enemy was strung up and a fire lit in front of the gallows. Then, as the mob roared, Despenser's genitals were cut off as punishment for 'unnatural practices with the king'.

His suffering was not over yet. Despenser was disemboweled while still alive. He had to watch his innards being burned in the fire. Finally, mercifully, he was beheaded and his body cut into four pieces. This was the grisly death accorded traitors – hanging, drawing and quartering. Despenser's son was well aware that the same horrific fate awaited him.

King Edward, too, realized the game was up. Accompanied by the younger Hugh Despenser, he tried to escape to Ireland by sea. They never reached their destination. They were ambushed at Llantrisant in Wales on 16 November. Hugh Despenser, as he had expected, suffered the same gruesome traitor's death as his father. His head was sent to London, where it was stuck on a pike on London Bridge. The four quarters of his body were displayed the same way in four other English towns. They remained on pikes until they rotted away, a terrible warning to anyone else with treason in mind.

King Edward's punishment was to be even more ghastly. Edward II was made to listen as a long list of his misdeeds and errors was read to him. He burst into tears as the list was read out. At one point he even fainted. When

A detail from the tomb of Edward II in Gloucester Cathedral, which is decorated with a portrait sculpture of the king.

he recovered, he sobbed that he 'was aware that for his many sins he was thus punished, and grieved for having incurred the hatred of his people, therefore (he) besought those present to have compassion on him in his adversity.'

Compassion for the ex-king, however, was in very short supply. He was locked up in a secure dungeon and systematically tortured. Then, on the night of 22 September 1327, his jailers prepared a fire and placed a plumber's soldering iron in it until it was red hot. Edward was held down, with cushions placed over his head.

Then, the soldering iron was pushed up his back passage and into his bowels – or, as one chronicler phrased it, through 'those parts in which he had been wont to take his vicious pleasure.' Edward's cries of agony could be heard all over the castle and even in the nearby town of Berkeley. The barbaric punishment was carried out – according to hearsay – on the direct orders of Queen Isabella.

The she-wolf bares her teeth

When the Despensers were exiled, the barons described them as 'evil counselors.' It was a surprisingly mild term for leeches who were taking King Edward for everything they could get. But for Queen Isabella, the Despensers were much more than that: they were symbols of her years of humiliation and neglect.

Isabella also had a personal reason for wanting revenge on the Despensers. In 1324, they had seized her lands in France. They had also taken her four children from her. They planted spies in her household to keep an eye on her. By this time, Isabella was no longer the helpless little girl who had married the king in 1308. Now a mature 28, she had become the so-called She-Wolf of France and she was about to show just how terrible the fury of a woman scorned could be.

> Isabella plundered the royal treasury. She made huge grants to herself and her lover. She used Parliament to rubber stamp any laws she wanted. It was clear that Isabella would have to go, and Mortimer with her.

Although he had neglected her shamefully, King Edward trusted Isabella's political abilities. In 1325, he sent her to France to negotiate a dispute between himself and her brother, the French King Charles IV.

While she was in Paris, Isabella met Roger Mortimer, the wealthy and ambitious seventh Baron Wigmore. Mortimer was just the sort of man to appeal to a new, vengeful Isabella – a man's man, rough, tough, brutal and arrogant. Mortimer became Isabella's lover and the two openly lived together. And together, they plotted the downfall of King Edward II.

Mortimer and Isabella raised an army and on 24 September 1326, they invaded England. The immediate targets were the Despensers, who were rounded up and duly murdered, brutally. The king, too, was ambushed and taken to Berkeley Castle, near Bristol Channel in southwest England. There, he was forced

King Edward III styled his court on the stories of King Arthur and the Knights of the Round Table that became very popular during his long reign. In 1348 Edward founded the Order of the Garter, an order of chivalry that still exists today.

to abdicate on 24 January 1327. The next day, his son, 14-year-old Prince Edward, was proclaimed King Edward III. Later that year, Edward II also met an almost inconceivably cruel end.

Insatiable greed

Isabella and Roger Mortimer, who was made the Earl of March in 1328, were now the rulers of England. Mortimer's main concern was to enrich himself and his family, and he did not care how he did it. He seized lordships, castles and estates and any other treasure he could lay his hands on.

Isabella was no better. She plundered the royal treasury. She made huge grants to herself and her lover. She used Parliament to rubber-stamp any laws and orders she wanted. The situation could not continue. Isabella would have to go – and Mortimer with her.

At first, though, the underage King Edward III had no authority to act against the regal pair. Not until he turned 16, in 1330, was he able to take on the full powers of king. One of his first acts was to destroy Roger Mortimer.

In October 1330, Mortimer and Isabella were staying at Nottingham Castle. They knew they were in danger and had ordered the gates locked. Guards were set to patrol the castle walls. But there was a secret passageway into the castle which led to Mortimer's bedroom. Together with a small band of men, the young king entered by the passageway, unseen.

The band cut down the two knights on guard and seized Mortimer. Isabella heard the scuffle and rushed into the room. When she saw what was happening, she screamed: 'Have pity on gentle Mortimer!' Regardless of her pleas Mortimer was taken to London, where he was hung, drawn and quartered on 29 November. Isabella's days of power and revenge were over. But she was not executed. Instead, she was retired to Castle Rising, in Norfolk.

A fresh start, but a sorry end

Now, in Edward III, England could look forward to a respectable king for the first time in 20 years. The third Edward knew just how to keep his barons happy.

REGAL PROFILES

THE DEMISE OF A HERO

IN THE LAST YEARS before his death, Edward spent long hours alone in his apartments, refusing to see members of his family or his household. In this pitiful state, Edward fell into the clutches of his mistress, Alice Perrers, the mother of at least two of his illegitimate children.

King Edward first met Alice Perrers when she became a maid-of-the-bedchamber to his wife, Queen Philippa of Hainault, in 1364. She became his mistress soon afterward. The Queen died in 1369. From then on, the greedy Alice could do anything she wanted with the king. He gave her manors, money and

Alice Perrers, King Edward III's mistress, was a very greedy woman. In 1377, the senile King lay dying. Alice, realizing that this was her last opportunity to enrich herself, stole the rings from his fingers.

jewels. He even gave her some of Queen Philippa's jewels.

Gossip circulated that Alice was a witch, and that she made wax images of Edward and herself to keep him in her power. Parliament tried hard to get rid of Alice, but the king was always there to rescue her. In 1376, when she was impeached by Parliament, he simply quashed the sentence passed on her.

But that same year, tragedy struck the king. Edward's heir, Edward the Black Prince, died. The prince had been a fearless warrior. The king never got over his son's death. He suffered a stroke and spent the rest of his life in mourning. After his stroke the king did not live long. When Edward III died on 21 June 1377, Alice Perrers was with him. Greedy and grasping to the last, she quickly removed Edward's rings.

He allowed them what they most wanted – to act as his advisers. He satisfied them even more by the splendid victories he and his son, Edward, the Black Prince, won over the French. The reign of Edward III was regarded as a glorious time in English history, despite the horrific Black Death, or bubonic plague, of 1349–1350, which killed a quarter of his subjects.

But Edward III lived too long. He became senile in the seven years before his death in 1377, aged 64, a sad shadow of the great warrior king he had once been.

A new king and a peasant uprising

Three weeks later, King Richard II, Edward's grandson and son of the Black Prince, was crowned at Westminster Abbey. He was 10 years old and at first seemed likely to be a good king. Four years later, Richard became a national hero when he rode out in person to confront the leader of the Peasants' Revolt, Wat Tyler. Tyler had 60,000 followers with him. They were protesting about a poll tax of a shilling, which had to be paid by all adults aged 14 and over. It was far more than many poor peasants could afford, So they rebelled, and three days and nights of anarchy and bloodshed followed.

The young king must have known how violent and dangerous the rebels were. But he showed no signs of flinching. He calmed the situation by offering to withdraw the poll tax and give the rebels a pardon. But Wat Tyler approached Richard in such a menacing way that, fearful for the king's safety, the Mayor of London, William Walworth, stabbed him with a sword. Tyler's head ended up on a pike on London Bridge.

As Tyler fell to the ground, menacing murmurs came from the crowd. They moved forward, as if to attack the king and his officials. But young Richard kept his cool.

'Sirs,' he cried, 'will you shoot your king? I am your captain, follow me!'

That was the end of the Peasants' Revolt. Many people came to believe that England now had a brave young king who would one day match the great deeds of his father, the Black Prince. Or so it appeared on the face of it. But the face was deceptive. The fact that Richard had given in to the rebels, and had offered to grant them pardons after all the killing, destruction and chaos they had caused, was not a promising sign. It suggested that basically he was timid and would crack under pressure.

Call me Your Majesty

Added to that, Richard lacked the temperament of a traditional medieval king. He was not interested in military matters; he was over-emotional and hot-tempered. And, like King Henry III before him, he thought royal commands should be instantly obeyed without question.

Because Richard was underage when he came to the throne, a regency council ruled for him. Meanwhile, he stayed at home with his mother, Joan of Kent. But at every opportunity, he demonstrated what a thoroughly spoiled brat he was.

In 1382, he dismissed his chancellor, the Earl of Suffolk, for failing to obey his commands. The following year he told Parliament that he would choose any adviser he wanted and insisted that Parliament accept his wishes without question.

Before long, Richard had made rather too many enemies – powerful ones. He surrounded himself with advisers, making it clear that any opposition to his will would be regarded as treason. He invented new, more exalted terms of address: anyone speaking to him had to call him Your Majesty instead of the usual Your Grace.

Richard was obviously a tyrant. But English nobles had seen it all before. They knew what had to be done. In 1387, five so-called Lords Appellant – the Dukes

---

They persuaded Parliament to charge Richard's most important supporters with treason. Richard was forced to watch as four of them were hung, drawn and quartered.

---

of Gloucester and Hereford, the Earls of Arundel and Warwick, and Thomas Mowbray, Earl of Nottingham, took a stand. They persuaded Parliament to charge Richard's most important supporters with treason. Richard was frightened. He gave in. He was forced to stand by and watch as four of his supporters, including his aged tutor Sir Robert Burley, were hung, drawn and quartered.

After this, Richard laid low. He did nothing to upset Parliament. He created a magnificent court

Though only 14 years old, Richard II faced up bravely to Wat Tyler, leader of the Peasants' Revolt in 1381. Tyler moved toward the young king in a threatening manner, and for this he was killed by William Walworth, Mayor of London.

and filled it with artists, writers and other harmless, non-military, types. But it was a smokescreen. All the while, Richard had been plotting his revenge.

By 1397, he was ready. Suddenly, without warning, the king ordered the arrest of the Lords Appellant. Three of them – the Duke of Gloucester and the Earls of Arundel and Warwick – were charged with treason. They were found guilty and executed. The Duke of Gloucester was arrested in Calais. He was smothered to death with a mattress.

Cousins at war

King Richard had a special punishment in mind for the fifth Lord Appellant, Thomas Mowbray. It was one that would also get rid of Richard's first cousin, Henry Bolingbroke. Richard had always been jealous

of Henry, who was the epitome of a chivalrous knight. He was well educated and spoke several languages. He was admired at royal courts throughout Europe. And he was heir to the magnificent Duchy of Lancaster.

But Henry was far too trusting. He did not realize how devious Richard could be. Henry fell straight into Richard's trap after Thomas Mowbray warned him that the king was plotting the downfall of the House of Lancaster. Bolingbroke accused Mowbray of speaking treason against Richard. Richard ordered that the dispute be settled the old-fashioned way: in a trial by battle.

On 26 September 1398, a huge crowd gathered to watch the combat. But as soon as Bolingbroke and Mowbray came out dressed for battle, Richard suddenly forbade them to fight. He exiled Thomas Mowbray for life. Henry Bolingbroke was exiled for 10 years.

Bolingbroke's bitter chalice

Five months later, on 3 February 1399, Henry Bolingbroke's father, John of Gaunt, died. The exiled

Bolingbroke succeeded him as Duke of Lancaster. But he was a duke without rights or lands. As soon as John of Gaunt was dead, Richard announced that Bolingbroke would be banished for life. He ordered that lands belonging to the Duchy of Lancaster be handed over to the Crown.

Henry Bolingbroke soon struck back. Within a few weeks, he sailed home from France. He landed at Ravenspur in Yorkshire, in the north of England, on 30 June 1399. Bolingbroke claimed he had returned only to reclaim the Duchy of Lancaster. But there

was a lot more at stake than that. Richard had finally gone too far. He had made too many enemies. And his enemies believed he was no longer fit to be King of England.

When Henry Bolingbroke landed in England, King Richard was in Ireland. He rushed back and shut

In this fifteenth century painting, the youthful Richard II sits with members of the Royal Council beneath an ornately decorated canopy. Richard was one of those kings who wanted absolute power – and paid the penalty for it.

himself up in Conway Castle, in Wales. But everyone had deserted him. He might have held out for a time inside the castle but for Thomas Arundel, brother of the executed Earl of Arundel, who assured him that if he came out he could make peace with Bolingbroke and still be allowed to remain king. It was a trap. On 20 August 1399, as soon as King Richard set foot outside Conway Castle, he was ambushed and taken prisoner.

Richard was taken to London, and imprisoned in the Tower. At the end of September, Parliament forced him to abdicate. Henry Bolingbroke claimed the throne of England.

After that, Richard did not have long to live. He was taken to Pontefract Castle, in west Yorkshire. There, it was said, he was slowly starved to death. But

This formidable fortress is Conway Castle, where Richard II attempted to hide from the forces of his cousin Henry Bolingbroke. The castle was fairly new in Richard's time, having been built in the thirteenth century.

This picture shows King Richard II abdicating his throne, surrounded by knights and courtiers. It was painted at some time between 1400 and 1425 and comes from *The History of the Kings of England* by French chronicler Jean Creton.

his end might have been much more violent. It seems that on 14 February, eight men armed with axes burst into Richard's cell in the castle. Richard was eating dinner at the time. He immediately overturned the table and grabbed an axe. He set about his attackers and managed to kill four of them. But there was no doubt about the outcome. The remaining four assassins overwhelmed the ex-king and hacked him to death.

By this time, Henry Bolingbroke had already been crowned King Henry IV on 13 October 1399. But Henry was not happy. He was a usurper and had stolen the crown from its rightful owner, King Richard.

Henry was well aware of it. 'God knows by what right I took the Crown,' he said later. Strictly speaking, Henry had no right, and he was tortured by guilt for the rest of his life.

INSANITY, CIVIL WAR AND CHILD MURDER

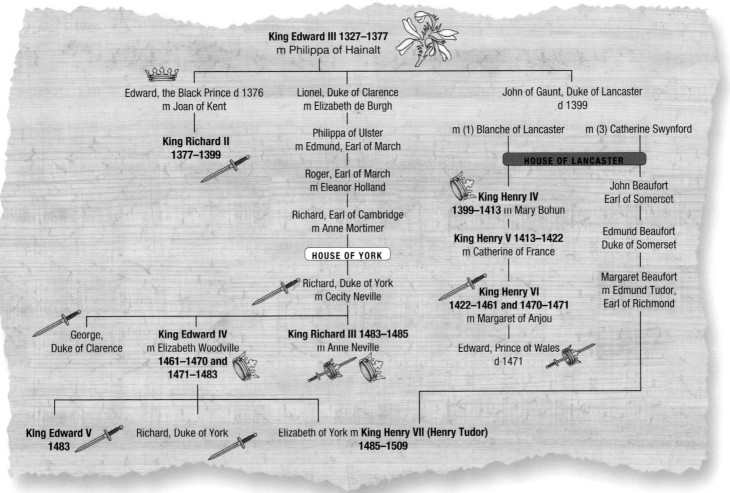

King Henry IV was always nervous, constantly watching his back. He could never be sure how long he would be able to hang on to his stolen throne.

✦

There were enemies lurking in the wings, many of whom had better claims to the throne. There was troublesome gossip, too. Henry had based his claim to the throne on the fact that he

The coronation of King Henry IV in 1399 was overshadowed by guilt and tragedy. Henry had usurped the English throne from his cousin, Richard II. The ex-king did not have long to live.

was the grandson of King Edward III. But according to hearsay, when King Edward's wife, Philippa, lay dying in 1369, she made a confession. She revealed that in 1340, she had given birth to a daughter while in Ghent, in present-day Belgium. But by accident, Philippa had killed the young princess. Philippa was terrified the king would find out. So she had a boy, the son of a porter, smuggled into her apartments.

REGAL PROFILES

THE BLUSHING KING

AS WELL AS LOATHING WAR, fighting and executions, the timorous King Henry VI was also a prude. Nudity made him blush and run. One Christmas, a guest of the king tried to please him by providing entertainment. Or so he thought. This guest brought along a troupe of topless dancing girls. Henry was shocked and stormed out of the room in a huff.

Nevertheless, like all sovereigns before him, Henry had a duty to provide at least one heir to the throne, so he was married, in 1445, to the fiery Margaret of Anjou. However, no children came along for eight years. Gossip provided the truth of the matter: one of Henry's advisers, William Ayscough, Bishop of Salisbury, had turned him off sex. For reasons known only to himself Ayscough advised the king not to have his sport with the queen. The bashful king was not hard to persuade.

Philippa passed this boy off as the child born to her in Ghent. King Edward was delighted with his new 'son'. But the child's real background was kept a secret. The boy grew up to become John of Gaunt, Duke of Lancaster. John of Gaunt was Henry IV's father.

Consumed with guilt and plagued by illness

If Henry IV had known the truth about his father, he kept it quiet. But there were other pressures. He was consumed by guilt over the murder of King Richard II. He tried to make up for it by paying monks to say prayers for Richard's soul. But it did not make him

---

When Edward was brought to him on New Year's Day, the king didn't know why. He'd forgotten he was the child's father. Instead, he thought the father was the Holy Ghost.

---

feel any better. Having stolen the English crown, he had laid himself open to conspiracies. There were several plots to kill him. There were many rebellions against him. King Henry survived them all. But the strain showed. Henry suffered the first of several strokes in 1406. Tales spread that he was suffering from leprosy, though he more probably had eczema.

He had epileptic fits. Henry IV was a physical and mental wreck when he died in 1413, aged 47.

Other Plantagenets had not forgotten their own claims to the throne. But they had to wait awhile to make their bids. There was no chance during the reign of Henry IV's son and successor, King Henry V. Henry V was one of England's greatest and most successful warrior monarchs and remains one of England's national heroes. But when he died suddenly in 1422, aged 35, his son and successor was just the sort of king his rivals had been waiting for.

Henry VI was still in his cradle when he became king. He grew up weak and timid. Anyone could push him around. He had no military skills and hated bloodshed. Sometimes, he stopped the executions of criminals or traitors – he could not bear to see them die. But Henry was very religious. When he had to wear his crown on feast days, he felt he had committed the sin of pride. So he wore a hairshirt next to his skin to make up for it.

The king loses his mind

By rights, Henry should have been a monk, or better yet, a hermit. He found being king very hard going, so much so that in August 1453, he went mad. He no longer knew where he was, what year it was or even who he was. But somehow Henry had escaped from Ayscough's influence long enough to conceive a child – Prince Edward, born in 1453. But when Edward was brought to him on New Year's Day 1454, the king did not know why. He had forgotten he was the child's father. Instead, he thought the father was the Holy Ghost.

Rival for the throne

All this was icing on the cake for King Henry's rivals. A mentally unbalanced king with an infant heir was a double gift to anyone who wanted to seize power. As a mad king, Henry had to have a protector. So up stepped Richard, Duke of York. Ten years older than Henry, Richard was everything Henry was not – proud, warlike, ambitious and greedy.

Richard of York had his own claim to the English throne, a better one than either King Henry's or Prince Edward's. King Henry VI was descended from John of Gaunt, Duke of Lancaster, the fourth surviving son of King Edward III. Richard of York was descended from Lionel, Duke of Clarence, King Edward's third surviving son and John of Gaunt's elder brother.

Richard's first move was to have himself appointed the mad king's protector, in March 1454. His next was to arrest Edmund Beaufort, Duke of Somerset. Somerset was King Henry's most powerful supporter. He was sent to the Tower of London.

Richard was also gunning for Queen Margaret. But he had to be careful. The bold, proud Margaret dominated her spineless husband. And beside being Queen Consort of England, she was also the mother of the heir to the throne. So however much Richard of York wanted to pack her off to the Tower of London, he did not dare.

Richard could remain protector only as long as King Henry's madness lasted. It did not last very long. By Christmas 1454 he was better and Richard lost his job. But by now, the power struggle had gone too far. The Plantagenet royal family had already split into two rival factions: King Henry's House of Lancaster and Richard's House of York. The only way to settle their rivalry was by civil war.

Their struggle was called the War of the Roses. This was because the badge of Lancaster was a red rose and the badge of York was a white one.

King Henry VI was as unlike his father, Henry V, as it was possible to be. Timid and weak-minded where Henry V was valiant and strong, Henry VI was like his maternal grandfather, Charles VI of France; Charles was mad, and so was Henry.

This formidable-looking woman was Queen Margaret, wife of King Henry VI, who was completely dominated by her. Margaret was the driving force behind the resistance of the House of Lancaster to the claims of the House of York.

The war began with the battle of Saint Albans, Hertfordshire, on 22 May 1455. The House of York won. Henry VI was such a weakling that he even forgave Richard. Afterwards, Richard's supporters were even given prestigious posts in the government. Richard could afford to let the harmless Henry VI remain king. As long as he did what he was told, that is. Henry VI was very good at doing what he was told. Even so, Richard took the precaution of imprisoning the king in the Tower of London.

But Richard had reckoned without Queen Margaret. Unlike her husband, she had never dreamed of giving in. Margaret raised an army and confronted the Yorkists at Wakefield, in Yorkshire. She won a great victory. Richard of York was killed in the fighting. Later, his skull was displayed from the walls of York, wearing a paper crown. Now the House of Lancaster had the upper hand – but not for long.

The Duke of York's son Edward, aged 18, took over his father's claim to the English crown. Of the two – Richard and Edward – Edward was by far the better man. He was handsome, charming and a fine military commander. Edward made far more headway than Richard had. He twice defeated the Lancastrian army. Afterwards, he was crowned King Edward IV of England on 28 June 1461.

Royals reduced to begging

King Henry, Queen Margaret and Prince Edward managed to escape to Scotland. But they arrived like beggars. On the way, Margaret was robbed of everything she had — her plate, jewels and gowns. At one point, she was reduced to borrowing money. A chronicler wrote of how 'the king her husband, her son and she had…only one herring and not one day's supply of bread. And that on a holy day, she found herself at Mass without a brass farthing to offer; wherefore, in beggary and need, she prayed a Scottish archer to lend her something, who half loath and regretfully, drew a Scots groat from his purse and lent it to her.'

While the royal fugitives were in this terrible state, King Edward IV was living it up in London. He was very popular and women adored him. They did not have much trouble attracting Edward's attention. He was a good-looking, lusty six-footer with a roving eye for beautiful women. Soon, everyone was gossiping about the number of women he had bedded. But before long, his roving eye got him into trouble.

A secret marriage

Edward IV's most powerful supporter was Richard Neville, Earl of Warwick. Warwick fancied himself as a 'kingmaker'. Edward owed much of his success to Warwick. So, when Edward became king, this was payback time as far as Warwick was concerned. Warwick decided he was going to control the king. He planned a brilliant marriage for him, to a French princess. But Edward had other ideas. He had set his heart on an Englishwoman: Elizabeth Woodville, a 27-year-old widow with children. Edward wanted her badly. At first, he tried to seduce her, but she refused him. The gossips said Edward put a dagger to her throat, but she still resisted him. There was only solution: the king had to marry her.

Queen Margaret and Prince Edward managed to escape to France. The deposed King Henry VI was left behind. He had to wander from one safe house to the next. Often, he disguised himself as a monk.

But Edward was still very young and afraid of Warwick. So he married Elizabeth Woodville in secret on 1 May 1464. Edward managed to prevent Warwick from learning about his marriage for four months. When Warwick found out, at the end of September 1464, he was furious. The king had made him look like a fool. But that was not all. Elizabeth Woodville's many relatives – including her seven unmarried sisters – were soon taking advantage and leeching off the king. They were given titles, grants of money, grants of lands – all of which Warwick had wanted for himself. Even more infuriating, King Edward preferred to go to the Woodville family for advice rather than to Warwick.

Meanwhile, in 1463, Queen Margaret and Prince Edward managed to escape to France. The deposed King Henry VI was left behind. He had to wander from one safe house to the next. Often, he disguised himself as a monk. But Edward IV's spies were after him. They found him at Waddington Hall in Lancashire in July 1465. True to form, Henry did not put up a struggle. He was taken to London, and made a prisoner in the Tower for a second time.

Richard Neville, Earl of Warwick – 'Warwick the Kingmaker' – was the most powerful English noble during the Wars of the Roses. In 1470, Warwick had the Yorkist king, Edward IV, imprisoned and the Lancastrian Henry VI locked up in the Tower.

The kingmaker and the queen

Now, King Edward had Henry in his power. But he still had to deal with the Earl of Warwick, who was a dangerous man. So, in March 1470, King Edward accused the earl of treason. Warwick fled for his life to France. There, he contacted the woman who had once been his greatest enemy, Queen Margaret. Six months after Warwick and the Queen had joined forces, Warwick brought an army to England. Margaret was to follow on with another army. Warwick was determined to topple Edward IV and pay him back for insulting him. Warwick pulled it off. King Edward was captured after a battle at Northampton, in central England.

Now, Warwick really was a kingmaker. He had King Edward IV imprisoned in his castle of Middleham in northern England. King Henry VI was in the Tower of London. Warwick could do what he liked with both. Warwick chose to put Henry VI back on the throne. He was easier to control than Edward IV. After all, he was called Henry the Hopeless, the king who would do as he was told.

But King Edward escaped from Middleham Castle and managed to reach France. He did not stay there long. Soon Edward was back in England, this time with a new army of his own. Edward's forces met Warwick's at the battle of Barnet, just north of London, on 14 April 1471. Warwick had brought King Henry from the Tower and sat him by a tree to watch the fighting. What Henry saw, however, was Warwick's defeat. Warwick fled from the battlefield. But the triumphant Edward IV was not about to let him get away. The earl was pursued and killed. Poor King Henry was then seized and sent back to the Tower for the third and last time.

Warwick the Kingmaker was killed at the Battle of Barnet when Edward IV's forces defeated the Lancastrians. Warwick began the Wars of the Roses fighting for the Yorkists, but he changed sides because of a quarrel with Edward IV.

The same day, Queen Margaret and Prince Edward returned to England. But Edward made short work of Margaret and her army. At Tewkesbury in Gloucestershire on 4 May 1471, Queen Margaret was defeated. Seventeen-year-old Prince Edward ran away from the battle, but was pursued and killed.

Margaret was devastated. But for her, worse was to come. The victorious King Edward IV could not afford to let Henry VI live any longer. On the night of 21 May 1471, around midnight, Henry was stabbed to death in his cell at the Tower of London. One of the killers was Richard, Duke of Gloucester, Edward IV's youngest brother.

Later, Henry's body was publicly displayed so everyone would know he was dead. According to the official story he had died naturally, 'of pure displeasure and melancholy'. But there was also talk that blood had spurted from his wounds, signifying what had really happened to him.

This was the end for Queen Margaret. She had lost everything – her husband, her son and her crown. Her father, King René of Sicily, ransomed her and she lived in France until her death in 1482.

The following year, Edward IV's days of enjoying high living and his scores of mistresses caught up with him. He suffered a stroke and died on 9 April. He was only 42. He left his throne to his 12-year-old son, who became King Edward V.

Queen Margaret was taken prisoner after the Battle of Tewkesbury in 1471 and her son, Prince Edward, was killed. Later Margaret's husband, Henry VI, was murdered in the Tower of London.

> **Richard of Gloucester would go down in English history as the evil uncle, a deformed monster and just about everything else bad.**

Edward V was an invitation for trouble. With a civil war simmering, the last thing England needed was a boy king. No king could actually rule until he grew up. A royal council ruled for him. And this gave ambitious men ideas about seizing power for themselves. The most ambitious of them was Richard of Gloucester.

'Woe to the land that's governed by a child!' Shakespeare wrote in *Richard III*. This was certainly true for Edward V. Robbed of his throne by his uncle, Richard III, Edward became the third English king to be murdered in the fifteenth century.

Tudors demonize Uncle Richard

Richard of Gloucester would go down in English history as the evil uncle, a deformed monster and just about everything else bad. This picture of Richard was pure propaganda. It was dreamed up by the Tudor royal family, which took over from the Plantagenets after the Wars of the Roses ended in 1485.

Like all propaganda, it was more powerful than true. The Tudors did a very thorough job in creating Richard's demonic image. They turned him into a hunchback. They said he had been born with teeth and born breech – legs first – which was considered extremely bad luck in highly superstitious times when any-thing 'unnatural' was seen as the work of the devil. And by the time the Tudors had finished with him, no one doubted Richard was one of the devil's own.

But Richard was not a hunchback. His por-traits show there was nothing wrong with him. During the Wars of the Roses, he had stuck loyally by his brother King Edward IV. Edward trusted Richard so completely that he sent him to rule the trouble-some north of England. He ruled it well and became very popular. Even today, more than five centuries later, people in the north of England look back on Richard of Gloucester with affection.

Elsewhere, however, the Tudor smears about Richard stuck – firmly. So did the idea, encouraged by the Tudors, that Richard had murdered his way to the throne. The list of accusations was a long one. To begin with, he allegedly had murdered King Henry VI in the Tower of London in 1471. The same year, so the story went, Richard killed Henry VI's son, 17-year-old Prince Edward, at the battle of Tewkesbury. Seven years later, Richard was blamed for the death of his own elder brother, George, Duke of Clarence, also in the Tower of London. It is a well-known story that Richard drowned George in a butt of Malmsey wine. The simple truth was that George was a habitual trai-tor, and King Edward IV had had him executed.

After George, only two people stood in Richard's way: the boy king Edward V and his 10-year-old brother, Richard, the Duke of York.

On 1 May 1483, Richard of Gloucester abducted Edward V while the boy was on his way to London.

THE LOST BOYS

RICHARD HAD PLACED the two young boys, Edward V and the Duke of York, in the Tower of London. There was nothing particularly suspicious about this. In the

This sinister looking passage is in the White Tower of the Tower of London where Edward V was lodged before his planned coronation.

fifteenth century, the Tower was a palace as well as a prison. English kings normally stayed there before their coronations. The difference was that King Edward V never came out. And he never had a coronation.

In 1513, Sir Thomas More published his *History of King Richard III*. This book contained More's account of what happened in the Tower on the night of 3 September. In the fifteenth century, it was easy to hire assassins. For a fee, they would quietly kill a victim, conceal the body and hide the evidence. According to More, Richard III had paid a Yorkist knight named Sir James Tyrell to do away with The Little Princes in the Tower.

'SMOTHERED AND STIFLED'

'For Sir James Tyrell,' wrote More, 'devised that they should be murdered in their beds. To the execution whereof, he appointed Miles Forest, one of the four that kept them, a fellow fleshed in murder before time. To him he joined one John Dighton, his own horsekeeper, a big broad, square, strong knave.

'Then, all the others being removed from them, this Miles Forest and John Dighton, about midnight (the innocent children lying in their beds) came into the chamber and suddenly lapped them up among the clothes, so bewrapped them and entangled them, keeping down by force the feather bed

This romantic portrait, painted in 1878 by pre-Raphaelite painter Sir John Millais, shows the 'Little Princes in the Tower' – King Edward V and his brother Richard, Duke of York.

and pillows hard unto their mouths, that within a while, smothered and stifled, their breath failing, they gave up to God their innocent souls into the joys of heaven, leaving to the tormentors their bodies dead in the bed.

'After that the wretches perceived, first by the struggling with the pains of death, and after lying still, to be thoroughly dead: they laid their bodies naked out upon the bed, and fetched Sir James to see them. Which, upon the sight of them, caused those murderers to bury them at the stair foot, meetly (suitably) deep in the ground, under a great heap of stones.'

AN ENDURING MYSTERY

Nearly two centuries later, in 1674, workmen rebuilding the stairs to the Tower's Royal Chapel came upon a wooden chest buried 10 feet below the stairs. Inside was an assortment of bones. Sir John Knight, chief surgeon to the then king, Charles II, decided they were the bones of 'two striplings' – in other words, Edward V and his little brother.

But in 1933, the bones were reexamined. The results were not so certain. There had been many deaths in the Tower over the centuries and the bones could have been anybody's. So, the mystery remains. Currently, the King Richard III Foundation Inc., which seeks to clear the king's name of murder, has asked for DNA tests to be made on the bones. If that happens, the riddle may be solved once and for all.

Richard had always hated Queen Elizabeth Woodville and her family. When the queen heard the boy king was in Richard's clutches she took fright and bolted, taking her younger son, Richard, Duke of York with her to the safety of Westminster Cathedral. There, under the protection of the Church, Richard could not get at her. Or so the queen thought. But Richard found a way. On June 16, he threatened the Queen so fiercely that she let him take the young Duke of York away. That was the last she saw of him. She never again saw her elder son, Edward V, either. From time to time, the boy king and his brother were seen playing in the gardens of the Tower. But by July 1483, the sightings had stopped. They were never seen alive again. There was no funeral. The boys had simply vanished. Later, they became known as the tragic Little Princes in the Tower.

Richard claims the crown

Meanwhile, Richard of Gloucester made preparations to seize the throne. He propagandized that Edward V and the Duke of York were illegitimate. This was because when their father married their mother, he was already betrothed to another woman. In other words, the marriage was illegal. It was a terrible smear on the boys, but Londoners just about believed the story. Richard was proclaimed King Richard III. His coronation took place on 6 July 1483.

It is possible that just then the boy king and his brother had still been alive. But once their uncle had

Shakespeare's Richard III is one of the great tragic parts in British theatre. Ian McKellen (below) played the role on film in 1995. Forty years earlier, Laurence Olivier starred in and directed another film version.

During a propaganda campaign against him, the Tudors presented King Richard III as an evil hunchbacked monster who was born unnaturally, with teeth. This portrait shows there to be nothing wrong with Richard.

usurped the throne, they were not going to be permitted to remain alive for long. The boy king and his brother were killed, possibly on 3 September 1483.

As a usurper, King Richard III had many enemies. After the deaths of the Princes in the Tower, people found it easy to believe he would do anything to retain the stolen throne. When his wife, Anne Neville, died in 1484, people said that Richard had poisoned her so he could marry his niece Elizabeth, daughter of King Edward IV. That marriage would have strengthened Richard's hold on the throne.

But that was just gossip. Richard's real enemy was Henry Tudor. Henry was the chief claimant to the throne from the House of Lancaster. He had spent most of his life in exile. For years, Henry moved from one secret place to another, dodging the thugs that Yorkists had sent to kill him. He escaped them all. And in 1485, he set out to remove Richard from his stolen throne.

It is told that during the battle Richard's crown fell from his head and rolled in the dirt. Supposedly, it was later found hanging from a bush, where Lord Stanley picked it up and then placed it on Henry Tudor's head.

Betrayal and suicide

On 7 August, Henry Tudor arrived with an army of 4,000 to 5,000 men at Milford Haven in South Wales. It was not a large force. So, on 22 August, when Henry Tudor confronted Richard and his army of 12,000 men at the battle of Bosworth, in Leicestershire, his chances did not look good. But what neither Richard nor Henry knew was that three of

The seal of King Henry VII, the first Tudor monarch. It shows King Henry with the royal coat of arms on either side. An official document was only valid if it bore this seal.

At the battle of Bosworth Field in 1485, two of Richard III's most powerful supporters changed sides. Richard was doomed. He then staked everything on a desperate attempt to reach his rival, Henry Tudor, and kill him, but he failed.

Richard's commanders were about to desert him.

One, Henry Percy, Earl of Northumberland, refused to move his troops when ordered. Two others, Sir William Stanley and his brother Lord Stanley, planned to switch sides. Richard was doomed.

All he could do in the circumstances was make a desperate attack. It proved to be suicidal. With a small force of men, Richard spurred his horse through the front line of Henry Tudor's army. His aim was to reach Henry and kill him. Richard never got that far. He managed to kill Henry's standard bearer, but Henry's soldiers closed in and trapped him. Before long, Richard was pulled from his horse and killed. Afterwards, his naked body was slung over the back of a packhorse. Then it was taken to Leicester for burial.

Richard III was indeed the unlucky 13th Plantagenet king of England. With his death, the Wars of the Roses came to an end. A famous story recounts that, during the battle, Richard's crown fell from his head and rolled in the dirt. It was later found hanging from a bush. Supposedly, Lord Stanley picked up the crown and placed it ceremoniously on Henry Tudor's head.

After an eventful 330 years, Plantagenet rule in England had finally come to an end. As Henry VII, Henry Tudor became the first king of a new dynasty.

6

CONSPIRACY AND BLOODSHED

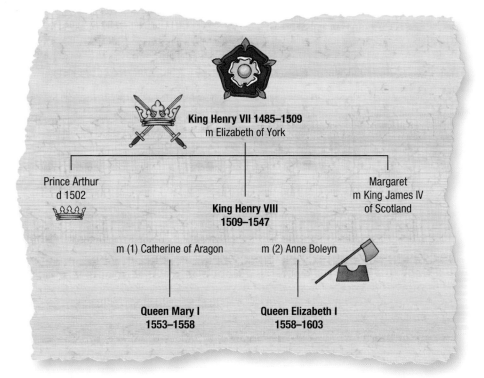

King Henry VII 1485–1509
m Elizabeth of York

Prince Arthur
d 1502

King Henry VIII
1509–1547

Margaret
m King James IV
of Scotland

m (1) Catherine of Aragon

m (2) Anne Boleyn

Queen Mary I
1553–1558

Queen Elizabeth I
1558–1603

The Plantagenet dynasty was gone. Now, the Tudors were in charge. But the Plantagenet family was still around. Henry VII, first king of the new Tudor dynasty, tried to heal the rift that had led to the Wars of the Roses.

◆

After the battle of Bosworth, he married Elizabeth of York, daughter of King Edward IV. This, King Henry hoped, would finally reunite the rival houses of York and Lancaster. But there was not a chance. The Yorkists were still out for revenge, and would try any trick in the book to dislodge the Tudors.

A 'king' with no crown

In 1487, a young man arrived in Ireland claiming to be Edward Plantagenet, Earl of Warwick. His real name

Cardinal Wolsey was Henry VIII's chief minister. The two were friends for the first twenty years of the king's reign, but Wolsey's relationship with Henry was soured by his failure to persuade the Pope to grant Henry a divorce.

was Lambert Simnel, son of a joiner in Oxford. The true earl was the son of George, Duke of Clarence, brother of King Edward IV. That gave Simnel a putative claim to the throne of England. He staked this claim on 24 May 1487: that day, he was crowned 'King Edward VI' in Dublin Cathedral. For a crown, the 'king' had to use a gold circlet 'borrowed' from a statue of the Virgin Mary.

The 'king's' humble end

When Henry VII heard about it, he responded vehemently. He knew this 'King Edward VI' was an impostor because he had the real Earl of Warwick imprisoned in the Tower. To prove Simnel was a sham, Henry brought the real Earl of Warwick out

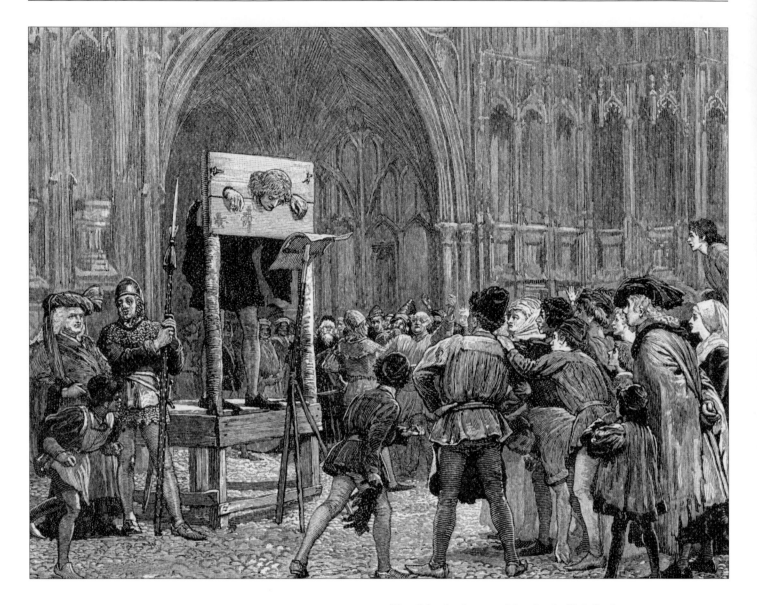

Perkin Warbeck, the second royal impostor of Henry VII's reign, is seen being put in the pillory where anyone was free to abuse him or throw missiles. Unlike the first impostor, Lambert Simnel, Warbeck was eventually executed.

of the Tower. He made a big show of parading him through the streets of London so everyone would know who he was. But this did not deter Simnel and his supporters. They landed an invasion force in Lancashire, in the north of England, on 4 June 1487, then marched south toward London.

King Henry was waiting for them at Stoke in Nottinghamshire, and won the battle that ensued. He also captured Lambert Simnel. Arguably, Simnel deserved to be executed for treason, but Henry decided to shame him instead. So he made Simnel a servant in the royal kitchens.

The 'king' who would not admit defeat

Lambert Simnel was not the only false claimant to the crown. In 1491, another young man turned up in Cork, Ireland, claiming to be the Earl of Warwick. Then he changed his story and said he was an illegitimate son of King Richard III. Finally, he settled for pretending to be Richard, Duke of York, one of the Princes in the Tower. The young Duke of York, so he declared, had not died in 1483; he had escaped and somehow made his way to safety. And here he was, in Ireland, ready to claim the throne of England that was rightfully his.

The young King Henry VIII was handsome and personable, with a flair for dancing. It was only later that he became a bitter, overweight, cruel and much feared despot with a reputation as a wife killer.

The Byward Tower at the Tower of London was meant to be the last in a series of strongholds for the complex. Even today, nighttime visitors have to give the right password to the sentry on guard before they can enter the Byward Tower.

The 'Duke of York' was, of course, another impostor. His real name was Perkin Warbeck. He was son of a customs official in the Netherlands. Warbeck was 19, about the same age the real duke would have been if he were still alive.

For Henry VII, this impostor was even more dangerous than Lambert Simnel. Henry sent agents to scour Europe and find him. Henry need not have bothered, for Warbeck fell straight into his hands. In 1497, he landed in Cornwall, in southwest England, with a force of 120 men. He gathered support and before long had raised an army of 8,000. Now, he felt secure enough to declare himself King Richard IV.

But Warbeck was no military leader. His followers were a rabble, with no idea how to fight a battle. Most of them fled when they encountered Henry's army at Taunton in Somerset. After that, Warbeck was easily captured and forced to confess that he was not really Richard IV. At first King Henry was kind to him. He made him one of his courtiers. It was only when Warbeck tried to escape that he was dispatched to the Tower of London.

King Henry VIII was obsessed with the Plantagenets. He set out to get rid of every Plantagenet he could lay his hands on.

That did not cure him. In 1499, King Henry's spies discovered that Warbeck and the real Earl of Warwick were planning to escape. It was the end for both of them. Warbeck was hanged. Warwick was beheaded.

There were no more impostors during the reign of King Henry VII, which ended with his death in 1509.

But his successor, King Henry VIII, was obsessed with the Plantagenets and their conspiracies. As king he set out to get rid of every Plantagenet he could lay his hands on.

Henry VIII's chief target was the De la Pole family. They were descended from George, Duke of Clarence, the brother of Edward IV and Richard III. Their claim to the throne was somewhat distant, but legitimate all the same.

During Henry's reign, the senior member of the family was Margaret Pole, Countess of Salisbury. Cardinal Reginald Pole, son of the countess, managed to escape into exile in Europe. But his brother Geoffrey Pole was arrested. He gave evidence against his mother the countess, another of his brothers, Henry Pole, Lord Montague and two other relatives, Henry Courtenay, Marquis of Exeter, and Sir Edward Neville. All were executed.

By this time, Henry had gained a very bloodthirsty reputation. Much later, he was given the nickname 'Bluff King Hal' – jolly, friendly, kindly and always

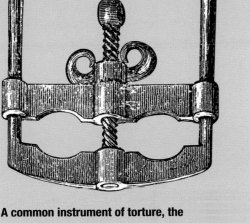

KING WITH A LUST FOR BLOOD

DEEDS *of* **POWER**

THERE WAS LITTLE DOUBT how the evidence against the Poles and their relatives was obtained. Geoffrey Pole was tortured. When the agony became too much for him, he 'confessed'. But he did not have to confess to much. Any excuse was enough for King Henry to order an execution.

Lord Montague was condemned to death for letting slip a piece of gossip about the king and his father: When Henry VIII was a boy, Montague said, his father did not like him. Sir Edward Neville was condemned because he once opined: 'the king is a beast and worse than a beast'. It was careless talk, nothing more. But both Montague and Neville were executed on Tower Hill on 9 December 1538. Henry Courtenay died with them.

By this time, Margaret, Countess of

A common instrument of torture, the thumbscrew was designed to extract information and confessions from prisoners.

Salisbury was in prison. She was a harmless lady in her late sixties. As with Montague and Neville, the evidence against her was trivial. Her crimes? She forbade her servants to read the Bible in English, and was once seen burning a letter. The truth was that her death sentence owed to her Plantagenet blood alone.

She, too, was executed on Tower Hill, outside the Tower of London, on 28 May 1541. Her death was grotesque. The countess was senile. When led out to the execution block, she did not know where she was or what was happening. She was told to lay her head on the block. Instead, she wandered around Tower Hill.

She was grabbed and forced back to where the block stood. Her head was pushed into place. Unfortunately, the executioner was young and inexperienced. The axe was probably blunt. He had to hack away at the countess's head three or four times before it fell off.

Margaret, Countess of Salisbury, a senior member of the Plantagenet royal family, was grotesquely beheaded for treason in 1541.

good for a laugh. The real King Henry VIII hardly matched that description. In truth he was terrifying. By 1541, Henry had married four wives, and each had had time to discover what he really was: a cruel despot who would not hesitate to torture and execute anyone in his way.

Blissfully wedded

Henry VIII's first wife was Catherine of Aragon, daughter of King Ferdinand and Queen Isabella of Spain. Catherine had been married before, to Henry's elder brother Arthur. But Arthur died in 1502, soon after the wedding. Little did Catherine know that

> Henry loved his daughter Mary and was very proud of her. But England was not yet ready for a reigning queen. Henry needed a new, young wife who could give him the son he so desperately craved.

this first marriage would later provide Henry with ammunition against her. Catherine was six years older than Henry. She had to wait for him to grow up before he could marry her. He was 18 and already King of England, and she was 24 when the ceremony took place on 11 June 1509.

At first, Henry and Catherine were very happy. 'My wife and I be in good and perfect love as any two creatures can be,' Henry wrote to Catherine's father, King Ferdinand. Their first child, a son, was born on New Year's Day, 1510. His delighted father held a tournament in celebration at Richmond Palace. Then, tragedy struck. The baby prince lived for only seven weeks. Henry and Catherine were devastated. But things would only get worse.

Dark clouds on the horizon

Catherine had several more children. All except one died in infancy or were born dead. The only survivor was a daughter, Princess Mary, born in 1516. Catherine had been a beautiful woman. But all those deaths had worn her down. By age 30 she had lost her

Catherine of Aragon, the first wife of King Henry VIII, was born a Spanish princess in 1485. She was trained and educated for her role as a Queen Consort and was capable of taking over from the king when he was absent abroad.

looks and her figure. Even her hair had turned silver. She became intensely religious. Most of her time was spent at prayer. She even wore a hair shirt under her gowns, in the manner of an ascetic or saint.

None of this appealed much to Henry. He liked young, lively women and Catherine was no longer young nor lively. But most of all, he longed for a son to succeed him.

Henry loved his daughter Princess Mary and was very proud of her. He also spoiled her. But England was not yet ready for a reigning queen. Henry needed a new, young wife who could give him the son he so desperately craved.

New flesh for the king

In 1522 Anne Boleyn came to court as one of Queen Catherine's ladies-in-waiting. She was 21, stylish, sexy and sophisticated. Although not beautiful, Anne knew how to attract men. She was a tremendous flirt with a few tricks up her sleeve. Even King Henry was taken aback by how much she knew about the arts of love.

Anne Boleyn was also ambitious. Once she arrived at the royal court, she aimed for the top prize: Henry VIII himself. But she was not going to make the same mistake as her sister Mary, who had once been Henry's mistress. Mary had learned a great deal at the royal court in France, which was in fact little more than an upscale brothel. She joined in the fun with such zest that even the French king, Francis I, considered Mary little more than a common prostitute. When Henry took her over, he thought he could benefit from such an experienced mistress. But maybe he hadn't been able to keep up with her: Anne Boleyn said later that he was not a very good lover. Even so, Henry had tired of Mary Boleyn after two years and thrown her out. Anne was not going to let that happen to her.

All or nothing

In 1526, Henry asked Anne to become his mistress. He was flabbergasted when she turned him down. He kept on trying, but the more he tried, the more Anne refused. He wrote her passionate love letters. She took her time answering, just to keep him on the hook. But

Catherine, seen in the foreground, knew about Henry VIII's romance with her lady-in-waiting, Anne Boleyn. In this 20th century illustration Henry and Anne are seen chatting in the background while a tearful Catherine walks alone in tears.

she would not budge. She knew she had driven the King of England into a frenzy of desire – just where she wanted him.

Meanwhile, Henry was having big trouble with Catherine. She had always been a great lady; calm, modest and gracious. It would not be difficult to get around her, or so Henry believed. Then, he could have Anne Boleyn. But in June 1527, when he told Catherine he wanted a divorce, he found out differently.

Henry had discovered a good reason for divorcing Catherine, a religious reason that should have done the trick. The 'Prohibition of Leviticus' in the Bible forbade marriage between a man and his brother's widow. King Henry could always persuade himself that whatever he wanted he should have. And the

Prohibition of Leviticus persuaded him that his marriage to Catherine had been cursed. That was why all their sons had died.

The queen digs her heels in

Catherine burst into tears when he told her. But that did not mean she was giving in – far from it. When she stopped crying, Catherine told Henry that he could not have a divorce. She claimed that her brief marriage to Prince Arthur had never been consummated and therefore had not been a marriage at all. The Prohibition of Leviticus did not, therefore, apply. This was the start of one of the most ferocious marital contests in English history.

Now that it was war, husband and wife lined up their ammunition. Henry tried to gather evidence that Catherine and Prince Arthur had slept together. He did not get far with that line of inquiry. Some courtiers said they had, others said they had not.

Henry was furious. But he tried to get around

the problem by sending his chief minister, Cardinal Thomas Wolsey, to Rome. Wolsey's orders were to obtain permission from the Pope for Henry to marry Anne Boleyn. But Catherine had better firepower. She had powerful relatives in Europe. The mightiest was her nephew, King Charles I of Spain, who had the Pope, Clement VII, in his pocket. There was no way Henry was going to get what he wanted from him.

When Catherine told King Charles what was happening, he sent a stern warning to Henry to forget about the divorce or prepare for the consequences. But Charles had other things on his mind, such as French invasions of Spain and his own lands in Italy. These problems distracted the Spanish king long enough for Pope Clement to slip his leash. Clement agreed to send a legate, Cardinal Lorenzo Campeggio, to England to judge the royal divorce case.

The pope steps in…diplomatically

Pope Clement was a cautious man. He told Campeggio to waste time by taking the longest route to England. When he arrived, Campeggio was told, he should start by trying to patch up the royal marriage. Above all, Campeggio was to delay, delay again, and make no decision.

Until 1529, Cardinal Thomas Wolsey was a very powerful man. He is shown here receiving petitions and requests from people who treat him with extreme deference, bowing and kneeling as he passes by.

In this nineteenth century illustration, Cardinal Campeggio, the papal legate, questions Queen Catherine at the inquiry into the divorce while her husband, King Henry (seated) glowers in the background.

The Pope need not have taken the trouble. When Campeggio reached England after a journey of four months, he found that Henry and Catherine were still at odds. Neither would back down. Catherine fought Campeggio all the way. No, she told him, she would not enter a nunnery. No, she would not leave the court. And she would rather die twice than admit her marriage to Henry was invalid.

Campeggio had no better luck with King Henry. He wanted Anne Boleyn and that was that. Clearly, it would be a fight to the finish. All the same, the cardinal convened a special court on 21 June 1529. He ordered King Henry and Queen Catherine to attend. But after they arrived, it was Catherine who captured all the attention.

In her speech to the court, she asked for justice as Henry's 'true and obedient wife.' Then, she asked – in all innocence – how she had offended him. It was a great performance. At the end, Catherine swept out of the court. Henry commanded her to return. She refused.

...a friend indeed

Henry exploded. In his fury, he turned on Cardinal Wolsey, his faithful minister since the beginning of his reign. But Wolsey's devotion did not matter now. What mattered was that he had failed to persuade the Pope to let Henry marry Anne Boleyn. Anne had already been running a slander campaign against Wolsey. She had Henry spellbound, and it was only a matter of time before he accused Wolsey of high treason. Wolsey was so upset he became seriously ill. In 1530, he died on his way to London where the treason trial was to have taken place. Anne Boleyn celebrated his death with a court entertainment called *The Going to Hell of Cardinal Wolsey*. Henry was disgusted. But he was so scared of Anne and her sharp tongue that he let her get away with it.

By now he had gone too far with the divorce to walk away from it. Meanwhile, King Charles of Spain had thrashed the French invaders. So the Pope was in his power again and Henry would have no joy there. He was also thoroughly bedeviled by his women. Catherine still defied him. So did their daughter, Princess Mary. And Anne Boleyn continually nagged him to marry her.

In 1531, egged on by Anne Boleyn, Henry separated Catherine from their daughter Mary. Anne believed the two had conspired against the king. Splitting them up might weaken their resistance. The king ordered Catherine to More House in Hertfordshire. Mary was sent to the royal palace at Richmond, Surrey. Mother and daughter would never see each other again.

After that, Catherine was moved from one house to the next. Each was more decrepit and unhealthy than the last. Wherever she was, Henry sent counsellors and other officials to crack her resistance. They tried threatening her. They terrorized her. They told her terrible things would happen to Princess Mary if she did not change her mind. They got nowhere.

Anne throws her weight around

Meanwhile, Anne Boleyn was showing off in London. She said she would rather see Catherine hanged than acknowledge her as Queen of England. Henry demanded that Catherine hand over her jewels. When she did so, he gave them to Anne.

Anne was already living in the royal apartments that had once belonged to Catherine. She had her own ladies-in-waiting. It was as if she were Queen Anne already. She was constantly with the king. They dined together, danced together, went hunting together. They did everything except sleep together. This stoked up Henry's passion even more. In addition to jewels, he sent Anne other luxurious gifts, such as hangings in cloth of gold and silver, and lengths of embroidered crimson satin. Henry also gave her a title – Marquess of Pembroke: lands worth £1,000 a year went with it. Anne Boleyn was riding high.

But she did not intend to hold off Henry forever. Around November or December 1532, she at last let the king take her to bed. A month or so later, she was pregnant. This was probably no accident. Anne was determined to be queen.

Her pregnancy was a warning

Born to a poor family in Ipswich, the son of a butcher, Thomas Wolsey rose to the greatest heights possible: he effectively governed England for the first twenty years of Henry VIII's reign. He also had ambitions to become Pope.

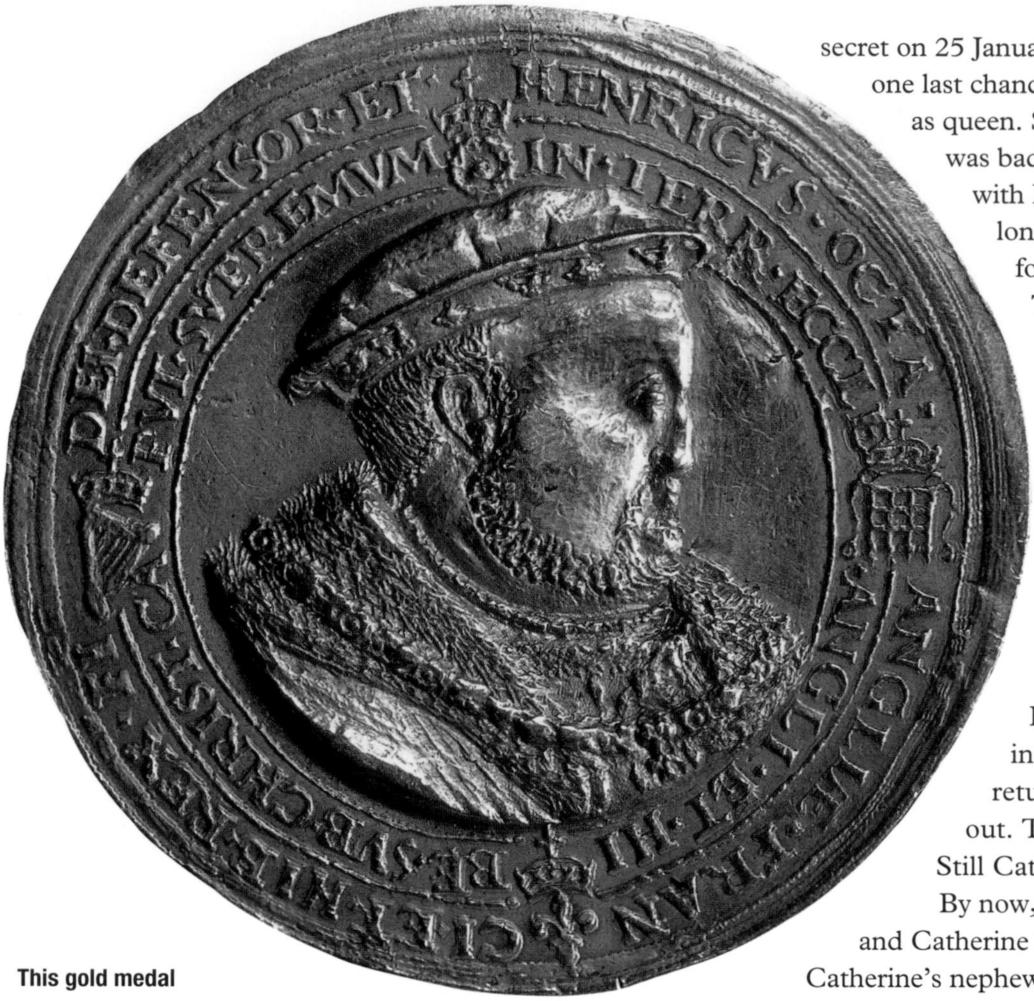

This gold medal
was minted in 1545 to
commemorate Henry VIII's
new role as head of the English church in place of the Pope.
Henry appears on the medal wearing an ermine robe and a
cap and collar studded with jewels.

to Henry to put his foot down and get that divorce.
Henry's response to Anne's demands was to change
England and the lives of its people forever.

A milestone in history

At this time in Europe, the Reformation was
underway. Protestants were breaking away from the
Pope and the Roman Catholic Church. Now, it was
Protestants against Catholics. King Henry was a
sincere Roman Catholic, but he broke with Rome just
the same. The Pope would not give him a divorce.
So he made himself Supreme Head of the Church of
England and granted himself the divorce he wanted.

Anne finally gets her way

King Henry VIII and Anne Boleyn were married in
secret on 25 January 1533. Henry had given Catherine
one last chance to give up her rights and title
as queen. She had still refused. The outlook
was bad for Catherine. After the break
with Rome, the English church no
longer needed the Pope's agreement
for anything. So it was easy for
Thomas Cranmer, Archbishop
of Canterbury, to declare that
Catherine's marriage was at an
end. At the same time, he decreed
that Anne's marriage was legal.
Catherine was ordered to
stop calling herself 'Queen of
England'. She had to use the
title 'Princess Dowager' instead.
It was a terrible insult. Once
more, Catherine refused. When
Henry sent her a document changing her title to Princess Dowager, she
returned it with the new title crossed
out. The furious Henry threatened her.
Still Catherine held out.

By now, the struggle between Henry
and Catherine had gone beyond a marital spat.
Catherine's nephew, Charles of Spain, threatened to
invade England. Moreover, Henry's subjects did not
like Anne Boleyn, but loved Catherine. Whenever
Catherine had to move from one house to the next,
people gathered by the thousands to cheer her. Anne
was often booed in public. There were public demonstrations against Anne. She was called a 'whore' and a
'witch'. A huge crowd gathered when she rode through
the streets of London on the way to her coronation on
1 June 1533. The crowd had been ordered to cheer.
Instead, they yelled: 'Nan Bullen shall not be our
Queen!'

His Majesty regrets

By this time, the King had become desperate.
Catherine and Mary were still defying him. As for
Anne, she was giving her husband a hard time. Anne
was a real tartar, demanding and vengeful. She

After the downfall of Cardinal Wolsey, Henry took over his
magnificent palace, Hampton Court, by the River Thames. He
was astounded and also infuriated at the luxurious fittings
and decorations, like those seen here in the Great Hall.

A LOVE TEMPERED BY DIGNITY

IN HER LAST HOURS, Catherine dictated a letter to the king. Even in the face of his great cruelty, as the last line clearly shows, she had always loved the king.

'My most dear lord, king and husband: the hour of my death drawing on, the tender love I owe you forceth me…to commend myself to you and to put you in remembrance…of the health and safeguard of your soul, which you ought to prefer before all wordly matters…for which you have cast me into many calamities and yourself into many troubles. For my part, I pardon you everything and I wish devoutly to pray God that He will pardon you also. For the rest, I commend unto you our daughter Mary, beseeching you to be a good father to her…. Lastly, I make this vow, that mine eyes desire you above all things. Farewell.'

Catherine needed help to hold the pen as she signed the letter. Her signature was shaky. It read 'Catherine, Queen of England.' She had defied King Henry to the last.

threw one tantrum after another. Her child, born on 7 September 1533, turned out to be another girl – the future Queen Elizabeth I. There were no celebrations.

Henry felt he had been made the laughingstock of Europe. In England, he had to face fearful slanders. It was said that the king was living in sin with Anne, that she was no more than a wicked woman with loose morals who deserved to be burned at the stake. Princess Elizabeth was condemned as illegitimate.

> **Catherine did not have much longer to live. By 1534, it was said she had dropsy. In fact, she was suffering from cancer. 'So much the better', retorted the king when he heard about it.**

Before long, Henry decided it was Anne's fault that their child was not the son he wanted. He began to call his second marriage his 'great folly'.

It certainly looked that way. Henry had no control over Anne. She would insult him in front of his courtiers. She never apologized. All Henry could do was to complain to Anne's father, Sir Thomas Boleyn, that Queen Catherine had never used such language to him.

The pressure brought out Henry's natural cruelty. He began to mull over the idea of getting rid of Anne. But, as long as Catherine lived, he was stuck with her.

Catherine, however, had not much longer to live. By 1534, it was said she had dropsy. In fact, she was suffering from cancer. 'So much the better', retorted the king when he heard about it. Catherine was then shortening whatever life she had left by refusing to eat. She was afraid Henry was going to poison her.

Meanwhile, there was opposition to his second marriage. Henry's answer was to execute anyone who spoke out against it. One of the condemned was Sir Thomas More, scholar and author, and once Henry's chancellor. More was beheaded on Tower Hill on 6 July 1535.

By that time Catherine was dying. Somehow she hung on over Christmas 1535 and into 1536. But she was in a terrible state. She was so wasted, wrote ambassador Chapys, 'that she could hard sit up in bed. She couldn't sleep. She threw up what food she managed to swallow.' Finally, she passed away on 9 January 1536.

Sir Thomas More, Henry's former chancellor, refused to acknowledge him as the head of the English church. Found guilty at his trial for high treason, More was executed in 1535. Here he is, saying good-bye to his daughter, Margaret Roper.

7
DECAPITATION AND DIVORCE

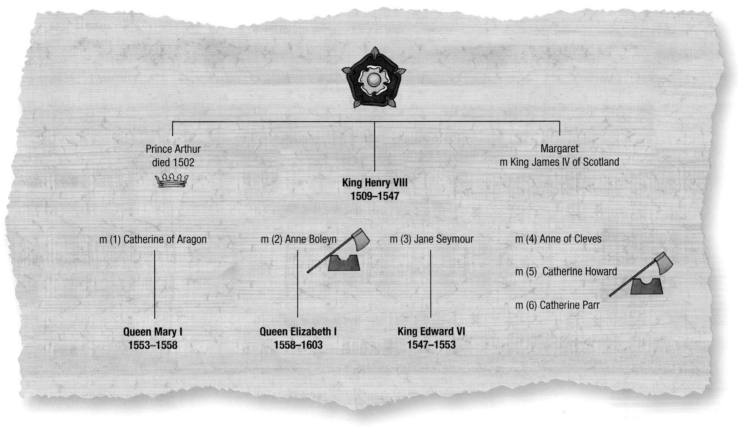

Prince Arthur
died 1502

Margaret
m King James IV of Scotland

King Henry VIII
1509–1547

m (1) Catherine of Aragon

m (2) Anne Boleyn

m (3) Jane Seymour

m (4) Anne of Cleves

m (5) Catherine Howard

m (6) Catherine Parr

Queen Mary I
1553–1558

Queen Elizabeth I
1558–1603

King Edward VI
1547–1553

Free of Catherine at last, King Henry began to think of ways to get rid of Anne. He was tired of clever, educated women like his first two wives. What he wanted now was a nice, placid girl who would not argue with him.

◆

Henry found his new wife in the same place he had found Anne Boleyn: among the queen's ladies-in-waiting.

The perfect partner

Jane Seymour, daughter of Sir John Seymour, appeared to fit the bill perfectly. She seemed quiet and modest with a nondescript personality. Nor was she very pretty: she had a long chin, a tight mouth and a

The Tower of London had been used as a palace, a prison and a place of execution since Norman times. Here Henry's second wife, Anne Boleyn, would meet her end.

large nose. She could hardly read and write, beyond signing her own name. Yes, dull, plain Jane Seymour was just what Henry wanted.

But Jane Seymour was much more calculating than Henry could have known. She quickly gathered that Anne Boleyn was on the way out. This was Jane's cue to step in smartly. She played the game perfectly. She accepted gifts Henry sent her. But she would not open his letters or accept money. Once, she kissed a letter sent to her on the king's behalf. Then she handed it back to Sir Nicholas Carew, who had brought it to her. She also gave back the purse of gold that came with it. Jane asked Sir Nicholas to tell the king she would only

351

accept money when God sent her a husband. Subtle hints were not Jane's style.

Poor fool Henry was taken in again. He was delighted that Jane had proven so virtuous and demure. But Anne Boleyn was not so easy to deceive. She knew exactly what was going on.

A minx at court

Jane heartlessly rubbed Anne's nose in the dirt. Henry sent Jane a portrait of himself in a locket. In front of Anne, she toyed with it. She opened and closed it and cooed over it. Anne was so furious that she tore the locket from Jane's neck. Several times she slapped Jane's face when gifts and messages from Henry arrived. Jane made no secret of where they had come from.

Now that Henry had found a new love, there was only one hope for Anne: to produce the longed-for son. She became pregnant three more times. She lost two of the babies, but near the end of 1535, she was pregnant again. Henry began to hope, but still carried on with Jane. Then, on the afternoon of 29 January the day Queen Catherine was buried, something happened to push Anne over the edge: she found her rival sitting on the king's knee.

Anne flew into such a wild fury that Henry began to

> ## Torture was used to obtain Smeaton's confession. Henry knew perfectly well that Anne was being framed. But he was satisfied.

---

fear for the child she was carrying. He tried to calm her down. But she raged on and on. A few hours later, the inevitable happened. Anne miscarried. When it was examined, her child appeared to be a son. For Anne, it was the end. She had a violent argument with the king. Each of them blamed the other for the miscarriage. Eventually, the king stormed out, vowing Anne would have no more sons by him.

This time, Henry did not have divorce in mind. Anne, he knew, would plague him for as long as she lived. There was only one answer: Queen Anne Boleyn had to die.

Anne Boleyn was the fiery, sexy and ambitious second wife of Henry VIII. She got away with treating him with little respect, but fell foul of fate when, instead of the longed-for son, her child born in 1533 turned out to be a girl.

Henry chose his weapons. He would accuse Anne of witchcraft, adultery and plotting his death. All these charges carried the death penalty. Henry set his chancellor, Thomas Cromwell, to gather the 'evidence' together. Thomas Cromwell was a highly inventive man. Gossip and reports from spies formed part of his dossier against Queen Anne. The rest he made up. Henry now learned that Anne supposedly had had four lovers: three courtiers and a court musician, Mark Smeaton. Cromwell also 'discovered' that Anne had committed incest with her brother, Lord Rochford.

As per usual in Tudor times, torture was used to obtain Smeaton's confession. The others all denied the charges. Henry knew perfectly well that Anne was being framed. But he was satisfied. He ordered Anne's arrest on the evening of 2 May 1536. She was taken to the Tower of London in a paroxysm of fear. She had to be helped out of the barge that took her to the Tower. By the time she stepped inside she was hysterical and sobbing wretchedly. In mid-May, her 'lovers' went on trial. The evidence given was full of holes. Anne and her 'lovers' could prove they were all in different places when the alleged adulteries had taken place.

No place for truth

It did not matter. Henry could always fall back on the supposed plot to kill him. It was 'guilt by accusation', but it did the trick. The four 'lovers' were all found guilty. They escaped the penalty for traitors: hanging, drawing and quartering. Instead, they were beheaded on Tower Hill on 17 May 1536. The same afternoon, Anne's marriage to Henry was annulled.

At her own trial, Anne was calm and dignified. She denied everything. But it did her no good. She was found guilty and condemned to death. From her apartments at the Tower, she watched workmen constructing her scaffold. They worked all night and by 9:00 A.M. the next morning, 18 May, the scaffold was ready. The queen was executed the following day.

While Anne's trial was going on, Henry was making arrangements to marry Jane. Their engagement was announced on the same day Anne Boleyn died. Eleven

DEEDS
of
POWER

A DEATH WITH DIGNITY

HENRY DID ANNE one last good turn. Instead of being beheaded with an axe, like a common criminal, she was given a more dignified execution: her head was cut off with a sword. On 19 May 1536, a swordsman was waiting as she walked out across Tower Green and climbed the scaffold steps. He had tactfully hidden his sword underneath straw.

With a priest, Anne knelt and prayed. In these last moments of her life, she was calm. She took off her hood and necklace. A blindfold was tied over her eyes. As she prayed again, the executioner swiftly sliced off her head. Her last words had been: 'Mother of God! Pray for me. Lord Jesus! Receive my soul!'

Thereafter, Anne Boleyn was wiped off the royal map. In the royal palaces, her portraits were removed from the walls. Masons, carpenters and seamstresses stripped her initials from sheets and cushions and everywhere else they had been applied.

Anne Boleyn bids farewell to her ladies-in-waiting in this illustration. Her executioner, a French swordsman, waits in the background (right), beside the execution block.

This picture shows the inside of Traitor's Gate, one of the entrances to the Tower of London. Traitor's Gate was close by the Thames and prisoners were rowed along the river to disembark at the bottom of the steps leading up to it.

days later, on 30 May 1536, Jane became Henry's third wife and queen in a ceremony at Whitehall Palace. Jane was also Henry's third chance to have the son he so greatly desired.

But by now, King Henry was no longer the handsome young man he had been in his youth. He was 45, nearly 20 years older than Jane. He had grown fat and had a troublesome ulcer on his leg. His temper was worse than ever. But Jane played the submissive wife, which made Henry feel a bit better. It is likely, however, that the king's bad health prevented Jane from conceiving quickly. It was January, 1537, before she could tell Henry she was expecting.

Henry became almost mad with joy. He was sure that the child would be a son. This time, he was right.

Ecstasy gives way to agony

Jane gave birth to Prince Edward on 12 October 1547. Henry's joy knew no bounds. Church bells pealed in celebration. Bonfires blazed. Twenty thousand rounds of ammunition were fired off at the Tower of London. Doors were decorated with garlands. Banquets were held throughout England. The party went on for 24 hours.

But something had gone wrong. Jane seemed to recover quite well from the birth. But four days later, she fell ill. It was soon clear that Jane had childbed fever. Her doctors were helpless. All they could conclude was that Jane's servants had given her too much rich food. After three days, Jane was delirious. Another three days passed, and she was dying. She hung on for a while, but passed away on 24 October.

Henry was demented with grief. He bolted to Windsor Castle and shut himself up, unwilling to see or speak to anyone. His ministers were, in any case, terrified of him. None dared come near him for some

German artist Hans Holbein came to England in 1526 and again in 1532 to paint a series of magnificent portraits of prominent men and women, including the original version of this picture of King Henry VIII.

time. Particularly not with the plans they had already laid for his fourth marriage.

Duty comes first

Henry's ministers were practical men. With his second and third marriages, the king had failed to do his dynastic duty: to make a marriage for political advantage. Also, one infant son as heir to the Tudor throne was not enough: babies and children died all too easily and far too early in the 16th century. Henry had to marry again.

But Henry had a terrible track record. One wife hounded to death; another executed. A third, Jane Seymour, had survived mainly because she knew how to keep her mouth shut. The remnants of the

Plantagenet family, and several high profile victims such as Thomas More, had all been beheaded. This King of England, it seemed, was dangerous. To marry him looked very much like a prescription for suicide.

The search for a willing bride

Likely brides in Europe were thoroughly alerted. Two were daughters of King Francis I of France. He refused to let them even think of marrying Henry. Another French princess, Mary of Guise, hastily married someone else – King James V of Scotland – upon hearing that Henry had been after her. Another, Duchess Christina of Milan, agreed to marry the king – as long as she could have two heads, one for the axeman and one for herself.

It was not just the risk of disgrace and death that put these women off. Nearly 50 years old, Henry was not much of a catch. He needed a nurse, not a wife. His health was poor, his temper worse than ever. He could no longer ride or joust in the lists, once his best-loved sport. All in all, he was a wreck.

Fortunately for Henry, there was still political advantage in marrying the King of England. In Europe, small Protestant states were under threat from the prominent Roman Catholic powers, Spain and France. One such state was Cleves, in Germany. For England, the Duchy of Cleves would be a useful ally against the French and the Spaniards. The ruling Duke of Cleves, John III, had two unmarried daughters. In 1538, Duke John offered the elder, Anne, as a bride for King Henry.

The nightmare bride

Anne of Cleves was ugly, skinny and loud-mouthed. Neither was she much concerned about personal hygiene. Anne was a problem. Henry liked his wives well-covered, good-natured and retiring. He had had enough of clever women with opinions of their own. But Henry's ministers, who approved of the match, got around this by lying to Henry about Anne. They

Jane Seymour, Henry VIII's third queen, was quiet, demure and ill-educated – just the sort of wife he wanted. Though pale-faced and plain, Jane looks magnificent in this portrait, which emphasizes her rich robes and jeweled headdress.

SVÆ ·21

described her as 'moderately beautiful'. They said she was tall, but did not mention she was skinny. To back this up, they commissioned a leading artist, Hans Holbein, to paint a portrait of Anne. It showed her as a dumpy young woman with dreamy eyes, but that was not all it showed. Most of the portrait was taken up with Anne's magnificent jewel-encrusted gown and headdress.

Henry fell for it. He soon was madly in love, and demanded to meet Anne as soon as possible.

A date with disappointment

The meeting was a disaster. Anne and her entourage arrived at Deal in Kent on 26 December 1539. She set out for London at once and arrived four days later. In a tizzy of love, King Henry rushed to see her. What he beheld was not the beautiful bride he anticipated, but an absolute fright. She was badly dressed and gawky. And she smelled awful. Henry was repelled. 'I like her not, I like her not,' he kept repeating. Henry was enraged.

Cromwell takes it on the chin

Henry summoned Thomas Cromwell, his chancellor, who had made the marital arrangements. The king habitually thrashed Cromwell, who was of low birth. Cromwell was often witnessed staggering out of meetings with Henry, his clothes awry and his hair askew. He also had at least one –more frequently two – black eyes. At their meeting to discuss Anne of Cleves, Henry was more violent than ever. But Cromwell kept his cool. He knew the alliance with Cleves was important and managed to convince the king that he was sincerely committed to this marriage. Henry, no fool, understood the significance of the alliance, too. So he gritted his teeth and married his ugly, foul-smelling bride on 6 January 1540.

But already, the king was trying to think of a way out. He had his lawyers look for loopholes in the marriage contract. The contract proved to be watertight. Next, Henry suggested that Anne was not a virgin when she married him. If she had been with other men, the marriage could have been annulled.

Catherine Howard looks a lot older than her 15 years in this portrait, based on a painting by Holbein. Catherine managed to ruin herself within two years of her marriage and suffered the same fate – execution – as her cousin Anne.

A marriage made in hell

Henry knew perfectly well that Anne was a virgin. He kept her that way by refusing to sleep with her. Poor Anne spoke little English and knew nothing of the 'facts of life'. She was bemused by the jokes that went around Henry's court about the virgin bride who did not know how to do 'it'. But Anne soon learned that she had failed to please. Her coronation as queen had been set for February 1540. Henry called it off without giving a reason.

Catherine Howard, a cousin of Anne Boleyn, was about 15 years old, but she was very beautiful and knew how to please men. She had had at least two lovers since the age of 12.

Then Anne's ladies-in-waiting explained to her what should happen when a husband and wife get into bed together. Anne could then hardly fail to realize that what was meant to happen was most definitely not happening. At last, it dawned on her that Henry was trying hard to get rid of her. And, as everyone knew, when Henry VIII got rid of a wife, she usually ended up in a grave.

Dumb but alluring

Alarm bells began to ring loudly for Anne when Henry started paying too much attention to one of her ladies-in waiting. Catherine Howard, a cousin of Anne Boleyn, was about 15 years old, but was very beautiful and knew how to please men. She had had at least two lovers since the age of 12. Although she could not read or write, and was interested in nothing but her own pleasure, Catherine was lovely to look at, young, flirtatious and ignorant – for King Henry, Catherine Howard filled the bill perfectly.

Anne was not jealous, it seemed, but was terribly frightened. Henry began to complain that she 'waxed wilful and stubborn with him'. Thomas Cromwell, just as scared, had to tell Anne not to antagonize the king or both of them would suffer.

REGAL PROFILES

JOY AT LAST FOR ANNE

AFTER THE DIVORCE ANNE remained in Britain. Henry gave her an allowance of £4,000 a year, a stupendous sum for the time. He also gave Anne two manors and a castle of her own. It was a wonderful ending for Anne; she was rich and independent for the first time in her life. Best of all, she was out of danger.

For the next 17 years, until her death in 1557, Anne led the life of a great lady. She staged huge banquets for her friends. She chose a different gown every day from her vast new wardrobe. She enjoyed every minute of it.

Holbein's portrait of the plain Anne of Cleves was meant to convince Henry of her 'beauty'. It succeeded – until the King met her in person.

Cromwell was the first to suffer. Six months after Henry married Anne, Cromwell had done nothing to get Henry off the hook. In the summer of 1540, Henry ran out of patience and set the dogs on him. On 10 June 1540, Cromwell was arrested and taken to the Tower of London. The same day, he was accused of treason and heresy. It was a trumped-up charge, but having framed Cromwell, Henry pursued it to the end. On 28 July, Cromwell was duly executed on Tower Hill.

Henry had already taken charge of ending his hated fourth marriage. He sent Anne to Richmond Palace, promising to join her in two days. He never showed up. Meanwhile, he pursued Catherine Howard. Every evening, the king could be seen sailing by barge along the River Thames to Lambeth, where Catherine had been given apartments.

At Richmond, Anne became more and more agitated. So it was a tremendous relief to her when, on July 6, Henry's counsellors arrived to ask if she would agree to a divorce. Anne had feared much worse. She grabbed the divorce with both hands. Her marriage to Henry ended three days later.

Just under three weeks after his divorce from Anne, on 28 July 1540, King Henry married Catherine Howard. He thought he had achieved bliss at last, but he was wrong, mainly because he had failed to read the tell-tale signs at the start. Catherine Howard had been on the 'good-time-girl circuit' – always looking for wild fun and not minding how she got it. She had lost her virginity long before Henry married her and her worldliness stood her in good stead when it came to seducing the aging, sickly king.

Catherine pretended to ignore Henry's huge bulk: he had a 54-inch waist. She also overlooked the oozing ulcer on his leg. Once, Henry had been able to dance

This document, dated 9 July 1540, set out the annulment of Henry's marriage to Anne of Cleves. Henry had not been able to bring himself to consummate the marriage, but he was fond of Anne and often visited her after their union ended.

Excellentissimo

all night and ride all day. Now, he could barely walk. Catherine paid no attention to that, either. Instead, she flattered him. She appealed to his vanity. He was hooked. He made a spectacle of himself in public, kissing and fondling her no matter who was watching. He called Catherine his 'rose without a thorn'. He pampered her, showering her with sumptuous gifts. In 1541 he presented her with jewels – 52 diamonds, 756 pearls and 18 rubies – to say nothing of furs, velvets, brocades and other finery.

Henry loved to show Catherine off. In July 1541, he took her on a 'progress', or tour, though the eastern and northern counties of Britain. But Catherine was

Catherine Howard was barely 17 years old when she was accused of adultery and beheaded in 1542. This illustration shows Catherine being rowed in some luxury to her imprisonment in the Tower of London.

in for a shock. When the 'progress' reached Pontefract in Yorkshire, Francis Dereham, one of her former lovers, showed up. Dereham knew far too much about Catherine, things that she did not want King Henry to discover. When Dereham asked to be allowed to join Catherine's household she had to agree. On August 27 Dereham became Catherine's private secretary.

If Catherine had hoped that would satisfy him, she was mistaken. Francis Dereham was the sort of young buck who could not keep his mouth shut. Dereham began to boast that he had known Catherine before King Henry. Everybody realized what he meant by 'known'. Sooner or later, the truth about Catherine's past was bound to come out.

Love is blind

It was sooner. In October 1541, Thomas Cranmer, Archbishop of Canterbury, received information about

DEEDS of POWER

A BRUTAL END FOR THE MOST BELOVED

CATHERINE WAS NOT GIVEN A TRIAL. That would have been too much for Henry, since his own folly would have been revealed in court. He would have looked like an old fool for having fallen for the wiles of a scheming harlot. Instead, charges were brought against Catherine in Parliament on 16 January 1542. She was presumed guilty and condemned to death.

Catherine was paralyzed with fear. When guards came to take her to the Tower of London, she refused to go. She had to be carried struggling to the barge that was to take her along the River Thames to the dreaded prison. By the time the barge reached there, Catherine was in a state of collapse.

Three days later, on 13 February 1542, she was led out to Tower Green. She could barely walk. Somehow, the executioner managed to get her to lay her head on the block. Then he swiftly chopped off her head with an axe.

An axe was normally used for executions by beheading, the fate of Catherine Howard in 1542.

Catherine's life before marriage. The information came from Mary Lascelles, who had lived in the same household as Catherine in Norfolk. Cranmer decided to investigate. He had a heart-to-heart talk with Mary Lascelles. She told him everything.

Cranmer turned pale as Mary described Catherine's noisy lovemaking sessions with Francis Dereham. He heard of how another lover, musician Henry Manox, boasted that he knew of a mark on Catherine's body where no man but her husband had a right to look. When Cranmer told King Henry, he refused to believe a word of it. It was just wicked gossip, he said. But just in case, he asked Cranmer to make further investigations. Meanwhile, Henry ordered Catherine to remain in her apartments. The

allegations, he was sure, would soon be disproven.

They were not. Cranmer's new investigations backed up everything the Archbishop already knew. Henry was devastated. He sat on his throne in the Council chamber and wept openly. He shut himself away in his palace at Oatlands in Surrey. He was eaten away with grief for his shattered happiness.

When Catherine was charged with 'misconduct', she became hysterical. She wept and wailed and threw herself about so violently that her attendants feared she was going to kill herself. When she calmed down, Catherine knew she had only one hope: she would have to beg Henry to forgive her.

Catherine waited until Henry passed close by her apartments on his way to prayers. She dashed past her

Van der Werff pinxit.   Hargrave sculpt.

This elegant portrait features Henry's sixth and last wife, Catherine Parr, who married the king in 1543. It is based on a painting by Hans Holbein, who died during an epidemic of bubonic plague in London the same year.

guards and ran towards the king. But she was unable get near him. The guards grabbed her before she could speak to him. Catherine was taken back to her apartments, screaming and struggling. She never saw Henry again.

Now Catherine and her lovers were quizzed relentlessly for evidence. Cranmer did not get much information out of Catherine. Whenever he tried to question her, she wept and became hysterical. However, she did mention another man she had known before marriage – Thomas Culpepper, now at Henry's court as a gentleman of the King's Privy Chamber. Culpepper was immediately arrested. His rooms were searched and a love letter from Catherine was found.

Cranmer was now hot on the trail. When he questioned Lady Rochford, one of Catherine's attendants, she told him everything about the love affair between Catherine and Culpepper. Lady Rochford disclosed how she had stood guard outside the bedroom door while the pair made love at Pontefract and elsewhere. Having sex before marriage was bad enough. But lovemaking at Pontefract meant that Catherine had committed adultery. And for that, there was only one penalty: death.

On 10 December 1541, Thomas Culpepper and Francis Dereham were executed. Afterwards, their heads were stuck atop pikes on London Bridge. The queen was executed two months later.

Finally, an enduring love

At long last, King Henry had learned his lesson. He would never find happiness by marrying young girls. The next time he chose a wife, in 1543, he chose well. Catherine Parr was a mature woman who had had two previous husbands. Thirty-one years old, she was more than 20 years younger than Henry. But she was level-headed, pleasant and kind-hearted. Henry married for the sixth and last time on 12 July 1543. During the next four years, Catherine Parr made a happy home for him and his three children. This was something none of them had ever known before.

But four years were all they would have. By the end of 1546, King Henry was in a worse state than ever. He found it difficult to walk. He had to be winched up and down stairs by a mechanical hoist. He was dying.

Gone, but never forgotten

Catherine stayed with him as he lay on his deathbed. So did his daughter by Catherine of Aragon, Princess Mary. But both became so upset that Henry told them to go away. For Catherine, it was a good thing. Before King Henry died on 28 January 1547, it was not her name that he cried out as he lay dying. Instead, he called for Jane Seymour, whom he had loved and lost ten years before. After his death, Henry was buried next to Jane at St. George's Chapel, Windsor.

This letter from Catherine Howard to Thomas Culpepper – probably dictated since she was almost illiterate – was open and affectionate, and became a vital piece of evidence against her when she was accused of adultery.

8

TURMOIL, TERROR AND FATAL ILLNESS

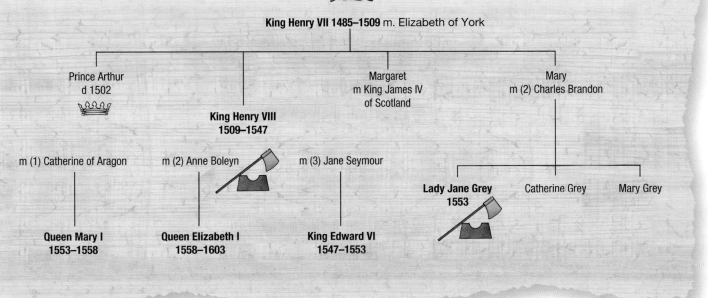

King Henry VII 1485–1509 m. Elizabeth of York

Prince Arthur
d 1502

Margaret
m King James IV
of Scotland

Mary
m (2) Charles Brandon

**King Henry VIII
1509–1547**

m (1) Catherine of Aragon

m (2) Anne Boleyn

m (3) Jane Seymour

**Lady Jane Grey
1553**

Catherine Grey

Mary Grey

**Queen Mary I
1553–1558**

**Queen Elizabeth I
1558–1603**

**King Edward VI
1547–1553**

The new king, Edward VI, was a boy of nine. His heirs were his half-sisters, Mary, daughter of Catherine of Aragon, aged 31, and Elizabeth, aged 13, daughter of Anne Boleyn.

◆

This was just the situation King Henry VIII had wanted to avoid. He had destroyed two wives in his search for a son to succeed him. Now, the Tudor throne was in the hands of a boy, a woman and a girl. And though it was not yet apparent, the last two had been badly affected by the turmoil of Henry's first two marriages.

This painting illustrates the scene at the execution of the unfortunate Lady Jane Grey, a victim of the plot that surrounded the succession to the English throne in 1553.

Princesses with a legacy of pain

Princess Mary had once been a bright, beautiful child, adored by her father. But she had suffered badly during her father's battle with her mother, Catherine of Aragon. Mary, aged 31 when Henry died, was left mentally scarred. Deprived of love, she craved it badly. Roman Catholicism was outlawed in England by this time. But Mary remained a devout Catholic. It all led to terrible mistakes and a sad, lonely end.

Princess Elizabeth could have gone the same way. But years of turmoil had hardened rather than

weakened her. She was unusually shrewd, even at 13. She was also very wary. She had been less than three years old when her father killed her mother. When Elizabeth was only eight, there was another execution: Catherine Howard, who had befriended Elizabeth, had her head chopped off. After that, Elizabeth came to believe that marriage was dangerous. Men were dangerous. These fears were to affect Elizabeth for the rest of her life.

Schemers 'protect' the boy-king

King Edward VI also had a problem: he was too young to rule on his own. He had to have a protector. This was the cue for two very ambitious men to seize the power they had always wanted: the boy-king's uncles, Edward and Thomas Seymour.

Edward Seymour was a fast mover. Two days after the death of King Henry VIII, he filled the Royal Council with his cronies. Then, with their help, he had himself proclaimed the boy-king's Protector. Next, Seymour gave himself a grand title – Duke of Somerset.

Meanwhile, Seymour's younger brother, Thomas, was plotting his own way to power. He planned to get it by the back door: if he could marry into the royal family, he would gain riches and a say in government.

There were three ways Thomas Seymour could ally himself to the royal family – he could marry Princess Mary, Princess Elizabeth or Henry VIII's widow, Catherine Parr. Mary and Elizabeth turned him down flat. They were princesses. Marriage to an upstart like Thomas Seymour would have been beneath their royal dignity. So Thomas fell back on Catherine Parr, who had in fact been betrothed to him before she married King Henry. Now he charmed her again. They married in secret in May 1547. Thomas Seymour had reached first base.

Not that his marriage stopped him from playing around. Seymour was particularly keen on Elizabeth. Seymour often went to her bedroom, wearing scanty clothes. He played suggestive games with Elizabeth. Seymour did not attempt to hide his activities. At court, he paid Elizabeth so much attention that Catherine, who was pregnant, became jealous.

Another Tudor family portrait by Holbein, this time of Edward VI, who succeeded his father, Henry VIII, in 1547. There was something wrong with the Tudor line – Edward was the third Tudor boy to die young, at just 15.

The unfortunate Catherine died in childbirth on 5 September 1548. This robbed Thomas Seymour of his precious royal connection. He became desperate. One night in January 1549, he was found outside King Edward's bedroom. He held a smoking pistol in his hand. The young king's pet dog lay dead at his feet. The only explanation offered was that Thomas had meant to kill the king.

> ## Edward Seymour was a fast mover. Two days after King Henry VIII's death, he filled the Royal Council with his cronies.

Protector Edward Seymour had never trusted his scheming brother. This was a chance to get rid of him. Thomas was accused of treason, and on his brother's orders, was executed on 20 March 1549.

No love lost between brothers

But Edward Seymour had himself made many enemies. He was hated for the way he grabbed power in 1547. The most deadly of his enemies was John Dudley, Earl of Warwick. Dudley was a cool customer. He was cunning, clever and much more ruthless than Edward Seymour. He had been planning the Protector's downfall for some time. On 6 October 1549, he struck.

Dudley arrived with a small armed force at Hampton Court Palace, near the River Thames. King Edward and Seymour were there at the time. The Protector hustled the boy-king onto a barge and ordered the bargemen to row downriver for Windsor – fast. Edward got there safely. But Seymour knew the writing was on the wall. Eight days later, he gave himself up and was sent to the Tower of London.

Subsequently, Seymour was charged with embezzlement and unlawful seizure of power. He was fined, and sacked from his role as Protector. He was released, and Dudley allowed Seymour to live a while longer, safe in the knowledge that sooner or later the former Protector would slip up. Then he could be accused of more serious crimes – crimes that carried the death penalty.

John Dudley, Duke of Northumberland, plotted to supplant Princess Mary, the rightful heir to the throne. His scheming ended in disaster and death for himself, his son Guildford Dudley and Dudley's wife Lady Jane Grey: all of them were executed.

England on the verge of bankruptcy

With both the Seymour brothers dead, John Dudley had a free hand to do as he pleased. He gave himself and his supporters grand titles. He became Duke of Northumberland. Dudley and his cronies plundered the monasteries and university libraries of their treasures. They grabbed royal estates worth a phenomenal £30,000 a year. By the time they had finished, England was almost bankrupt.

Meanwhile King Edward, now 14, was feeling the strain. The Seymour brothers had pressured him and torn his loyalties back and forth. But John Dudley was much worse. He was a pure brute. He treated the boy-king like a puppet, bullying him mercilessly. He nagged him to sign documents and laws. Edward had no say in anything: Dudley was all powerful.

Then, at the end of January 1553, Edward became seriously ill. He had a high fever, his lungs were congested, he could barely breathe. When Princess Mary came to visit him, he failed to recognize her. Edward, aged 15, was clearly dying. Alarm bells rang for John Dudley. If Edward died, Catholic Mary would become reigning queen. That would be the end of Dudley's power. He had no intention of letting that happen.

Swift marriages to aid plans

The plot he laid to hang on to power was truly dastardly. Dudley arranged three marriages. Sisters Lady Jane Grey, Catherine and Mary were members of the Tudor royal family, descended from Henry VIII's sis-

Seymour gave Dudley the chance he wanted in 1552. The Catholic Princess Mary had refused to have anything to do with Protestant church services. The Royal Council tried to bully her, but she would not give in.

Unfortunately for Edward Seymour, he had a fondness for Mary and supported her. With that, John Dudley pounced. He accused Seymour of wanting to restore the Roman Catholic Church in England. To back that up, Seymour was also charged with conspiring against the Royal Council.

It was a lethal package. Seymour was found guilty and sentenced to death. King Edward was horrified. He begged Dudley to spare Seymour's life. Dudley ignored his pleas and Edward Seymour was executed on 22 January 1552.

Jane Seymour's brother Edward made himself Protector to her son, King Edward VI, but was outmanoeuvred by the more brutal and ambitious John Dudley. Accused of treason, Edward Seymour was sent to the Tower and executed in 1552.

ter Mary. Jane Grey was considered most important of the three. Dudley married her off to his own son, Guildford Dudley. Catherine and Mary married powerful nobles, both Dudley's allies. That done, Dudley went to King Edward and bullied him into agreeing that if Princess Mary became Queen it would be a disaster for England. Poor Edward was too ill to resist. On Dudley's orders, the young king changed the succession to the throne. Now, his successor was to be Lady Jane Grey.

But Dudley had not finished with Edward. The boy was now a ghastly figure. He looked like a skeleton. His lungs had been eroded by tuberculosis. There were running sores all over his body. Dudley decided that he had to be kept alive. He called in a quack doctor who dosed Edward with arsenic. This drastic treatment revived the boy for a time. It was just long enough, Dudley thought, to trap Mary and Elizabeth. He invited both to Greenwich, in London, to see their dying half-brother.

Elizabeth immediately suspected a trap and refused to come. She guessed, correctly, that Dudley meant to imprison her and Mary. Mary was not quite so astute. She set out for London. But when she reached Hoddesdon, 25

The order for the execution of Lady Jane Grey that took place in 1554. Queen Mary shrank from executing her after the failure of Northumberland's plot, but the rebellion against Mary's planned marriage to Philip of Spain meant Jane had to die.

The escape of Elizabeth and Mary foiled Dudley's plan. But there was nothing he could do about it. Late in the evening of 6 July 1553, Edward VI died. At the end, he had been too weak to speak, or even cough.

Subjects loyal to Mary

John Dudley was in a fix. In Norfolk, nobles rushed to support Princess Mary, escorted by their armies. Soon, Mary's forces numbered 30,000 men. On 9 July Dudley had Lady Jane Grey declared Queen. But Mary's support kept growing.

Mary was now safeguarded in the fortress at Framlingham. Dudley set out from London to capture her. With Dudley gone, his supporters became so frightened they shut themselves up in the Tower of London. Lady Jane Grey and her husband were among them.

'Long live the queen!'

On his march to Framlingham, things went from bad to worse for Dudley. His troops started to desert. He heard that Londoners had declared their support for Mary. He himself was branded a rebel and realized his plan was hopeless. Overnight, his power had vanished. Dudley became hysterical. He tossed his cap into the air and shouted: 'Long live Queen Mary!' Tears ran down his cheeks as he said it. Against the odds, Mary was queen, the first reigning queen England had known.

John Dudley was arrested on 21 July, accused of high treason. Guarded by 4,000 soldiers, he was taken back to London. The people of England had come to hate Dudley. All the way, people lined his route to the capital. They jeered at him. They cursed him. They threw stones, shook their fists, shouted insults. When he reached London, he was imprisoned in the Tower.

John Dudley was arrested on 21 July, accused of high treason. Guarded by 4,000 soldiers, he was taken back to London.

---

miles (40km) from the capital, she received a warning that Dudley was up to no good. Mary fled to Kenninghall, her house in Norfolk. It was a much safer 85 miles (136km) from London.

Although she has since acquired the nickname 'Bloody Mary', Mary I began as England's first ever reigning queen with an act of mercy: she pardoned five prisoners incarcerated in the Tower of London.

Mary's triumph

Meanwhile, on 3 August 1553, Queen Mary entered London. It was a triumph all the way. Huge crowds gathered to cheer her. Some were so happy they wept. The noise was deafening. No monarch of England had ever received such a greeting.

Mary dressed for the occasion. Her gown was of royal purple. Her neck was circled with jewels. Even her horse had trappings made of cloth of gold. But she was now 37 and looked even older. All her sufferings now showed on her lined, pale face. Mary was not a cruel woman. She tried to see good in everyone. She was remarkably forgiving. But she could not forget what she had endured during the reigns of her father and brother.

As the cheering Londoners would soon learn, Mary's reign would be payback time for those sufferings. Her subjects would suffer in turn.

Queen of hearts

Queen Mary was on a high. And it was typical of her to begin her reign with an act of mercy. She pardoned five prisoners from the Tower of London. Mary's ministers expected her to punish the conspirators who had tried to cheat her of her throne. Mary confounded their expectations by pardoning all but three. Only John Dudley and two cronies were executed, on 22 August 1553.

But what to do with Lady Jane Grey, who had been 'queen' for only nine days? What about her husband, Guildford Dudley? People expected that they, too, would soon lose their heads. But Mary would not execute them, though they did remain imprisoned in the Tower.

Mary's primary aim was to restore England to the Roman Catholic Church. Unfortunately, she did not understand that her subjects were solidly Protestant. They wanted nothing to do with Catholics or with the Pope. With this, the stage was set for a major clash between the queen and her people. It became even bigger when news leaked out of Mary's marriage plans. Mary had chosen Philip, the son of King Charles of Spain – a Catholic, and a foreigner.

Wyatt's rebellion, which protested against the planned marriage of Queen Mary and Philip of Spain, was a terrifying experience for Londoners. Wyatt's army was massing, ready to march on the beleaguered city.

Mary was not as free to choose her own husband as she thought. Reaction against the 'Spanish Marriage', as it was called, was violent. Parliament was against it. Mary's ministers were opposed. Protestant bishops of the English church disapproved. Most of all, the people were against it. But foolishly, Queen Mary ignored them all. On 29 October 1553, she announced that she was betrothed to Philip. She would 'never change,' she said, 'but love him perfectly...'

Panic spreads

A wave of alarm spread through England. There were fearful stories doing the rounds that a Spanish army

DEATH OF AN INNOCENT

MARY HAD WANTED to let Lady Jane Grey and Guildford Dudley live. But the queen was not a soft touch any longer. The day after Wyatt surrendered, she signed death warrants for both. They were led out to execution on 12 February 1554. Guildford Dudley died first.

Later a chronicler wrote: 'His carcase thrown into a cart, and his head in a cloth, he was brought to the chapel within the Tower, where the Lady Jane...did see his dead carcase taken out of the cart.... '

The seventeen-year-old Lady Jane Grey died bravely and with dignity. The chronicler continued: 'She gave...(her attendants) her gloves and handkerchief, and her book...she untied her gown. The hangman went to her to help her therewith...giving to her a fair handkerchief to (tie) about her eyes.

'Then feeling for the block she said, "What shall I do? Where is it?" One of the standers-by guiding her thereto, she laid her head down upon the block, and stretched forth her body and said: "Lord, into thy hands I commend my spirit!" And so she ended.'

A fanciful illustration of the execution of Lady Jane Grey: the blow of the axe was normally administered to the back, not the side of the neck.

8,000 strong was en route to England. The Spaniards sought to take over the Tower of London, ships of the English Navy and England's ports.

None of these stories were true, of course. But rebellions were being planned all over the country. The rebels' leader, Sir Thomas Wyatt, was ready to march on London. Once there, Wyatt planned to use his military might to force Queen Mary to put a stop to the Spanish Marriage.

Wyatt and his followers set out for the capital on 25 January 1554. There was panic in London. Watchers were posted at every gate into the city. Mary ordered the bridges over the River Thames destroyed. Soldiers guarded the streets. Lawyers, priests and tradesmen wore shirts of mail beneath their robes for protection.

About the only one who did not panic was Queen Mary herself. She refused to leave London. She told Londoners: 'Good subjects, pluck up your hearts and like true men, stand fast against. . . our enemies and yours, and fear them not, for I assure you I fear them nothing at all!'

That cheered up Londoners for a while. But panic soon returned. The bridges had been destroyed, as Mary had ordered. But on the night of February 6, Thomas Wyatt swam across the icy River Thames. He found a boat and used it as a floating platform to repair one of the bridges.

Battle in the heart of London

That done, some 7,000 rebels marched across and on to London once again. On 17 February they reached the gates of the city. There, waiting for them, stood 10,000 soldiers, 1,500 cavalry and row upon row of heavy cannon.

Despite her bravery, Mary was badly shaken by Wyatt's rebellion. She realized that she could no longer afford to be merciful. There would be no pardon for the rebels this time.

As the rebels advanced, the lines of soldiers parted. Wyatt rushed through with his vanguard of about 400 men. But it was a trap. The soldiers closed in behind him. Now Wyatt had to fight it out in the streets of London with only a small force to help him. At first, he met no resistance. But when he reached Charing Cross, he came up against a force of the Queen's Guards. But they did not fight. They ran for safety to the nearby Palace of Whitehall. Wyatt and his force followed. They peppered the windows of the palace with arrows.

Queen Mary, inside, heard the noise. One of her senior commanders, Edward Courtenay, was quivering with fear.

'Well then, fall to prayer', the queen told him scornfully. 'And I warrant you, we shall hear better news anon.'

Better news soon arrived. A troop of Mary's cavalry attacked Wyatt and his followers. Before long, Wyatt's men were cut down. The streets were stained with their blood. At last, with only a handful of men left standing, Thomas Wyatt surrendered.

Despite her bravery, Mary had been badly shaken by Wyatt's rebellion. She realized that she could no longer afford to be merciful. There would be no pardon for the rebels this time. Nearly 200 were condemned to death. Forty-six were hanged in London in a single day. Lady Jane Grey and Guildford Dudley were executed soon thereafter.

The unfortunate Lady Jane had had to die, but she was an innocent victim. The same could not be said of Princess Elizabeth, Queen Mary's half-sister. At least, Mary did not think so. What made Mary suspicious was the way Elizabeth avoided contact with her. She would not come to court. She would not attend Catholic Mass. Mary was sure Elizabeth had conspired with Thomas Wyatt and the rebels.

Today, the Tower of London is no longer a place of terror and death. It is one of London's most popular tourist attractions: the spot where the scaffold once stood is marked out for visitors to see the place where so many people were beheaded.

Queen Mary I was an attractive young woman before frustration, disappointment and a failed marriage embittered her and aged her before her time. She was particularly fond of jewels, fine brocaded fabrics and delicate lace ruffs and collars.

Surprising support for Elizabeth

Then, on 17 March 1554, Elizabeth was arrested and taken to the Tower of London. But she denied knowing anything about Wyatt's rebellion. There was no real evidence against her. After two months, she was released, and taken under guard by barge to Woodstock in Oxfordshire.

Queen Mary was alarmed to see how popular Elizabeth was. All the way, people lined the banks of the river. They cheered her loudly. Church bells rang out. Guns were fired in celebration. Women baked special cakes for Elizabeth. Before long, her barge was piled high with gifts.

Meanwhile, the leaders of Wyatt's rebellion were heavily punished. One of them, the Duke of Suffolk, was beheaded on February 23. Wyatt himself was hung, drawn and quartered.

Members of Parliament had protested violently against the Spanish Marriage. But the day Wyatt died, they gave in. The Royal Marriage Bill became law. Gritting their teeth in fury, Parliament told Mary that Philip would be welcome in England.

Reluctant groom

But Philip was not too happy about the marriage, either. The last thing he wanted was to marry a scrawny, ageing queen 11 years older than he. But he had to go along because his father, King Charles, wanted to ally Spain with England. That way, Charles could get his hands on English money and troops for his war with France.

Mary knew nothing of all this. She imagined her marriage was going to be a great romance. She longed to be loved. She looked forward to showing off her handsome young husband. Philip, Mary thought, had been given to her by God. Poor Mary. It was all a dream.

DEEDS *of* POWER

THE REMORSEFUL COWARD

IN ALL, SOME 300 PEOPLE WERE BURNED at the stake during Mary's reign. Most were ordinary men and women. Some were very high profile. Thomas Cranmer, Archbishop of Canterbury during the reigns of Henry VIII and Edward VI, was burned on 16 October 1555. Cranmer had been terrified of burning to death.

To avoid it, he admitted he had been wrong to become a Protestant, even signing a confession saying so. But he was condemned to burn just the same. When he realized what a coward he had been, he decided to make up for it. When the fire was lit, he thrust his hand into the flames. He held it there until it completely burned away. It was the hand he had used to sign his confession.

Thomas Cranmer, Henry VIII's Archbishop of Canterbury, seen here at Traitor's Gate at the Tower of London, later died bravely at the stake.

Philip left Spain for England on 4 May. He took his time getting there. It was not until 21 July that he met Mary for the first time. It was not a happy meeting. Philip found Mary repulsive and could not stand

A devout Catholic, Queen Mary I longed to return the English church to the jurisdiction of the Pope in Rome, and during her reign some 300 Protestants were burned at the stake for resisting her demands.

being near her. But he endured it and didn't let his real feelings show.

Philip and Mary were married in Winchester Cathedral on 25 July 1554. Within days, Mary became pregnant – or at least she thought so. Great preparations were made for the birth. A religious service was held to give thanks for the queen's quickening, the moment when her baby showed its first signs of life. Mary sat there, proud and happy.

PHILIPPE II. CATHOLIQVE ROY D'ESPAGNE, DES INDES, ET MONARQVE DV NOVVEAV MONDE

Moncornet ex.

Philip of Spain was 11 years younger than Queen Mary when, very reluctantly, he agreed to make a political marriage with her. Later, as King Philip II, he became the sworn enemy of Mary's Protestant half-sister, Queen Elizabeth I.

She let her swelling belly show, so that 'all men might see she was with child'.

'Bloody' Mary

But Mary's plans to return England to the Catholic faith were not going well. There was a lot of resistance, so much that Mary resorted to burning the resisters in public. That was a mistake. The watching crowd howled with anger. Each burning inspired more ugly scenes than the last. Hatred for Queen Mary increased. Now, she had a new name – 'Bloody Mary'.

Philip tried to put a stop to the burnings. Unlike Mary, he realized the more people she burned, the more she was hated. Even for his sake, however, she would not stop. The burnings went on.

A blow for the queen

But a terrible humiliation awaited her. The birth of her baby had been expected on or near 23 May 1555. But the date passed and there was no sign of a baby. There had been nothing by the end of June. There were suggestions that the Queen was not pregnant at all, that she had imagined the whole thing.

At first, Mary refused to believe it. But months passed. Still nothing happened. In the end, Mary had to admit she had been wrong. There was no baby. She became deeply depressed. At this point, just when she needed him most, Philip decided to leave England. Mary begged him not to go. But Philip had had enough of England, the English and their queen. On 22 August 1555, he left for his own territory, the Spanish Netherlands. Mary wept bitterly as she watched him leave.

Happy husband on the loose

Soon, gossip reached England that Philip was having a great time in the Netherlands. He was going to parties, attending weddings and dancing until dawn. He was also playing around with other women – all in all, acting as if he had been freed from prison. No one dared tell Mary what was going on. But that was not all they dared not tell her. Mary's doctors had now discovered the truth of her 'pregnancy': she had a tumor in her womb.

Philip kept promising Mary that he would soon return to England. But he had no intention of returning. Mary became more and more depressed. She could not perform her duties as queen. She shut herself away and mourned for Philip as if he were dead.

Joy for the queen

Time passed, and Philip showed no signs of coming back. Then, in 1556, his father, King Charles, gave up the throne of Spain. Philip was now king in his own right, King Philip II of Spain and of its huge, rich empire in America.

For hours, Mary lay in a coma. When she spoke, she talked of seeing little children in her dreams. A priest came to give her last rites. While he was saying the prayers, she died. When news got out that 'Bloody Mary' was dead, England celebrated.

To defend his vast territories, Philip needed money. And for money, he needed England. Philip returned at last in 1557. Mary greeted him with joy. But joy soon faded. Once Philip had the money, troops and ships he needed, he was gone. Mary never saw him again. All she had for comfort was the belief that she was pregnant again. But it was another phantom pregnancy. Philip had not gone near his wife while he was in England. The truth was that Mary's tumor had returned.

The end of a hated sovereign

By November 1558, Mary was dying. For hours, she lay in a coma. When she spoke, she talked of seeing little children in her dreams. A priest came to give her last rites. While he was saying the prayers, she died.

When news got out that hated 'Bloody Mary' was dead, people all over England celebrated. They sang and danced in the streets. They rang bells. For many years thereafter, the day Mary died, 17 November, was celebrated in England as a public holiday.

GLORIANA AND GORE

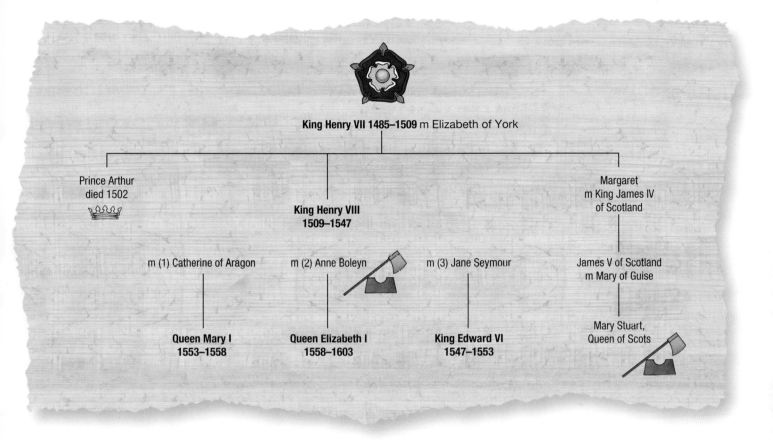

King Henry VII 1485–1509 m Elizabeth of York

Prince Arthur
died 1502

King Henry VIII
1509–1547

Margaret
m King James IV
of Scotland

m (1) Catherine of Aragon

m (2) Anne Boleyn

m (3) Jane Seymour

James V of Scotland
m Mary of Guise

Queen Mary I
1553–1558

Queen Elizabeth I
1558–1603

King Edward VI
1547–1553

Mary Stuart,
Queen of Scots

Now Elizabeth was Queen of England, at only 25. The journey to the throne had been a hazardous one. Queen Mary had hounded Elizabeth and imprisoned her in the Tower of London.

✦

King Charles of Spain wanted her executed. English Catholics believed she was Protestant and hated her. To them, she was illegitimate, not only by birth, but also as queen.

But if Elizabeth's life was in peril before she came to the throne, it was far more dangerous for her afterward. More enemies were lying in wait. On England's

Elizabeth I's richly embroidered robes and magnificent jewels disguised the weakness of her realm and made her look more powerful.

northern border, Scots were making trouble. Catholic kings of France and Spain wanted to invade England and remove Elizabeth from the throne. Pope Pius V was Elizabeth's avowed enemy, too. He excommunicated her in 1570.

Tolerance wins over the people

But Catholics at home and abroad were not Elizabeth's only problems. England was a small, poor country. Its armed forces were below par. Its people were exhausted and confused by 25 years of religious dispute.

(continued on page 135)

REGAL PROFILES

GLORIANA, THE VIRGIN QUEEN

WATCHING ELIZABETH'S 'PROGRESSES', her travels through her realm, no one would ever have guessed that the royal treasury was bankrupt. The courtiers who accompanied the queen were richly dressed. Their horses were magnificently attired. And there in the midst of it all, was Elizabeth herself. She rode in a splendid litter, swathed in sumptuous brocade gowns, covered with the finest ornaments and dazzling jewels.

Wherever she went, people rushed to see her. They were thrilled by the splendid sight of Elizabeth riding by. They began to look upon their queen as more of an icon than a human being. This was exactly what Elizabeth wanted.

Furthermore, playwrights, artists and balladeers endorsed Elizabeth's magical image. Edmund Spenser, for example, turned her into 'Gloriana', the heroine of his fantasy The Faerie Queene. Artists produced dazzling portraits of her – smothered in jewels and richly dressed.

Elizabeth was also an inspiration to famous seamen, including Sir Francis Drake and Sir John Hawkins. They sailed across the Atlantic to raid and rob Spanish colonies in America. The Spaniards called them pirates. The English welcomed them home as heroes.

Elizabeth's image as a glorious queen, surrounded by pomp and glory, was a great propaganda job. But there was one thing Elizabeth would not do for her people. She refused to get married. Her ministers nagged her constantly. They told her a monarch had to have heirs to the throne. She told them she was 'married' to England. She preferred to remain the 'virgin queen'.

Opposite: The famous scene in 1580, when Queen Elizabeth knighted Sir Francis Drake on the deck of his ship *Golden Hind* after his voyage round the world.
Below: This scene from a manuscript dedicated to Elizabeth I shows the queen in a procession.

Hundreds had been executed for their beliefs. Now, they looked to Queen Elizabeth I to find a cure for their years of trouble.

Fortunately, Elizabeth was just the package they needed. In matters of religion, she did not make the mistakes of Protestant Edward VI or Catholic Mary I. Instead, she sat on the fence. Personally, she was not all that interested in religion. Certainly, she did not intend to persecute anyone because of it.

Religious tolerance was part of Elizabeth's plan to make herself attractive to her subjects. She put on a magnificent show. No monarch had ever made so many public appearances.

'We princes', Elizabeth told the English Parliament 'are set as it were upon stages in the sight and view of the world.'

In spite of Elizabeth's refusal to consider marriage, several betrothals were arranged for her. But she kept all her suitors dangling. One, François, Duke of Alençon, tried for years to persuade the queen to marry him. Alençon, 21 years younger than Elizabeth, was not a pretty sight. He was squat and ugly. His face was covered with scars and his nose was misshapen.

All the same, he seemed to imagine that Elizabeth, who called him her 'frog', was indeed willing to marry him. But she would not say 'yes' and she would not say 'no'. She just kept putting Alençon off. In the end, the poor man was still trying to marry Elizabeth when she was in her forties. He never succeeded. No one did. Elizabeth gave all her suitors the brushoff.

The Queen's fears of marriage

Elizabeth had several reasons for doing so. First, she was frightened of marriage. And she was scared of childbirth. Childbirth was still very dangerous for women in the 16th century. Elizabeth had seen Jane Seymour die after giving birth in 1537. In 1548, Catherine Parr had died the same way.

But that was not all Elizabeth was afraid of. Her father, King Henry VIII, had executed two of his wives. The first was her own mother, Anne Boleyn. The other was the king's fifth wife, Catherine Howard,

Amy Robsart, wife of the Earl of Leicester, lies dead at the foot of the stairs. It was said by some that Amy was murdered so that her husband could marry the queen.

who had befriended Elizabeth as a child. Elizabeth's half-sister, Queen Mary, had made enemies among her subjects by marrying Philip of Spain. No wonder Elizabeth thought marriage was dangerous.

Unrequited love

Another reason was that Elizabeth had already been in love long before she became queen. Robert Dudley had known Elizabeth since both were children. They might have been in love even at that early age. But Dudley had a terrible family history. His father had been John Dudley, Duke of Northumberland, who was executed for plotting to cheat Queen Mary of her throne. His grandfather, Edmund Dudley, had also been executed, in 1510. His crime was treason.

On 8 September 1560, Amy Robsart died in suspicious circumstances. Her servants returned from a day out and found her dead at the bottom of the stairs. Her neck was broken. It might have been suicide....

With such a family background, Robert Dudley did not have a chance of marrying Elizabeth. She did make him her closest companion at court, showering him with gifts and a title, Earl of Leicester. But that was as far as Robert Dudley got. There was something else, too. In 1550, Dudley had married Amy Robsart. He kept Amy hidden away in Oxford while he spent most of his time at court. It is possible that Elizabeth did not even know about her.

A scandal that ruled out marriage

But, on 8 September 1560, Amy Robsart died in suspicious circumstances. Her servants returned from a day out and found her dead at the bottom of the stairs. Her neck was broken. It might have been suicide; Amy had been suffering from breast cancer. But gossip soon went around. It was said Amy had been murdered so Robert Dudley could marry the queen. Dudley was known to visit his wife from time

DEEDS
of
POWER

LOVE, JEALOUSY, REVENGE AND MURDER

MARY, QUEEN OF SCOTS is often pictured as a beautiful, desirable young woman. It was not true. Mary was no romantic heroine. She was an ignorant, foolish, indiscreet airhead. She managed to do almost everything wrong and was certainly not the queen 16th century Scotland needed. The country was in constant turmoil. Scottish lords were out of control. All Mary did was make a bad situation worse. In 1565, for example, she married Henry Stuart, Lord Darnley. The lords hated him. But Mary went further. She made court 'pets' out of men the lords detested, resulting in at least one untimely end.

One of Queen Mary's 'pets' was her Italian secretary, David Rizzio. Lord Darnley, Mary's husband, was jealous of him. He believed Rizzio was Mary's lover. So Darnley plotted, with others, to have Rizzio killed. The murder took place at Holyrood House in Edinburgh on the evening of 9 March 1566. The Queen, six months pregnant, was dining with Rizzio and one of her ladies-in-waiting when Lord Darnley and other conspirators burst into the room. They seized David Rizzio. As they dragged him away, the Italian tried to grab Mary's skirts, screaming 'save me, my lady, save me!'. Mary was helpless. One of the murderers kept a pistol pointed at her as Rizzio was pulled into the room next door.

The daggers came out and Rizzio was stabbed 56 times, dying in a spreading pool of blood. Later, the conspirators kept Mary a prisoner, but she managed to keep her head. She calmed them by promising a pardon. Two days after the murder, she managed to escape from Holyrood through underground passages in the chapel where the Scots' royal tombs were situated. From there she rode 20 miles to Dunbar – and safety.

Soon there was gossip that Mary wanted revenge for Rizzio's death by having Darnley killed. The truth was worse than that, Mary had fallen in love

Mary, Queen of Scots was the focus of plots to depose and kill Queen Elizabeth and replace her on the throne of England.

This 19th century illustration depicts the murder in 1560 of David Rizzio by Mary's jealous husband, Lord Darnley, and her unruly nobles.

with a Scottish noble, James Hepburn, Earl Bothwell. Another reason for getting rid of Lord Darnley.

Bothwell, it seems, made arrangements for Darnley to die. On the night of 10 February 1567, Mary left Kirk o'Field, her house near Edinburgh, to attend a wedding. Darnley, who was ill, remained at home.

Sometime during the night, there was a huge explosion at Kirk o'Field. The building was flattened. Darnley was not killed in the explosion. He tried to escape.

But conspirators were waiting for him. Later, Darnley was found dead outside the house. He had been strangled. Three months later, Mary married Bothwell. He had already made her pregnant – with twins. But the Scottish lords hated Bothwell. The marriage was the last straw. Mary had to go – and Bothwell with her.

On 24 July 1567, at Loch Leven Castle, Mary was forced to abdicate. Later, she suffered a miscarriage. Scotland was now a dangerous place to be. So Mary headed for England. She arrived there on 16 May 1568. Bothwell fled to Denmark. They never saw each other again. Bothwell went mad and died in a Danish prison in 1578.

to time. Just before she died, Amy had ordered a new dress, maybe because she was expecting to see her husband. But during his visit, so the gossips said, Dudley killed her.

Nothing was proven. But the scandal had been too great. Elizabeth had to send Robert Dudley away from her court. After a time he returned and became Elizabeth's pet once again. But marriage was out of the question.

Even so, it seems that Dudley still wanted to marry the queen. In 1563, Elizabeth suggested he might marry her cousin, Mary, Queen of Scots. At that time, Mary was heir to Elizabeth's throne. So Robert

In 1568, Mary, Queen of Scots was imprisoned in Loch Leven Castle, where she was forced to abdicate. She managed to escape, but there was nowhere safe for her to go but England, where she became Elizabeth's prisoner.

Dudley could have become King of England had he played his cards right. But he had not. He refused to marry Mary. He preferred to stay in London, close to Elizabeth…and hope.

Mary, Queen of Scots became a big problem. She was Catholic. The French and the Spanish wanted her to become Queen of England once they had removed Elizabeth from the throne. Catholics in England wanted the same thing. But in 1568, the problem grew bigger. Mary was forced to abdicate and fled south, where she placed herself under Elizabeth's protection.

Elizabeth granted Mary the protection she sought. Mary wanted Elizabeth to help her to get back her Scottish throne. Elizabeth agreed to consider it. But she did not like the idea. Mary on the loose in Scotland would be more trouble than Mary in England. So Elizabeth stalled, and went on stalling.

Mary pushed her plan several times. In the end, it

William Cecil, Lord Burghley, served both Mary I and Elizabeth, who appointed him Secretary of State when she became Queen in 1558. Burghley was the principal architect of Elizabeth's policies for the next forty years, until his death.

was foiled by her son, King James VI of Scotland. He grew up cold-hearted and cunning. He did not want his mother around. James was, after all, the second heir to the throne of England after Mary. If he played his cards right, he could have two crowns instead of one.

Safe, but never free

If Mary was not about to return to Scotland, what was Elizabeth to do with her? Elizabeth decided that Mary must be kept under house arrest. She would be comfortable and have servants. But she would be watched. English spies planted in Mary's household could read letters and messages she received. Even more important, they could find out who sent them.

Of course, Catholics and other sympathizers might try to rescue Mary. As a precaution, from time to time Elizabeth had Mary moved from one house to another. Catholics were not fooled. Several attempts to rescue Mary were made. All were unsuccessful.

Fending off rescuers was largely the work of Sir Francis Walsingham, Elizabeth's Secretary of State. Walsingham was really a secret agent, and a very good one, too. He had 53 agents planted in foreign courts. Another 18 worked for him in Europe. Between them, Walsingham's spies kept him well fed with information from 42 European towns and cities. Thus he was always one step ahead of conspirators who wanted Mary free and Elizabeth dead. Walsingham hated Mary. He called her 'that devilish woman'. His aim in life was to destroy her.

Mary always claimed she knew nothing of the plots against Elizabeth. The truth was that she was involved up to her neck. The first serious plot against Elizabeth occurred in 1571. It was hatched by Robert Ridolfi, a Catholic banker from Florence, Italy. Ridolfi wanted to see Mary on the throne of England. So did his supporters in Europe. They included King Philip II of Spain and the Pope himself.

Elizabeth's enemies hatch a plot

Ridolfi planned to invade England with a force of around 6,000 men. Meanwhile, rebels in Norfolk, in

eastern England, would kidnap Elizabeth and hold her hostage. It was also planned that Mary should marry a Catholic, Thomas Howard, Duke of Norfolk. Together, they would rule England and Scotland.

One day, Babington received a letter from Mary. He was immensely flattered. But it was a ploy and Babington fell for it.

But Ridolfi ruined his own plot. He could not keep his mouth shut. He talked of his plans to the wrong people. The plot thereby reached the ears of Elizabeth's Chief Minister, William Cecil, Lord Burghley, who put a tail on Ridolfi. Burghley's spies got their hands on messages he sent and letters he wrote. The letters were in code, but the code was broken and all was revealed.

Soft-hearted queen saves Mary

The Ridolfi Plot, as it was called, never got off the ground. Subsequently, the Duke of Norfolk was accused of treason. He was executed in 1572. But Ridolfi got away scot-free. So did Mary. Elizabeth's ministers begged her to have the Queen of Scots executed. But she refused. The English queen did not like spilling blood – especially royal blood. She simply could not bring herself to sign a death warrant for another queen.

This might not have been wise, however. As long as Mary lived, plots against Elizabeth would go on. But Sir Francis Walsingham had plans of his own. It has been said he turned double agent and hatched his own 'plot' against the English queen. Walsingham's plan was to involve Mary. He knew Mary was vain and empty-headed and loved being the focus of intrigue. Walsingham was sure she would fall for his plot. Then, he could trap her. And when her guilt was revealed, Elizabeth would have to execute her.

Reputedly very beautiful, Mary, Queen of Scots, became a tragic heroine after her execution in 1587. In reality, Mary was foolish, lacked royal dignity, and had a fatal penchant for political conspiracies.

But this scheme was to be unlike other secret agent operations. Walsingham's plans for getting rid of Mary coincided with Spanish preparations for invading England. King Philip of Spain had wanted to invade England ever since Elizabeth became queen. Now, the time had come.

What Philip did not know was that his security screen had already been broken. English spies in Spain knew all about Philip's huge fleet, the Armada. But combined with Walsingham's plot against Elizabeth, this put England in double peril.

A fool for love

Walsingham needed a fall guy to head his plot. Sir Anthony Babington was just the man for it. He was only 25 and a secret Catholic. Among 'young bloods' of his kind, it was fashionable to be in love with the Queen of Scots. Babington was head-over-heels about her.

One day, Babington received a letter from Mary. He was immensely flattered at such attention from the beautiful Mary; it quite turned his head. But it was a ploy, and Babington fell for it. He started smuggling letters and packages to and from the Queen of Scots. These letters contained news of secret Catholic activities in England.

At the end of May 1586, one of Mary's agents, John Ballard, told Babington of the secret plot. Catholics in England would revolt. England would be invaded. Elizabeth would be murdered. Mary would be released from house arrest and placed on Elizabeth's throne.

Treachery at every turn

At first, Babington was frightened by all this. He decided to get out of England. Better to plot against Elizabeth from outside the country, he thought. But in order to leave England, Babington needed to get special travel papers from Sir Francis Walsingham.

A certain Robert Poley volunteered to help Babington get his documents. Poley was one of Walsingham's agents. He made friends with Babington, who came to trust him. This proved most unwise, for Poley managed to get details of the plot out of Babington and passed the information to Walsingham.

Babington, meanwhile, wrote to Mary, and told her about the plot. Walsingham, of course, had read it before it was delivered to the Scottish queen. Walsingham had devised a foolproof method of delivering letters to and from Mary: they were hidden

In 1586, Mary was put on trial at Fotheringhay Castle in Northamptonshire for plotting against Elizabeth. Questioning the court's authority over her, she pleaded innocence, but was nevertheless condemned to death.

in a cask of beer. When Mary replied to Babington, her letter was thereby smuggled out. And when Walsingham read it, he knew that at last he had Mary where he wanted her. He sketched a gallows on the letter.

Duped, and condemned to die

Babington went into hiding in St. John's Wood, in north London. But Walsingham's agents soon found him. Babington was taken to the Tower of London. The young man was scared witless. It soon turned out he would say anything, betray anybody, to save himself.

At their trial for treason, Babington put all the blame on John Ballard. It did him no good. Babington was sentenced to be hanged, drawn and quartered. So was Ballard. Terrified at this gruesome prospect, Babington begged Queen Elizabeth for mercy. He offered the huge sum of £1000 to a friend if the friend could get him off the charge. This did not work either.

On 20 September 1586, Babington and Ballard were dragged through the streets of London to where a huge gallows had been specially built. Babington was forced to watch as Ballard suffered the tortures of a traitor's death. Somehow, during this ghastly procedure, Babington found courage. Instead of

The Palace of Holyroodhouse in Edinburgh was the official residence of Mary, Queen of Scots. Building began in the reign of King James IV (1473–1514), and later the palace was improved and enlarged several times.

praying on his knees as Ballard died, he stood upright, hat in hand. When his turn came, he died bravely.

When Elizabeth heard of the great cruelty the executioners had employed, she was horrified. Seven other conspirators awaited execution. Elizabeth ordered that, unlike Ballard and Babington, they should not be taken down from the gallows while still alive. Only once they were dead could the drawing and quartering proceed.

Mary, Queen of Scots went on trial at Fotheringhay Castle in Northamptonshire the following 14 October. Mary was defiant from beginning to end. The court had no right to try her, she protested. She was not going to admit to anything, except to a desire to be free.

'I came into this kingdom under promise of assis-tance, and aid, against my enemies and not as a subject...instead of which I have been detained and imprisoned....I do not deny that I have earnestly wished for liberty.... Can I be responsible for the criminal projects of a few desperate men, which they planned without my knowledge or participation?'

She was, of course, lying through her teeth. The judges were not impressed. Mary was found guilty of treason and sentenced to death. William Davison, Elizabeth's secretary, drew up the death war-rant. Predictably, Elizabeth refused to sign it. But Walsingham, Burghley and other ministers were not going to let her off the hook.

They nagged and pleaded with Queen Elizabeth. They argued that if Mary were allowed to live, other

REGAL PROFILES

BRAVERY AT THE BLOCK

On 8 February 1587, Mary entered the Great Hall at Fotheringhay Castle, in procession with her groom holding a large crucifix in front of her. She was wearing a black dress with a red petticoat underneath and a veil around her head and shoulders. Three hundred people were there to watch her die.

One of them, Robert Wynfielde described what happened.

'She (knelt) down upon the cushion most resolutely, and without any token or fear of death.... Groping for the block, she laid down her head, putting her chin over the block with both her hands.... Lying upon the block most quietly, and stretching out her arms cried, *In manus tuas, Domine* (Into your hands, Oh God, I give myself), three or four times.

'Lying very still upon the block, one of the executioners holding her slightly with one of his hands.... She endured two strokes...of the axe...and so the executioner cut off her head...which being cut asunder, he lifted up her head to the view of all.... Her lips stirred up and down a quarter of an hour after her head was cut off.

'...One of the executioners...espied her little dog which had crept under her clothes, which could not be gotten forth but by force, yet afterward would not depart from the dead corpse, but came and lay between her head and her shoulders, which (were) soaked with her blood.'

---

potential traitors would believe they too could get away with treason. They reminded the queen that before long Spaniards were going to invade her realm. If the invasion succeeded, Mary would become Queen of England.

That finally did it. The idea of Mary on her throne, as a puppet of Philip II of Spain, was too much for Elizabeth. She signed the warrant and on 8 February 1587, Mary, Queen of Scots was duly executed.

In London, bells rang and bonfires were lit to celebrate the execution. But when Queen Elizabeth learned that Mary was dead, she had a fit of hysterics. She wept, she wailed, she threw herself about dramatically. She blamed her ministers, calling them 'criminals'. But Lord Burghley told the queen to stop play-acting. No one, he said, was going to be convinced by her antics. Everyone knew she had hated Mary and was glad to be rid of her at last.

Spain defeated, thousands killed

The following year, 132 ships of the Spanish Armada left Spain for the invasion of England. King Philip was sure that his 'Enterprise of England' would succeed. But he was wrong. The English navy had a secret weapon. When the Armada entered the English Channel on 31 July, the English fleet kept its distance and raked the Spanish vessels with gunfire. Several were wrecked. Many were set on fire. Thousands of Spaniards were killed.

Then the weather in the English Channel turned stormy and violent. Ferocious winds drove the Spaniards to the eastern end of the Channel. From there they limped back to Spain around the tip of Scotland. Of the Armada's 132 ships, only 60 made it home. Of the Armada's 30,000 crew, more than a third – 11,000 men – perished.

The English had scored a tremendous and unexpected victory. They celebrated with dancing in the streets, bonfires and fireworks. A vast quantity of beer was drunk as the English toasted their queen. Elizabeth celebrated more quietly. On 24 November she held a service of thanksgiving in St. Paul's Cathedral in London.

Despite her misgivings, Elizabeth I finally assented to the execution of Mary, Queen of Scots at Fotheringhay Castle in 1587. It was a violent end to nearly 20 years of exile and imprisonment in England.

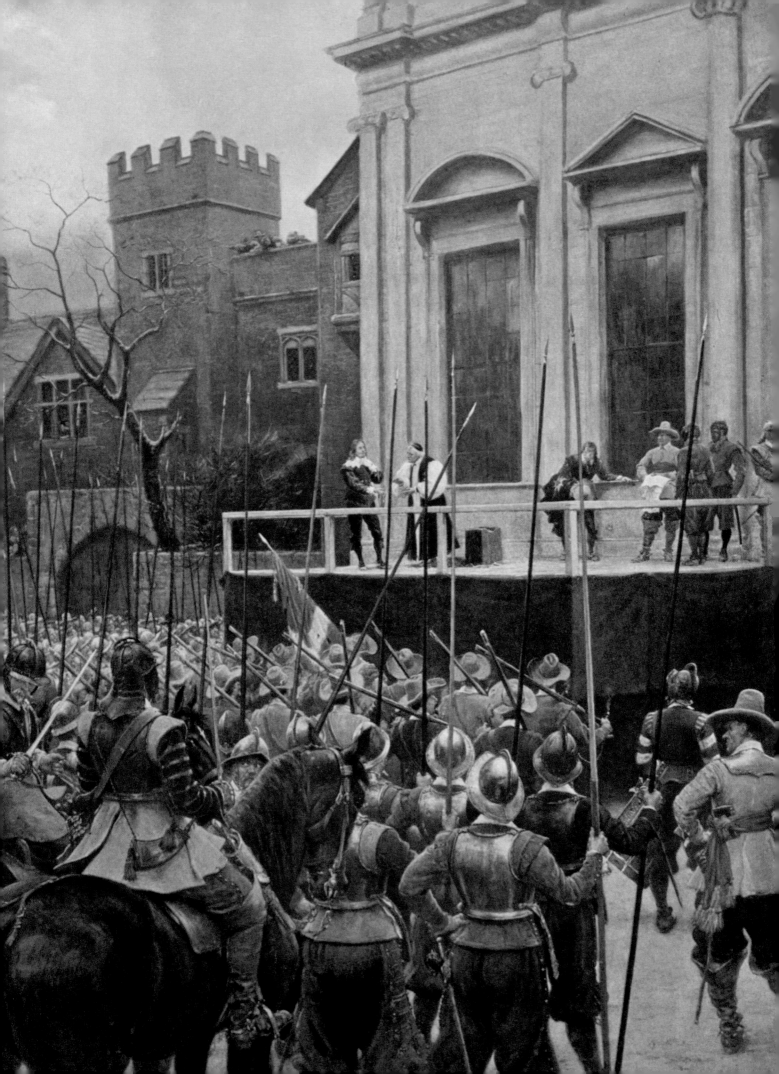

10
ROUNDHEADS AND REGICIDE

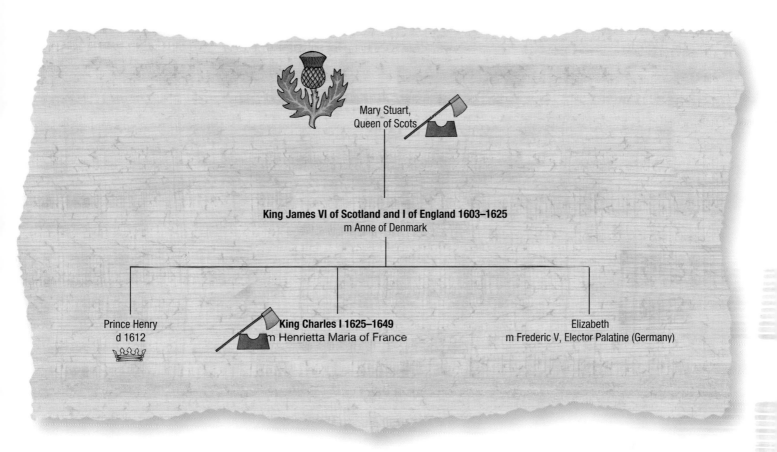

Mary Stuart,
Queen of Scots

King James VI of Scotland and I of England 1603–1625
m Anne of Denmark

Prince Henry
d 1612

King Charles I 1625–1649
m Henrietta Maria of France

Elizabeth
m Frederic V, Elector Palatine (Germany)

Queen Elizabeth I lived longer than any other Tudor monarch. She lost her hair and her teeth, but she kept her guts. In 1601, when she was 67, her beloved Robert Devereux, the Earl of Essex, rebelled against her.

◆

She was furious…so furious that she declared she would step out onto the streets of London to see if any rebels dared to shoot her. Her ministers barely prevented her from doing it.

But by late in 1602, Elizabeth was not well. She refused to eat. She would not take any medicines. She even refused to go to bed. She thought if she went to bed, she would die. There was not long to go until the end. Elizabeth died sitting in a chair on 24 March 1603, the last of the Tudor monarchs. It was only at the very last moment that she named her heir – King James VI of Scotland. In a historic event which united the monarchies of England and Scotland, he then became James I of England, first of the Stuart kings.

Charles I was the first and only king of England to be publicly beheaded. A special scaffold was built at London's Whitehall for the execution that took place on 30 January 1649.

Rapturous welcome for the new king

James set out for London in May 1603. He was so eager to get there that he rode 40 miles in less than

A GROTESQUE ODDITY WITH REPULSIVE HABITS

THE ENGLISH DISCOVERED that King James was extremely strange. He looked creepy. He had spindly legs. His tongue was too big for his mouth. It slopped about when he ate or talked. He drooled. He did not wash very often. His hands were always black with dirt. He looked scruffy because he dressed so badly.

James was terrified of being assassinated. Many Scottish kings in the century or two before had been murdered. So he always wore dagger-proof padded clothes, giving him an alarmingly lumpy shape. As if this were not enough, King James I had some shocking habits. He played with himself in public. He loved crude jokes. In front of his courtiers, he would make statements such as 'God's wounds! I will pull down my breeches and they shall also see my arse.' When he went hunting, he would jump feet first into the innards of animals he had killed and mingle in their blood and gore.

But his unpleasant appearance and habits aside, and idiosyncratically for his time, James I was tolerant about religion. Many contemporaries were not. English Protestants detested Roman Catholics. Catholics feared persecution. Many had gone into hiding. James decided to put an end to all this. He decreed that Catholics should be allowed to follow their faith openly. But so many Roman Catholics came out into the open that James became frightened. Hastily, he withdrew his decree. It was back to square one.

In this illustration, King James I looks neater and cleaner than he actually was. He hardly ever washed, was always itching and scratching and smelled bad.

four hours. That was fast going for the time, but too fast. On the way to London, James fell off his horse, injuring himself. His doctors thought he had broken his collarbone.

When James reached London at last, he received a great welcome. Thousands turned out to see their new king enter the city. Celebrations went on far into the night. But the excitement soon wore off when the public discovered its new monarch not only looked weird, but that his personal tastes and habits were truly repugnant.

An ambitious plot fails

King James soon found, however, that he was in a no-win situation. After their disappointment, a group of Catholics led by Guy Fawkes hatched the famous Gunpowder Plot of 1605. It was very ambitious, involving nothing less than blowing up the Houses of Parliament when King James and his ministers were in attendance.

The plot never got going. Guy Fawkes was discovered red-handed in the cellars of the Houses of Parliament, together with his stock of gunpowder. The plotters were hung, drawn and quartered as traitors. Ever since, Guy Fawkes Day has been celebrated in England on 5 November. Dummy models of Fawkes are displayed in the street. Children ask passersby to give them 'a penny for the Guy'. Fireworks displays take place all over England.

Guy Fawkes was caught red-handed with several barrels of gunpowder and was arrested on the spot. Though not the leader of the Gunpowder Plot, he has since become the focus of its commemoration in England on 5 November each year.

James believed in witchcraft. There had been a Witchcraft Act in Queen Elizabeth's time. But that was not enough for James. He changed the act to include cannibalism among the dark practices performed by witches.

'If any person or persons shall use, practice or exercise any invocation or conjuration of any evil or wicked spirit…or take any dead man or child out of his or her grave, or the skin, bone or any part of any dead person, to be employed or used in any manners of witchcraft…they shall suffer the pains of death.'

The king prefers gentlemen

Though he was married and had children, James was also homosexual. He used to prowl around his court looking for beautiful young males as lovers. When James took a fancy to one, the king would plant sloppy wet kisses on his cheeks. He would fondle him in full view of the court.

One who received this royal treatment was handsome George Villiers, who became Duke of Buckingham. Villiers was canny enough to know that being the king's lover was more than just a guarantee of a grand title. It could lead to wealth and power as well. James adored Buckingham. He pawed and petted him in public. He called him his 'sweet Steenie'. In letters to him, King James addressed Buckingham as 'sweetheart'. When Buckingham went abroad on a foreign mission, James wrote to him, saying: 'I wear Steenie's picture on a blue ribbon under my waistcoat, next to my heart.'

> **Sooner or later, the king would run out of cash. Then, Parliament could hit back. The king spent money like water. His coronation cost £20,000. His wife, Anne, went overboard with expensive clothes and jewels.**

But the king's advances were not always welcomed. The Earl of Holland, for example, turned aside and spat after James had 'sladdered' in his mouth. James's courtiers, looking on, were disgusted. A later historian, Thomas Babington Macaulay, called King James 'a nervous drivelling idiot'. He was not far wrong.

'Kings are chosen by God'

The English could just about put up with all this. After all, they had had some peculiar kings before and England had survived. What they could not stand, however, was a highly dangerous notion James had brought with him from Scotland. This was the Divine Right of Kings, which belief implied that James had been appointed as king by God. Only God could judge

King James I of England was also King James VI of Scotland. This illustration shows him dressed in state robes, holding the orb and sceptre that were part of the Crown Jewels and the regalia that signified his royal powers.

what he did. James considered himself above the law and told Parliament so in 1610:

'The state of monarchy', said James, 'is the supremest thing on earth. As to dispute what God may do is blasphemy...so it is seditious in subjects to dispute what a king may do.... ' He went on: 'Kings are not only God's lieutenants upon earth and sit upon God's throne, but even by God himself they are called gods.'

This was alarming rhetoric. English kings had never before been allowed to carry on in such a way. Parliament and its predecessors, the English barons, had fought a long battle for the right to advise the monarch. Now here was King James telling Parliament that they could 'go to hell': he chose his 'sweet Steenie', the Duke of Buckingham, as his one and only adviser.

Luxury lifestyle funded by the public purse

James also found a way around Parliament's chief power: their right to grant the king money. James obtained funds in other ways: he imposed taxes on imported goods, forced the aristocracy to accept loans, and sold offices to the highest bidder. All of this was illegal.

Parliament fumed. But they settled down to wait: sooner or later the king would run out of cash. When he did so, Parliament had the chance to hit back. The king spent money like water. His coronation had cost £20,000. His wife, Queen Anne, went overboard with expensive clothes and jewels. James gave cash away in handfuls to courtiers. Entertainments at his court were always lavish. The most popular, the masque, cost a fortune. Many such masques were staged at the court of King James.

King's surprising turnaround

Eventually, in 1621, James needed money so badly that he was forced to call a Parliament. The members got their shots in first. For a long time they had been angered by the partiality James showed to Roman Catholics. They wanted England to be Protestant through and through. Above all, they wanted an end to James's friendship with Catholic Spain. Their

Charles I looks very dandified in this portrait, wearing a long wig and broad-brimmed hat. The horse was posed with its head down, with its groom leaning to one side, to conceal the fact that the king was only 4 feet 7 inches tall.

demands, in the form of a 'Protestation', were entered into Parliament's journal. James was furious. He sent for the journal. He tore out the pages where the Protestation was printed. Parliament knew what they could do with their Protestation.

Then, quite suddenly, King James gave in. In 1624 he let Parliament have everything they had ever wanted. A say in foreign policy; an end to preference toward Catholics – even the right to make war.

'If I take a resolution, upon your advice, to enter into a war,' James told Parliament, 'then yourselves… shall have the disposing of the money. I will not meddle with it.'

Parliament, triumphant at last, voted the king the enormous sum of £30,000. James's turnaround had been amazing. But there were good reasons for it. He was only 57, but getting old. He had suffered a stroke. He was becoming senile and did not have long to live. Letting Parliament have what it wanted was the only way to get a quiet life. James died on 27 March 1625 at his country home, Theobalds in Hertfordshire.

Thirteen years earlier, James's heir, Prince Henry, had died of typhoid fever. This was not only a tragic loss for his parents, but for England as well.

Henry, only 18, had been a bright young man. He had up-to-date ideas about working with, instead of against, Parliament. He was a devout Protestant. When Henry came to the throne, so it was said, all the problems his father had caused would be cured. But it was not to be.

The runt of the litter

What England got instead of Henry was a new version of King James. King Charles I, James's second son, was a very small man, four feet seven inches tall. He was stubborn, shy, slow and stupid. All his life, he stammered. Worse, he took over the Duke of Buckingham as his own lover. Worse still, Charles was another 'Divine Right of Kings' adherent. Parliament cringed when Charles said: 'I must avow that I owe the account of my actions to God alone'. It might have been his father James talking.

There were all sorts of bad omens on 2 February 1626, the day Charles was crowned king. One of the wings on the dove topping Charles' sceptre broke off. A jewel popped out of the coronation ring. Most frightening of all, there was an earthquake. Superstitious people began speculating that there would be trouble ahead.

There certainly was trouble ahead. In the reign of James I, Parliament had argued fiercely with him. But they had always been loyal to him as king. Charles' Parliament was different. It was full of extreme Protestant Puritans. They were not willing to put up with King Charles – or any king. To them, all kings were tyrants.

Duke haters unite

This placed Charles in a very dangerous position. He made it worse by employing all his father's tricks. He imposed taxes on his people – some illegal. He clung to Buckingham, who practically controlled the king and so controlled England.

George Villiers, Duke of Buckingham, was widely hated. Slanderous ditties were written about him. Rude ballads were sung. On 28 June 1628, a mob gathered in London for a 'we-hate-the-Duke' meeting.

The duke was widely hated. Slanderous ditties were written about him. Rude ballads were sung. Seditious pamphlets were written. Then, on 28 June 1628, a mob gathered in London for a 'we-hate-the-Duke' meeting. Nearby was a playhouse where a performance had just ended. Someone spotted John Lambe, the duke's doctor, coming out one of the doors. The mob howled. Lambe ran. He darted from one tavern to another, desperately seeking shelter. But the mob caught up with him. They seized Lambe and beat him to death on the pavement.

Murdering the duke's doctor was the next best thing to killing the duke himself. But it wasn't good enough for one John Felton, who had a personal grudge against Buckingham.

The Duke of Buckingham was murdered by John Felton, who held a grudge against the duke. Felton became a hero: the death of Buckingham was welcome to many people who disliked his influence over King Charles.

he became a national hero. Londoners cheered and celebrated when they heard Buckingham was dead. Parliament was pleased, for they had wanted to get rid of Buckingham for years. Now he was gone, and King Charles was on his own.

By now his disputes with Parliament had reached new heights. They were on a collision course. Inside Parliament, on 2 March 1629, Charles' supporters and opponents actually brawled in the House of Commons chamber.

Charles soon put a stop to that. He dismissed Parliament and ruled without it for eleven years. He kept his cash flow going in the same way as had King James. A tax called 'Ship Money' became the most hated of his fundraising schemes. Ship Money was supposed to be a tax paid by coastal towns for building ships in times of national danger. There was no national danger when Charles demanded the tax. Furthermore, he demanded Ship Money from inland towns.

Ship Money was not sufficient, however. In 1640 Charles needed £300,000 for a war against the rebellious Scots. He summoned Parliament. Nothing had changed. All the old quarrels were still there: the king must stop imposing taxes, he must be tougher on Catholics, his ministers must be controlled by Parliament. King Charles refused to give in. Instead, he dissolved Parliament once again.

A heroic murderer

In 1627 Buckingham had refused to make Felton a captain in the Navy – and had been very insulting about it, too. Felton vowed revenge. On 23 August 1628, Felton waited for Buckingham outside the Greyhound Inn in Portsmouth. Buckingham had just finished breakfast when Felton rushed up and stabbed him in the chest. That one blow was enough. Buckingham fell to the ground dying.

John Felton was hanged for his crime, but

Ship Money and other taxes went on. Hatred of the king increased, and Parliament lost patience. On 23 November 1641, the Grand Remonstrance was passed by the House of Commons by a margin of 159 votes to 148.

The Remonstrance was the work of John Pym and four other members of Parliament. It contained a list of the many ways in which King Charles had abused his power. Nearly six weeks later, on 4 January 1642, King Charles went in person to the House of

In 1642, Charles I went to the Houses of Parliament hoping to arrest five members who had accused him of abusing his royal powers. He failed. A tradition followed of the monarch not being permitted to enter the House of Commons.

Commons. He took a strong guard of soldiers with him. His intention was to arrest the five authors of the Grand Remonstrance. They would then be charged with treason.

Charles told the Speaker of the House of Commons, William Lenthall:

'By your leave, Mister Speaker, I must borrow your chair a little.'

The Speaker's chair was on a raised dais. The king stepped up on it and scanned the faces in front of him. John Pym and his four friends were not there. They had been warned not to go to the Commons that day.

Charles asked Lenthall where they were. Lenthall replied: 'May it please Your Majesty, but as the House is pleased to direct me, whose servant I am

here.' In other words, Lenthall intended to give nothing away.

The king knew he had lost. 'Well,' he said, 'since I see all the birds are flown, I do expect from you that you shall send them unto me as soon as they return hither.' Then he left. John Pym and others returned a week later, but no one was about to hand them over to King Charles.

Royalists versus Roundheads

Civil war looked certain now. King Charles, his queen, Henrietta Maria, and their children fled from London to Hampton Court Palace in Surrey, where it was safer. England's third and last civil war began on 22 August

A royalist stronghold under assault during the English Civil War, showing one woman deafened by the artillery barrage. Civil wars are often regarded as the most savage of all: this one brought terror to thousands of ordinary people.

1642. That day, King Charles 'raised the royal standard' in Nottingham. Now it was his supporters, the Royalists, against Parliament, the Roundheads.

The war began well for King Charles and the Royalists. They won the first big battle, at Edgehill, in Warwickshire. But after that, it seemed neither side could finally defeat the other. Too many battles ended as draws. Sieges dragged on and on.

Families took sides in the civil war. Some members supported the king, others Parliament. Many had no choice. Royalists and Parliamentarians both introduced conscription: young men were forcibly hauled off to fight. In 1643, one of the Parliamentary leaders, Oliver Cromwell, recruited a troop of women. They were known as 'the Maiden Troops'. Their job was to 'stir up the youth' to fight for Parliament.

Many of the troops did not want to go to war. A group of them attacked one recruiting officer, Lieutenant Eures, in a tavern. They forced Eures to

BRAVE BRILLIANA

WIVES WERE LEFT TO defend their homes when their husbands went to war. One was Brilliana, Lady Harley. Brampton Bryan, her home in Herefordshire, in western England, was besieged for six weeks by Royalist forces. Royalists led by the Marquess of Hartford ordered her to surrender. She refused.

Before long Lady Harley, her servants and followers were in a fearful state. They ran short of food. Royalist soldiers entered the park surrounding her house. They stole cattle, sheep and oxen. They burned buildings and cottages. They killed one of her servants, Edward Morgan. Lady Harley's cook was also shot dead.

Royalists pounded Brampton Bryan with cannon fire, destroying most of the roof. The rain leaked in. Every room in the house was soaking wet.

But Lady Harley hit back. She had only 50 soldiers, but she ordered them to destroy the Royalists' defenses. She stole back much of the food the Royalists had taken. But the effort cost Lady Harley her life. She had an apoplectic fit on 29 October 1643, and died two days later. In the end, the Royalists gave up and withdrew.

crawl out on a beam attached to the tavern sign. He was beaten. Stones were thrown at him. Then he was flung onto a heap of rubbish. But he was not dead – not yet. He managed to stagger out, but his attackers spotted him and beat him savagely about the head until he died.

New Model Army stormtroopers

Cromwell was a country gentleman and farmer. He came from the same family as Thomas Cromwell, Henry VIII's doomed minister. He had fought in the civil war from the beginning. He soon recognized important facts about the Parliamentary army. It was untrained. It was undisciplined. Parliament was not going to win this war with an army like that.

In 1645, Cromwell set about creating a New Model Army. This was much more professional. They trained hard, lived hard, fought hard. All this made an enormous difference. On 14 June 1645, the New Model Army won the battle of Naseby in Northamptonshire. This was the beginning of the end for King Charles. He fled for safety to Hereford. But he knew his cause was lost.

King throws himself on Scottish mercy

Charles cut his hair short, put on a false beard. Then, disguised as a servant, he went north, to Scotland. There he gave himself up. As King of Scotland as well as King of England, Charles hoped the Scots would help him. But the Scots Presbyterians had no intention of doing

so, unless Charles agreed to their terms. They wanted him to impose their Presbyterian faith in England, but for Charles this was anathema: Presbyterians believed that kings should be accountable to the people, who held supreme power in the land. A monarch like Charles, who believed in the Divine Right of Kings, wasn't going to swallow that, and he refused. The Scots lost patience and handed him back to the English. Parliament placed Charles under arrest at Hampton

> **Charles cut his hair short. He put on a false beard. Then, disguised as a servant, he went north, to Scotland. There he gave himself up. As King of Scotland...Charles hoped the Scots would help him.**

Court Palace. But he became afraid that his guards meant to kill him. On 11 November 1647, he escaped. He rode south as fast as he could go. After three days, Charles reached Carisbrooke Castle on the Isle of Wight, off the south coast of England. He demanded protection from the governor of the castle, who let him in.

A year later, on 1 December 1648, army officers arrived at the castle. They forced King Charles to go with them. He ended up in Hurst Castle on the English south coast. His room was small and dark with only a slit for a window.

England's first royal trial by subjects

Meanwhile, Oliver Cromwell had given orders for the king to be tried in London's Westminster Hall. No king of England had ever been tried by his own subjects before. The trial opened on 20 January 1649.

The reenactment of Civil War battles is a popular activity among historically minded societies in England. Recreating the seventeenth century setting requires a great deal of careful research into costumes, hairstyles and weaponry.

Charles was accused that 'out of a wicked design to erect...an unlimited and tyrannical power...traitorously and maliciously levied war against the present Parliament and the people (they) represented.' The judges refused to call the king by his title. Instead, they called him plain 'Charles Stuart'.

THE STUARTS PART I: ROUNDHEADS AND REGICIDE 411

DEEDS
of
POWER

ENGLAND'S FEMALE SNIPERS

KING CHARLES FORBADE WOMEN to fight in battle. But some of them did so, just the same. One was Jane Engleby, a farmer's daughter, who disguised herself as a man and fought alongside her husband at the battle of Marston Moor in 1644. Other women acted as snipers in Chester, Leicester and other towns. One woman, Lady Wyndham, took a potshot at one of the Roundhead leaders, Oliver Cromwell, during the siege of Bridgewater, in Somerset. She missed. If she had managed to kill him, the civil war might have turned out differently.

Defeat at the battle of Marston Moor on 2 July 1644 lost the royalists their support in northern England. Prince Rupert's men were defeated so severely that he had to hide in a bean field.

Charles I's death warrant, signed by 59 Parliamentary soldiers, including Oliver Cromwell. Many more were summoned to attend Charles's trial at Westminster Hall, but most of them baulked at the idea of passing a death sentence on their king.

Charles would not defend himself, since he did not recognize that the court had any right to try him.

'I would know by what power I am called hither....' Charles said. 'I would know by what authority, I mean lawful.... Remember, I am your king, your lawful king…a king cannot be tried by any superior jurisdiction on earth.'

The court was not impressed. All that remained now was to find Charles guilty and pass sentence. The sentence was death. Fifty-nine soldiers, including Oliver Cromwell, signed the death warrant. A large scaffold was built outside the Banqueting Hall in London's Whitehall.

30 January 1649 was a bitterly cold day. Charles asked for two shirts to keep him warm because, he said: 'The season is so sharp as probably may make me shake, which some observers may imagine proceeds from fear.'

Charles was taken to the scaffold. A vast crowd was there to watch. When he spoke to them, it was clear that for Charles, the Divine Right of Kings was still very much in force:

'I must tell you that the liberty and freedom [of the people] consists in having of Government, those laws by which their life and their goods may be most their own. It is not for having share in Government, that is nothing pertaining to them. A subject and a sovereign are clean different things.'

Charles laid his head on the block. The executioner's axe swung. He cut off the king's head with a single blow. As he did so, wrote an eyewitness, 'there was such a groan by the thousands then present, as I never heard before, and desire I may never hear again!'

Eight days later, Parliament abolished the title and office of king. On 19 May the monarchy was abolished, too. For the first and only time in its history, England had become a republic.

This painting by an anonymous Victorian artist depicts the future Lord Protector, Oliver Cromwell, gazing at the body of the executed Charles I. The king's head would have been reattached to his body before it was placed in the coffin.

11
A NOT-SO-MERRY MONARCHY

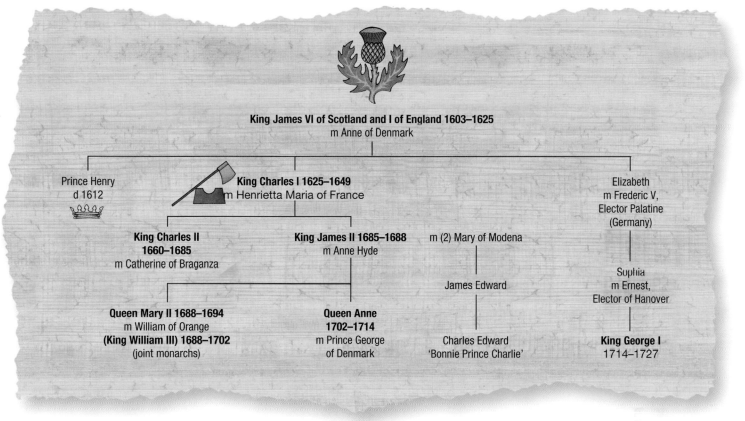

King James VI of Scotland and I of England 1603–1625
m Anne of Denmark

Prince Henry
d 1612

King Charles I 1625–1649
m Henrietta Maria of France

Elizabeth
m Frederic V,
Elector Palatine
(Germany)

King Charles II
1660–1685
m Catherine of Braganza

King James II 1685–1688
m Anne Hyde

m (2) Mary of Modena

James Edward

Sophia
m Ernest,
Elector of Hanover

Queen Mary II 1688–1694
m William of Orange
(King William III) 1688–1702
(joint monarchs)

Queen Anne
1702–1714
m Prince George
of Denmark

Charles Edward
'Bonnie Prince Charlie'

King George I
1714–1727

The English Republic was ruled by Parliament, which was dominated by Puritans. Strict believers, they sought to purify the country from sin and the excessiveness of remaining Roman Catholic practices.

◆

Adultery meant a death sentence. If a man killed his rival in a duel, he could be charged with murder. Puritans made special targets of swearing, gambling and drunkenness. They closed public houses on Sundays and fast days. Swearing was punished by fines. The amount depended on who had done the cursing. A duke was fined thirty shillings, a baron twenty shillings, a country squire ten and everyone else three shillings and four pence.

The crown, orb, sword and other regalia used at the coronation of Charles II had to be newly made for the event, because Parliament had sold off the existing regalia.

That was only for the first crime. All fines were doubled the second time around.

Fun is banned
Puritans were always on the lookout for wickedness and opportunities for same. This was why the playhouses – 'dens of vice and immorality' – were closed. Traditional pastimes such as bear baiting and cockfighting were stopped. So was 'lewd and heathen' maypole dancing.

Dyed clothing of any kind was out. It was against the law to be caught wearing lace, ribbons or decorative buttons. Puritans frowned on long hair, too.

415

England and its people had a very dismal time while Puritans ruled.

Public yearns for royal 'magic'

But the Puritans had made a big mistake when they abolished the monarchy. Monarchy and love of the monarchy were deeply ingrained in English tradition. There was a certain magic about the monarchy. People missed it so much that in 1657, Parliament made an unusual offer: they invited Oliver Cromwell, now Lord Protector, to become king. He laughed off the very idea. Cromwell knew the people did not want any old king: they wanted the real thing. And that meant Prince Charles, son of King Charles I, who was in exile.

Beyond this, Puritanism had a serious weakness. It depended on Cromwell and Cromwell alone. Once he died, in 1658, their regime fell apart.

England under 'Idle Dick' turns to anarchy

Cromwell's successor as Lord Protector was his son, Richard. Richard Cromwell was not the man his father had been. During the 20 months he was in charge, England sank into anarchy. One of the worst aspects was that many soldiers went unpaid. They began to wander around England, stealing food, money and anything else they needed.

Richard Cromwell was so useless that he was given the nickname 'Idle Dick'. He knew he was out of his depth. So he bolted. On 16 May 1659, Cromwell disappeared from London. He fled to Paris, then Italy. He even took a false name: John Clark. His wife never saw him again.

With Idle Dick gone, there was no one to rule England. It was now imperative that the king return. Charles had waited 11 years to get his throne back. He had made one attempt to seize it by force, in 1651, but it failed. After Charles' army was defeated at the battle of Worcester on 14 October, Charles had to go on the run. Oliver Cromwell published a poster offering £1,000 for his capture. Charles was forced to hide in an oak tree to escape his pursuers. Today, the many English pubs called 'Royal Oak' are reminders of this incident.

Hundreds of English public houses are named 'Royal Oak' after an incident that took place on 14 October 1651, when Charles II was forced to hide in an oak tree while escaping from his defeat at the battle of Worcester.

King returns in triumph

After his defeat in 1651, Charles disguised himself. He blackened his face and donned a shabby old suit of clothes. After skipping from town to town, with Cromwell's men in hot pursuit, he managed to sail back to France. But nine years later, Charles's great moment arrived at last: General Monck, a senior officer in the Army, invited him to return as king. On 29 May 1660, Charles's 30th birthday, he entered London in triumph. Londoners turned out by the thousands to welcome him. John Evelyn, the diarist, wrote:

'The triumph of above 20,000 horse and foot brandishing their swords and shouting with inexpressible joy: The ways were strewed with flowers, the bells ringing, the streets hung with tapestry, fountains ran with wine …trumpets, music and myriads of people flocking…so they were seven hours in passing the City (of London) even from two in the afternoon till nine at night.'

That night, there were fireworks and illuminations

A great moment for Charles II after 11 years of exile: he is being rowed towards Dover, where he landed back on English soil after being restored to his throne. Charles received a joyous greeting from his subjects.

over the River Thames. Spectators crowded into boats and barges. There were so many, Evelyn wrote, 'you could have walked across (the river)'.

King Charles had his own way of celebrating his return. Nine months later, on 15 February 1661, Barbara Villiers, one of his many mistresses, gave birth to a daughter. Known as Anne Palmer, she was one of the king's 15 illegitimate children.

'Pretty, witty Nell'

Taking mistresses was almost the only entertainment Charles had while in exile. He was not fussy about his choices. Any curvy, good-looking woman who caught his eye was invited to share the royal bed. The most humble, and the most delightful, was Nell Gwynn. She

Nell Gwynn was the most famous and least pretentious of Charles II's many mistresses. Charles first saw her at the theatre in London, where she was selling oranges to the audience. Later, Nell became one of England's first actresses.

came from the slums of London's East End. Her first job was hawking fish around the richer parts of London. She was spotted by one Madame Ross, a brothel keeper. So, at only 12 or 13, Nell became a prostitute.

But she was no ordinary prostitute. Nell Gwynn was a lively and amusing charmer. Later, Samuel Pepys, the diarist, called her 'pretty, witty Nell' and it suited her. She was ambitious, too. She did not intend to remain just another disposable girl in a brothel. London's stage gave her the chance to move on.

The playhouses reopened after King Charles' return. They showed new, sexy 'Restoration' comedies. These rude, crude, suggestive plays made Puritans rigid with disapproval. But King Charles loved them. He was often among the audience at one of the newest, The King's House, which opened in 1663. There he first saw Nell Gwynn. She sold oranges to members of the audience.

The charming Nell was eyed appreciatively by almost every man within range. She was an accomplished flirt and took several lovers. One was an actor, Charles Hart. He realized Nell would make a splendid actress. At this time, actresses were quite new to the English stage. Previously, female roles had been played by males.

Nell ruins rival's night of love
Another actress was Moll Davis, one of King Charles' mistresses. Moll hated Nell Gwynn and Nell hated her back. To get revenge on Moll, she played a wicked trick. One night early in 1668, Moll was about to sleep with King Charles. A few hours earlier, Nell invited Moll to eat some sweetmeats she had prepared. Moll did not know that the sweetmeats contained a hefty dose of the laxative jalap.

That night, the jalap went to work. Moll was seized by violent attacks of diarrhea. There was no lovemaking. What the king thought is not known. But he was probably amused by the joke – and the delightful young woman who had played it. Soon he had added Nell to his roster of mistresses.

Another 'prank' – though this one considerably more dramatic – that appealed to Charles' sense of fun was an attempt, in 1671, to steal the Crown Jewels from the Tower of London. The would-be thief was Colonel Thomas Blood, son of an Irish blacksmith. Blood had led a vivid life. In 1670, he kidnapped the Duke of Ormonde, Lord Lieutenant of Ireland. Blood was sentenced to death and was about to be hanged at Tyburn in London when a last minute reprieve arrived. Blood fled. A reward of £1,000 was offered for his capture. But he was not caught and set out to steal the Crown Jewels.

Blood brothers
Colonel Blood disguised himself as a parson. He spent time getting friendly with Talbot Edwards, Master of the Jewel House at the Tower. Their friendship went so far that the two men agreed to a marriage between members of their families. This marriage was to have taken place at the Tower on 9 May 1671.

> **Colonel Blood seized the king's crown and used the mallet to flatten it so it would fit into the pocket of his cassock. One of his accomplices seized the orb and hid it inside his breeches.**

That day, with two accomplices, Blood arrived at the Tower. Talbot Edwards suspected nothing until Blood produced a mallet from beneath his cassock and began to beat him over the head. Edwards fell unconscious to the floor.

Blood seized the king's crown and used the mallet to flatten it so it would fit into the pocket of his cassock. One of his accomplices seized the orb and hid it inside his breeches. Meanwhile, the other gang members tried to file the sceptre in half.

Just then, Edwards' son Wythe arrived unexpectedly. When he found his father lying on the floor bleeding, he raised an alarm. At this, Blood and his accomplices fled. But they were caught before they got away.

The Merry Monarch is amused
When King Charles was told what had happened, he was so amused he gave Blood a pardon. He also gave

VENGEANCE, EVEN AFTER DEATH

THERE WAS ALSO REVENGE against the dead. Puritans who had died before the King's return were dug up and their bodies thrown into a pit. Among them were Oliver Cromwell and John Bradshaw. Bradshaw had been the presiding judge at Charles I's trial. There was a special punishment for this pair.

On 30 January 1661, their corpses were dragged on hurdles to Tyburn, near London's Marble Arch. There they were hanged on a gallows until the sun went down. After that, their heads were cut off and stuck on poles on top of Westminster Hall. Cromwell's head remained there for 25 years until it was blown down by strong winds.

A portrait of the young Charles II, who fled to France in 1648, the year before his father, Charles I, was executed.

him a large pension of £500 a year and invited him to come to court. It was all part of the 'fun and games' that returned to England when Charles, the 'Merry Monarch', came back as king.

But the Merry Monarch's reign was not all fun. There was a vicious campaign of revenge against the men who had signed his father's death warrant. Ten of these king-killers were hung, drawn and quartered at Tyburn in London on 20 October 1660. One, a soldier, sat up while he was being drawn and hit his executioner.

Cunning scheme to oust Parliament

But King Charles had other scores to settle. His main purpose in life was 'never to go on his travels again'. He would do anything to keep hold of the throne he had waited for so long. The most important item was to get rid of Parliament.

Kings had always relied on Parliament for money. If Parliament did not like a king's policy, they would refuse to pay up. The solution was for Charles to obtain his own store of cash. In 1670, he signed the Treaty of Dover with King Louis XIV of France. Parliament was supposed to believe that with this treaty, Charles would help Louis with his wars in Europe. But there was a secret clause: Louis agreed to give Charles large sums of money. When Parliament became suspicious, Charles lied, declaring there were no secret clauses. But his hands trembled as he spoke.

All the same, Louis' money gave Charles what he wanted. He was able to dissolve Parliament in 1681. He ruled without it for the rest of his life. This killed two birds with one stone. Parliament could no longer blackmail the king by refusing him money. But they also could not stop his heir, his brother James, Duke of York, from succeeding to the throne.

James was a Roman Catholic. When he became

Titus Oates received far worse punishment than simply being pilloried, as shown in this illustration. Found guilty of perjury, he was imprisoned for life in 1685, but was released in 1688 after the dethronement of James II.

DEEDS *of* POWER

SADIST JEFFREYS'S BARBAROUS DECREES

THE EXECUTION OF THE MOVEMENT'S leader did not mean the end of revenge for Monmouth's rebellion. Even more gruesome punishments followed. In a series of trials, 300 people who had supported Monmouth were sentenced to death. One was Alice, Lady Lisle, aged 70: she was sentenced to burn for sheltering two of the rebels.

The trials became known as the 'Bloody Assizes'. George Jeffreys, one of James II's most brutal agents, presided over the trial in Bristol. He was already known as a bloodthirsty sadist. Jeffreys even profited from the deal. He made a fortune selling pardons to some of the rebels. But hundreds were flogged. Hundreds more were transported to the American colonies – a terrible punishment at the time. It was revenge on a grand scale.

The sentences given out by Judge Jeffreys at the 'Bloody Assizes' remain the benchmark for cruel and unusual punishment.

king, he sought to return England to the Catholic Church. This caused an uproar in Parliament. Several attempts were made to exclude James from the succession. None succeeded. James's most powerful backer was King Charles himself. James was the rightful heir, so he argued, thus James must be king.

Plots and intrigue

But anti-Charles conspirators were also at work. In 1678, two jokers, Titus Oates and Israel Tonge,

The Catholic James II caused tremendous upheaval and much violent protest with his attempts to return England to the jurisdiction of the Pope in Rome. He escaped the fate of his father, Charles I – execution on the block – but was forced into lifelong exile.

decided to stir things up. They hatched the 'Popish plot'. This plot was all hot air. It never existed. But people were so nervous that many believed it was true.

The 'plotters' were Catholic Jesuit priests who planned to kill King Charles. This would make sure Catholic James became king. Then the Popish Plot became known to a London magistrate. He looked into it and came to the conclusion that it was all lies. All the same, Titus Oates went on trial for perjury and was sentenced to life imprisonment.

Next, in 1683, a group of conspirators hatched another plan, the 'Rye House Plot'. This time they really meant to kill. Their targets were not only James, but King Charles as well. That, they thought, would eradicate the risk of having a Catholic king on the throne of England.

Rye House near Hoddesdon in Hertfordshire, which was at the centre of a republican plot hatched in 1683 to kill Charles II and his brother, James, Duke of York, on their way back from the horseracing at Newmarket.

One of the conspirators was James, Duke of Monmouth, King Charles' first illegitimate son. He was vain, stupid and ambitious. Monmouth wanted to be king himself and thought that this was the way to do it.

The plot focused on Rye House farm at Hoddeston, Hertfordshire. King Charles, a keen racegoer, was a regular visitor to the Newmarket races. A narrow lane near Rye House was on the route to Newmarket from London. When King Charles and his brother James used it to return from the races, the plotters intended to ambush and kill them.

But things did not work out as planned. A fire broke out at Newmarket while Charles and James were there. Racing was abandoned. This meant they left Newmarket and rode along the lane much earlier than expected. That, of course, saved their lives.

The conspirators were arrested. One, the Earl of Essex, committed suicide before his trial. But three others were found guilty of treason. There were suspicions that much of the evidence had been made up, and that some of the prosecution witnesses had lied. All the same, the conspirators were beheaded – except Monmouth. King Charles was too fond of him to punish him.

A new king, an old rebellion

Two years later, on 5 February 1685, Charles died. Just as he had always wanted, James became King James II. But soon thereafter, Monmouth tried again to seize the throne. He headed an armed rebellion against the new king. Monmouth's army was overwhelmingly defeated at the battle of Sedgemoor,

DEEDS *of* POWER

A SIMPLE MISTAKE LEADS TO CARNAGE

THE DISASTROUS EVENTS of January 1692 occurred purely due to a simple mistake about location, followed by hazardous weather. The chief of the MacDonald clan, Alisdair McIain, went to the wrong place, Fort William, to swear his oath of loyalty to William and Mary. Upon discovering his error he set off for the right place – Inverary – but snowstorms delayed him. He did not reach Inverary until January 6.

The Government would not listen to excuses or explanations. Instead, they took a savage revenge. On 13 February 1692, at Glencoe, soldiers of the Argyll regiment butchered the MacDonalds. They shot, stabbed and clubbed them to death. Their commander, Robert Campbell, lined up seven MacDonald prisoners and shot them in turn. Then he finished them off with his bayonet.

Alisdair McIain was shot in the back as he was getting out of bed. Dung was smeared over the bodies of the dead. Then they were thrown into the nearby river. Alisdair McIain's wife's fingers were bitten off so that soldiers could steal her rings.

In 1692, Glencoe in the Scottish highlands saw the most appalling massacre to take place on British soil, when the MacDonald clan was slaughtered by soldiers of the Argyll regiment.

ulielmus Rex Maria Regi

in Somerset, on 6 July 1685. He managed to escape from the battlefield and went on the run.

Monmouth was found a week later, hiding in a ditch. He was accused of treason and executed on 15 July. But axeman Jack Ketch was a bungler. He chopped away at Monmouth's neck five times. Even then, he did not kill him. Monmouth's body was still twitching. Ketch threw down the axe in disgust. 'I cannot do it,' he said. 'My heart fails me.' In the end, a knife was used to hack off Monmouth's head.

Even though he had fought hard to make sure James succeeded him, King Charles knew exactly what would happen when he did. He predicted that James would ruin himself within three years. His calculation was perfect.

James lost no time returning England to the Catholic faith. Protestants seethed as he gave Catholics important government and other official posts. They gritted their teeth in rage as James opened negotiations with the Pope to return the English church to his jurisdiction.

The only comfort James' opponents had lay with his two daughters, Mary and Anne. Both were Protestants. Mary was married to the prominent Dutch Protestant, William of Orange. So even if they had to put up with the Catholic James for now, he would be succeeded in time by a Protestant reigning queen – maybe two.

An unwanted surprise

Then, in 1688, something happened that changed the whole picture. On 10 June, King James's second wife, Mary of Modena, gave birth to a son, James Edward, after 15 years of marriage. James Edward's birth after such a long time surprised everyone, even his parents. It also placed James II's enemies on alert.

James Edward was now heir to his father's throne. That meant an endless line of Catholic monarchs on the throne of England. It was too much. James had to go. A group of seven prominent Englishmen sent a secret message to William of Orange. They asked him to bring an army to England and throw James out.

This painting shows the joint monarchs William III and Mary II. William was invited by Parliament to save England from the Catholic 'menace' that threatened the country because of the 'popish' policies of King James II.

England must be saved

It was a desperate move. Undoubtedly these men were committing treason. But no one was going to accuse them of that when England had to be saved from the Catholic 'menace'.

William of Orange landed at Torbay, Devon, on 5 November 1688. As he advanced toward London, James's army retreated. During the retreat, they began to desert. James knew he was on a losing streak. He became terrified. He thought he was going to be beheaded, as had been his father, Charles I.

Now, nothing stood between Mary and the throne – except that her husband William did not want to be a mere consort.

James tried to escape. He attempted to cross the English Channel to France on 11 December 1688. Though disguised as a woman, he was recognized by fishermen who took him back to England.

William and Parliament did not want James back. They would have preferred it if he had escaped into exile. James was given every chance to try again. He managed to get to France on his second attempt, Christmas Day, 1688.

'The throne or nothing' for William

Now, nothing stood between James's daughter, Mary, and the throne – except that her husband William did not want to be a mere consort. He wanted to be king. It was King William or no William, he told Parliament. Otherwise, he threatened to return home and let the English stew.

Parliament had to agree, even though Mary was true heir to the throne. Parliament could not sidestep her, so the throne was offered jointly to William and Mary. They became King William III and Queen Mary II. It was the first and only time England had two monarchs at the same time.

Parliament's offer was not without strings, however. They had had more than enough of monarchs who ranted on about the Divine Right of Kings and did as they pleased.

In 1689, Parliament solved this problem by creating a 'constitutional' monarchy. Meaning that monarchs lost some of their rights, such as to make war or raise taxes. The only income they could have was that granted by Parliament. The polite way of describing constitutional monarchy was that the monarch reigned but did not rule. What it really meant was that Parliament 'fixed' the monarchy so it could no longer rock the boat.

The 'woman' descending the steps in this picture is no woman at all, but the fleeing King James II in disguise. Despite the deception, James was recognized the first time he tried to flee, but he was helped to get away a second time.

The first order of business for William and Mary was to get rid of ex-King James once and for all. In 1690, James brought an army to Ireland. But William easily defeated him at the Battle of the Boyne on 1 July. James fled back to France. He never tried to invade again.

In 1689, the Scots had tried to fight for him. They rebelled against the new king and queen. They were defeated, and the English were very suspicious of them. The Scottish clans were ordered to declare loyalty to William and Mary. The deadline was New Year's Day, 1692. But a terrible misunderstanding occurred and because of it, a shocking slaughter took place.

Scots never forgave King William for the Massacre

Queen Anne, second daughter of James II, was the last Stuart monarch. In 1694, after her elder sister Queen Mary II died, Anne waived her right of succession and allowed her brother-in-law, William III, to take the throne. She succeeded him after he died in 1702.

of Glencoe. But William's problems were getting worse. He had no children. And there was no hope of any children after Queen Mary died of smallpox in 1694. William was heartbroken. Outwardly, he was something of a cold fish. But he collapsed in tears when told Mary had smallpox. The shock was so great that William became paralyzed for a time.

William refused to marry again. This meant that Mary's sister, Anne, became his heir. Unlike Mary, Anne had given birth to many children – 17 in all. But something was terribly wrong with each of them. All died while still young. The last, William, Duke of Gloucester, survived longer than the others. But in 1700, when he was 11, William died, too. He suffered from water on the brain and was weak, slow and stupid. But as long as he lived, he was the last hope of the Protestant Stuart monarchy.

A Scottish toast to the heroic mole

Two years later, on 21 February 1702, William III was riding in Richmond Park, near London, when his horse stumbled on a molehill. At first, William's doctors thought the only damage was a broken collarbone. But the accident was much more serious than that. William's hand became swollen. He could not sign documents and instead had to use a stamp. His doctors tried everything – powdered crab's eyes, pearled julep and sal volatile. Nothing worked. William died on 8 March. For centuries afterwards Scots drank toasts to the mole – 'the little gentleman in the black velvet coat' – because it had caused the hated king's death.

Queen Anne – a ladies' woman

The plain, dull and obstinate Anne, who now succeeded to the throne, was the last of the Stuart monarchs. Although she was married and had given birth to many children, Anne was probably a lesbian. All her close companions were women. A crude pamphlet was written about Queen Anne's 'orientation':

> When as Queen Anne of great renown
> Great Britain's sceptre swayed
> Beside the church, she dearly loved
> A dirty chambermaid.

Anne, it seems, was the 'girl' in lesbian relationships. She was completely dominated by her most famous female companion, Sarah Churchill, Duchess of Marlborough, a very strong-minded woman and ancestor to Winston Churchill.

Sarah and her husband John had Queen Anne just where they wanted her. Anne and Sarah had been childhood friends. Sarah used their friendship to grab all sorts of titles and rewards. These titles came with plenty of money and land. Sarah also engineered a dukedom for her husband: he became Duke of Marlborough in 1689. Later, when Anne was queen, the duke won four splendid victories against the French. With this he shot to fame as England's greatest soldier. Blenheim Palace in Oxfordshire was built especially for him as a reward.

A game goes horribly wrong

Queen Anne disliked pomp and pageantry. She hated the formality of the royal court. So she relaxed by playing a game with Sarah Churchill. Anne called herself 'Mrs. Freeman'. Sarah called herself 'Mrs. Morley'. They pretended they were not queen and subject, rather two ordinary women who enjoyed a chat and gossip and a game of cards.

This was a mistake. Sarah took the game seriously. Anne was a bit of a mouse, plain and awkward. Sarah was a beauty and knew it. So it was not long before she was boldly ordering the queen around and throwing her weight about.

This could not go on indefinitely. In 1707 Anne and Sarah had a big row. Sarah stormed out of the court. The quarrel was so serious that Sarah and her husband left England, too. They did not come back until after Anne's death.

But someone else was waiting to take over from Sarah Churchill. Mrs. Abigail Masham was a relative of Sarah's. Indeed, it had been Sarah who arranged for Mrs. Masham to be appointed 'Woman of the Bedchamber' to Queen Anne. Sarah soon found it was the wrong move: Abigail Masham wormed her way into Queen Anne's affection, telling terrible tales about Sarah to the queen.

Sarah was furious. She wrote of 'the black ingratitude of Mrs. Masham, a woman that I took out of a garret and saved from starving.'

But Abigail remained Queen Anne's closest companion for seven years. In that time she lined her

own pocket with profits from financial deals. She kept other would-be friends of the queen away by plotting against them. But when Anne died, Mrs. Masham's power vanished overnight.

Anne's health had never been good. It was made worse by her long series of miscarriages and stillbirths. The deaths of her children depressed her greatly. In 1708 her husband, Prince George of Denmark, died.

> **Queen Anne hated Sophia. She would not even allow her name to be mentioned at court. So she was delighted when Sophia died in June 1714.**

Anne had adored him and was never the same again.

Anne's childlessness was not just a personal problem. It was a national one as well. In fact, it was an emergency. The Catholic Stuarts were still around, still aiming to seize the English throne. To prevent them from succeeding, a Protestant heir had to be found. The nearest was Sophia, Electress of Hanover in Germany. Her mother Elizabeth had been a daughter of King James I, the first Stuart monarch.

Queen Anne hated Sophia. She would not even allow her name to be mentioned at court. So she was delighted when Sophia died in June 1714, since she now would not be Queen of England. But within three months, Anne herself was dead.

German George gains Crown

The king who now succeeded to the throne as the first Hanoverian monarch of England was Sophia's son George, Elector of Hanover. George was Protestant, which is what Parliament wanted. It was enough to keep the English loyal to him when James Edward Stuart and his followers, the Jacobites, attempted but failed to seize the throne in 1715.

But George did not have much else about him to appeal to his subjects. They had endured bad kings, mad kings, despots, usurpers and weaklings. But, as the English were soon to discover, the Hanoverians were something else.

Queen Anne was the last of the Stuart monarchs. When she failed to produce an heir, the country was thrown into intense debate. Her eventual successor, George I, was only 52nd in line to the throne, but at least he was a Protestant.

12
MISTRESSES AND MADNESS
A FEUDING FAMILY

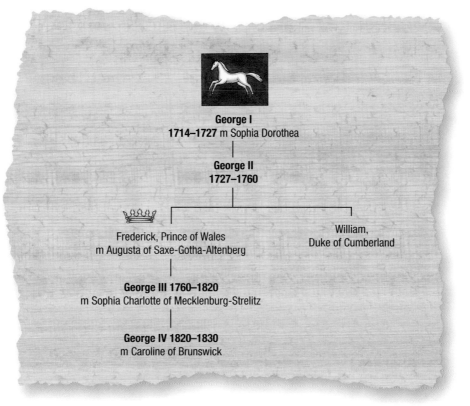

George I
1714–1727 m Sophia Dorothea

George II
1727–1760

Frederick, Prince of Wales
m Augusta of Saxe-Gotha-Altenberg

William,
Duke of Cumberland

George III 1760–1820
m Sophia Charlotte of Mecklenburg-Strelitz

George IV 1820–1830
m Caroline of Brunswick

All but one of the Hanoverian Kings were among the crudest, coarsest monarchs that England ever had. Their manners were dreadful and they showed little idea of how to behave.

✦

In an age when the English expected monarchs to be gracious and dignified, the Hanoverians had no concept of what the words meant.

Even worse, King George I started a terrible family tradition. Each Hanoverian monarch clashed violently with his heir. These were not just family spats. They were vicious contests. Real harm was intended – and real harm was done.

George II was the last king of England to lead his troops into battle, at Dettingen in 1741. At the time he was 60, a lot older than this illustration makes him appear.

A boor with two gruesome girlfriends

The English were shocked to find out what George I was like. He was a dull man, with reddish features and bulging eyes. He was something of a savage – boorish and uncultured. He spoke very little English and had only three interests in life: women, horses and food.

George came to England with two mistresses. Both were incredibly ugly. One was Melusina von Schulenberg, the other Charlotte Sophia Kelmanns. King George was very fond of both. He lost no chance to show them off at court. This trio soon became a national joke in England.

433

This portrait of George I, the first Hanoverian monarch of Britain, was copied from a painting by a fellow German, Sir Godfrey Kneller. King George is shown in his robes of state, his crown on his head, and an ermine cloak.

The contrast between the two mistresses was hilarious. Schulenberg was nearly 60 years old and thin as a reed. She became known as 'the maypole'. Kelmanns was a huge mass of wobbling fat. She was called 'Elephant and Castle' after a district in south London. Both were dubbed 'ugly old trolls'. There was even extra-spicy gossip about Kellmanns: it was widely hinted that she was King George's half-sister.

George I was the first divorced King of England since Henry VIII. The tragedy surrounding his divorce fed gossips with endless tittle-tattle. George's marriage in 1682 had been a disaster from the start. George and his wife, Sophia Dorothea of Celle, had hated each other since they were children. But their marriage was a business arrangement: both families gained new lands because of it.

A marriage made in hell

Unfortunately, Sophia Dorothea was looking for happiness in her marriage. She found the opposite. George was dour, lumpish, and could not take a joke. Sophia, by contrast, was a bright spark. She was very pretty, lively and full of fun. George did not understand her, nor did he try. He was often away from Hanover, fighting wars. When at home, he preferred to play around with his mistresses.

Sophia was too young and impetuous to put up with such a situation. In 1686, while pregnant with her second child, she burst into George's study and demanded he get rid of his mistresses. George was furious. He

---

George took a terrible revenge on Sophia. In 1694, they were divorced. Sophia was forbidden to see her son and daughter.

---

seized Sophia and shook her violently, almost strangling her. Sophia became hysterical. Fortunately, her child, a daughter, was safely born in March 1687.

Prince Charming falls for queen

Around this time a Swedish count, Philip von Königsmarck, arrived at the court of Hanover. Königsmarck was everything George was not. He was 22 years old, very handsome and a real charmer. Men liked him. Women adored him. Königsmarck, a soldier, had come to Hanover for a job. Instead, he became Sophia Dorothea's lover. The two became attracted to each other at a ball given in Hanover in 1688. Königsmarck looked wonderful in a suit of pink and silver. Sophie wore a beautiful white dress and flowers in her hair.

It was all very romantic, even magical. Before long, Königsmarck was hopelessly in love with Sophia. He wrote her passionate love letters every day, sometimes twice a day.

Sophia kept trying to send him away. She realized taking a lover would be very dangerous. But eventually, he broke down her resistance. Sophia and Königsmarck became lovers sometime in 1691. The gossips soon got hold of the

story. From there, George's family learned about it. They placed Sophia under constant surveillance.

Tragedy for the lovers

On the night of 1 July 1694, the lovers met in Sophia's apartments at Leine Palace in Hanover. Königsmarck begged Sophia to run away with him. Apparently someone had seen him going into the apartment. But no one saw him coming out. In fact, no one ever saw Count Königsmarck again.

What had happened to him? People said that he was murdered on George's orders, and his body was chopped into pieces. The pieces were supposedly buried beneath floorboards at the royal country house, Herrenhausen.

George took a terrible revenge on Sophia. On 28 December 1694, they were divorced. Sophia was forbidden to see her son and daughter and was shut away for life in the Castle of Ahlden. She remained there for 32 years until her death in 1726.

Sophia Dorothea haunted George for the rest of his life. He was terrified she would escape from Ahlden. He destroyed all documents concerning their divorce. No one was allowed to speak of Sophia in his presence.

Herrenhausen Palace, in Hanover, Germany, was the summer residence of the Electors of Hanover. It was completed by Electress Sophia, mother of King George I. Destroyed in an air raid in 1943, it was rebuilt in 2013.

The son eclipses the father

George's son and heir, George Augustus, had been only 11 when he last saw his mother. But he never forgot her. And never forgave his father. When he came to England with his wife, Caroline, he kept two portraits of Sophia Dorothea hidden in their apartments. George Augustus became very popular in England. Unlike his father, he spoke English. Caroline was beautiful and gracious. It was no wonder people liked them.

Not so with King George. His subjects never liked him. They made fun of him and his mistresses. They wrote rude pamphlets about him. Journals published cartoons that made him look ridiculous. But George Augustus

A portrait of King George II. Throughout his long reign George hated England and did not travel very far in the country, preferring his beloved Hanover. Unpopular at first, he eventually gained the respect of his subjects.

and Caroline did not suffer this way. They were welcomed wherever they went.

The king grew jealous of them. When he hit back, he hit hard. Just before Christmas, 1717, he ordered George Augustus and Caroline to leave St. James's Palace in London. Worse, the king ordered them to leave their four young children behind. Unfortunately, the youngest child, a boy, died soon thereafter: he was only four months old. The autopsy showed he had a faulty heart. Even so, his parents blamed King George.

Rival court in the heart of London

George Augustus and Caroline set up a new home of their own in London. It became a popular meeting place for politicians and others who disliked King George and his ministers. People said that many plots to overthrow the king were hatched in Leicester House. If they were, nothing actually happened. But the rival 'royal court' increased the hatred between father and son.

The pair never truly reconciled. On occasion, they made a great show of affection in public, to convince everyone everything was all right. But it was not. This show was more difficult to sustain after Sophia Dorothea died in Ahlden on 2 November 1726.

After the news reached London, King George went to see a play with his mistresses. He showed every sign of enjoying himself. The 18th century was not an

The beautiful and lively Sophia Dorothea of Celle, the neglected wife of the future King George I, paid a terrible price for her infidelity – imprisonment for life in the Castle of Ahlden, where she died in 1726 after 32 years.

This illustration shows the execution of the defeated Jacobite rebels at Tower Hill after the Battle of Culloden. It had been a decisive victory for George II's second son William, the Duke of Cumberland.

age of tender feelings. It was a cruel, crude time. Even so, the audience was shocked. They did not expect their monarch to behave like such a cad.

Royal death foretold

King George and Sophia Dorothea had seemed linked in a curious way. George came to hear of a prophecy about them: when one died, so said the prophecy, the other's death would follow within a year. In June 1727, King George went back to his Electorate of Hanover for a visit. Some said that a letter written by Sophia Dorothea was thrown into his coach. It reminded him of the prophecy.

The letter was right. On the way to Hanover, the king suffered a stroke. His entourage managed to reach Osnabrück safely on 11 June. But that same night King George died.

The news took four days to reach England. Prime Minister Robert Walpole rode all the way from

Sir Robert Walpole, painted by John Wootton against a rural background in the guise of a country gentleman. Walpole, usually regarded as Britain's first Prime Minister, was chief minister to George I and George II for a total of 20 years.

London to Richmond, Surrey, to inform George Augustus – now King George II. The new king received the news without emotion.

New king damns his new kingdom

George II's first act was to order portraits of his mother, Sophia Dorothea, brought from their hiding place. The portraits were to be hung where all could see them. The new king seemed a welcome change from his father. He was much friendlier and much more gracious. But that was just a show. In fact King George hated England, the English and everything about them.

'I wish with all my heart that the devil take your (Prime) Minister,' he once exploded in a rage, 'and the devil take the Parliament, and the devil take the whole island, provided I can get out of it and go to Hanover!'

Hanover, of course, was his sanctuary. There, he could be free from 'that damned House of Commons'.

Hanover would allow him to rule as an absolute monarch, by Divine Right.

Queen and Walpole unite and rule

George's wife, Queen Caroline, was a great asset to her husband. She was beautiful, charming and clever. George adored Caroline. Even in public, he could hardly keep his hands off her. Caroline could easily have dominated him, but George would not have it. He wanted everyone to see he was boss. But everyone knew otherwise.

The truth was that Caroline, together with Prime Minister Robert Walpole, had the king on a string. The two used to discuss the latest political questions in private, and together would decide what the government's policy was to be. Then, Walpole would arrive at the palace to see King George. Queen Caroline would be in the room, stitching quietly at her embroidery.

While Caroline remained in the background, the two men talked. But the queen and Walpole prearranged a set of secret hand signals. During his conversation with the king, Walpole played with his hat. Or he took snuff. Or pulled out his handkerchief. Caroline sent a signal back by raising her fan or threading a needle. George never noticed a thing. Once he and Walpole had agreed about policy, he imagined it was all his own idea.

But there was something George and Caroline did agree about. Both detested their eldest son, Prince Frederick. They began to dislike him almost as soon as he arrived in England from Hanover in 1728.

The gentle prince with a brute of a brother

The trouble was, Frederick was not the heir to the throne his parents wanted. He was not the military type. He preferred writing poetry to fighting wars, and

These miniature portraits are of George III and his queen, Charlotte. The couple, who married in 1761, were devoted to each other and had a very large family of 15 children. George III was unusual among British monarchs in not having any mistresses.

was a talented musician. As far as King George was concerned, Frederick was a weakling. He far preferred his second son, William, Duke of Cumberland.

William was a soldier first and last. He was also very uncouth. He gained a terrible reputation for cruelty in the second Jacobite Rebellion in 1745. Then, the Stuart who tried to reclaim the English throne was Charles Edward, son of James Edward. Charles was known as 'Bonnie Prince Charlie'.

Wholesale slaughter at Culloden

The rebellion came to a shocking end at the Battle of Culloden in 1746. Highlanders who supported Charles were slaughtered by the hundreds, mainly by lowland Scots soldiers. Later there were executions and massacres. Scottish homes were looted and burned. Whole communities were destroyed.

Bonnie Prince Charlie had managed to escape back to Europe, aided by one Flora MacDonald. She disguised him as a woman, 'Betty Burke', an Irish spinning maid. Once it was all over, Scots dubbed William 'Butcher Cumberland' for his cruelty. Frederick presumably would not have acted like his brother. He was too kind-hearted. When Flora MacDonald was taken to London and locked up in the Tower of London, Frederick visited her and offered help. Because of Frederick, Flora was set free.

That, of course, did not please the king one bit. Here was his hated heir actually helping his Scottish enemies. Soon history began to repeat itself. King George and Frederick had vicious quarrels. Frederick was banned from his father's court and the royal palaces. A rival court gathered around Frederick and his wife, Princess Augusta. When told of it, King George flew into one of his violent rages.

'He is a monster and the greatest villain ever born,' he ranted. 'My first-born is the greatest ass and the greatest liar...and the greatest beast in the whole world, and I most heartily wish he was out of it!'

Unloved and unmourned

Tragically, Frederick soon fulfilled his father's wishes. Quite suddenly, in 1751, Frederick became seriously ill. While he was working in his garden, it began to rain and Frederick was soaked to the skin. Before long, he was suffering from pleurisy. Pleurisy turned to pneumonia. Then, on the night of 20 March 1751, he suddenly clutched his chest and cried out: 'I feel death!' Minutes later, Frederick was dead. He was 44.

An anonymous poet had the last word about Frederick – and the Hanoverian family.

'Here lies Fred,
'Who was alive and is dead.
'Had it been his father,
'I had much rather;
'Had it been his brother,
'Still better than another.
'Had it been his sister,
'No one would have missed her.
'Had it been the whole generation,
'Still better for the nation.'

King George was playing cards when told his son was dead; he continued his game. He was glad Frederick was gone, and the son was not given a proper funeral for an heir to the throne. Suspicion was that King George had ordered it that way. No member of the Royal Family attended. Nor did any English lord or bishop. There was only a brief ceremony, without music.

Frederick's successor as heir was his eldest son, 13-year-old Prince George – the future King George III. George was forced to live with his grandfather at Hampton Court Palace. He was a stubborn boy. The king often complained that his grandson 'lacked the desire to please'. In other words, he would not do as he was told. George frequently had his ears boxed for disobedience.

Cleaning up the act

Although young, Prince George had learned much from watching his father and grandfather. Though both were devoted to their wives, they were also great womanizers. Young George vowed that when he became king, he would clean up the royal act. There would be no mistresses, immorality at court, gambling or extravagance. George III set the pace himself. He was still unmarried when he became king at age 22 in 1760. But he immediately gave up his teenage love, Lady Sarah Lennox. Although Sarah was aristocratic – her brother was Duke of

A rival court gathered around Frederick and his wife, Augusta. When told of it, King George flew into a violent rage.

Richmond – her rank was not high enough to become queen. Giving up Sarah caused George a great deal of pain. But he was also mindful of the dignity of the British Crown. So the woman he married in 1761 was much more highly ranked: Princess Charlotte of

George, Prince of Wales, the future Prince Regent and George IV, was the embarrassing heir every royal parent dreaded: an irresponsible renegade, undignified, profligate, selfish and immoral.

Mecklenburg-Strelitz. King George was totally faithful to her for the 57 years their marriage lasted.

A motley crew

George and Charlotte had 15 children – seven sons and eight daughters. But if George thought he was going to bring back good old-fashioned family values with his many offspring, he was sadly mistaken. The king kept his daughters at home, ostensibly to save them from the so-called wicked world. But his sons were a disgrace.

One of them, William, Duke of Clarence, seduced two of the queen's Maids of Honour when he was only thirteen. Later, he had ten illegitimate children by his mistress, the married actress Dorothea Jordan. Another son, Ernest, Duke of Cumberland, had a child by his own sister, Princess Sophie. The youngest son, Edward, Duke of Kent, lived for 30 years with his French mistress, Madame Laurent. Two other sons were eccentric and badly behaved, frequently making nuisances of themselves in the House of Lords. On one occasion they had to be removed, swearing and making rude gestures.

The worst of a bad bunch

Undoubtedly the worst of the sons was the eldest, George, Prince of Wales. No vice seemed beyond him. He was vain, arrogant and inconsiderate. He bedded a long series of unsuitable mistresses, including other men's wives. He was already an experienced hand at gambling, drinking and creating scandal by age 17.

As if this were not enough, the Prince of Wales was wildly extravagant. 'Spend, spend, spend!' might have been his motto. In 1787, he was in the red to the tune of £220,000. This was not merely a personal problem, it was a matter of royal prestige. It did not look good to have tradesmen and other creditors pounding on the door of the heir to the throne, demanding payment. Or, just as bad, refusing him credit.

REGAL PROFILES

CURED – ALMOST TO DEATH

THE FIRST SYMPTOM of King George's strange illness was a painful jaw. It was so painful it prevented him from sleeping. Next, he had a stomach upset, shooting pains in his back and breathing difficulties. Things got worse. His eyesight failed. He became deaf. He started talking nonsense incessantly. He talked to trees. He talked to his dead ancestors. Before long Queen Charlotte became terrified of being alone with her husband. His veins stood out on his face. His eyes had a dangerous glint. He foamed at the mouth.

The king's doctors were baffled. Possibly, he had been affected by the loss of the American colonies in the War of Independence that had ended five years before. George had become deeply depressed at what he saw as his failure as king, and that might have affected his mind. Whether or not this was so, no one knew, but one thing appeared evident: the king, the doctors decided, had gone mad. But they had no idea how to cure him. So a quack, the Reverend Francis Willis, was called in. Willis had some very drastic 'cures' up his sleeve. First, he had the king bound to a chair. Then he threatened him. King George became very frightened. He burst into tears and sobbed bitterly.

Willis's strategy continued. Every time King George had a problem – difficulty in swallowing, loss of appetite, or sweating – he was strapped into a straitjacket. Then he was tied down to his bed and left there for hours.

Willis raised blisters on the king's legs to 'drive out the evil humours'. The blisters caused King George agonizing pain. He tore them off only to be strapped into a straitjacket once again. The blisters were reapplied by force. Before long, King George came to believe Willis was trying to murder him. He began to pray for a cure. If he could not be cured, he prayed instead for death.

But somehow, King George started to recover. Early in 1789, his crazy talk began to stop. His personality returned. He was able to shave himself again. He was given back his knife and fork at mealtimes. Soon the king was back to normal.

Nigel Hawthorne brought the troubles of the British monarchy to life in Alan Bennett's 1991 play *The Madness of George III* and its subsequent film adaptation.

King George did not have sufficient funds to pay his son's debts. So Parliament had to bail out the prince and pay his bills. But the prince was not cured – far from it. He kept on spending, fancying himself as something of a dandy and expending vast sums on clothes. The prince was also fond of building projects, jewels, expensive parties and expensive women.

The son breaks all the rules

Then, in 1784, Prince George committed the greatest of all his follies. He fell madly in love with Mrs. Maria Fitzherbert, a twice-widowed commoner. He asked her to become his mistress. But she was a devout Roman Catholic and a respectable woman. She refused. It was marriage, or nothing. So George and Maria were married in 1785 – in secret. The parson who performed the ceremony was released from debtors' prison for the specific purpose.

> **It was thanks to his sons and their mistresses that King George III had an army of illegitimate grandchildren. But what he did not have was a single legitimate grandchild to continue the Hanoverian dynasty.**

With this marriage, George had broken two very important laws in England. One was the Act of Settlement of 1701, which stated that no one in line of succession to the throne could marry a Roman Catholic. The other was the Royal Marriage Act of 1772, which banned royals from marrying before age 25 without the monarch's permission. George was 23 when he married Maria. This did not stop him from living openly with his wife. From time to time, he found a new mistress and wandered off. But he always returned to Maria. He called her 'the wife of my heart and soul'.

Maria was undoubtedly good for the Prince. She civilized him. She made him cut down on his drinking. She put a stop to some of his more boorish habits – such as picking his teeth in public.

Then, in 1788, King George became very sick. No

Caroline of Brunswick, wife of King George IV, was even more outrageous than her husband. The couple lived together for barely a year until after the birth of their daughter, Princess Charlotte, in 1796. Afterwards, Caroline embarked on a career of blatant adultery and scandal.

one knew what was wrong. He had to endure many months of bizarre and painful 'quackery' before he recovered fully.

Parliament strikes deal with prince

By 1794, the Prince of Wales was in big trouble again. He had built up another huge mountain of debts. He became bankrupt, owing £630,000. Once again he had to ask Parliament to pay. Parliament agreed, but with strings attached.

Thanks to his sons and their mistresses, King George III had an army of illegitimate grandchildren. What he did not have was a single legitimate grandchild to continue the Hanoverian dynasty. Parliament offered the Prince of Wales a deal: his debts would be paid, but he had to marry legally and produce legitimate heirs to the throne.

The Prince was trapped. He had to agree – and Mrs. Fitzherbert therefore had to go. Instead, he would marry the wife his father now chose for him. Princess Caroline of Brunswick was the king's niece and the prince's first cousin. But she was the worst possible choice the king could have made. Her family background said it all. She came from an unhappy home. Her parents were constantly at war with each other. Two of her brothers were mentally retarded.

Trouble in store

Caroline had grown up thoroughly spoiled. Her conversation was peppered with swear words. She was vain, rebellious and immoral. It was as if King George was allowing his son to marry a wild beast.

Prince George knew nothing of any of this. He and Caroline had never met before she arrived in England for their wedding. But when he saw her for the first time, he went into shock. 'Harris,' he gasped to his attendant, Lord Malmesbury, 'I am not well, pray get me a glass of brandy!'

But the shock the prince received at Greenwich was nothing compared to what followed. He did not know it yet, but the stage was set for the most outrageous royal scandal England had ever known.

13
BATTLE ROYAL

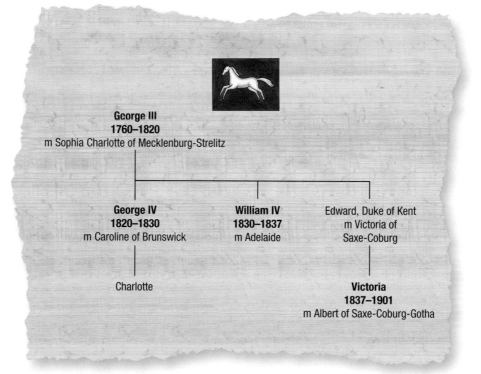

George III
1760–1820
m Sophia Charlotte of Mecklenburg-Strelitz

George IV
1820–1830
m Caroline of Brunswick

William IV
1830–1837
m Adelaide

Edward, Duke of Kent
m Victoria of
Saxe-Coburg

Charlotte

Victoria
1837–1901
m Albert of Saxe-Coburg-Gotha

A glass of brandy may have dulled the shock for a time, but an awful reality was still there when the effect wore off. Prince George's future bride stood before him at their first meeting looking an absolute fright.

◆

Caroline was dressed in a robe and cloak with a beaver hat on her head. The robe was in a shade of sickly green with satin trimmings, festooned with fussy loops and tassels. This was the best her attendants could do to hide her pudgy figure.

A frump decked out in finery

Caroline's face was covered with garish makeup. Somewhere underneath were her fine, fresh complexion and rosy cheeks. She looked like a clown.

The Royal Pavilion, Prince George's exotic home in Brighton, East Sussex, was greatly influenced by oriental styles of architecture, with an Indian exterior and a Chinese interior.

And that was not all. Close up, Caroline reeked. She smelled unwashed. Prince George reeled. He was very strict about hygiene and regular bathing.

Somehow, Prince George managed to compose himself and behave graciously. But it took a stupendous effort. The prince had to contain himself again when he took Caroline to a pre-wedding dinner. She prattled on and on about the latest gossip, including talk about the prince's latest mistress, Lady Jersey. Her language was crude, coarse and smutty.

After a while, George could stand the situation no longer and got thoroughly drunk. He was still hung over when the marriage ceremony took place on 8 April 1795. George spent most of his wedding night in a drunken stupor, asleep on the floor next to the fireplace. But somehow – though he probably never remembered how – he fulfilled his royal duty. Caroline, the new Princess of Wales, became pregnant on her wedding night.

Royal pair make an effort

In truth, Caroline was not all that impressed with George, either. At one time, he had been a slim young man, and handsome too. Not any more. At age 33, years of self-indulgence and overeating had taken a toll. Caroline was disappointed to see how fat and puffy he had become.

In spite of having a distinct aversion to one other, George and Caroline made some effort to live together. They spent the summer and autumn of 1795

Cartoonists often caricatured Prince George. His huge bulk was due to constant overeating. He fancied himself as a dandy and wore exotic clothes. This contemporary caricature shows him with an equally gross 'friend'.

Maria Fitzherbert was the great love of King George IV's life. He broke the law in 1785 when he married her without his father's permission. George left her from time to time to dally with mistresses, but he always returned.

at Brighton Pavilion, on England's southern coast. This lavish, oriental-style building – still one of the major sights of Brighton – had once been George's most expensive extravaganza. But while the couple were there, George's drinking pals descended on them, along with their women. The quiet honeymoon in Brighton turned into a riotous drinking party.

This did not help George and Caroline learn to tolerate each other, and soon they stopped trying. Caroline was spoiled, rebellious and vain. It had once been said that unless she were kept on a tight leash, she would go wild. George did not bother trying to rein her in.

Once their daughter, Princess Charlotte, was born on 7 January 1796, Prince George made moves to distance himself from his marriage. Charlotte was

but a few days old when her father drafted a will disinheriting Caroline.

After his fling with Lady Jersey, George was struck with a yearning for Maria Fitzherbert once again. In a nearly hysterical mood, he wrote vowing eternal love for 'my wife in the eyes of God and who is and ever shall be mine.' Another letter, this time to Caroline, was totally different. It began 'Madam', and went on to state his desire for a total and permanent separation.

George and Caroline never lived together again. But they were never divorced, nor was this the end of their relationship. The couple would be bound together in mutual hatred for the next 25 years.

The Queen's amorous adventures

Caroline was not the sort of woman to retire to a quiet, discreet life in the country, where everyone might forget about her. She was too vulgar, too outlandish, for that. She did move to the country, but that was about it. Her new home was in Blackheath, on the southern edge of London.

Before long, Caroline was shocking the locals with her antics. She received a stream of 'gentleman callers'. Tales of multiple adultery began to circulate and spread. Caroline got her clutches on one William

---

With Parliament against him, the prince had to give in. But he hit back by throwing Caroline out of her Kensington Palace apartments. He also forbade Charlotte to see her – no matter what Parliament said.

Austin, young son of a dockyard worker, and claimed he was her and Prince George's son. Fortunately, government investigators proved the story false. They went on to dig up evidence about Caroline's sex parties. But they were unable to prove anything, despite the gossip.

The indecisive lover

Meanwhile, Prince George's longing for Maria Fitzherbert had worn off again. He took a new

mistress, Lady Horatia Seymour. After that, it was back to Maria again. She held George off for four years, possibly to teach him a lesson. But in 1801, she agreed to live with him again. Maria managed to hang on to George for ten years – a record for him. But he wandered off again, this time with yet another mistress, Lady Hertford.

King loses his mind – for good

In 1811 King George III's illness returned and he became permanently mad. He had violent fits. He refused to eat. He imagined that his son Augustus, who had died in 1783, aged four, was still alive. He lost all sense of time, place or reality and lived in a dream world. The one thing he remembered, it seems, was how to play the harpsichord.

This time, it was hopeless. The king was declared incurably insane in 1812. He was shut away in his palace and spent his days wandering around his rooms, mumbling to himself and clutching the Crown Jewels.

Caroline senses trouble ahead

George was appointed Prince Regent at last. He took the oath on 6 February 1811. But he still had to deal with the troublesome Caroline. The king's madness had been a disaster for her, for in spite of everything, King George had protected her. Now, that protection was gone, and she was in the hands of a husband who detested her. He soon made the most of it.

He used Princess Charlotte as a psychological weapon with which to beat his wife, refusing to let her see their daughter. Caroline was up to the challenge. She had allies in Parliament and used them to force a Parliamentary debate. The vote went to Caroline.

With Parliament against him, the prince had to give in. But he hit back by throwing Caroline out of her apartments at Kensington Palace. He also forbade Charlotte to see her – no matter what Parliament said.

Queen wins public's affection

Caroline's response was to make several well-publicized public appearances. She posed as the victim of a cruel husband, but cheerfully so. The ploy worked. Crowds cheered her. At the same time, they booed the Prince Regent.

The warfare between George and Caroline moved on to the next round. George decided that Princess Charlotte should marry Prince William of Orange.

This cartoon shows 'the Royal Extinguisher' – King George IV – who finally triumphs over his dreadful wife Caroline by placing a cone made of paper over her and a crowd of Jacobites – supporters of the ousted House of Stuart.

William was an unpleasant young man. Even so, Charlotte was expected to obey her father. But, as was her mother, she was stubborn and loud-mouthed. It was not long before she had picked a quarrel with William.

Charlotte fled to Caroline's house in Connaught Place, London. Caroline was not there. She was at Blackheath. The Prince Regent's brothers came after her. They badgered her to obey her father. By this time her war with the Prince Regent had exhausted Caroline. This latest fight was too much. She joined in and told Charlotte to stop making trouble and marry William.

Charlotte had her own cunning way of dealing with William. She blackmailed him by demanding that, as second in line for the English throne, she must remain in England after their marriage. Next she told William that Caroline must come and visit whenever she wanted. That was it. The very thought of sharing living space with Europe's most scandalous mother-in-law was the last straw for William. He refused her requests. Charlotte broke off the engagement.

Princess Charlotte eventually married another prince, Leopold of Saxe-Coburg-Gotha, in 1816. However, she died after giving birth to a stillborn son. Caroline was in Italy when she heard the news and immediately went into deep mourning for her daughter. In England, the Prince Regent collapsed in a dead faint on hearing the tragic news. He recovered, but was so distressed he was unable to attend the funeral.

THE PARTY QUEEN WHO LOVED TO SHOCK

BY 1814, AFTER NEARLY 20 YEARS OF FIGHTING her husband, Caroline longed to get away. The time was right. England's long wars against Napoleon Bonaparte and the French were coming to an end after 22 years. It was now safe to travel in Europe. Despite her experiences in England, Caroline still had plenty of bounce left in her. She wanted to be free to enjoy herself.

But for Caroline, that meant she would spin even more out of control than before. News soon reached England of a long series of spicy scandals. Bonaparte's family were now in disgrace. Caroline went out of her way to seek them out. They became so friendly that Caroline even took Joachim Murat, Napoleon's brother-in-law, for her latest lover.

Caroline moved on to Italy. There, she squeezed her fat bulk into skimpy dresses with necklines down to her waist. The skirts rose well above her plump knees. Caroline appeared at parties and gala balls wearing a huge black wig. She painted her cheeks blood red and stuck sequins on them.

Caroline became an attraction wherever she went. She went about wearing long pink feathers, riding in a coach shaped like a shell. Somewhere along the way, Caroline acquired an extraordinary companion. Bartolomeo Bergami had flashing eyes, curly black hair and an outsized moustache. He was an Italian adventurer of mysterious origins.

Bergami became Caroline's secretary and, of course, her lover. The pair journeyed around the Mediterranean, ending up in the Middle East. There Caroline made a pilgrimage to Jerusalem mounted on a donkey. Considering her vast bulk and the donkey's small size, it was a sight to behold.

Caroline and Bergami settled down to live together in Pesaro, Italy.

Like her husband, Princess Caroline was a frequent target of cartoonists and pamphleteers. Here she is cavorting around with her lover Bartolomeo Bergami and, right, on the arm of Alderman Wood. Caroline died in 1821, the year these caricatures were published.

Urgent quest for an heir

This, though, was not merely tragic family loss. It created a crisis. Charlotte had been the only heir to the throne in her generation. The other heirs to mad King George III were Charlotte's elderly uncles and aunts, none of whom had any legitimate children.

So Parliament sent a petition to four of Charlotte's uncles to marry and produce legitimate heirs. It meant leaving their mistresses, which caused them pain. All the same, they did their duty for the sake of the Hanoverian line. They took wives and had children. Unfortunately, many of the infants died.

For a time, even the Prince Regent considered divorcing Caroline and marrying again. But Caroline refused to let him. She did not think her sexual adventures in Europe were sinful, and prepared to fight any divorce action the prince might bring.

> **Time for the new king to act was limited. He had to get rid of Caroline before his coronation. In fact, the coronation was postponed while the king made yet another attempt to unhitch himself.**

The prince set up a commission to find grounds for divorce. Caroline responded by promising to create a storm of protest in England. It was a shrewd move. Details of the prince's own private life were bound to come out. All the same, Caroline tried another tack. She offered to set aside her rank as Queen of England when George became king. In return, she wanted George to give her a large sum of money. He refused, ending thoughts of divorce. The couple remained married, shackled together in mutual loathing.

Death of a pitiful old man

Caroline was still on course to become Queen of England. As long as King George III was still alive, that remained a remote possibility. But on 29 January 1820, King George died. He had become a tragic figure, far

This drawing of King George III depicts him at the age of 72, in his Golden Jubilee year of 1810. But tragedy was fast approaching at this time: King George went mad once again, and this time there was no chance that he would recover.

gone into madness. He was deaf and blind. His white, gaunt face was sometimes observed, staring out the palace window, seeing nothing. His beard had grown long and straggly. He knew nothing about the death of Princess Charlotte, or the marriages of his sons. He was even unaware his queen, Charlotte, had died in 1818.

George fails to ditch Caroline

The Prince Regent succeeded his father as King George IV. As far as her rights were concerned, Caroline was now queen. But as far as her husband was concerned, he was not going to let her anywhere near the throne.

Time for the new king to act was limited. He had to get rid of Caroline before his coronation. In fact, the coronation was postponed while the king made another attempt to unhitch himself from his outrageous queen. He asked Parliament to pass a Bill of Pains and Penalties. This set out Caroline's numerous sins. The attempt failed. The only evidence offered was circumstantial – albeit Caroline's sexual antics had been the subject of frequent gossip. The Bill of Pains and Penalties had to be dropped. Londoners, who loved Caroline, went wild with joy and celebrated for three days and nights.

The toast of London once more

Caroline chose this moment to make a triumphant return to England. Everywhere she went she was fêted and saluted. George IV, by contrast, was subjected to vile insults. Obscene graffiti were scrawled on the walls of Carlton House, his private London residence. And not only there. 'The queen forever! The king in the river!' were slogans scrawled on the walls of the Russian Embassy in London. George IV got the message. He left London for his country cottage at Windsor, Berkshire. There, he waited for 'Caroline fever' to die down.

Nine weeks passed before George thought it safe to return to London. To make sure, he took a troop of Life Guards with him. He was relieved that the crisis seemed to have passed. When he went to a play at London's Drury Lane, he was applauded. The same happened when he went to see another play at Covent Garden.

DEEDS *of* POWER

NO ENTRANCE TICKET FOR THE QUEEN

ON CORONATION DAY, the interior of Westminster Abbey was decorated with brocade, lace, silks and satins, velvet and feathers – an opulent display for a great royal occasion. Outside, the crowd of sightseers was large and excited. Sellers of coronation souvenirs did a vast trade. Pickpockets moving unnoticed among the sightseers also had a very good day.

Suddenly, a row broke out at an entrance to the abbey. Caroline was there, but the doorkeeper had orders from the king. He was to stop the queen from getting in. His reason?, The queen did not have a ticket. Caroline tried another door. It was locked. She could not get in that way, either. It was the same at each of the abbey's many doors. Stone-faced doorkeepers barred her. They were not the least impressed when she told them who she was.

Caroline was not going to stand for this without making a big fuss. But the crowds soon tired of her. Caroline was making a nuisance of herself and spoiling the fun. They hissed and booed her. No one helped Caroline as she desperately went from door to door, trying to get in.

The row became so great that guards were called in. They stood in a line in front of every doorway. Finally, the last door was shut in Caroline's face. By this time Caroline was red-faced with shame and fury. In the end she was forced to return to her carriage and drive home to Brandenburg House. Two days later, she wrote a furious letter to the king.

'The queen must trust that after the public insult Her Majesty has received this morning, the king will grant her just right to be crowned next Monday....' There was no reply.

Determined to be acknowledged as queen, Caroline attempted to gate-crash the coronation of her husband, King George IV, in 1821. He managed to stop her from getting in and she had to return home, frustrated.

King bans queen from his coronation

After this, the king felt confident enough to fix another date for his coronation – 19 July 1821. Queens of England had their own special coronation, after the king's. But George was confident enough now to tell Caroline she could not take part. Her name had already been removed from the prayers to be said at the coronation ceremony. She had been pestering him to have her name put back, to tell her what robes she should wear, to name the attendants who would carry her train.

But George IV was determined that his coronation would be a one-man show. Caroline was not deterred. She was determined to crash the ceremony, planned for London's Westminster Abbey. Failing that, she would create mayhem. Caroline was counting on her popularity with London crowds. The king knew she would make a terrible scene, so he took precautions to prevent her even from entering the abbey.

The end of a feisty queen

Twelve days after his coronation, George IV went aboard the royal yacht for a state visit to Ireland. The yacht was at anchor off the Isle of Anglesey, north Wales, on 6 August 1821, when news arrived that Caroline was dying. She had been taken ill at Drury Lane. Medical treatments at this time were extremely brutal, often causing the patient's death. But such treatments were all Caroline's doctors knew. So they bled her and gave her hefty doses of calomel and castor oil.

William IV succeeded his brother George IV on the throne in 1830. He had never expected to become king and was so delighted that he drove around London in his carriage greeting his subjects and shaking them by the hand.

Queen has the last word

The doctors believed she would somehow recover. Instead, she died on 7 August. For once, George IV acted decently. He remained on Anglesey during the week of Caroline's funeral. Five days of official mourning had been declared. The king waited until they had passed before making his entry into Dublin.

But it was Caroline who had the last word. At her own request, her coffin was inscribed with the words: 'Caroline of Brunswick, the Injured Queen of England'. Even the King of England was unable to do anything about that.

George IV was King of England for ten years, until his death at Hampton Court on 26 June 1830. His heir was his brother William, Duke of Clarence, who became King William IV.

An unruffled royal oddball

Like other sons of King George III, William was a bit of an oddity. He even looked peculiar. Aged 64, William had a round face, very red cheeks and a distinctly unroyal quiff. When the coins of his reign were minted, designers deliberately left out the quiff.

William was awakened at six in the morning and told he was king. He showed no emotion. Instead, he shook the messenger's hand and went back to bed. His only comment was that he had 'always wanted to sleep with a queen'. His wife Adelaide had, of course, just ascended from Duchess of Clarence to Queen Consort of England.

Later the same day, he stuck a small piece of black crepe in his hat and went out riding at Windsor. But William IV was not as nonchalant about succeeding to the throne as he pretended to be. As a younger son of a king, he had never really expected to be king himself. When it actually happened, he was thrilled.

No heir but Victoria

A few days later, he went riding around London in his coach. He stopped here and there to buttonhole passers-by, shake them by the hand and tell them how delighted he was to be their king. It was embarrassing, but somehow heartwarming.

Unfortunately, William IV came to the throne without legitimate heirs of his own. As Duke of Clarence, William had married Adelaide in the royal rush for a wife after the death of Princess Charlotte. They had two daughters, but both died in infancy, and there were no children after that.

William's heir was his niece, Princess Victoria. She was the daughter of his younger brother, Edward, Duke of Kent – another participant in the royal rush to marry. Victoria's mother, Victoire of Saxe-Coburg, kept her daughter strictly under her control. Victoire's

Victoria, niece of George IV and her predecessor William IV, came to the throne at age 18 in 1837 determined to repair the good reputation of the royal family after the outrageous activities of the Hanoverian kings. The result was an era of strict morality.

main aim was to keep the girl well away from the influence of disreputable Hanoverian relatives.

Predictably, William IV became at odds with Victoria's mother. His greatest wish was to live long enough for Victoria to reach the age of majority, 18: if he could do that, he could prevent her mother from becoming Regent. The king just made it. William IV died on 20 June 1837. Victoria had turned 18 the month before, on May 24.

A pair of right royal prudes for England

Not surprisingly, Princess Victoria grew up to be narrow-minded and self-opinionated. She was also a terrible prude, and tended to be obsessive. In 1840, she married her first cousin, Prince Albert of Saxe-Coburg-Gotha, who was even more of a prude than she was. He once said that the thought of adultery made him feel physically sick.

Victoria's heir, the future King Edward VII, was pure Hanoverian. Strict morality meant nothing to him. Both as Prince of Wales and as king, he became the greatest royal womanizer since Charles II.

Albert set the pace for his wife's reign and for their private life. Hanoverian sleaze was out. Strict Puritan-style morality was in. Family respectability was to become the motto of Victorian England. More than that, the nine children of Victoria and Albert were to be role models for a new society: their example, so their parents resolved, would stand as a lesson on how to be royal, yet lead a pure life.

But there was one great big flaw in this plan. Victoria's heir, the future King Edward VII, was pure Hanoverian. Strict morality meant nothing to him. Both as Prince of Wales and as king, he became the greatest royal womanizer since King Charles II. He gambled, he drank, he smoked – all to excess. His life was one long round of scandal that horrified his parents and left their high-minded plans in ruins.

14

SCANDAL BEHIND CLOSED DOORS

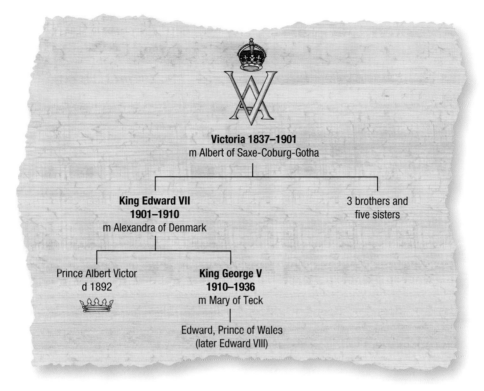

Victoria 1837–1901
m Albert of Saxe-Coburg-Gotha

King Edward VII
1901–1910
m Alexandra of Denmark

3 brothers and
five sisters

Prince Albert Victor
d 1892

King George V
1910–1936
m Mary of Teck

Edward, Prince of Wales
(later Edward VIII)

**Edward, Prince of Wales, known in the royal family as Bertie, began his
life of scandal at a young age. In 1861, when he was 19, he was sent for
military training to an army camp at the Curragh, in Ireland.
It was there that he lost his virginity.**

◆

Bertie had spent his childhood in confinement at home, with his family. He was held captive by a very strict system of education. But more study and more application were required of him than he could reasonably manage. Bertie was not stupid, he was simply unacademic. Book learning, which he came to hate, meant nothing to him. He reacted by throwing tantrums, attacking his tutors and working himself into wild rages.

**Three royal generations: Queen Alexandra and King Edward
VII (standing), the future George V and Queen Mary, and their
son Edward (later King Edward VIII and, after his abdication
in 1936, Duke of Windsor).**

'Bertie's Fall'

But in 1861, this repressed young man had his first taste of what the outside world was really like. First of all, he met other young men, all training to be army officers. He found they had habits he had never heard of. One was making use of the services of the camp prostitute, a pretty young actress named Nellie Clifden.

One night, officers at the Curragh moved Nellie into the prince's bed. The inevitable happened. Nellie made a man of him. But when the news reached Bertie's parents, they were horrified. The incident became known as 'Bertie's Fall', and Bertie was never allowed to forget it.

Prince Edward shocked his parents and Victorian society with his sexual antics and his association with high-life scandal. Less prudish types, however, had a sneaking admiration for Bertie, who broke the rules and got away with it.

Bertie gets the blame

Even worse, there was a tragic sequel. Not long after 'Bertie's Fall', his father, Prince Albert, fell seriously ill. His doctors had no idea what was wrong. He had probably caught typhus from faulty drains at Windsor Castle.

Albert died on 14 December 1862, aged only 42. Queen Victoria went half-mad with grief, for she had idolized him. She went into mourning and remained so for the next 40 years, until she died. Bertie and his 'Fall' were blamed for causing Albert's death. Victoria never forgave him.

But before Albert died, a cure for 'Bertie's Fall' had already been arranged: marriage to a sensible wife who would keep tabs on him and stop his straying.

A hand-picked beauty

The royal houses of Europe were searched for a suitable bride for Bertie. Finally, the choice became the 18-year-old Princess Alexandra of Denmark. She had the one asset Bertie's parents most wanted: she was extremely beautiful. Victoria firmly believed Alexandra's physical beauty alone would make Bertie mend his ways. Victoria – and Alexandra – soon discovered differently.

REGAL PROFILES

FUN-LOVING PRINCE WITH GIRLFRIENDS GALORE

BERTIE WAS NATURALLY ATTRACTED to fun-loving, pleasure-seeking high society types. He could dance until dawn. He would gamble and bet on horses and play flirtatious games all night. Bertie loved every minute of it. Before long, Bertie and Alexandra were leading separate lives.

Alexandra stayed at home with their children. She supported many charities. Meanwhile, Bertie lived it up. He was off to the races. He went to Paris, where he took a French princess for a mistress. He cavorted openly with opera stars and actresses. When he came back to England, he brought with him semi-pornographic pictures of popular French singers. Gossip soon did the rounds about his illegitimate children. Bets were placed on who his next mistress would be and how long she would last.

Although Bertie was pure Hanoverian, he was not irresponsible, like his ancestors: he had a strong sense of royal dignity and the need to maintain it.

Bertie and Alexandra were married on 10 March 1863 at St. George's Chapel, Windsor. Queen Victoria cast gloom over the ceremony by attending clad entirely in black and observing from a high balcony.

What Victoria had not realized was that in having Bertie married, she was freeing him from her apron strings. Now, he would have his own household. In fact he had two homes, Marlborough House in London and Sandringham in Norfolk. He also soon had his own family: his first son, Prince Albert Victor, known as Eddie, was born in 1864. Above all, Bertie could now make his own social life. And a very riotous – not to say scandalous – social life it would be, too.

> **John Brown was often alone with the queen. He came to her bedroom after breakfast and sat with her while she looked through papers in confidential government 'boxes' – a task she had to perform every day.**

Queen Victoria, meanwhile, was involved in a scandal of her own. Victoria was a very emotional woman given, on occasion, to melodramatic conduct. She had not simply loved her husband, Prince Albert, she had adored and worshipped him. It was the same – according to gossip of the day – with her personal servant, or gillie, Scotsman John Brown. Brown was never anything but a best-liked servant. But after Albert's death Victoria became so attached to him that it gave rise to gossip.

Courageous and well-respected companion

John Brown was based at Balmoral, the royal home in Scotland. He was no ordinary gillie. His intelligence was above average and he was a very good judge of human nature. Besides that, he had a way of talking Victoria liked. She hated all the bowing and scraping when royals were around. Brown, by contrast, spoke his mind. And he knew how to do it without being rude. For Victoria, he was a breath of fresh air.

Brown was unusually thoughtful and considerate. He knew Victoria loved white heather. So he kept an eye out for it in the countryside around Balmoral. Victoria was thrilled to receive bouquets of her beloved flower from her much-loved servant.

Despite her high position as Queen of England, Victoria was a dependent type of woman. She liked and needed to be cared for. Brown fulfilled her requirements. He became her constant companion, accompanying her wherever and whenever she wanted.

Brown also saved her life. On 29 February 1872, Victoria was about to go through the garden entrance to Buckingham Palace when a man named Arthur O'Connor pointed a pistol at her. John Brown leapt on him and knocked the weapon out of his hand. Brown pinned the man down until police arrived.

Later the queen awarded Brown a gold medal for his courage.

John Brown was often alone with the queen. He came to her bedroom after breakfast and sat with her while she looked through papers in confidential government 'boxes' – a task she had to perform every day. She saw more of Brown than of her own children.

Victoria's children became jealous. They spoke of Brown as 'Mama's lover'. They may even have believed the gossip that Victoria and John Brown were secretly married. For a while, it became an 'in' joke to refer to the queen as 'Mrs. Brown.'

'Mrs. Brown' widowed again

After more than 20 years of devotion to the queen, John Brown died in 1883. Victoria was almost as distraught as when Prince Albert died. Her reaction was, of course, excessive. She put up a statue to Brown at Balmoral. She planned to write a poem in his praise. She ordered that Brown's room should be kept exactly as it had been when he died. A fresh rose was to be placed on his pillow every day. The orders were carried out: a new rose appeared on the pillow every day for 18 years, until Queen Victoria died in 1901.

Bertie, of course, thoroughly disapproved of all this 'romantic nonsense' over John Brown. Victoria, in turn, thoroughly disapproved of Bertie. If anyone was disgracing the royal family name, so she thought, it was he.

Judi Dench as Queen Victoria and Billy Connolly as John Brown in *Mrs Brown*, a film made in 1997 about the relationship between Victoria and her 'gillie', or Highland servant. Some said that Victoria and Brown were married.

Bertie's near-miss

She had a point. Bertie, as always, lived dangerously. Mostly his activities were kept under wraps. But it was inevitable that sooner or later, there would be a scandal that could not be hidden. The time arrived in 1870.

In February of that year, Lady Harriet Mordaunt confessed to her husband, Sir Charles, that she had committed adultery with several men. One of them had been Bertie.

Bertie protested his innocence. He knew the Mordaunts well. It was true he had written several letters to Harriet. But they were friendly, so he said, no more than that. Unfortunately, Sir Charles Mordaunt was not like other members of the English aristocracy. Most did not mind if the prince bedded their wives. They regarded it as a sort of compliment. But Sir Charles did not see why Bertie should get away with it. He threatened to name the prince as a co-respondent in his divorce case. This caused horror all around. It was one thing to gossip about royal goings-on, quite another to have it all spelled out in public.

But Bertie was saved when Sir Charles' divorce case

Bertie and Alexandra, Prince and Princess of Wales, photographed in 1882. Alexandra was famous for her beauty, which lasted all her long life, but her physical attractions were not enough to keep her husband faithful or virtuous.

This did not mean he was out of trouble. Bertie was never out of trouble. Six years later, he had another lucky escape. In 1876, the Earl of Aylesford sued his wife for divorce. Bertie was not named as co-respondent this time. The man named by the earl was Lord Blandford, heir to the Duke of Marlborough. But Bertie had written letters to the Countess of Aylesford. Read a certain way, some suggested a very close, maybe sexual, relationship.

Unfortunately for Bertie, Lord Blandford had a fiery younger brother, Lord Randolph Churchill. When Lord Randolph worked himself into a temper, sparks flew. Randolph threatened to publish Bertie's letters. But then the Duke of Marlborough stepped in and put a stop to the divorce proceedings. It had been a narrow escape.

Another close call for Bertie

By now, there was talk that Bertie was not fit to succeed his mother on the throne. That faded after a while. But in 1890, Bertie added fuel to the fire once again. In September that year, the prince was staying at Tranby Croft, country home of his rich friend Arthur Wilson and his wife.

On 8 September, after dinner, it was decided to play a round or two of baccarat, the card game. Baccarat was illegal in England at the time. Even so, bets were placed, and the game commenced.

One of the players was Sir William Gordon Cumming, a distinguished army officer with many medals to his name. Cumming had been a friend of Bertie's for 20 years. They shared interests in womanizing and gambling.

During the evening, other players thought they

failed. Not because his wife was not guilty, but because she had been declared insane. Her 'lovers', royal and otherwise, were found to be in her imagination. It was a tragic outcome, but it got Bertie off the hook. After the divorce case, he had to put up with booing, hissing and catcalls whenever he appeared in public. But at least he had not been named as an adulterer by the court.

had seen Cumming cheating. At that time, cheating at cards was one of the worst social crimes possible to commit. It was made even worse because the prince was there. Bertie was told what had happened.

First thoughts were to protect him from a 'horrible scandal'. Two courtiers had accompanied Bertie to Tranby Croft. One, Major Owen Williams, thought of a way out. Gordon Cumming had to sign a document saying he would never play cards again. It made him sound guilty. But that could not be helped.

Gordon Cumming signed the document, but under fierce protest. He claimed he was innocent. But he was assured nothing more would be said on the matter. He had to be content with that.

But the story got out. Late in 1890, Gordon Cumming received an anonymous letter from Paris. This revealed that far from being hidden, gossips were

The Baccarat or Tranby Croft Scandal, in which Bertie was involved in 1890, shocked society both because his friend Cumming was accused of cheating and because baccarat was illegal. It hardly reflected well on the prince's probity.

having a field day talking about the 'baccarat scandal'. No one ever found who had talked. But Gordon Cumming was furious. He decided to clear his name through the courts. He would demand that his hosts at Tranby Croft, the Wilsons, withdraw the accusation of cheating. Otherwise, he would sue them for slander.

The case was to be heard in English civil court. This meant Bertie could be subpoenaed as a witness. For a member of the royal family to appear in a witness box was unheard of. It was a scandal in itself. Desperate attempts were made to persuade Gordon Cumming to withdraw the case. But he refused.

The case opened at the Chief Justice's Court in London on 1 June 1891. Press and public were packed tightly in galleries above the courtroom. Bertie entered the witness box on the second day of the trial. Other witnesses, including Gordon Cumming himself, had been mercilessly cross-examined by prosecution lawyers. But they went gently when it came to Bertie. They did not try to pin him down, but attempted to gather his evidence as quickly as they could.

But there was one man on the jury, Goddard

Clarke, who was not prepared to pussyfoot around. He stopped Bertie just as he was leaving the witness box. In a sharp cockney voice, he asked the prince questions the lawyers had avoided.

There was one last cure Eddie's parents had not tried yet. They would find him a nice, sensible wife to act as his minder.

Had the Prince actually seen Gordon Cumming cheating at cards?

'No,' the Prince replied.

'What was your Royal Highness' opinion… about the charges of cheating made against Gordon Cumming?' Goddard Clarke wanted to know.

All Bertie could say was: 'I felt no other course was open to me but to believe what I was told'. It was a lame answer and it made him look foolish. But it turned the case against Gordon Cumming. The jury decided if the heir to the throne of England believed his friend was guilty, then he must be. Gordon Cumming lost the case. The consequences were dire.

Bertie tainted by grubby trial

Cumming's social life was at an end. He was thrown out of clubs. He was banished from the British Army. No one in high society would speak to him, or of him. He might as well have been dead. And all because he had dared to involve a future king of England in a grubby court case.

But Bertie did not get away scot-free. He received much criticism from the press – for gambling, for keeping bad company, for betraying his friend, for setting a bad example.

'If he is known to pursue in his private visits a certain round of questionable pleasures', thundered The Times of London, ' the serious public…regret and resent it.'

This was mild compared to a cartoon in German newspapers ridiculing Bertie's emblem – the tall, white, Prince of Wales feathers. The Prince of Wales' motto was also depicted, but the inscription had been changed from 'I Serve' to 'I Deal'.

The French press made the most of the scandal. They printed gossip that hinted Bertie was about to leave his mother's court and abdicate, giving the crown to his eldest son, Prince Eddie. But what even the prying French press did not know was that Eddie on the throne of England would have been a downright disaster, for he was the royal family's darkest, most embarrassing secret.

Utterly hopeless Eddie

Born in 1864, Prince Eddie grew up idle, weak and backward. His tutors found it impossible to teach him anything. He was unable to concentrate for any length of time. And he did not give a damn. If anyone tried to discipline Eddie or give him instructions, he replied with an idiotic grin or a shrug of the shoulders.

Experts and specialists were called in. But they could not tell what was wrong. Eddie's parents, Bertie and Alexandra, were in despair. They tried a few cures of their own. Eddie was sent to Cambridge University in the hope that somehow it would spark an interest in something. But this idea failed. One of Eddie's tutors described him as 'abnormally dormant'. Another remarked: 'He hardly knows the meaning of the words "to read".

Next, Eddie was placed in the army. But his instructors soon realized he could not manage even the simplest parade ground drills. After that, Eddie became a cadet in the Royal Naval College, Dartmouth, in 1877. The results were no better.

Final attempt to stabilize son

There was one last cure Eddie's parents had not tried yet. They would find him a nice, sensible, down-to-earth wife who would act as his minder. This was the same trick Queen Victoria had used on Bertie himself. It had not worked then. But Bertie and Alexandra were so desperate by this time, they could not think of anything else to do.

The wedding that was never to be

The girl they chose was Princess May of Teck, a cousin of Eddie's and a descendant of George III.

The Prince of Wales is pictured here in 1901, just before he succeeded to the throne. He loved the pomp and ceremony of royalty and relished wearing medals and orders, carrying his sword and wearing his plumed hat.

May was 25; young, but not too young. She was very disciplined and dutiful. She would make a first-class watchdog. Eddie and May became engaged on 3 December 1891. Their wedding was fixed for the following February. But it never took place. Eddie went down with influenza the day before his 28th birthday, on 7 January 1892. The following day, he only just managed to stagger downstairs to look at his birthday presents.

From then on, his health became worse and worse. Later, Princess May remembered the scene at Eddie's

---

When the king and Mrs. Keppel were invited to a weekend house party in the country, their hosts quietly gave them adjoining rooms. Everybody knew what was going on. But no one breathed a word.

---

bedside. It was like some ghastly tableau. The grieving mother, Alexandra, the tormented patient, Eddie, the helpless doctor and the family watching it all over a specially erected screen. Eddie died at 9:45 A.M. on 14 January while his mother held his hand. Later, at Eddie's funeral, Princess May's wedding bouquet decorated his coffin.

It was all very sad. Eddie's short life had been wasted. His parents became ill with grief over the tragedy. But it had surely crossed several minds that tragedy now was better than disaster later. Many people, including Queen Victoria, believed that if Eddie had ever become king, the English monarchy would have come to an end.

Bertie becomes king

With Eddie's death, his younger brother Prince George became their father's heir. In 1893, George married Princess May. Eight years later, Queen Victoria, last of

The aged Queen Victoria in this photograph did not appear on her postage stamps. Throughout her 63-year reign, she appeared as the pretty 21-year-old she had been in 1840, when Britain's first stamp, the Penny Black (right), was issued.

the Hanoverian monarchs, died. Bertie, by now almost 60, became King Edward VII, first king of the House of Saxe-Coburg-Gotha. The name of the ruling dynasty was changed in memory of Prince Albert, who hailed from the Duchy of Saxe-Coburg-Gotha in Germany.

But nothing else changed for the new king. His high-flying social life went on. He still journeyed to Biarritz every spring. He still visited the health resort of Marienbad later in the year. Then there were the shooting season in England, regular visits to the races, rounds of golf, card-playing sessions and a new royal craze – motoring.

Throughout the year Edward VII would play host at enormous banquets. The menu typically consisted of turtle soup, salmon steak, chicken, mutton, snipe stuffed with goose liver, fruits, ices, caviar and oysters. There was plenty of claret, champagne and brandy to drink. At the end of the banquet large cigars and cigarettes were passed out. King Edward himself was a very heavy smoker: he could get through twelve cigars and twenty cigarettes a day. That was in addition to heavy drinking and overeating.

The king still had his mistresses, notably the charming Mrs. Alice Keppel. As with all his affairs, Edward's liaison with Mrs. Keppel was carefully protected by their friends. When the couple were invited to a weekend house party in the country, their hosts quietly gave them adjoining rooms. Everybody knew what was going on. But no one breathed a word.

Alexandra's generous gesture

Queen Alexandra, of course, knew all about Mrs. Keppel. She also knew that King Edward truly loved her. In 1910, the king's long years of overeating and high living at last caught up with him. He suffered a series of heart attacks. Alexandra remained with him until he died on 6 May at 11:45 P.M.

Before his death, however, Queen Alexandra called in many of his good friends to say a last goodbye. Among them was Mrs. Keppel. Alexandra knew how to be generous.

Edward VII loved the theatre. Here he is in the front row of the audience, sitting between his mistress Mrs. Keppel and the Duchess of Devonshire at a theatrical event at Chatsworth, the Devonshires' country mansion.

King George V and Queen Mary in full coronation robes. George V, who succeeded his elder brother Eddie as their father's heir in 1892, came to the throne after the death of Edward VII on 6 May 1910.

Diplomatic name change for new king

Edward was succeeded by Prince George, who became King George V. Princess May became known as Queen Mary. King George began as the second monarch of the House of Saxe-Coburg-Gotha, but the name would be changed again, in 1917.

The world war with Germany and its allies was being fought at the time. Horrific tales of slaughter were coming back from the battlefields in France. In England, this caused such hatred of Germany that it became embarrassing for members of the royal family to have German names and titles. So George V changed the family's name again – to Windsor, after the royal castle in Berkshire.

King George was the opposite of his father. He was very shy and did not like the high life. He was utterly devoted to Queen Mary, so much so that if he didn't see her for a while he felt physically ill. He took no mistresses.

Although he had loved his father, Edward VII, George had strongly disapproved of his way of life. Like the young King George III before him, he was determined to wipe out the disreputable image of the king as playboy and make the royal family respectable once again.

But like George III, his plans went haywire. The culprit was exactly the same; the heir to the throne. George V's eldest son and heir, Prince Edward, was arguably worse than all the other troublesome heirs put together. He very nearly destroyed the monarchy.

15
A LOOSE CANNON

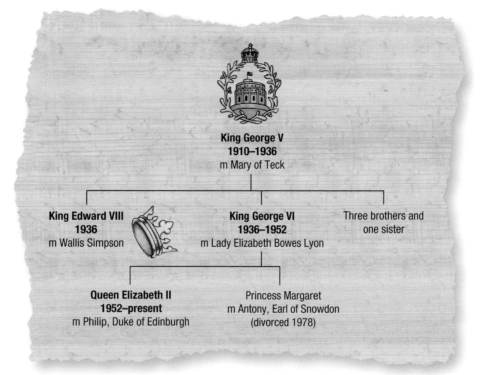

King George V
1910–1936
m Mary of Teck

King Edward VIII
1936
m Wallis Simpson

King George VI
1936–1952
m Lady Elizabeth Bowes Lyon

Three brothers and
one sister

Queen Elizabeth II
1952–present
m Philip, Duke of Edinburgh

Princess Margaret
m Antony, Earl of Snowdon
(divorced 1978)

Quarrels between monarchs of England and their eldest sons had been going on for almost two centuries when King George V came to the throne in 1910. George and his son and heir, Prince Edward, would carry on in the same way.

◆

But their quarrel was much more serious than any before. So grave, so fundamental was this particular dispute that the royal family themselves believed they were finished.

The unwilling royal

Essentially, the problem with Prince Edward – known as David within the royal family – was that he did

Edward VIII came to the throne determined to make divorcee Wallis Simpson his queen. He met stern, unyielding opposition that ultimately forced him to abdicate.

not wish to be a prince. He wanted nothing to do with the pomp and pageantry that went with being royal. Royal duties bored him. He hated formality. He hated privilege. What he wanted was to be ordinary, something no royal could ever hope to be.

All this set David on a collision course with his parents, King George V and Queen Mary. Their devotion to duty was total. If it meant making personal sacrifices – lack of privacy, limited choice of friends – that was too bad. Rules had to be obeyed.

David, of course, wanted to toss out royal rules. The first public sign of how he felt came in 1911. That year, aged 16, he was invested Prince of Wales at a grand

Glum-looking Prince Edward, known as David, is seen here with his parents, King George V and Queen Mary at his investiture as Prince of Wales at Caernarvon Castle in 1911. He later referred to the robes as a 'preposterous rig'.

ceremony at Caernarvon Castle in Wales. Photographs of the event show him looking sulky and glum. Later on, David did everything he could to test the limits placed upon him by royal birth. During World War I, he insisted on going to France and the front line of the fighting. Everyone was horrified. Suppose David were taken prisoner by the enemy? Suppose he were killed? It would not do. The heir to the throne had to be protected.

Battling prince is 'one of the boys'

David would have none of it. He went to France. He went right to the front line. And he was there, in the trenches, while British soldiers were under fire.

'The prince is always in the thick of it,' one soldier wrote home to England. 'Only last night he passed me when the German shells were coming over.'

Despite the dangers and risks, David loved every minute of it. At last, he could be with ordinary men, sharing their problems, talking with them as if he were their equal. The king definitely did not approve. He believed royals should remain aloof and dignified. He told David: 'The war has made it possible for you to mix with all manner of people. But don't think this means you can act like other people. You must always remember... who you are.'

The king was already too late. In 1918 David had taken refuge in an air-raid shelter in London while German Zeppelins were dropping bombs. There, he met a young married woman, Freda Dudley Ward. David fell madly in love with her. Within a short while, they were all but living together.

Playboy prince revels in high life

For a prince to have a mistress was, of course, nothing new. But Freda Dudley Ward was David's entree to the sort of social life where he at last felt at home . It was not the stiff, starchy circle of 'good' families approved by his parents. It was the so-called *'demi-monde'*, the 'twilight' world of wild all-night parties, fashionable nightclubs, loose morals and shady people. They included social climbers, gold diggers and profiteer millionaires. These were not the sort,

according to the king, that his son should have had anything to do with.

David's parents tried to 'cure' him by sending him on overseas tours, but the cure never worked. On his return to England David simply took up again where he had left off. He was back at the parties and night-clubs almost as soon as he got off the ship.

After a while, David took on another mistress, a beautiful American, Thelma, Lady Furness, a sister of Gloria Vanderbilt. Thelma, too, had a large circle of fun-loving friends. In 1931, she introduced David to two of them, Wallis Simpson and her second husband, Ernest.

Prince falls for Mrs. Simpson

At first, the Simpsons were just two more of David's acquaintances. But in 1934, Thelma had to return to

David, seen here in army uniform, relished the chance to mix with ordinary young soldiers in the trenches of World War I. He longed above all to be ordinary himself, but his royal birth made that impossible.

During Edward VIII's brief reign as king, only one set of stamps was issued for Great Britain, including this one.

the United States. She left 'the Little Man', as she called David, in the care of Wallis Simpson. It seemed a safe bet. Wallis was plain, scrawny and a little sour-faced. Thelma reckoned she was no competition.

Little did she know. While Thelma was away, David fell in love with Wallis. She was more womanly, more protective and a much stronger character than his other women. At a time when England was hard hit by the Depression, she shared David's concern for the plight of ordinary people.

'Wallis,' David told her, 'you're the only woman who's ever been interested in my job!' She was just what David wanted.

But Wallis Simpson was just what David's parents did not want. It was not because she was American, it was because she was a divorced woman and, as David's passion for her grew, was likely to be divorced again. At this time, divorce was considered immoral in England. Members of the royal family were not supposed to know or even speak to anyone who had gone through a divorce.

Now here was the heir to throne involved in a romance with a divorced woman while she was still married to her second husband. The shock was tremendous. But Wallis was no passing fancy. Edward wanted to marry her and make her his queen.

Father despairs over the future king

King George and Queen Mary were helpless. They forbade David to bring Wallis to the royal palace. David thought his father was a stuffy old prig. The king thought his son was a cad. Queen Mary thought Wallis an 'adventuress'. This seemed to be a general opinion about Wallis, who was branded a fortune hunter and a loose woman out to get as much as she could grab from her royal connection. The British secret services, who kept Edward and Wallis under close surveillance, certainly thought so. Early in 2003, their reports were made public for the first

time, and revealed that Wallis was very careful to feed Edward's infatuation for her. She kept secret from both the prince and her husband, Ernest Simpson, that she was having an illicit affair with a car salesman

---

Now that he was king, Edward VIII did not have to worry that the royal family, royal officials – and his mother – did not like Wallis. Far from it. He could show Wallis off to everyone.

---

named Guy Trundle, and fended off all other women who might get near her royal lover. Meanwhile, the public in England knew nothing of the growing royal crisis. There was no television. Cinema newsreels were carefully censored, so too were radio broadcasts. Few people took holidays abroad, where the foreign press was full of the story. By general agreement, newspapers in England kept quiet about the whole affair. But sooner or later, the truth was bound to come out.

On 20 January 1936, King George V died. David, the queen and other members of the royal family were at his bedside. Queen Mary curtsied to her son, in recognition of him as the new king, Edward VIII. But she could not help remembering what her husband had once said: 'The boy will ruin himself within the year'. How right he was.

King parties on regardless

Now he could show Wallis off to everyone, and the way he did it was outrageous. In May 1936, when he hired a yacht, the *Nahlin*, for a cruise in the eastern Mediterranean, he and Wallis were accompanied by several of their 'unsuitable' friends. What happened next filled the foreign newspapers with smut and scandal for many weeks. The *Nahlin's* passengers,

This illustration of Wallis Simpson flatters her. The British public found it almost impossible to understand how the sour-faced, middle-aged woman pictured in their newspapers could rock the throne of England and the royal family.

According to royal officials, this was not how the King of England should appear in photographs: a bare-chested King Edward VIII is pictured with Wallis Simpson during the cruise of the yacht *Nahlin* in the Mediterranean.

According to royal officials, this was not how the King of England should appear in photographs: a bare-chested King Edward VIII is pictured with Wallis Simpson during the cruise of the yacht *Nahlin* in the Mediterranean.

'To oppose him over doing anything,' Queen Mary wrote, 'is only to make him more determined to do it. At present, he is utterly infatuated (with Mrs. Simpson), but my great hope is that violent infatuations usually wear off.'

Plans to wed Wallis

It did not wear off. In July 1936, while the king and Wallis were still cruising on board the *Nahlin*, her divorce proceeding was already underway. The case was due to be heard in court on 27 October. Simple arithmetic was all that was needed to guess what was in King Edward's mind. The divorce would be final in six months, on 27 April 1937. The king's coronation was fixed for 12 May. There was just enough time for Edward and Wallis to get married and be crowned king and queen soon thereafter.

Royal affair sparks national crisis

The royal scandal became a serious national crisis. Prime Minister Stanley Baldwin was called in. He tried to persuade the king to give up Mrs. Simpson. He failed. The king's own relatives tried. They failed. So did the Archbishop of Canterbury. And the governments of the Dominion countries of the British Commonwealth – Australia, New Zealand, Canada and South Africa – all failed.

By early December, King Edward VIII had become a man none of his friends wanted to know anymore. They realized the biggest royal scandal of the century was about to break and did not want to be involved. Suddenly the king's friends started turning down invitations to Fort Belvedere, his personal home. They made excuses not to attend parties, or go on royal picnics. They had never liked Wallis Simpson, they said. As for the king, they thought he must be crazy.

including the king, arrived at various ports of call drunk and barely dressed. They gave noisy parties on board the yacht. King Edward and Wallis did not care who saw them kissing and cuddling. All of it was considered a grossly undignified way for the King of England to behave.

The king could not have cared less. What he wanted to do, he did – and damn what anyone else thought.

This is the abdication document signed by Edward VIII on 10 December 1936. Edward signed himself 'RI': Rex Imperator (King Emperor), but it would be for the last time. His three brothers, Albert, Henry and George, signed the document as witnesses.

INSTRUMENT OF ABDICATION

I, Edward the Eighth, of Great Britain, Ireland, and the British Dominions beyond the Seas, King, Emperor of India, do hereby declare My irrevocable determination to renounce the Throne for Myself and for My descendants, and My desire that effect should be given to this Instrument of Abdication immediately.

In token whereof I have hereunto set My hand this tenth day of December, nineteen hundred and thirty six, in the presence of the witnesses whose signatures are subscribed.

SIGNED AT
FORT BELVEDERE
IN THE PRESENCE
OF

THE KING STEPS DOWN FOR LOVE

DESPITE HIS RELUCTANCE TO BE KING, there was no escape for Bertie. His brother signed the Document of Abdication on 10 December. Having done so, he became Prince Edward once more. The next day the former king made an historic broadcast from Windsor Castle:

'A few hours ago I discharged my last duty as king and emperor, and now that I have been succeeded by my brother, the Duke of York, my first words must be to declare my allegiance to him. This I do with all my heart.

Britain's new King, the Duke of York, arriving home at 145, Piccadilly, last night, after dining at Fort Belvedere with his brother. Huge crowds gave the new Monarch a great welcome to his capital. (See back page).

'You all know the reasons which have impelled me to renounce the throne. But you must believe me when I tell you that I have found it impossible to carry the heavy burden of responsibility and to discharge my duties as king as I would wish to do without the help and support of the woman I love.

'…This decision has been made less difficult to me by the sure knowledge that my brother, with his long training in the public affairs of this country and with his fine qualities, will be able to take my place…. And he has one matchless blessing, enjoyed by so many of you, and not bestowed on me – a happy home with his wife and children.

'…And now, we all have a new king. I wish him and you, his people, happiness and prosperity with all my heart. God bless you all! God save the king!'

A historic edition of the London *Daily Mirror*. The trepidation on the face of the new king, George VI, was genuine.

Wallis begs to be set free

All this happened within a few days. The English poet Osbert Sitwell dubbed it 'Rat Week'. But as the rats deserted the ship, the ship was sinking. When the silence of the English newspapers was broken on December 3, the king was on his own. The next day, Wallis fled for safety to France after stones were thrown at the windows of her home in London. From there, she begged the king to let her go rather than give up his throne for her sake.

He would not even think of it. 'No matter where you go,' he told Wallis, 'I will follow you!'

What Edward VIII wanted was the throne of England and Wallis, but if he had to choose between them, then the throne would have to go. The throne went on 10 December 1936 when Edward VIII became the first king of England to abdicate of his own free will.

His decision caused anguish in the royal family. The heir to the throne, Edward's younger brother Bertie, became terrified at the thought that now he would be king. He burst into tears and sobbed on his mother's shoulder. His wife, Elizabeth – the late Queen Mother – said, 'It was like sitting on the edge of a volcano.'

Another unwilling king

Bertie had never been trained to be king. He was nervous. His health was poor. He suffered from a stammer. Appearing in public was agony for him. He had a nice, quiet life with his lovely wife and two daughters, Elizabeth and Margaret. Now all that was to end. No wonder Bertie was so upset.

Royal snub for Wallis

The former king crossed the English Channel into lifelong exile on the night of his abdication. On 3 June 1937, he married Wallis Simpson at a château in northern France. No member of the royal family was there. The couple were given new titles – Duke and Duchess of Windsor. But there was one thing they did not get. Bertie, who took the name King George VI, refused to make Wallis a 'Royal Highness'. He reasoned that, with two failed marriages behind her, the chances of the third one lasting weren't all that good.

Edward and Wallis never forgave King George or his family. Although Edward had no authority to do so, he himself gave Wallis the title which King George had kept from her. He insisted that everyone address his wife as 'Her Royal Highness, the Duchess of Windsor'.

Government wants the Windsors out of the way

Back in England the duke was offered the governorship of the Bahama Islands. The position carried little prestige. The Bahamas were the most insignificant colony in the whole British Empire. Usually, its governor was a minor civil servant or a retired army officer. But the islands had one great advantage: they were well away from the war zone. It was a good place to park the Windsors for as long as the war lasted.

After the war ended, the Windsors returned to Europe. Still shut out by the royal family, they became stars of the rich social scene, moving from one fashionable resort to the next.

Trouble follows wherever they go

Once in the Bahamas, the Duke of Windsor still could not stay out of trouble. The worst thing that happened while he was governor was the murder of Sir Harry Oakes, a mining millionaire. Oakes was a shady character. He lived in the Bahamas to avoid paying taxes and had secret arms dealers for friends.

In 1943, Sir Harry was savagely murdered. The duke personally took charge of the investigation. He had no experience in such matters. As a result, he bungled the case so badly that an innocent man – Oakes' son-in-law – was framed for the crime. Fortunately, he was found not guilty at his trial. The real killer was never discovered. But there were hints about Mafia involvement in the affair.

Champagne lifestyle for globe-trotting pair

Ever since his abdication, the duke had wanted to serve his country in a 'top job'. But yet again, he had become embroiled in scandal. The sordid business of Oakes and his kind had rubbed off a little on him. Beside this, he had proven himself incompetent. The mess he made of the Oakes affair made sure that the duke was never offered an official post again.

After the end of the war in 1945, the Windsors returned to Europe. Still shut out by the royal family, there was only one place for them to go. They became stars of the rich, well-heeled social scene. They moved from one fashionable resort to the next – Biarritz, Venice. They dined at Maxim's, the Paris restaurant, twice a week. Photographs of them enjoying themselves in nightclubs and luxury hotels appeared in newspapers. They lived the high life to the fullest.

Sad Wallis can never say goodbye

But it all came to an end in 1972, when the duke died in Paris. After that, if anyone still thought of Wallis as a greedy gold digger, out for all she could get, they were proven wrong. For a time, she refused to admit that the duke was dead and had to be forcibly removed from his bedside.

'He was my entire life,' she said at her husband's funeral at Windsor.

'He gave up so much for me. I can't begin to think what I shall do without him.'

She could not do without him. Wallis was never able to put her life back together again. She would sit alone for hours in the duke's room, which was kept exactly as it was when he died. 'Goodnight, David!' she would say before going to bed.

Wallis went into a steady decline. She ended up paralyzed and crippled. She spent her last years lying in bed surrounded by pictures of herself and her husband. She lived in the past, dreaming of the years they had spent together. Wallis died in 1986, aged 89. She was buried next to Edward at Windsor. Queen Elizabeth II and her family attended the ceremony.

The duke had always wanted Wallis to be accepted into the royal family. In death, she had managed it at last. But there was still no official 'HRH' title. The

The Windsors' nightlife was avidly followed by the press. The duchess was of particular interest to newspaper readers. She was usually wearing magnificent jewels from the collection showered on her by the duke.

plate on her coffin read simply 'Wallis, Duchess of Windsor 1896–1986'.

A dutiful king

George VI had died 20 years before his elder brother, in 1952. The good name of the English royal family had taken a frightful battering in the abdication crisis of 1936. The royals themselves believed they were finished. But in his reign of 15 years, King George and his admirable Queen Elizabeth had done a first-

As Duke and Duchess of Windsor, David and Wallis concentrated on an energetic social life, appearing in all the 'right' fashionable places in the 'right' fashionable company. Here they are following the play at a golf tournament.

DID THE DUKE SUPPORT THE NAZIS?

EVEN IN EXILE, the Windsors had a knack for creating sensational headlines wherever they went. In 1938 they were invited to visit Nazi Germany, where they met Führer Adolf Hitler and his henchmen. There was outrage in England when newsreels showed the duke giving the Nazi salute. Stories arose that the duke and duchess were Nazi sympathizers, but secret surveillance reports released in 2003 contained no evidence that this was true.

The Nazis, however, didn't require proof. The former king of England gave them a chance to spread innuendoes about his supposed Nazi sympathies. There was also gossip about a Nazi plot to kidnap the Windsors. Then, so the story went, once they had invaded and conquered England, the former king would be placed on the throne again – as a Nazi puppet.

The Germans never invaded England. But the duke and duchess showed no interest in their plans anyway. They just wanted to get away from the war zone. They managed to escape to neutral Spain. From there, they returned to England. But they were not to stay.

Pictures such as this showing the Windsors meeting Hitler gave rise to gossip that the duke and duchess were Nazi sympathizers.

The seemingly perfect royal family. George VI and Queen Elizabeth (later the Queen Mother) with their daughters, Princess Elizabeth and Princess Margaret. This picture of domestic bliss was in total contrast to the high jinks of the duke and duchess.

class repair job. The royal family became respectable once again. This time there was no troublesome heir to ruin the effort. The love and affection King George felt for his heir, Princess Elizabeth, was so great that his eyes filled with tears whenever he spoke of her. The long series of royal quarrels was over.

Dark cloud in a clear blue sky

This did not mean that Elizabeth II was going to escape trouble and scandal. Trouble made its appearance very early on, on the day of Elizabeth's coronation, 2 June 1953. That same day, outside Westminster Abbey, her younger sister Margaret was caught on camera picking a piece of fluff off the uniform of Group Captain Peter Townsend of the

Royal Air Force. It seemed the sort of thing a woman did when she regarded a man as 'hers'.

Townsend was a royal servant, a former wartime fighter pilot and an equerry to the new queen. Beady-eyed journalists watched the scene and took note. A new royal romance was in the air. But so was a new scandal. Peter Townsend was a divorced man and an untitled commoner. By the royal rules of the time he had no business romancing the sister of a queen.

16

A MODERN MONARCHY?

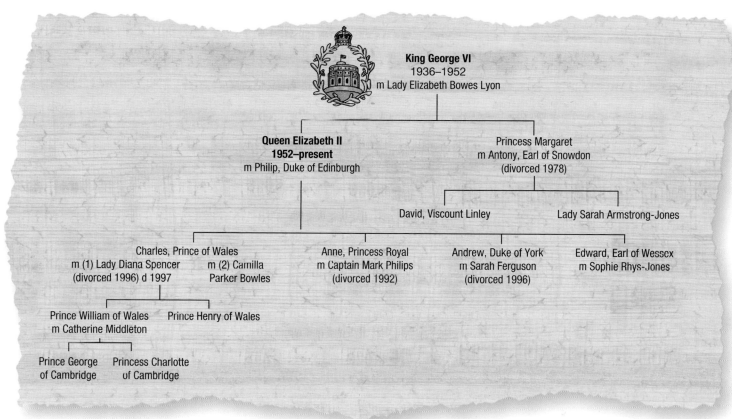

King George VI
1936–1952
m Lady Elizabeth Bowes Lyon

Queen Elizabeth II
1952–present
m Philip, Duke of Edinburgh

Princess Margaret
m Antony, Earl of Snowdon
(divorced 1978)

David, Viscount Linley

Lady Sarah Armstrong-Jones

Charles, Prince of Wales
m (1) Lady Diana Spencer
(divorced 1996) d 1997
m (2) Camilla
Parker Bowles

Anne, Princess Royal
m Captain Mark Philips
(divorced 1992)

Andrew, Duke of York
m Sarah Ferguson
(divorced 1996)

Edward, Earl of Wessex
m Sophie Rhys-Jones

Prince William of Wales
m Catherine Middleton

Prince Henry of Wales

Prince George
of Cambridge

Princess Charlotte
of Cambridge

Princess Margaret was the live wire of the royal family. If she had not been born a princess, she could have had a brilliant career on the stage – as a mimic, singer or pianist.

✦

She had charm, she had zest. She had personality. And, as Peter Townsend himself said, she was 'intensely' beautiful. What Margaret did not have was luck. Margaret first met Peter Townsend in 1945, when she was 15. He had just become equerry to her father, King George VI. Townsend was handsome and charming. He was a war hero. Margaret fell deeply in love with Peter Townsend and set her heart on marrying him.

24 February 1981 was the day that years of royal wedding speculation ended. Charles, Prince of Wales announced his engagement to the pretty 19-year-old Lady Diana Spencer.

Forced to choose between duty and love

Margaret was delighted when she found that Townsend loved her in return. But there were tremendous obstacles. Townsend was divorced. The social barriers divorced people faced were bad enough. But the English church did not even recognize divorce. It was an impossible idea that the queen's sister should marry a man whose first wife was still living, and become stepmother to his children.

The queen, supreme head of the Church of England, could not possibly give permission for such a marriage. The only way it could go ahead was for Margaret to give up her royal title, cut herself off

Peter Townsend (left) and Princess Margaret were often photographed together during royal engagements. But their romance was doomed from the start. It was not yet acceptable for royals to marry commoners.

love would cool. That did not happen. When Townsend returned to England in 1955, the romance was still very much 'on'.

English newspapers went into a frenzy of speculation. Would the couple marry or not? 'Come on, Margaret, make up your mind!', ran one newspaper headline.

But Margaret was not in a position to make up her mind. She was bombarded with reasons not to marry Townsend. The church was against it. The royal family did not like it. The people were divided. Some thought that as a war hero, Townsend would make an admirable husband for a royal princess. Others believed that Margaret should put her royal duty first.

Royal duty won in the end. The announcement came on 31 October 1955. Margaret had decided not to marry Peter Townsend.

'Mindful of the Church's teaching that Christian marriage is indissoluble, and of my duty [to the queen], I have decided to put these considerations before all others.'

from her family, and leave England to live abroad for the rest of her life.

Queen Elizabeth did not want that to happen to her beloved sister. So she tried another way. Peter Townsend was given a job in Belgium. It was only just across the English Channel, but far enough away to separate him from Margaret. The queen hoped their

Margaret parties to forget sorrows

It was the worst moment of Margaret's life. She never got over it. She plunged into a frantic round of parties. She became the star of the fun-loving jet set. She went to nightclubs. She shocked everyone by drinking and smoking in public. She made friends with people royals were not supposed to mix with – actors, actresses and pop stars.

Then, in 1959, Townsend wrote to Margaret that he was going to marry a Belgian girl, Marie-Luce. No one was surprised that Marie-Luce looked almost exactly like Princess Margaret. Margaret, meanwhile, had received a proposal of marriage from the English society photographer, Antony Armstrong-Jones.

'I received the letter from Peter in the morning,' she said later, 'and that evening, I decided to marry Tony. I didn't really want to marry at all. Why did I? Because he asked me!'

A marriage doomed to failure

In time, the reason proved not to be good enough. Margaret and Tony, as they came to be known, were married at Westminster Abbey on 6 May 1960. It was

Margaret never got over the Townsend affair, though her marriage to photographer Antony Armstrong-Jones in 1960 concealed that fact. Ironically, Margaret became the first of the Windsors to divorce when that marriage ended in 1978.

a splendid royal occasion. The couple later had two children, but the marriage was doomed. Armstrong-Jones, who became Lord Snowdon, came to hate his link with the royal family. It got in the way of his career. The couple had terrible rows. Each took lovers. At last, in 1976, they decided to give up. Margaret and Tony separated and in 1978 they were divorced.

Margaret never married again. She drank and smoked even more than before. She took much younger men as lovers. She held high-life parties at her villa on the island of Mustique.

A sad life and an untimely end

At home in England, Margaret received occasional visits from Peter Townsend. But he died in 1995. At last, it all caught up with her. Her health began to fail. She suffered a series of strokes. Outside her family and

friends, no one knew how badly she was affected until 4 August 2001, the day her mother, the Queen Mother, celebrated her 101st birthday. There was the Queen Mother, looking fit and sprightly, waving to crowds cheering her outside her London home, Clarence House. And there was Princess Margaret, sitting in a wheelchair, half-paralyzed and partially blind. Princess Margaret died six months later, on 9 February 2002, at the age of 71.

By that time, the royal family had been rocked by another scandal even greater than the Townsend affair, and almost as serious as the abdication of King Edward VIII. It was a story of betrayal, bad faith and hole-in-the-wall affairs. Once again, people wondered if the English monarchy would survive. Once again, they watched with a mixture of horror and fascination as the fearful story unfolded.

A fairy tale for the nation

This, though, was the last thing on anyone's mind on 29 July 1981, when Prince Charles, heir to the throne, married Lady Diana Spencer at St. Paul's Cathedral in London. The press pronounced it the 'fairytale'

After the end of the Townsend affair, Princess Margaret indulged in the high life. Her excessive smoking and drinking produced serious health scares and she was accused, quite unjustifiably, of neglecting her royal duties.

The kiss on the balcony at Buckingham Palace, the romantic climax to the 'fairytale wedding' of the Prince and Princess of Wales. The marriage, however, was no fairytale: for the Windsors, it marked an era of unprecedented scandal.

marriage of the century. The fresh-faced 20-year-old Diana became an overnight star. Everywhere she went, she was greeted by huge crowds. She was the most famous, most photographed woman in the world. The public loved her. The press loved her. Everyone loved her. Except for her husband, Prince Charles.

Groom still loves 'ex'

No one knew it at the time, but Charles was in love with someone else: Camilla Parker-Bowles, who had once been his girlfriend. Charles could have married Camilla as far back as 1973. But he had thought she was not quite 'pure' enough for a future queen of England. She had had lovers. She was too much of a 'go-getter' to settle down to the dull round of royal duties. So Charles let her go and Camilla married someone else. Even then, Camilla was not completely out of Charles's life. They remained friends and occasional lovers. Camilla boosted Charles's confidence, made him feel good and accepted him as he was. Before long, Charles realised that by marrying Diana, he had married trouble.

Insecure Diana craved love

Lady Diana Spencer, youngest daughter of Earl Spencer, was the child of a broken marriage. When she was only six, her mother, Frances, suddenly disappeared from home and never came back. The divorce that followed was so brutal that Frances would never speak about it. In a fight for custody of their four children, Earl Spencer won by blackening his wife's character. The effect on Diana and her younger brother, Charles, was devastating.

Diana grew up insecure and longing for love. She wanted a husband who would be hers and hers alone, who would love her and protect her, and always be there for her. But Charles could not give Diana the attention she craved. Being Prince of Wales was not a nine-to-five job. Charles had royal duties to perform and was often away from home.

> **There was plenty of media speculation that all was not well in the household of the Prince and Princess of Wales. It was easy to laugh off the talk as gossip, but in fact, the media were right. By 1986 Charles and Diana's marriage was crumbling fast.**

Little in common

Moreover, Charles and Diana were very different people. Charles loved opera. Diana preferred pop music. Charles liked reading books about philosophy or history. Diana read romantic novels. None of this would have mattered had there been enough goodwill between them. But goodwill was difficult when Charles' friends thought Diana was 'an airhead'. Her friends thought Charles was stuffy and dull.

It did not take long for relations between Charles and Diana to become strained. Diana came to believe that if only she could get Charles away from Camilla, everything would be all right. But the more Diana nagged him to give up Camilla, the more Charles clung to Camilla.

Charles runs from rows

Diana staged dramatic tantrums. While she was expecting their first child, Prince William, Diana threw herself downstairs to prevent Charles from going out riding.

Unfortunately, Charles was not the sort of strong-minded man to cope with a wife who behaved like this. Charles's solution was to run to Camilla, which only made matters worse.Royal duty demanded that, in public, Charles and Diana must put a brave face on the situation. Even so, there was plenty of media speculation that all was not well in the household of the Prince and Princess of Wales. It was easy to laugh off the talk as gossip, but in fact, the media were right. By 1986 Charles and Diana's marriage was crumbling fast. Charles later confessed that by that time he was no longer sleeping with his wife. In 1987 Diana seemed to give up hope that Charles would ever give her the attention she wanted. She began to look for it elsewhere, with other men.

No joint celebrations

In 1991 came the tenth anniversary of Charles and Diana's wedding. A date to celebrate? No, it was not. No one felt like celebrating. On their wedding anniversary, they were apart, Charles in London, Diana in Wales. The tenth anniversary party Queen Elizabeth wanted to give for them never took place.

The mouse finally roars

Meanwhile a time bomb was ticking that would burst the bubble of the so-called 'fairytale' marriage forever. Sometime in the winter of 1991–2, Diana gave the royal reporter Andrew Morton long, detailed interviews about what was really going on in her marriage. She told him everything. No holds were barred. Morton's book *Diana: Her True Story* was published in London on 7 June 1992. It was a bombshell. Morton painted a picture of Charles as cold and arrogant. He was supposedly jealous of Diana's success and popularity.

Even worse was to come. The book revealed that Diana had attempted to commit suicide five times. She suffered from the eating disorder bulimia. She had mutilated herself on several occasions.

Diana colluded with author

When Morton's book was published, there were denials all around that Diana had had anything to do with it. But who else could have known about the marriage in such detail? Morton's fellow journalists and others with inside information guessed the truth, but the public was unaware for another five years, until shortly after Diana's death.

Public reaction to *Diana: Her True Story* was extraordinary. Many readers were convinced it told the truth. If Diana had taken lovers – which she had – Charles's behaviour had driven her to it. Nothing seemed to be too bad to say about Prince Charles, who was now cast as Public Enemy Number One.

The queen's terrible year

But even this was not the end of the scandals of 1992, which Queen Elizabeth later described as her *annus horribilis* – horrible year. On 19 March, the queen's second son, Prince Andrew, Duke of York, separated from his wife, Sarah Ferguson. They had married in 1986, but the marriage soon degenerated into a terrible tale of neglect, irresponsibility and adultery. Then, on 13 April, the queen's only daughter, Princess Anne, began a divorce action against her husband, Captain Mark Phillips. With that, the marriages of three of the queen's four children were on the rocks.

But the main spotlight was on Charles and Diana. *Diana: Her True Story* had been the end of the line. There could be no forgiveness. Prince Charles felt grossly betrayed. The queen was angry at all the dirty linen Diana had washed in public.

Media feeding frenzy

Charles's friends responded to Morton's book in a magazine article written by the journalist Penny Junor. This told the prince's side of the story. It pic-

tured Diana as paranoid and jealous. She had kept Prince William and Prince Harry away from their father. She swore at Charles and pulled every dirty trick known in the annals of shrewish wives.

By this time, the media were daily reporting accusation and counter-accusation, claim and counter-claim. No one knew any longer who was telling the truth and who was lying. Scandalous revelations came thick and

'Camilla,' Diana said, 'was always there.' Camilla Parker-Bowles had been an important presence in Charles's life since 1973, and their relationship continued even after his marriage to Diana.

Diana, Her True Story by Andrew Morton first appeared in 1992. After Diana's death in Paris in 1997, the book was re-published and the fact, formerly denied, that she had fully cooperated with Morton became public knowledge.

fast. Smutty conversations on secret tapes, involving both Charles and Diana, were transcribed and published. The headlines were lurid. 'My Life of Torture', 'Love Tapes Upset Diana', and worse.

The end of a fantasy

After all this it was impossible for the 'fairytale' marriage to go on. The end came near the close of 1992. On 9 December, Charles and Diana's separation was announced in the House of Commons by Prime Minister John Major. The divorce followed nearly four years later, on 28 August 1996.

Now that Diana was no longer royal, she lost her title of 'Her Royal Highness' and no one had to curtsey to her any more. But she was still a headline-

maker and was going to make more sensational news after July 1997, when she received an invitation from the Egyptian billionaire Mohamed Al Fayed, owner of Harrod's, the luxury London store. Al Fayed offered Diana and her two boys his villa at St. Tropez, complete with his yacht, *Jonikal*, and a companion, his handsome and personable son Dodi.

No sooner had Dodi and Diana got together in St. Tropez than the press was weaving a romance about them. Sensing a major story, boatloads of newsmen and photographers descended on St. Tropez. Dodi and Diana fled, first to the Mediterranean island of Corsica, then to Sardinia and finally, on 30 August, to Paris. But word of their arrival had gone ahead of them and the paparazzi, who made a living taking and selling photographs of celebrities, were waiting for them.

Dodi and Diana were the greatest celebrities the paparazzi had encountered in a long time. A group of them followed the couple to their Paris hotel, and then laid siege to it. The couple managed to escape by a back entrance, but the paparazzi were soon on their tail.

Death of an Icon

It was nearly midnight. Dodi ordered his driver, Henri Paul, to step on it and a high-speed chase began through the streets of Paris. As Henri Paul reached an underpass close to the Place d'Alma, his Mercedes was doing close to 135 miles per hour. The Mercedes shot into the underpass. Soon Henri Paul, who, according to reports, was drunk, lost control of the car. It skidded across the tunnel, crashed into a pillar, bounced off and hit the opposite wall. The car ended up a tangle of twisted metal and broken glass.

Dodi was killed at once. So was Henri Paul. Diana lived through the crash, but her injuries were too severe for her to survive. She was pronounced dead at the hospital at 4:00 A.M. the next morning. She was 36.

A nation in mourning

When the news reached Britain, people went into shock. They stood in the streets, tears pouring down their cheeks. Thousands descended on London, and laid so many flowers for remembrance outside the royal palaces that the sidewalks disappeared under a thick carpet of blooms. Many of the mourners stood in line for hours to sign books of condolence. There was open criticism of the 'cold-hearted' Queen and her family who were spending their regular holiday at Balmoral in Scotland and were still there, instead of heading immediately for the capital.

Eventually, the royals gave in. They returned to London and the Queen gave a short tribute to Diana on television. For her pains, members of the public pronounced her speech 'not emotional enough'.

Queen Elizabeth suffered appalling embarrassment over the revelations contained in Andrew Morton's book. In it, she was pictured as aloof and unhelpful toward her daughter-in-law, the Princess of Wales, although in fact the opposite was true.

THE CAMPAIGNING PRINCESS

EARLY IN 1997 DIANA HAD ASKED the media to become her allies in a new cause on behalf of the Red Cross. The recent civil war in Angola, West Africa, had left behind acres of land thickly strewn with anti-personnel mines. Although the fighting was over, the mines were still there and thousands of local people were dying, losing legs, hands, eyes whenever they stepped on one.

With the press looking on and taking photographs and making newsreels, Diana went into the minefield area. She was protected by a visor and bulletproof vest. As the cameras rolled, she walked past notices placed every few yards which read: 'Danger! Mines!' Above each notice was the warning sign of a skull and crossbones.

The pictures were shown all over the world, on television, in cinemas and in newspapers. The Red Cross could not have had better publicity. Eight months later, in August 1997, Diana went to Bosnia, in southeast Europe, Here, too, a civil war had recently ended. Here, too, the land was filled with mines. Here, too, the press took pictures of Diana continuing her campaign.

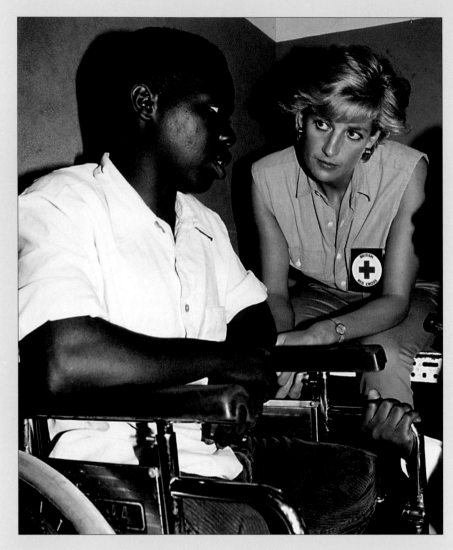

In the last year of her life, Diana worked to promote public awareness of the injuries inflicted by anti-personnel mines and campaigned against their continued use.

'GOODBYE, ENGLAND'S ROSE!'

Diana's funeral took place on 6 September. London virtually closed down for the day. Huge crowds lined the streets as Diana's coffin was driven to Westminster Abbey for a short service. They were still there when the cortège made its way out of London heading for Northamptonshire and Diana's childhood home. Althorp House. There, in a private family ceremony, she was buried on an island in the middle of a lake.

'Goodbye, England's rose,' said the next day's headlines as newspapers were filled, page after page, with reports of one of the most emotional, most tear-filled days England had ever seen.

Charles still cast as villain

But this was by no means the end of the Diana story. The intrusive, gossip-hungry media soon saw to that. Charles and his long-time love Camilla Parker-Bowles were still around and therefore still susceptible to reports that Diana's army of fans had never, and would never, forgive the Prince for the way he had treated his wife.

Even six years after Diana's death, millions were still willing to feed on any 'news' that painted the Prince as a villain. In January 2004, for example, a newspaper report appeared about a letter purportedly written by Diana. In this, she stated that Charles was planning a car accident in which she would suffer 'a serious head injury'. The letter was later revealed as a crude forgery, but not before it had convinced millions that Charles was a potential murderer.

The public were regularly polled for their opinions, and these showed that a majority rejected Charles as their future king. They preferred his son William as heir to the throne instead.

Over seven years after Diana's death, when Charles at last married Camilla Parker-Bowles on 9 April 2005, the numbers who wanted William for king had dropped, but still stood at 42 per cent, 8 per cent higher than in 2001.

Diana's continuing influence was evident from the moment Charles and Camilla became engaged on 10 February 2005. It was announced that instead of being called 'Princess of Wales' after the marriage, Camilla would take her future title, HRH the Duchess of Cornwall, from Charles's estate, the Duchy of Cornwall. She would not be Queen when he became King, but 'Princess Consort'.

These efforts to avoid comparisons with Diana did not prevent the late Princess's fans from sending

hundreds of pieces of hate mail to Camilla before the wedding. It was feared that on the day there might be demonstrations against the newlyweds outside the Registry Office in Windsor, Berkshire, where the ceremony was performed. Consequently, Charles and Camilla bypassed the crowd of spectators waiting to greet them, and drove off as soon as the ceremony was over.

Butler's revelations

Charles and Camilla were by no means the only avenue through which the media kept the Diana story going. In 2002, for example, there was the sensational

The marriage of Charles and Camilla in 2005 was a very quiet affair compared to his state wedding to Diana in 1981. The ceremony took place a day later than originally planned, because Charles had to travel to Rome to represent the Queen at the funeral of Pope John Paul II.

trial of Diana's butler, Paul Burrell, who was accused of stealing items belonging to Diana, Charles and their two sons. The trial was stopped and Burrell acquitted after the Queen recalled a conversation in which the butler told her he was keeping safe

---

in January 2005 Harry was pictured at a fancy-dress party wearing German Army uniform – complete with an arm-band bearing the Nazi swastika.

---

the items he was later charged with appropriating. Rumours soon flourished that the Burrell trial had come too close to revealing evidence that might have embarrassed Her Majesty.

Harold Brown, another royal butler whose trial on similar charges was also halted, refused to 'sell his story' to the Press. Paul Burrell had no such qualms. He became a headline celebrity with fresh revelations of royal misbehaviour. According to Burrell, Diana's erstwhile father-in-law, Prince Philip, wrote her insulting letters, calling her a 'harlot' and a 'trollop'. Philip, backed up by Rosa Monckton, Diana's close friend, hotly denied these allegations.

Was love-rat major Harry's father?

The year 2002 also produced one of the most titillating of Diana stories. James Hewitt, one of her ten alleged lovers, was known to the tabloid press as a 'Love-Rat' for going public about their affair. A former major in a cavalry regiment of the British Army, Hewitt was forced to resign over the revelations. In 1998, Hewitt announced that he would never sell the 64 love letters Diana had written him, but four years later he was asking a massive £10 million for them. The price included some salacious titbits, including the nicknames Diana gave to their private parts and details of the sex toy she sent him while he was serving

Prince Harry, furious at the intrusion into his private life, attacked a photographer who was trying to take his picture outside a London nightclub in October 2004. During the scuffle that followed, Harry was hit in the face by a camera.

in Kuwait during the first Gulf War in 1991. Although Hewitt received offers, they fell far short of his asking price: the highest bid reached only £4 million.

Also in 2002, a rumour circulated that Hewitt, not Prince Charles, was the father of Diana's second son, Prince Harry. There was certainly a resemblance between Hewitt and Harry, who was born on 15 September 1984. They had the same neat facial features and both of them had red hair. In September 2002, Hewitt publicly denied the rumours. Then news came to light that in 1985, the Royal Family had ordered a DNA test to prove paternity. Diana, it was said, was incensed, but the test proved that, after all, Prince Charles, not Hewitt, was Harry's father.

Harry the 'Nazi'

By this time Prince Harry was 18, old enough for some hell-raising of his own. Harry gave the press plenty of material. He indulged in drinking while below the legal age. He smoked 'pot'. He scuffled with a photographer outside a nightclub. But none of these compared with the furore that ensued in January 2005 when Harry was pictured at a fancy-dress party wearing a World War II German Army uniform – complete with an arm-band bearing the Nazi swastika.

Harry was savaged in the press for his insensitivity regarding the Holocaust and for insulting the memory of his great-grandparents, King George VI and Queen Elizabeth (the Queen Mother), who had been symbols of British defiance of the Nazis during World War II. Harry apologized, but the criticisms continued. A furious Prince Charles ordered him to visit Auschwitz-Birkenau, the largest of the Nazi concentration camps.

In July 2006, stories emerged about Harry's infidelity towards his long-term girl friend, Chelsy Davy. This time, the tabloid newspaper *The Sun* reported that Chelsy was 'putting a brave face' on the news that the Prince had enjoyed a wild night out at a party at the Art Bar in London where he romanced an older woman, Catherine Davies, a 34-year-old mother of two. To make matters worse, this was apparently the fourth time her boyfriend had 'seduced' another woman, leaving Chelsy 'furious'. It was June 2010 before another British newspaper, the *News of the World*, reported that Harry and Chelsy had finally broken up. Subsequently, Harry went on as he had begun – more boisterous behaviour in nightclubs and bars. In July of 2011, Hollywood News, which normally specializes in movie star gossip, reported that he was dating a lingerie model, Florence Brudenell-Bruce. Then, in 2012, he was photographed in Las Vegas playing strip billiards with six young women.

Not all partying

But while in his youth Prince Harry was much more of a party animal than his elder brother, Prince William, what the two princes did have in common was an active preoccupation with charity work. This reflected the interest which made their late mother, Diana, Princess of Wales, such an icon during and after her marriage to their father, Charles, Prince of Wales, heir to the English throne. The two princes carried on the British Royal Family's philanthropic traditions as presidents or patrons of several organizations and in September 2009 set up their

Harry is often perceived as the 'party prince' and he is living up to his name in this photograph. His wild behaviour in his youth reflected badly on the Royal Family.

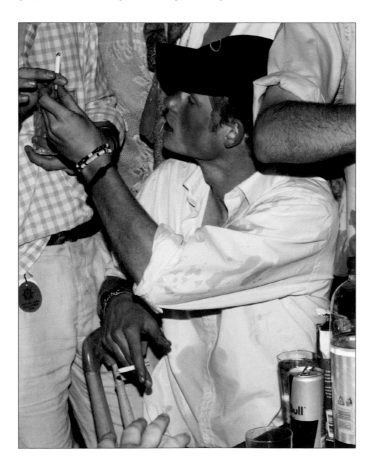

own foundation to co-ordinate their work in this area. A further royal tradition that the two princes shared was military service. Despite his wishes, as second in line to the throne, William's long term military career was considered out of the question, so after officer training at Sandhurst he went on to become an RAF search and rescue helicopter pilot, allowing him an active role in the armed forces without risking combat operations.

Harry, on the other hand, followed officer training at Sandhurst with active service in Afghanistan. He first served there for 77 days, only being pulled out when an Australian magazine made him a target by publishing news of his presence there. Four years

William had the advantage of a long relationship with a steady girlfriend, Catherine Middleton, who, unlike Diana, came from a happy family background.

later, he returned to Afghanistan for a 20-week deployment with the Army Air Corps, reaching the rank of captain and serving as an Apache helicopter co-pilot/gunner.

By the time he left the Army in 2015, Harry was already working on one of his new causes. The previous year he had launched the Invictus Games, an international Paralympic-style sporting event for injured servicemen and women. Following the first games in London in 2014, the second event was held two years later in Orlando, Florida.

While the Royal Family could at times be faulted for being stiff and out-of-touch with the country, a more mature Harry was proving to have a winning cheek and, like his mother, a more natural touch at connecting with people beyond royal circles.

The future King

Harry might have been forgiven for his more wayward moments, but Prince William, two years older than Harry, was destined for an onerous responsibility: in the course of time he would become King of England, as William V.

William was mindful of the sufferings his mother, Princess Diana, had endured from a rabid popular press during and after her marriage. He promised Catherine's parents that he would never allow such a thing to happen to their daughter.

Fortunately, in contrast to his brother, William had the advantage of a long relationship with a steady girlfriend, Catherine Middleton, who, unlike Diana whose parents went through a painful divorce, came from a happy family background. William and Kate, as they were popularly known, first met in 2002, when they were students at St. Andrew's University in Scotland. William had first seen Catherine when she appeared in a fetching see-through dress at a university fashion show, and was riveted by her superb figure.

In 2008, during their courtship, William got himself into trouble with the RAF authorities by landing his £10 million helicopter in a field close to the Middleton family home in Berkshire. The same year, he used a Chinook helicopter to fly himself and Harry to a stag party on the Isle of Wight.

Despite these pranks and a brief period in 2007 when William and Kate apparently parted, their relationship had a happy ending when they married on 29 April 2011 at London's Westminster Abbey. A popular person with the public, Kate, now known as the Duchess of Cambridge, gave birth to a son, George, in 2013, and a daughter, Charlotte, in 2015.

Prince William, Catherine, George, aged 2, and Charlotte, seven months, on the Christmas card sent by the Duke and Duchess of Cambridge in December 2015. Like Diana, Kate has become a style icon and the embodiment of a 'People's Princess'.

Nearly pipped by Pippa

The Duchess, though, risked being upstaged at her own wedding by her younger sister Pippa, whose eye-catching figure and bridesmaid's dress made her suddenly world famous. She seemed to love the attention and soon picked up deals writing books and magazines articles, and work as a television presenter.

But she was to feel the downside of fame, too. Her party planning book received negative reviews and sold poorly. Also, her television career didn't take off and her private life was closely scrutinized.

By 2016, she had wound down her media career. Reports suggested that she had been reined in by Prince William, who was sensitive to the poor publicity her work in the commercial sphere might bring to the Royal Family. Instead, she shifted her focus to charities, working as an ambassador for The British Heart Foundation, among other causes.

'Air Miles' Andy

Controversy would continue to surround Prince

Upstaging the bride? With her figure-hugging dress, bridesmaid Pippa Middleton drew almost as much attention as her sister at Kate's wedding to Prince William in 2011.

Andrew whose role as United Kingdom's Special Trade Representative involved him travelling the world promoting British business, but this led to accusations that he was too close to countries such as Azerbaijan and Kazakhstan, both with poor human rights records, and that he personally profited from the deals that followed. Andrew was also dubbed 'Air Miles' Andy by the British tabloid press for his frequent global trips, including tacked on golfing jaunts, many of them at public expense.

Then there was the matter of his Berkshire home. After the break-up of his marriage, both he and his former wife, Sarah Ferguson, had, by 2006, left their marital home, Sunninghill Park, a house built for them near the Queen's residence at Windsor Castle. The following year the house was sold for £15 million in 2007 – £3 million over the asking price – to an offshore trust in the British Virgin Islands. It was later revealed that the buyer was Timur Kulibayev, the billionaire son-in-law of the Kazakh president, Nursultan Nazarbayev. Why Kulibayev paid so much for the property isn't clear, but it fuelled speculation about the close links between Andrew and Kazakhstan's ruling elite. Then, Kulibayev allowed the empty house to fall into ruin, becoming,

Following accusations of poor judgement in his continued friendship with an American billionaire sex offender and also his business links to Kazakh oligarchs, Prince Andrew stepped down from his position as UK Special Trade Envoy in 2011.

for some, a symbol that there was something wasteful and rotten about the relationship. With permission granted to replace it with a larger property, the dilapidated house was finally demolished in 2015.

Andrew's reputation suffered again through his friendship with American billionaire hedge fund manager and philanthropist Jeffrey Epstein. In 2008 Epstein was sentenced to 18 months imprisonment after agreeing a plea bargain over child prostitution charges. Although Epstein lost many of his friends in the scandal, Prince Andrew wasn't among them. Following the sex offender's release, he was photographed in 2011 strolling through Central Park with the prince. The furore that this caused led to Andrew finally quitting his role as trade envoy.

However, it seems that Andrew hasn't completely ceased his business links with Kazakhstan. In 2016,

it was alleged that he had been on course to earn £4 million in commission in helping facilitate a Greek-Swiss consortium pursue a £385 million contract to build water treatment works in Kazakhstan — a deal which ultimately fell through. Does the Prince struggle in finding a role for himself, one wonders? And is he too easily dazzled by the super wealthy?

This other Eden

In 2015, the Queen surpassed the reign of her great-great-grandmother, Queen Victoria, to become the longest-reigning British monarch and the longest-reigning queen regnant in world history. The following year, she celebrated her 90th birthday.

Whether happy or sad, deplorable or felicitous, these royal episodes and the personalities involved in them provide the latest happenings to add to the long tale of dark deeds, dirty doings and foolish fancies that have marked a thousand years of English royal history.

Her family may have suffered very public marriage breakdowns, drunken mishaps and questionable friendships, but Queen Elizabeth II has maintained her dignity throughout and is still held in high regard. The longest-reigning British monarch, in 2016 she celebrated her 90th birthday.

INDEX

References to illustrations are shown in *italics*

PICTURE CREDITS